TAKING SIDES

Clashing Views in

Gender

THIRD EDITION

TAKING SIDES

Clashing Views in

Gender

THIRD EDITION

Selected, Edited, and with Introductions by

Jacquelyn W. White
University of North Carolina

Mc Graw Hill **Contemporary Learning Series**

A Division of The McGraw-Hill Companies

*To the countless students who have challenged me to
learn, relearn, unlearn, and learn anew.*

Photo Acknowledgment
Cover image: Photos.com and Suza Scalora/Getty Images

Cover Acknowledgment
Maggie Lytle

Library of Congress Cataloging-in-Publication Data
Main entry under title:
Taking sides: clashing views in gender/selected, edited, and
with introductions by Jacquelyn W. White—3rd ed.
Includes bibliographical references and index.
1. Sex (Psychology). 2. Sex Differences. White, Jacquelyn W., *comp.*
306.7

0-07-304401-6
978-0-07-304401-9
ISSN: 1526-4548

Printed on Recycled Paper

Preface

Issues having to do with females and males, "femaleness" and "maleness," are omnipresent in Western culture and around the world. Our lives revolve around presumed distinctions between females' and males' attitudes, characteristics, emotions, behaviors, preferences, abilities, and responsibilities. We have clear definitions of what females and males can and should do differently from one another. In some cultures, there are third and fourth gender categories, complete with their own expectations and proscriptions. What has triggered such a deep gender divide? Is it rooted in our biology? Is it a cultural creation that gets reproduced through socialization practices and interpersonal interaction? What is the future of gender? Controversy abounds.

Taking Sides: Clashing Views on Controversial Issues in Gender is a tool for stimulating critical thought about females and males, femaleness and maleness, and beyond. Consideration of the complexity of sex and gender necessitates a multidisciplinary perspective. Thus, you will learn about definitions and views of sex and gender from such fields as sociology, ethnic studies, women's studies, men's studies, gay and lesbian studies, queer studies, gender studies, transgender studies, education, language, political science, global studies, religion, history, medicine, law, psychology, and biology. The multidisciplinarity of inquiry on sex and gender has created a rich, exciting, and emotionally and politically charged body of theory, research, and practice. The study of sex and gender is so dynamic that it is one of the most fast-paced areas of inquiry, characterized by great fervor and rapid growth. It is also one of the most contentious areas of thought, distinguished by deep theoretical and philosophical differences. Such division also marks public discourse on sex and gender.

This book contains 20 issues, organized into 6 parts, that are being hotly debated in contemporary scholarly and public discourse on sex and gender. They are phrased as yes/no questions so that two distinct perspectives are delineated and contrasted. Each issue is prefaced by an *issue introduction* containing background material contextualizing the dual positions. Additional perspectives are presented in a *postscript* following each issue to enrich and enliven debate and discussion. No issue is truly binary, adequately represented by only two points of view. Considering other perspectives will broaden your understanding of the complexity of each issue, enabling you to develop an informed ideology. The *suggestions for further reading* that appear in each issue postscript should help you find resources to continue your study of the subject. At the back of the book is a listing of all the *contributors to this volume,* which will give you information on the various writers whose views are debated here. Also, on the *On the Internet* page that accompanies each part opener, you will find Internet site addresses (URLs) that are relevant to the issues in that part. These Web sites should prove useful as starting points for further research.

You begin this quest with an existing personal gender ideology of which you may not even be aware. It serves as a filter through which you process information about females and males, femaleness and maleness. It draws your attention to some information and points of view and allows you to disregard other more dissonant perspectives. Your challenge is to probe your personal gender ideology (and intersecting ideologies such as ethnicity, sexual orientation, social class, gender identity) so that you can open your mind to other perspectives and information and develop a more informed ideology. To do so takes courage and active thought. As you work through this book, note your reactions to different points and perspectives. Exchange reactions and relevant experiences with your peers. "Try on" different perspectives by trying to represent a view with which you initially disagree. Explore *suggestions for further reading* and Web sites provided for each part or issue. Challenge yourself to explore all angles so that your own theories or views become more reasoned and representative.

No matter what field of study, career path, and/or other personal choices you pursue, issues of sex and gender will be pervasive. Great sociohistorical change in sex and gender marked the twentieth century, catalyzing even greater momentum for the twenty-first century. The goal of this book is to help you develop an ideological toolchest that will enable you to intelligently and responsibly navigate the changing gender landscape. Collectively, you will chart the course of the future of gender.

Changes to this edition. This edition contains 20 issues organized into six parts. The book outline has changed substantially, with the addition of 16 new issues, and all new, more current selections added to reflect the YES and NO perspectives. Four issues are the same, but both the YES and NO selections have been replaced with more recent articles. Part openers, issue introductions, and issues postscripts have been revised accordingly. Part openers, issue introductions, and issue postscripts have been revised as necessary.

A word to the instructor. An *Instructor's Manual With Test Questions* (multiple-choice and essay) is available through the publisher for the instructor using *Taking Sides* in the classroom. A general guidebook, *Using Taking Sides in the Classroom,* which discusses methods and techniques for integrating the pro-con approach into any classroom setting, is also available. An online version of *Using Taking Sides in the Classroom* and a correspondence service for *Taking Sides* adopters can be found at http://www.mhcls.com/usingts/.

Taking Sides: Clashing Views on Controversial Issues in Sex and Gender is only one title in the Taking Sides series. If you are interested in seeing the table of contents for any of the other titles, please visit the Taking Sides Web site at http://www.mhcls.com/takingsides/.

Acknowledgements. First and foremost, the contributions of Elizabeth Paul, editor of the first two editions, are acknowledged. The insights and knowledge she brought to this project have provided a solid platform from which to move forward into the third edition. Her understanding of the issues facing the study of gender and her ability to cogently frame the issues set a high standard, one to which I hope the third edition can measure up. I also want to express great appreciation to my many undergraduates who helped me understand which issues resonate most with them. Many colleagues in the Women's and Gender Studies program at UNCG provided an articulate sounding board as I debated which issues to include and how to frame them. Also, the comments and feedback from my doctoral students Kelly Kadlec, Darcy McMullin, and Stacy Sechrist have been invaluable in developing the set of issues selected for this edition. I must also acknowledge Jill Peter at McGraw-Hill/Contemporary Learning Series who provided me with expertise, support, and encouragement at each step of the process. Lastly, my husband and children Ian and Elaine were enormously supportive and patient, filling in for all those household tasks I simply ignored. I have learned much from them about what it means to have an equal partner and to attempt to raise children free of gender constraints in a society that really does not want that to happen.

Jacquelyn W. White
University of North Carolina at Greensboro

Contents In Brief

Contents

PART 4   FROM 9 TO 5: GENDER IN THE WORLD OF WORK   181

Author Sarah Drescher contends that welfare reforms have inadequately addressed gender inequalities and have reinforced sex-segregated work and family roles, thereby worsening the "feminization of poverty." Hilda Kahne makes the argument that incomplete education and few training programs makes it more difficult for low-wage single mothers to raise their earnings.

Gerald Mackie takes a scientific approach to challenge the argument that female genital cutting is not always harmful, citing multiple examples of physical and psychological harm. Carla M. Obermeyer argues that a lack of research precludes us from fully understanding female circumcision and claiming that it is responsible for a variety of harmful health outcomes. She includes examples of no harm.

Bridget E. Maher argues that far too much funding has gone into programs that teach young people about sexuality and contraception— programs that she concludes are ineffective. Debra Hauser, in an evaluation of numerous abstinence-only-until-marriage programs that received funding under the Title V Social Security Act, concludes that they show few short-term benefits and no lasting, positive effects; rather such programs may actually worsen sexual health outcomes.

Elizabeth Sheff conducted an ethnographic study that suggests that engaging in nontraditional relationships can help women reject sexual objectification and enlarge their sexual subjectivity. Cheryl B. Travis and her colleagues argue that society's social construction of beauty has so deeply affected the socialization of girls that it plays a key role in controlling women's sexuality. Their analysis of the impact of the beauty myth calls into question whether any woman can truly have a sexual self that has not been shaped by societal ideals.

Sonja Grover argues that any sexual contact with a minor by an adult under any circumstances violates the human rights of a child. Bruce Rind suggests that it is important to distinguish adult-child from adult-adolescent sexual relationships, suggesting that the latter may not be harmful because adolescents are likely to interpret the relationship differently than children.

PART 6 GIRL INTERRUPTED: GENDER AND MENTAL HEALTH 321

Torbjörn Bäckström describe the relationship between hormones and premenstrual syndrome, also discussing the effects on the brain and various treatment options. Joan C. Chrisler argues that PMS is a culturally constructed disorder whose symptoms are tied to cultural meanings and social norms. PMS, as understood in U.S. women, does not manifest itself the same in all cultures.

Robert L. Spitzer reports on a study that identified a subgroup of gay men and lesbians who reported at least some minimal change in some aspect of their sexual orientation. Helena M. Carlson and Lisa M. Diamond, in separate critiques, note numerous flaws in Spitzer's methods and conceptualization of sexual desire. Both conclude that his conclusions are flawed.

The DSM-IV, the official manual of the American Psychiatric Association, presents the diagnostic criteria that must be met in order for a person to be diagnosed with a gender identity disorder. Carla Golden argues that the diagnosis of gender identity disorder is problematic. It is the socially constructed nature of sex and gender that has problematized some forms of gender expression while privileging others.

Introduction

Sex and Gender: Knowing Is Believing, but Is Believing Knowing?

As people go through their day-to-day lives, when is their sex or gender relevant, that is, in the foreground, and when is it in the background? Think about this question regarding your own life. Are you always aware of being a female or a male? Probably not. Does your femaleness or maleness cause you to behave the way you do all the time? Probably not. Thus, we arrive at the perplexing and complicated question: When do sex and gender matter? To begin to answer this question we need to consider what we mean by the terms *sex* and *gender*. We also need to identify and make explicit the fundamental assumptions that lead us to put so much importance on questions regarding sex and gender.

Within any species of living organisms, there is variation. In Western thought, a primary individual difference is sex. What do we "know" about the ways in which individuals differ by sex? Of course, an obvious response is that individuals are either female or male. We treat it as fact. What else do you *know* about human variation by sex? Are there other *facts* about human females and males? Perhaps you will state such facts as males' greater physical strength than females, males' taller stature than females, and females' unique capacity for childbearing. Make a list of what else you *know* about human variation by sex.

Most of us have a vast network of knowledge about human variation by sex. Many of the claims stem from knowledge of the differential biology of females and males and extend to variation in human emotion, thought, and behavior. In fact, some individuals maintain that females and males are so different that they are from different planets! For most of us, this is an interconnected network of "givens" about the far-reaching effects of femaleness and maleness. Given that we consider human sex variation to be an undeniable fact, we rarely question these claims. Instead we see them as essential truths or facts—unquestionable, unchangeable, and inevitable. The goal of this book is to guide your critical evaluation of this network of knowledge. What you may discover as you critically consider the controversial issues in this book is that many of the things we believe to be factually true and objectively provable about human sex variation are instead unsupported beliefs.

Consider what constitutes "proof" for you. What are your standards of "truth"? How do we know that a piece of information is a fact rather than a belief? Do we base our classification on evidence? What kind of evidence do we require? What constitutes enough evidence to classify a claim as a fact rather than a belief? Starting with what we *know* to be the most basic fact about human variation by sex, that humans are either female or male, how do you know that? Did someone tell you (e.g., a parent, a teacher)? Did you observe differences between yourself and others or among others? How did this information or observation get generalized from a few individuals to all humans? Is this kind of generalization warrantable, based on human variation? Are there any exceptions (i.e., individuals that do not fit neatly into the categories of female or male? Would such exceptions lead you to question the *fact* of sex as female or male? For something to be fact, must it be universally true of all individuals within a given species? Have you ever thought critically about this before?

What is the difference (if any) between facts and beliefs? Do we treat knowledge differently if we classify it as fact versus belief or opinion? Are facts more important to us than beliefs? Do we question the veracity of facts as much as that of beliefs? Why not? What are the ramifications of not submitting facts to critical questioning? Rethink the facts you listed about human variation by sex. How do you know these are facts? What is your evidence? Does your evidence indisputably support the claim as fact? Do you detect defensiveness about or resistance to critically questioning facts? Why?

Knowledge and Beliefs in the Study of Sex and Gender

For decades, in public discourse and in numerous academic disciplines, there has been widespread debate and discussion of the extent of human variation by sex. In addition, there is extensive consideration of the cultural meaning and significance attached to femaleness and maleness. The terms *sex* and *gender* are used to refer to these various phenomena. Although sex and gender are commonly thought to be synonyms, many scholars attempted to assign different meanings to these terms. Sex was often used to refer to the biological distinction between females and males. Gender referred to the social and cultural meaning attached to notions of femaleness and maleness. Depending on one's theory of how sex and gender were related, there were varying degrees of overlap or interconnection between these two terms. Many scholars now question the usefulness of the distinction, suggesting that the notion of biological sex itself is socially constructed. This more contemporary view rests on two arguments. First, biological organisms cannot exist or be studied devoid of a social context, making the sex and gender dichotomy arbitrary. Second, as Myra Hird has suggested, there is a persistent, yet unchallenged belief that biological sex is the "original sign through which gender is read." That is, what we know about a person's anatomy provides the basis for prescriptions and proscriptions regarding appropriate behaviors.

Gender has been employed in theory and research in various ways and toward various goals. The study of gender has been used to assess the validity of claims of human sex differences. It has also been used to challenge assertions of biological roots of gendered behavior by testing alternate causal theories (e.g., environmental, learning, cognitive theories). Some studies of gender aim to analyze the social organization of female/male relations, elucidating gendered power dynamics and patterns of dominance and subordination. Gender studies have also been used to show how burdens and benefits are inequitably distributed among females and males in society. Other scholars have used conceptions of gender to explain the structure of the human psyche, individuals' sense of self, identity, and aspiration.

How are elements of gender produced? Biological essentialists believe that biological sex differences directly lead to behavioral, cognitive, and emotional differences (i.e., gender affects) between females and males. In other words, there are *essential* differences between females and males that stem from biology and pervade human psychology and sociality. Evolutionary theorists believe that ancestral responses to environmental challenges created physiological differences between females and males that underlie contemporary behavioral differences. In contrast, social constructionists believe gender to be a social or cultural creation. Infants and children are socialized and disciplined so as to develop sex-appropriate gender attributes and skills. As individuals mature, they develop a gender identity or a sense of self as female or male. They internalize the dominant cultural gender ideology, develop expectations for self and other, and assume sex-congruent gender roles, behaving in gender-appropriate ways. Symbolic interactionists point to the power of pervasive cultural gender symbolism in the production and reproduction of gender in cultures. They show how gender metaphors are assigned to cultural artifacts and how language structures gender meanings and dynamics creating to a dominant cultural meaning system. Standpoint theorists show us how our position in the social hierarchy impacts our perspective on and involvement in cultural gender dynamics. Throughout all the issues in this book, you will see these various perspectives being contrasted.

The concept of gender has been construed in many ways, spawning a highly complex field of inquiry. Some scholars perceive gender as an attribute of individuals or something we "have." Others see gender as something we "do" or perform; gender is seen as a product of interpersonal interaction. Gender has also been construed as a mode of social organization, structuring status and power dynamics in cultural institutions. Some see gender as universal; others believe gender to be historically—and culturally—specific. The latter perspective has yielded a proliferation of investigations into how, why, when, where, and for whom gender "works." Recently similar logic has been applied to biological sex. That is, the concept of biological sex itself is a social construction.

Biological features of sex have been assumed to include genetic factors of female and male chromosomes, hormones and the endocrine system, internal and external sexual and reproductive organs (appearance and functionality) and central nervous system sex differentiation. The assumption or the defined norm was that there is consistency among these different biological factors, differentiating individuals into females and males. However, research with transgendered people and intersexed individuals challenges the assumption that various biological features of organisms "naturally" co-occur. Research suggests that variations among these features occur naturally. Defining these variations as "normal" or "deviant" is a social construction.

Adding to the complexity is a growing appreciation that what it means to be female or male in a given culture is affected by one's race, ethnicity, and social class, with some scholars arguing that these too are social constructs. Contemporary analyses suggest that the fundamental construct is *oppression*—that is, those in power have the authority to declare who is and is not "acceptable," with access to resources (such as education or political influence) based on criteria defined by the powerful. Thus, gender is seen as one system of power intersecting with other systems of power (such as race, ethnicity, and social class).

As you can see from this brief review of many of the ways in which gender has been construed and studied, there are differences and even contradictions among the various perspectives and approaches. Some individuals champion gender as stimulating complementarity and interdependence among humans; others see gender as a powerful source of segregation and exclusion. Some scholars emphasize differences between females and males; others allow for greater individual variation that crosses sex and gender boundaries or they even emphasize similarity between females and males. Some people think of gender as invariant and fixed; others think of gender as malleable and flexible. Some scholars see gender as politically irrelevant; others see gender as the root of all social and political inequities. Some view "gender-inappropriate" behavior with disdain and fear, labeling it problematic and pathological and in need of correction; others see gender variance as natural and cause for celebration. Some individuals believe "traditional" differentiated sex roles should be preserved; others believe that these conventional notions of gender should be redefined or even transcended. Some individuals view gender processes and dynamics as personally relevant; others have little conception of the role of gender in their lived experience. How do we deal with this controversy? How can we evaluated and weigh different assertions and arguments?

Tools for Argument Analysis

Each pair of selections in this volume present opposing arguments about sex and gender. How do you decide which argument is "right" or, at least, which argument is better? Argument analysis is a field with many approaches and standards. Here a few major components and criteria are briefly presented to help you in making judgments about the quality of the arguments advanced in the book.

To assess an argument's quality it is helpful to break it down into seven components, including its *claim, definitions, statements of fact, statements of value, language and reasoning, use of authority,* and *audience.* However, first we must touch on the issue of *explicit versus implicit elements* within an argument. Real-world arguments contain many implicit (unstated) elements. For example, they may use unstated definitions of key terms or rely on value judgments that are not made clear within the body of the argument itself. Occasionally these elements are left out because the author wants to hide the weaknesses of her or his argument by omitting them. However it is probably more often the case that they are omitted because the author assumes the audience for their work knows about the missing elements and already accepts them as true. The job of the argument analyst begins with identifying implicit elements in an argument and making them explicit. Since we usually do not have direct access to the argument's author, making implicit elements explicit requires a good deal of interpretation on our part. However, few arguments would stand up to analysis for long if we did not try our best to fill in the implicit content. Specific examples of making implicit elements explicit are provided in what follows.

Claim

The first component one should look for in an argument is its claim. What, specifically, are the authors trying to convince us of? The notion of a claim in an argument is essentially the same as that of a thesis in a term paper. In almost all cases it is possible to identify a single overarching claim that the authors are trying to get their audience to accept. For example, in Issue 3 Thornhill and Palmer claim that males' propensity to rape has an evolutionary basis. Once the claim of an argument is identified, the analyst can begin to look for and evaluate supporting components. If no claim can be identified, then we do not have an argument that is well formed enough to evaluate fairly.

Definitions

At first thought, an argument's definitions might not seem a very interesting target for analysis. However, definitions are often highly controversial, implicit, and suspect in terms of their quality. This is especially the case in the study of sex and gender. How are the key terms in an argument's claim and supporting reasons defined, if at all? Does the author rely on dictionary definitions, stipulative definitions (offering an original definition of the term), definition by negation (saying what the term does not mean), or definition by example? Dictionary definitions are relatively uncontroversial but rare and of limited application. Stipulative definitions are conveniently explicit but often the subject of controversy. Other types of definitions can be both implicit and not widely accepted. Once you have identified definitions of the key terms in an argument's claim and supporting reasons, ask yourself if you find these definitions to be acceptable. Then ask if the argument's opponent is using these same definitions or is advocating a different set. Opposing arguments cannot be resolved on their merits until the two sides agree on key definitions. Indeed many long-term debates in public policy never seem to get resolved because the two sides define the underlying problem in very different ways. For example, in Issue 19 on repartive therapy consider the centrality of each author's definition of "sexual desire."

Statements of Fact

Claims have two fundamentally different types of supporting reasons. The first type is statements of fact. A fact is a description of something that we can presumably verify to be true. Thus the first question to be answered about an argument's factual statements is how do we know they are true? Authors may report original empirical research of their own. With an argument that is reporting on original research, the best means of checking the truth of their facts would be to repeat, or replicate, their research. This is almost never realistically possible, so we then must rely on an assessment of the methods they used, either our own assessment or that of an authority we trust. Authors may be relying on facts that they did not discover on their own, but instead obtained from some authoritative source.

Aside from the question of the truth of facts is the question of their sufficiency. Authors may offer a few facts to support their claim or many. They may offer individual cases or very broad factual generalizations. How many facts are enough? Since most arguments are evaluated in the context of their opponents, it is tempting to tally up the factual statements of both arguments and declare the one with the most facts the winner. This is seldom adequate, although an argument with a wealth of well-substantiated factual statements in support of its claim is certainly preferable to one with few statements of fact that are of questionable quality. In persuasive arguments it is very common to see many anecdotes and examples of individual cases. These are used to encourage the audience to identify with the subject of the cases. However, in analyzing these arguments we must always ask if an individual case really represents a systematic trend. In other words, do the facts offered generalize to the whole or are they just persuasive but isolated exceptions? On the other hand, it is also common to see the use of statistics to identify general characteristics of a population. The analyst should always ask if these statistics were collected in a scientific manner and without bias, if they really show significant distinct characteristics, and how much variation there is around the central characteristics identified. Debates about the gender pay gap are highly influenced by how the pay gap is measured (see Issues 12 and 13).

A final question about statements of fact concerns their relevancy. We sometimes discover factual statements in an argument that may be true, and even interesting reading, but that just don't have anything to do with the claim being advanced. Be sure that the forest is not missed for the trees in evaluating statements of fact—in other words, that verifying and tallying of factual statements does not preempt the question of how well an author supports the primary claim.

Statements of Value

The philosopher David Hume is famous for his observation that a series of factual statements (that something "is" the case) will never lead to the conclusion that something "ought" to be done. The missing component necessary to move from "is" to "ought," to move from statements of fact to accepting an argument's claim, are statements of value. Statements of value declare something to be right or wrong, good or bad, desirable or undesirable, beautiful or ugly. For example, "It is wrong for boys to play with dolls."

Although many people behave as if debates can be resolved by proving one side or the other's factual statements to be true, statements of value are just as critical to the quality of an argument as are statements of fact. Moreover, because value statements have their roots in moral and religious beliefs, we tend to shy away from analyzing them too deeply in public discourse. Instead, people tend to be *absolutist,* rejecting outright values that they do not share, or *relativist,* declaring that all values are equally valid. As a result, statements of value are not as widely studied in argument analysis and standards of evaluation are not as well developed for them as for factual statements.

At the very least, the argument analyst can expect the value statements of an argument to be part of what has been referred to as a "rational ideology." A rational ideology is one in which value statements are *cogent* and *coherent* parts of a *justifiable* system of beliefs. A cogent value statement is one that is relevant and clear. Coherent value statements fit together; they are consistent with one another and help support an argument's claim. A system of beliefs is justifiable if its advocate can provide supporting reasons (both facts and values) for holding beliefs. A morality that makes value judgments but refuses to offer reasons for these judgments would strike us as neither very rational nor very persuasive. Although we rarely have the opportunity to engage in a debate with authors to test their ability to justify their value statements, we can expect an argument's value statements to be explicit, cogent, coherent, and supported by additional statements of fact and value as justification. As in the case of definitions, it is also fruitful to compare the value statements of one argument with those of the opposing view to see how much the authors agree or disagree in the (usually) implicit ideology that lies behind their value statements.

Throughout the issues in this book you will see an implicit clash of values: The sexes *should* be different versus opportunity for variations should be encouraged.

Language and Reasoning

There are a vast number of specific issues in the use of language and reasoning within arguments. Any introductory book on rhetoric or argumentative logic will provide a discussion of these issues. Here just a sample of the most common ones will be touched on. The analyst gives less weight to arguments that use language that is overly emotional. Emotional language relies on connotation (word meanings aside from formal definition), bias or slanting in word choice, exaggeration, slogan, an cliché. Emotional language is sometimes appropriate when describing personal experience but it is not persuasive when used to support a general claim about what should be believed or done in society.

The analysis of reasoning has to do with the logical structure of an argument's components and usually focuses on the search for logical fallacies (errors in logic). A common fallacy has already been discussed under statements of fact: hasty generalization. In hasty generalizations claims are made without a sufficient amount of factual evidence to support them. When authors argue that one event followed another and this proves the first event caused the second, they are committing the *post hoc* fallacy (it may just be a coincidence that the events happened in that order). Two fallacies often spotted in arguments directed at opponents are *ad hominem* and straw man. The first involves attacking the person advocating the opposing view, which is generally irrelevant to the quality of their statements. The second is unfairly describing an opponent's argument in an overly simplified way that is easy to defeat. Fallacies directed at the argument's audience include false dilemma, slippery slope, and *ad populum*. Authors commit the fallacy of false dilemma when they argue that only two alternatives exist when, in fact, there are more than two. Slippery slope is an unsupportable prediction that if a small first step is taken it will inevitably lead to more change. An appeal to public opinion to support a claim is an *ad populum* argument if there is reason to believe that the public is prejudiced or plain wrong in its views, or if what the public believes is simply not relevant to the issue. In general, the argument analyst must not only look at the individual statements of an argument but must also ask how well they are put together in an argument that is logical and not overly emotional.

Use of Authority

The issue of authority is relevant in argument analysis in two places. The first has to do with the authority of the argument's author. Analysts should use whatever information they can gather to assess the expertise and possible biases of authors. Are authors reporting on an issue that they have only recently begun to study, or have they studied the issue area in considerable depth? Do they occupy a professional position that indicates recognition by others as authorities in the field? Do you have reason to believe that their work is objective and not subject to systematic biases because of who pays for or publishes their work? Be careful not to commit *ad hominem* on this one yourself. The brief biographies of contributors to this volume give you a bit of information about the authors of the arguments that follow.

The second place authority enters into analysis is the citation of authorities within the body of the argument itself. To a greater or lesser degree, all arguments rely on citation of outside authorities to support their statements. We should ask the same questions of these authorities as we ask of authors. In general, we want authorities that are widely accepted as experts and that do not have systematic biases. Even if we do not have the time or resources to check out the authorities cited in an argument, it is reasonable to expect that an argument makes very clear whom it is citing as an authority.

Audience

The final component of argument analysis is consideration of an argument's intended audience. Clues to the intended audience can be found in the type of publication or forum where the argument is presented, in the professional standing of its author, and in the type of language that the author uses in the argument itself. Knowledge of audience is critical in evaluating an argument fairly. Authors writing an argument for an audience that shares their core values and general knowledge of the subject tend to leave definitions and statements implicit and use language that is highly technical, dense, and symbolic. This applies equally well to scientists writing for a journal in their field and politicians addressing their supporters. Authors writing for an audience that is very different from them tend to make the various components of their arguments much more explicit. However if an author believes the audience disagrees with them on, for example, an important value statement, they tend to make statements that are both explicit and yet are still very general or ambiguous (this is a skill that is highly developed in politicians). It is difficult to make a fair judgment across these two basic types of author-audience relationships, since the former requires much more interpretation by the evaluator than the latter.

Analyzing arguments by evaluating their quality in terms of the seven components listed above is by no means guaranteed to give you a clear answer as to which argument is better for several reasons. The relevant criteria applicable to each component are neither completely articulated nor without controversy themselves. In the process of making implicit elements explicit, analysts introduce their own subjectivity into the process. It should also be clear by this point that argument analysis is a very open-ended process—checking the truth of statements of fact, the justifiability of statements of values, the qualifications of authorities—could go on indefinitely. Thus the logic of argument analysis is underdetermined—following each step exactly is still no guarantee of a correct conclusion. However, if you apply the analytical techniques outlined above to the essays in this volume you will quickly spot implicit definitions, hasty generalizations, unsupported value statements, and questionable authorities as well as examples of well-crafted, logical, and persuasive argumentation. You will be in a much stronger position to defend *your* views about the arguments you find in this book.

Issues in This Volume

The critical examination of sex and gender in this text is segmented into six parts. In Part I, fundamental assumptions about sex and gender are considered, revealing that "simple" definitions of sex as female or male and gender as directly derivative from biology are shortsighted. Moreover, debate over these fundamental assumptions has yielded some of the most contentious controversy in this field. In Part II, the "difference model," the primary paradigm for conceptualizing and studying sex and gender is critically analyzed. Sex and gender are usually construed as binary oppositions: female versus male, feminine versus masculine. Thus, a primary way in which sex and gender are studied is the comparison of groups of females and males (i.e., sex comparison or sex difference). In this section, you will grapple with underlying theoretical rationales for excavating such differences (including biological, evolutionary, and learning theories), and you will critically evaluate the difference model in terms of methodology, social meaning and significance, and political impact. Is the search for differences between females and males a useful approach to elucidating gender or is it meaningless and even politically dangerous?

Part III examines gender in a critical social domain—family. Gender is influential before conception, in making decisions to carry a fetus to term, and in the life expectancy of female and male children. Sex selection is a common practice in many cultures, including Western cultures. Why is higher value placed on female versus male offspring? From some theoretical perspectives, gender begins with early socialization and is affected by family composition. One of the most gendered social institutions is the family. Traditional Western family ideology is heterosexist (regarding the heterosexual union as the only acceptable family context) and sexist (prescribing different roles for husbands and wives). In Part III these fundamental values and assumptions are examined. Gender ideology riddles the construction of parenthood. Does gender influence women's and men's capacities for and approaches to parenting? How are traditional family gender ideologies challenged by same sex parents?

In Part IV the world of work is explored. It is a well-established fact that women on average earn 75 cents for each man's dollar. We want to know why. Is it career choice, and if so, what factors determine individuals' career choices? It is highly likely that advanced training in mathematics and the sciences opens more doors of opportunity and increases the likelihood of a larger paycheck. And we know that there are more men in mathematically and scientifically based careers than women. How do gendered factors, be they biological or societal, affect girls' and boys' interest in math and science? Do these factors justify the gender wage gap? It is well understood now that most families cannot achieve a comfortable lifestyle without two paychecks. What are the implications of this for single parents, especially poor women?

In Part VI issues of gender and sexuality are explored. In particular, this section is interested in exploring the double-standard and double-bind that women and men often find themselves in. What does it mean to be a sexual person and how can society go about teaching young people about responsible sexual behavior? Throughout history there has been greater acceptance of female than male sexuality. Some societies have practiced female circumcision as a means of blunting female sexual desire. Some have argued that there are circumstances under which adult-child sexual relationships may be healthy. Even without such extreme measure societies traditionally have endorsed various explicit and implicit means of controlling sexual expression. For example, sex education programs in the schools are explicitly aimed to control adolescent sexuality whereas media messages about beauty and sexuality provide more subtle, yet very pervasive and often harmful, messages about sexuality.

The final section Part VI addresses mental health issues. We can ask how does gender affect one's mental health, or alternatively does one's gender affect perceptions of mental health? There are a number of mental health problems that are more pervasive among women (such as the internalizing disorders) and others that are more pervasive among men (such as externalizing disorders). The debate is whether these differences are "real." It has been argued that these differences may be the result of biological differences between women and men, gender-related biases in diagnosis, diagnoses based on deviations from expected gender roles, or the experience of sexism. Some scholars have argued that mental health, like many other constructs, is socially constructed, that those in power get to define what is healthy and what is unhealthy. In a classic study done in the 1970s by the Broverman's it was found that descriptions of a "healthy man" were similar to descriptions of a "healthy person," which matched the prevalent masculine stereotype of the time, whereas the description of a "healthy woman" did not match that of a "healthy person," but did conform to the feminine stereotype of the time. Although things might not be as extreme today, there is still evidence that a social understanding of gender shapes definitions of mental health, with the belief that women's hormones are responsible for many of their problems, as exemplified in the discussion of premenstrual syndrome. Sexual orientation and transgenderism offer two more cases whereby issues of what constitutes normal behavior can be explored.

Conclusion

Equipped with your new tools for analyzing arguments, begin your exploration of knowledge and belief in the study of sex and gender. Remain open to considering and reconsidering beliefs and knowledge in ways that you never imagined. Your "gender quest" begins now; where you will end up, no one knows!

On the Internet . . .

The True Story of John/Joan

This Info-Circumcision Web site by the Circumcision Information Resource Centre includes John Colapinto's original article entitled, "The True Story of John/Joan," *Rolling Stone* (December 11, 1997). This article reveals details of the John/Joan case.

http://www.infocirc.org/rollston.htm

Gender Talk

Gendertalk.com is a resource for trans persons and folks interested in learning about trans persons. Gendertalk.com provides comprehensive access to GenderTalk Radio, the leading radio program on transgender issues. GenderTalk is the leading worldwide weekly radio program that talks about transgenderism in the first person. News and information are presented that challenge traditional views of gender.

http://www.gendertalk.com/radio/about.shtml

The Office on Violence Against Women

The Office on Violence Against Women (OVW) handles the Department of Justice's legal and policy issues regarding violence against women, coordinates Departmental efforts, provides national and international leadership, and receives international visitors interested in learning about the federal government's role in addressing violence against women. The website provides several links to information about violence against women.

http://www.usdoj.gov/ovw/

Association of American Colleges and Universities

This Web site of the Association of American Colleges and Universities offer a selected bibliography of feminist science studies, with many of the classic papers critiquing traditional scientific approaches to the study of sex and gender listed.

http://www.aacu-edu.org/womenscilit/
bibliographies.cfm

Juvenile Justice and Delinquency Prevention

The Web site of the Office of Juvenile Justice and Delinquency Prevention offers a comprehensive bibliography of scholarly research and literature relating to juvenile sex offenders.

http://ojjdp.ncjrs.org/juvsexoff/sexbibtopic.html

PART 1

Definitions and Cultural Boundaries: A Moving Target

*W**hat is sex? What is gender? What is gender identity? Must there be congruence between biological aspects of sex (chromosomes, hormones, internal organs, and genitals) and social aspects of gender (assigned sex, gender identity, sexual orientation)? These are controversial questions with a diversity of answers. In fact, the vast array of conradictory "answers" loosens the boundaries of these concepts to the point of losing any sense of certain definition. Definitions often reveal important theoretical standpoints underlying much of the controversy in the study of sex and gender. Moreover, they raise the question of cultural relativity of definitions. Can these concepts be objectively defined or is the most objective and scientific definition still a product of culture? This section will explore the limits and limitlessness of definitions and boundaries of sex and gender within biology, psyche, and culture.*

- Is Anatomy Destiny?

- Is Gender Identity Innate?

- Is the Motive to Rape Biological?

ISSUE 1

Is Anatomy Destiny?

YES: Anne Campbell, from "X and Y: It's a Jungle Out There," *Psychology, Evolution, and Gender* (August 2001)

NO: Richard Wilson, from "Puncturing the Genome Myth: Why the Genetic Code Fails to Explain Gendered Behaviour," *Psychology, Evolution, and Gender* (December 2001)

ISSUE SUMMARY

YES: Psychologist Anne Campbell argues that gene-level discoveries about the X and Y chromosomes give insight into differences between females and males.

NO: Richard Wilson suggests that environmental and social factors explain gendered behavior better than the genetic code.

Do we really know what constitutes one's "sex" and "gender"? Typically people assume that being male or female is a clear and absolute distinction. Biologically based theories of sex differentiation support the argument that genetic make-up and resultant hormonal influences determine fundamental differences between women and men. Given the ethical constraints associated with doing research on humans, researchers have had to rely on animal experimentation to demonstrate that hormones contribute to sexual dimorphism (i.e., sexual differentiation) on neural systems, brains, temperament, and behavior. The assumption is that sexual is an unquestionably natural dichotomy rooted in an organism's genetics.

In contrast, a large body of research with numerous species of animals, as well as with humans, suggests that environmental factors provide the major determinants of gender-related patterns of behavior. That is, gender is a socially constructed constellation of feelings, attitudes, and behaviors, thus, strongly influenced by cultural forces.

Critics have begun to question the immunity of biological constructs from cultural analysis, urging that we must recognize that the practice of science occurs within a sociopolitical context. Therefore, biological notions of sex are cultural, social, and political creations.

The dominant Western definition of sex delineates two "normal" categories: male and female. Notions of gender follow suit, typically contrasting masculine and feminine behavior patterns. Is this dichotomy universal? Anthropologists have uncovered compelling evidence that dichotomous definitions of sex are not universal, arguing instead that many cultures have multiple genders. They argue that when looking for binaries, we observe a dichotomous reality. But what remains unseen—gender diversity—is also an important reality. Will Roscoe argues that gender diversity is a natural, worldwide phenomenon.

Some revisionists have begun to "reinvent sex" by replacing dichotomous conceptions of sex with arrays reflecting the complexities of sexual variability naturally characteristics of humans. For example, concepts such as "gender-crossing" have been coined. The problem with such concepts is that they still rely on the fixed binary of male/female, and they problematize deviations. In contrast, construing diversity as multiple genders enables the transcendence of this binary and notions of deviance associated with nonmale and nonfemale genders.

In the following selections, two different perspectives on the human genome project are presented. On the one hand, Campbell marvels at how a very small number of genes, and the very small and outnumbered Y chromosome, can accomplish so much with regard to masculinizing a male fetus. Her view of the differences between women and men are clearly rooted in an evolutionary perspective. On the other hand, Wilson bemoans the fact that the human genome project has revealed so little with regard to gendered behavior. First, he questions whether the practice of science can immune to social influences. Second, he questions the claim that genes are determinants of behavior in humans—that expressions of gender differences are "hardwired into the fabric or our being."

Anne Campbell

 **YES**

X and Y: It's a Jungle Out There

Almost as astonishing as the modest number of human genes uncovered by the human genome project (a mere 31,000) is confirmation of the astonishing disparity between the size of the X and Y chromosome. The Y has a humble 231 genes compared to a generous 1,184 on the X. From the point of view of evolution, size matters. It tells us much about the conflict between males and females.

The Y chromosome now carries little else but the gene complex called testes determining factor (TDF). Its job, as you might reasonably suppose, is a straightforward but very significant one—it instructs genes on other chromosomes to build the testes. From the testes comes a significant quantity of testosterone, starting in the second trimester of foetal growth and continuing for several months post-partum. From this testosterone come a variety of morphological changes to the brain as well as the body. It builds a brain with greater lateralization of function and smaller channel of communication between the two hemispheres. It builds a larger bed nucleus of the stria terminalis from which comes the ineffable sense of being male.

These masculinizing alterations to the female 'default' option are substantial yet they are accomplished by a very small number of genes. Sex differences are principally sex limited (dependent on the effect of hormones on autosomal genes) rather than sex linked (residing on the X or Y). How and why did the Y shrink to its current size? The answer seems to be that it is hiding.

It's hiding partly because it is unable to generate new versions of itself with the speed and efficiency of the X. The Y chromosome cannot recombine as the X can. To see why, we have to consider the notion of sexually antagonistic genes. These are genes that benefit one sex but are a burden for the other. Wide hips help females give birth but slow down running speed in males. Growing antlers is an efficient use of calories for a stag (who needs them for intrasexual competition) but a waste of calories for hinds. So antler genes link themselves to Y chromosomes but not to X chromosomes. During meiosis (the production of sex cells) most pairs of corresponding chromosomes line up together and exchange segments of genetic material ensuring variability in the gamete. But if X and Y were allowed to do this it would

From *Psychology, Evolution & Gender*, 3.2 August 2001, pp. 191–196. Copyright © 2001 by Taylor & Francis Journals. Reprinted by permission.

produce all sorts of inappropriate combinations—wide-hipped males and antler-bearing females. So selection operates against genetic recombination between X and Y (except on a very small section called the pseudoautosomal region). The Y chromosome now has a real problem—evolutionary biologists call it Muller's Ratchet. A gene that cannot recombine starts to degenerate and has no way to fix itself. Take a high resolution photograph, now make a photocopy of it and a photocopy of the photocopy. . . . That is the fate of the Y chromosome. It accumulates deleterious mutations much faster than beneficial ones and there is no recombination available to patch them back up. So there is selection for non-expression of these degenerate genes. The human genome project has discovered large repeated chunks of genetic material on the TDF. Perhaps they are extra insurance against the loss of accurate instruction for testes building.

The Y chromosome is not only undersized but also outnumbered. For every one Y chromosome in a population, there are three Xs. The Y is under attack from a strong army and one that has the advantage of recombination— the two X chromosomes can exchange genes during meiosis and the result is variability which is the fodder of natural selection. And there is evidence that the recombining X does indeed mount attacks on the Y. Biologists use the term 'driving' to describe a gene that behaves in such a way as to increase its chance of being transmitted to the next generation. It is a lawless gene and the law that it is breaking is Mendel's. Instances of driving X have been found in many species. An X-linked gene that killed Y-bearing sperm would be doing itself a good turn by decreasing the number of Ys and increasing the number of Xs in the next generation. Fortunately when the sex ratio veers in favour of females the results are not catastrophic—it takes just a few males to impregnate many females. Some species survive with a 97 per cent female population. When sex ratios depart from parity, it is usually in the female direction that they move. And they usually return to 50:50 because a male mutation that can fight this driving X has massive reproductive success and this version of Y sweeps across the male population.

But although Y may be small and outgunned, it does have the advantage of never finding itself in a female body. This means that it can be quite ruthless about exploiting females. If females were not good at fighting back, the Y would have killed us long ago. William Rice used fruit flies, who have a conveniently short lifespan for experimental purposes, to demonstrate the selfish strategies of males and the crucial importance of female resistance. Seminal fluid not only kills off rival males' sperm, it also carries proteins that make their way to the female's brain where they increase her rate of ovulation and diminish her interest in having sex again: This is good for a male but not so good for the female. Worse still is the fact that the fluid is toxic to her. Rice took a group of females out of the evolutionary process for forty-one generations while the males were allowed to continue competing, mating and evolving. When he returned the original females, he found that sex literally killed them. The experimental males had got better and better at producing sperm that caused the female to reject matings with other males and better at overcoming the females' reluctance to mate with them after a previous mating with a rival. Their sperm had also become more and more toxic. The males were killing the females who had been denied the opportunity to co-evolve and develop resistance. The relationship between males and females is an antagonistic one in which both sexes lose if one fails to keep up their side of the hostilities. It is like two upright wrestlers locked together—it only takes one to release their grip for both to collapse.

This same principle has been demonstrated in another genetic discovery called genomic imprinting. Here a gene is expressed or silenced ('imprinted') depending on which parent donated it. From a polygynous, mammalian male's viewpoint, reproduction involves installing his genes in a foetus which resides in a female body. From then on, the female takes responsibility for pregnancy, parturition and lactation. He may never have another child with this particular woman and so he is indifferent to her long-term reproductive success. But his genes do want to look after their own—in the form of the foetus. He wants to ensure that it is well nourished even if that costs the mother more than she can afford. (Mothers are not callous but they are cautious. They have to think ahead—they will have other children, who they can be certain will carry their genes, and they cannot squander everything on this one foetus.) The father wants more calories given to this foetus than to any other she will carry, while the mother must ration out her energy over a whole career. It is for this reason that the father's placenta-building gene is expressed over the mother's. As Matt Ridley puts it '. . . the father's genes do not trust the mother's genes to make a sufficiently invasive placenta; so they do the job themselves'. The father also tries to take control of the growth of the embryo—at least in mice. IGF2 (insulin-like growth factor two) promotes the transition of metabolites across the placenta and so is vital in acquiring resources from the mother. Predictably enough, it is the father's version of this gene that is activated. But this time, the mother fights back. Her gene for a receptor that mops up IGF2 is expressed and the father's is imprinted. And the necessity of this female counter-ploy is evident in individuals who lack the maternal receptor gene—they are 16 per cent larger than normal.

And while the father concerns himself, genetically speaking, with building a bigger body, the mother devotes a greater part of her genetic energy to controlling the growth of the brain. Keverne and his colleagues created mice where two different genomes were fused into the same body. To build a chimerical baby, they fused a normal embryo with an embryo made from two egg pronuclei. The result was a mouse with a very large head. But when they fused the normal embryo with one derived from an embryo made from two sperm pronuclei, they grew a mouse with a big body and small head. Indeed the body of the paternal chimeras grew so large that they had to be delivered by Caesarean section. So fathers contribute more to bodies and muscle while mothers specialize in brains.

But not just brains—particular parts of them. By biochemically marking the maternal and paternal cells, the researchers were able to see where they ended up. The input of the paternal cells to brain construction was to the hypothalamus, amygdala and preoptic area—the areas that control emotion and evolutionarily critical 'automatic' behaviours such as sex, reproductive behaviour, aggression and fear. The mother's cells migrated and proliferated in the cortex, striatum and hippocampus—areas implicated in reasoning, thought and behavioural inhibition. (If you are now blaming your father for inheriting his emotional tempo remember that half the hypothalamus-building genes that he bequeathed to you came from his mother. They may not have been expressed in him but they were inherited from his mother, re-tagged in him as paternal instead of maternal and then passed on to you.)

For me, these gene-level discoveries reflect the complicated and paradoxical relationship between men and women; distinctive and yet complementary, at war yet in alliance, so similar in areas where natural selection has worked and so different where sexual selection has been the driving force. The preferred sexual strategy of masculine prehistory has been sexual opportunism and with that has come selection for dominance, aggression and men's more causal regard for their own safety and longevity. For women it is offspring survival, not insemination, that has been paramount and with it has come commitment to the long haul and a cautious approach to danger. Women are no less competitive than men but their genes have 'learned' through differential reproductive success that, while cohabiting fathers are not obligate for children's survival, mothers are. I do not doubt that this tension in reproductive priorities is reflected in evolved psychological differences mediated through genes. (Nor do I doubt that they are usually embellished and occasionally opposed by culture.) But it is not all unalloyed competition. The altricial nature of human infants has also selected for a degree of paternal investment that is much higher than that seen in other primates. And the advantages of monogamy, how ever much self-denial it requires, have been elegantly shown at the gene's eye level.

The humble house fly is normally promiscuous. But Brett Holland and William Rice randomly selected some of these flies to have monogamy forced upon them. The experimenters acted as marriage brokers, teaming up and housing together individual males and females over thirty-two generations. Monogamy means not only that the reproductive success of males and females is identical but also that their reproductive interests should converge. While polygyny means that males can exploit females quite ruthlessly without suffering themselves, monogamy means that anything that hurts a female (prevents her from achieving her reproductive potential) hurts her male partner just as much. After several generations of monogamy, Holland and Rice performed the key tests. First, they introduced non-experimental, traditional females to make with the monogamous 'new males'. They found that monogamy had led to a decrease in the toxicity of the male's seminal fluid and also to a reduction in male courtship—an activity that is harmful to females. Then they looked at the effect of monogamy on the experimental females. During monogamy, these females' male partners had behaved in a less exploitative way toward them and so the monogamous females had not needed to evolve counter-strategies of resistance. As expected, when these monogamous females mated with normal males, a larger proportion died than among traditional females that had been allowed to co-evolve with male polygyny. Freed from the antagonistic tussle, monogamous males became more benign and females produced more offspring and suffered lower mortality.

Men and women are different morphs but they are not from different planets. They both have representational thought—they see into each other's minds, recognize their differences and manage to bridge them more often than not. And they both have foresight, a uniquely human gift. The combination of these two human abilities mean that men and women, unlike genes, can choose to cooperate rather than compete.

NO ⤺

Richard Wilson

Puncturing the Genome Myth: Why the Genetic Code Fails to Explain Gendered Behaviour

I have been following the developing and ongoing story of the human genome project, admittedly at a distance, for a few years now. The project seemed to promise, on the one hand, the possibility of cures for all known (and probably some unknown) ills and, on the other, to provide definitive answers to thorny questions of human social behaviour, explaining, for example, the differences between the sexes in their social presentation, and many others.

In arriving at a sceptical approach to the genome project there have been two lines of critical analysis which actively fuelled my doubt and disbelief. The first of these concerns the actual practice of science itself as the process by which this knowledge is generated and passed back into the wider social world. The second is related to the genetic code and the influence that it has, or might have, on human behaviour.

It often seems, or at least is often implied, that the scientific process is the only means by which a reliable and accurate understanding of the physical world may be generated. Scientific practitioners might advance many reasons for this contention but may well include the following: an inquiring and experimental approach to knowledge determining and gathering; an openness to testing and discarding ideas or theories about the way the world works if they are shown to be false; and a commitment to search for and work with facts rather than conjecture. Looking at the facts is an important component of the scientific method, and Chalmers notes that there is a conception of scientific knowledge being '. . . based on the facts established by observation and experiment . . .' and that this sets it apart from knowledge created by other means.

There is then still the question of whether this process of observation and experiment does produce something that is true in an objective sense or indeed whether science can ever produce a final truth. It is a debatable point. For Popper these are not possibilities. He talks of science not being knowledge and says '. . . it can never claim to have attained truth, or even a substitute for it. . . .' Science is, in his eyes, a painstaking process of groping toward the truth without necessarily ever arriving at it. The ideas science generates

From *Psychology, Evolution & Gender,* 3.3 December 2001, pp. 273–277. Copyright © 2001 by Taylor & Francis Journals. Reprinted by permission.

about the world can be considered nets within which to trap 'reality' and the ongoing task is to make the mesh of those nets '. . . ever finer and finer.' Work taking place on the genome project, and the theories which underpin this, is one of those nets which, while it may trap some little extra bit of reality, is also going to miss many other bits in the process. Whatever the knowledge that comes out of this whole project it will not present a complete answer, only a partial and probably poorly understood picture.

Nor can one ignore the wider social context within which scientific study is undertaken. Whatever claims may be made about open-minded approaches and impartiality it cannot be denied that scientists are social beings like all other members of society. They are steeped in the thinking, beliefs and attitudes of the wider society and their approach to science will reflect this. It is one thing to claim an open-minded attitude to the 'facts' and theories that might explain them but it is still necessary to define what things count as facts and then to specify what questions need to be asked in order to generate the theories that explain the facts. A particular orientation to the world is needed, one that is shared among the community of scientists, that gives structure to the ways of thinking and questioning that are permissible and defines those ways of thinking and questioning that are not. It is this common orientation that provides the framework or paradigm through which questions of science can be determined. Yet this paradigm is itself a social construct, prone to periodic destruction and rebuilding, shadowing the social developments and thinking of the era in which it was created.

This means that science, as a human endeavour, despite its claims to knowledge generation of a special kind, is no more immune to social influences than any other human activity. It is not particularly surprising if genomic research throws up evidence which is then used to support arguments that there are in-built differences in the presentation of gender. The genomically inspired claim that men and women are different in some fundamental, God-given and unalterable way would be well received by some (because they already believe it to be true) and accepted by others because of its cloak of scientific legitimacy. Now the science ripples back in to the social fabric by serving as a useful justification for maintaining the status quo and continuing the differential treatment of men and women in the workplace or in society generally. This in turn perpetuates inequalities in earnings and life chances. If science is finding genetically ordained differences of this type it is, to a greater or lesser extent, only reflecting the structural inequalities inherent in a conflictual capitalist society.

Taking all this into account I do not believe that science can be seen as a black box that takes phenomena in one end and churns out explanations from the other in some magical way that ultimately guarantees the absolute truth of the explanations produced. If it functions as a black box at all it is as one that owes its existence to the dominant scientific paradigm of the day; a paradigm which in turn is the product of the complex social forces and currents of opinion already present in society.

So, I regard science, and the knowledge it generates, as simply one more biased, partial and idiosyncratic human endeavour like any other and of no greater validity than any other. That claims are going to be made on the back of the apparently greater understanding of human genetic composition regarding gender attributes and the extent to which these may be built in and not acquired, to me, simply reflects the social milieu from which scientists are drawn from the current of beliefs in the wider society.

However, suppose one were to accept that the information we (or at least geneticists) now possess about the genome were true, what then? Does that mean that our genetic composition really is the ultimate determinant of all that we are, in terms of our social presentations and behaviour? Again, I find some quite real problems with the knowledge, and the claims made for it, even when taken at face value.

There has been, and there continues to be, a degree of hype and spin about the genome project (although there are dissenting voices to be heard). For many it seems to come across as one of the most profound events to have happened in human history and one which will transform all our lives. Take these comments made by an MP, Dr Ian Gibson, in the House of Commons in January 2000. In speaking of the genome project he says, 'The results of that have been described as revolutionary by scientists around the world and its implications equated with the discovery of the wheel.' Hardly a modest description but one which is accepted by a government junior minister speaking in the same debate. She follows him by saying, 'The scientific and technological achievements so far associated with the human genome project are arguably some of the finest to have been seen in the previous millennium—and the potential is greater still. . . . The potential of the human genome project cannot be overestimated.' These two members of the political elite are in no doubt as to the truth and value of genomic research. A commentator in the *Daily Telegraph* enthuses that 'it really is BIG NEWS' (his emphasis) and goes on to say that thanks to genome research we will be able 'to solve old mysteries of determinism and free will.'

All very inspiring. But despite this, and looking at the information that has now been gleaned on the genetic code, there are, I think, real problems with the thesis that genes can be considered as determinants of behaviour in humans.

It was initially thought that there may be up to 140,000 different genes in the human genome. Now, with the mapping complete, this figure seems to have been considerably over-estimated. The two bodies involved in the mapping process say that the true figure is likely to lie between around 26,000 and 40,000. Still a lot of genes, it is true, but many fewer than had been expected. And not only are there fewer genes than expected but we appear to hold most of them in common with all other living creatures. Humans apparently share 85 per cent of their genetic sequence with the dog, something that may explain the occasional urges I feel to urinate against lamp-posts and chase after sticks.

Lamp-posts aside, this reduced genetic number does have implications for explanations of human behaviour which rely on the scale and complexity of the genome to govern all aspects of our being. With the genes that are known to exist and the relationships between them, the way in which they work together must be of a complexity and subtlety that geneticists have barely begun to grasp. The influences that genes have on behaviour would be even harder to determine. It seems unlikely that it will be possible to identify one gene that can with certainty be seen to code for one protein that in turn governs one clearly identified facet of human behaviour, even if claims are being made to the contrary. Richard Lewontin chides geneticists who take this line (that genes can be said to govern behaviour) saying that they are 'supposed to know better' and arguing that if genes are determining anything at all about an organism it is patterns of variation, not of similarity.

That being the case, it seems to me that the door to environmental and social factors as primary determinants to behaviour is left wide open. I do not consider tenable the argument that our varying expressions of gender differences (that is, historically and in other human societies apart from our own) result from being hard-wired into the very fabric of our being. As discussed above, even if one ignores the validity or accuracy of the claims made about the genome, there seems insufficient 'wiring' to allow any aspect of human behaviour to be so simply or deterministically explained. That differences in the outward manifestation of genders exist is not in dispute. My final argument would be that gender attributes are the product, possibly including some inherent genetic predisposition, overwhelmingly of the complex and continuous interplay of the many social and cultural factors and influences to which we are exposed from the moment of our birth. It is here that I would seek for explanations of gender differences, not in the coiled helices of our DNA.

POSTSCRIPT

Is Anatomy Destiny?

Nature versus nurture? Biology versus social determinism? Just as some scholars argue that we need to move beyond gender binaries to better understand human complexity, we must also move beyond neat either/or propositions about the causes of sex and gender. Traditional thought dictates that biology affects or determines behavior, that anatomy is destiny. But behavior can also alter physiology. Recent advances explore the complex interaction between biology (genes, hormones, brain structure) and environment. We have learned that it is impossible to determine how much of our behavior is biologically based and how much is environmental. Moreover, definitions of gendered behavior are temporally and culturally relative. Yet why do researchers continue to try to isolate biological from environmental factors?

Advancements in the study of biological bases of sex and critiques of applications of biological theory to human behavior, such as Wilson discussed, challenge some of Campbell's assertions. Many traditional biologists recognize species diversity in hormone-brain-behavior relationships, which makes the general application of theories based on animal physiology and behavior to humans problematic. Moreover, species diversity challenges male/female binaries. The validity of the presence/absence model of sex dimorphism has been challenged. In embryonic development, do females "just happen" by default in the absence of testosterone? No, all individuals actively develop through various genetic processes. Moreover, the sexes are similar in the presence and need of both androgens and estrogens; in fact, the chemical structures and derivation of estrogen and testosterone are interconnected.

Suggested Readings

Dina Anselmi, *Questions of Gender: Perspectives and Paradox* (New York: McGraw-Hill, 2006).

Anne Fausto-Sterling, *Sexing the Body: Gender Politics and the Construction of Sexuality* (New York: Basic Books, 2000).

David C. Geary, *Male, Female: The Evolution of Human Sex Differences* (Washington, DC: American Psychological Association, 1998).

Michael S. Kimmel, *The Gendered Society* (New York: Oxford Press, 2000).

Steven Rhodes, *Taking Sex Differences Seriously* (San Francisco: Encounter Books, 2004).

ISSUE 2

Is Gender Identity Innate?

YES: David B. Cohen, from *"Stranger in the Nest: Do Parents Really Shape Their Child's Personality, Intelligence, or Character?"* (Wiley & Sons, 1999)

NO: Bernice L. Hausman, from   Do Boys Have to Be Boys? Gender, Narrativity, and the John/Joan Case," *NWSA Journal* (September 2000)

ISSUE SUMMARY

YES: Clinical psychologist David B. Cohen argues that genetic and other biological factors have a relatively more important role than parental influences on gender identity and discusses the John/Joan case as an example.

NO: Associate professor Bernice L. Hausman examines the narratives or stories told about the John/Joan case to reveal biases and oversights about nonbiological contributions to John/Joan's experiences.

Imagine you or your partner is giving birth. When the baby is delivered, you anxiously await the doctor's declaration of the baby's sex. The doctor excitedly begins to say, "It's a . . ." then stops, her or his demeanor changing to one of feigned unconcern. Both female and male genitalia are observed in the baby and thus your child is diagnosed with a form of intersexuality. The next morning the hospital clerk comes in for the completion of the birth certificate. The designation of the child's sex, male or female, is required by law. In the afternoon, your neighbor excitedly calls to hear the details of the baby's birth. The first question she asks is, "What did you have?" The only acceptable answers are male or female. Later that evening, the volunteer nurses' aid comes in to offer you a handknit cap for your infant—pink or blue?

The term <u>*intersex*</u> has been used in medical literature to refer to three major subgroups of individuals with both male and female biological characteristics: (1) true hermaphrodites have one ovary and one testis, (2) female pseudohermaphrodites have ovaries and partial male genitalia (except testes), and (3) male pseudohermaphrodites have partial female genitalia (except ovaries) and testes.

Physicians now diagnose most intersexuals at birth, immediately entering them into a program of surgical and hormonal management. The goal is to "restore" one's "true" sex—to return the body to what it naturally ought to have been had normative sexual differentiation taken its course. The leading researcher of intersexual infant case management is John Money, whose theory of gender continues to dominate medical case management practices. He advocates assigning sex as early as possible (at the latest by 18 months when gender identity is no longer malleable) so that gender identity (sense of self as belonging to a female or male category) can develop successfully. Surgical correction should also be undertaken as soon as possible so that genitalia conforming to the chosen (i.e., "true") sex can be created. After all, the theory goes, the genitals will determine the way parents will interact with the child.

There is considerable controversy over Money's theory that gender identity is socially constructed, not innate. Money's theory is generally uncontested by medical professionals but challenged by psychologists studying the effects of prenatal hormones on brain structure, gender identity, and gendered behavior. Money has spent his career conducting psychological research on children who were born intersexual and were surgically "corrected" soon after birth. His aim was to document the successful accommodation of the child and family to sex assignment resulting in a secure gender identity—a gender identity that may not match chromosomal sex. Recent critical analyses of this research, however, alert us to research design flaws that call for a reconsideration of the biological underpinnings of gender identity.

A pivotal case is that of John/Joan, a boy (with a twin brother) who at eight months of age was injured in a botched circumcision and subsequently reared as a girl. This created the opportunity to study "naturalistically" whether or not gender identity could be socially constructed, hoping to offer strong evidence once and for all against the innateness of gender identity. But at the age of 14, upon learning the facts of his birth and sex reassignment, the child rejected his reassigned sex and began living as a man. In May, 2004 he committed suicide.

In the following selections Cohen asserts that prenatal androgen has a profound and unalterable effect on one's desire to be a boy and argues that the John/Joan case makes this point. The case provides evidence of the innateness of gender identity. In contrast, Bernice L. Hausman examines the narratives or stories told about the John/Joan case to reveal biases and oversights about nonbiological contributions to John/Joan's experiences. She also observes that the specialized and heightened medical attention and differential parental treatment of children born as intersexuals (of which parents may not be consciously aware) may profoundly impact gender identity outcomes.

David B. Cohen  **YES**

Stranger in the Nest: Do Parents Really Shape Their Child's Personality, Intelligence, or Character?

Sex Beyond Our Sex Chromosomes

A lost Y chromosome is one way a male zygote can become a female. Another is through a mutation of the *SRY* gene, or sex-determining region of the Y chromosome. Normally, SRY sends a special signal to other genes for the development of testes, the major source of androgen. However, when mutated, SRY can't send the signal and the testes fail to develop. So, despite having a Y chromosome, the embryo develops female characteristics. Such rare anomalies remind us of how even a tiny DNA difference between people can sometimes make all the difference in the world.

Even with androgen, an XY embryo can still become female. This will happen if a genetic defect on the X chromosome creates an insensitivity to the hormone—a kind of biochemical blindness. The insensitivity doesn't apply to estrogen, a female hormone that in both sexes is produced in tiny amounts by the adrenal glands. Available estrogen means that upon reaching puberty, androgen-insensitive XY females will have a feminine appearance.

According to medical psychologists John Money and Anke Ehrhardt, an XY female typically has a lifelong feminine orientation, with dreams of being a wife, mother, and homemaker. She can be an attractive, statuesque woman with long legs, large breasts, radiant complexion, winning smile, and feminine ways. She may even look like a movie star or a fashion model. Her condition is usually not discovered until after puberty when a medical investigation of absent menstruation and an inability to bear children reveals two singular facts: the presence of undescended testes and a nonfunctional vagina, a short cavity or tube that dead-ends because no uterus exists.

⁓⊙⁓

While a genetic male (XY) fetus can become a female, a genetic female (XX) becoming a male almost never happens. Still, a female fetus can develop strikingly masculine characteristics. In the 1950s, some pregnant women took synthetic hormones to prevent miscarriage. Female offspring of these mothers were prenatally masculinized by such hormones. The girls developed a tomboy style complete with preference for cars and trucks over dolls, competition over cooperation, rough and tumble play over quiet talk, and blue jeans over frilly dresses. Whatever the social influence, fetal hormones had clearly made a big difference.

The influence of prenatal androgen on female development is evident in female fraternal twins with male co-twins. On tests of spatial ability that generally favor males, such women outperform female fraternals with female co-twins. They also show a greater preference for novel experiences, nonconformist or uninhibited behavior, and mind-altering drugs. Why would having a co-twin brother make a girl more masculine rather than more feminine? A biological answer—exposure to androgen during fetal development—fits what is known about animals. By chance a female mouse or gerbil fetus may develop between two male fetuses rather than between a male and a female or two females. A double dose of male neighbor means an extra dose of androgen, which in turn explains why such females tend to show more aggression and less sexual interest in males. It also explains why they are sexually less attractive to males.

The impact of prenatal androgen is illuminated by an unusual story of identical twin boys. At age 7 months, they underwent circumcision with a cauterizing needle rather than the usual scalpel. Unfortunately, one of the twins was the victim of a bizarre accident whereby his little penis was electrocuted, eventually drying up and falling off. After much anguish, the parents agreed to a sex reassignment, meaning that the victim's genitals would be surgically reconstructed to look female. She would be reared as a girl named Joan, and at puberty, estrogen therapy would be used to encourage mature female development.

This case has appeared in professional journals and psychiatry textbooks, but mainly to illustrate alleged parental power to shape a child's sex-appropriate behavior and sexual identity. Yet a follow-up of this and other cases suggests that, quite the contrary, the genetically determined influence of androgens during fetal brain development is paramount. Far from being sexually neutral, newborns are strongly biased toward maleness of female-ness, some even more strongly than others. Social pressures merely reinforce this bias, they do not create it.

From the outset, even despite hormone replacement therapy and being reared as a female, Joan was unable to adopt a female sex role. In her mind, she was a boy, not a tomboy, with tendencies toward stubbornness and dominance. The masculine self-image was evident in her rejection of dresses, dolls, and any attempt to get her to imitate her mother's makeup ritual; if anything, she preferred to mimic her father shaving and to play with boys. These and other masculine qualities inspired her peers to call her "cave woman" and "gorilla."

Alas, encouraged by experts, Joan's parents continued to press for feminine behavior, all of which went against the grain of instinct and feeling. No wonder that by early adolescence, she was having serious psychological problems including conflict over her sexual identity, a sense of helplessness, and attempted suicide. Then, at age 14, Joan renounced her false female identity, deciding to live as a man named John and eventually to undergo extensive sex reassignment surgery including mastectomy with reconstruction of male genitals. It was at this point that John's father revealed the truth that John was a genetic (XY) male. "For the first time everything made sense," said John, "and I understood who and what I was." By age 25, he was happily married. Though still somewhat bitter, he was finally at reasonable peace with himself.[1]

While John's case is exceptional, others make the same point. Regarding a group of six XY males born without penises castrated during infancy, and reared as girls, one researcher noted that all six were basically male in their mind and behavior. "They don't say, 'I wish I was a boy,' or 'I'd really rather be a boy,' or 'I think I am a boy.' They say, 'I *am* a boy.'" Additional evidence further suggests the paramount power of biological events to shape a person's psychological development despite unremitting social pressure from parents, peers, and professionals. The best known come from the testimony of homosexuals, but truly exotic phenomena make the point more convincing and memorable.

Consider genetically male (XY) children with a genetic deficiency of dihydrotestosterone, a male hormone that the body normally product from testosterone. Because of the deficiency, such children have ambiguous, somewhat feminine external genitals with a clitoris-like penis, a labia like scrotum, and a pouchlike vagina. However, because of their norm levels of testosterone, they have internal male genitals including seminal ducts and undescended testicles. With puberty comes a remarkable Kafkaesque transformation. The usual surge of testosterone that normally causes masculine development has similar effects in these children including enlarged penis, descended testicles, deepened voice, more muscle mass, and a new capacity for erection and ejaculation.

With these biological changes, and despite a lifetime of female upbringing, most such children living under reasonably tolerant social conditions develop a normal male-gender identity and adopt male role including husband and (adoptive) father. Apparently, much of what they have learned—much of the parental influence imposed during the so-called formative years—sloughs off, making clear just how superficial gender socialization can be in the face of powerful inborn dispositions from prenatal testosterone.

In a rare condition affecting about one person in 15,000, an overactive adrenal gland produces too much prenatal androgen. Congenital adrenal; hyperplasia, or CAH stems from a double dose of a recessive gene locate on chromosome 6. Compared to normal females, CAH girls tend to be somewhat masculine in their preferences and behaviors. They are in tensely energetic, enjoy rough and tumble play, and are seen as tomboys. When given a choice, they tend to display a preference for traditionally male toys: cars and blocks, for example, rather than dolls and crayons. While most CAH girls identify themselves as females, some show little enthusiasm for that role. While most become heterosexual, some become bisexual or homosexual. On personality tests, they tend to score more like males in attitudes toward aggression and in reactions to stress. So, too, on tests of spatial ability, for example recognizing an object rotated in space CAH females tend to perform more like males.

These observations on sexual and gender development support our main theme: Parental and peer influence is limited, even blocked, by strong inborn potentials involving intelligence, personality, gender identity, vulnerability to mental illness, and special talents. We have seen this power of nature over nurture, not just in the findings of twins and adoption studies but in the striking effects of even slightly altered DNA and in marked differences that siblings show right from birth. Finally, despite the most unremitting pressure from families and communities, unconventional sexual and gender development could not be altered in the child.

~◌~

With CAH, masculine behavior occurs despite social influences that encourage feminine behavior. With male homosexuality, feminine behavior occurs despite even stronger expectations and demands for masculine behavior. Looking forward, roughly 75 percent of strikingly effeminate boys become homosexual men; looking back, 85 percent of homosexual men responding to questionnaires endorse one or more questions about early effeminacy. Some of these are aversion to rough and tumble play, preference for the company of girls, interest in dolls, dressing in women's clothes, and being considered a sissy.

In males, the homosexual disposition is about 50 percent heritable, with estimates varying between 30 and 75 percent. That at least some of the disposition is transmitted by the mother is evident in a relatively high rate of male homosexuality on the maternal side of the family. This in turn implicates the X chromosome that a male inherits only from his mother. Genetics researcher Dean Hamer searched the X chromosome of 40 pairs of homosexual brothers. From each subject he isolated and identified the same set of 22 genetic markers—short, easily distinguished stretches of DNA that vary from person to person and that geneticists use to flag a particular spot on a chromosome. If two brothers shared a marker, chances were pretty good that they also shared genes in the neighborhood of that marker—genes presumably involved in their homosexual disposition. Thirty-three of the 40 pairs of brothers did indeed share the same set of five markers located in a region on the X chromosome called q28—far too many matches to be coincidental.

A follow-up study found essentially the same thing: 67 percent of homosexual brother pairs shared genetic markers in the same region of the X chromosome, compared to 22 percent of heterosexual brother pairs. Since 50 percent sharing is expected by chance, one or more genes in the q28 region of the X chromosome may very well contribute to male homosexuality. If homosexuality is indeed a heritable disposition, then those with its most obligate form have no more freedom to choose their sexual orientation than those whose heterosexual disposition is likewise obligate. A similar point can be made of other dispositions—for example, cigarette smoking—that in some are powerfully addictive while in others, though pleasurable, are nevertheless dispensable when circumstances and good judgment prevail.

Heritability implies differences in brain, physiology, and psychology. Some structures in the male homosexual's brain look more female than male, for example the hypothalamus, a structure that regulates needs, drives, appetites, and circadian rhythms, and the anterior commissure, a structure that helps the left and right cerebral hemispheres communicate with each other. Physiological differences have also been found: For example, in response to an injection of the female hormone estrogen, women react with a big increase in another hormone called luteinizing hormone (LH); males have little or no increase. Male homosexuals show either the strong female pattern or an intermediate one involving a modest increase in LH. As for psychological differences, male homosexuals tend to perform more like heterosexual females on certain psychological tests that normally tend to differentiate males and females. Males tend to outperform females and male homosexuals on test of spatial rotation, for example the ability to recognize a target object that has been rotated left to right and front to back and placed among other similar objects.

Absent direct genetic evidence, a convincing argument that homosexuality is as inborn as heterosexuality would have to be founded on a definitive study of people adoptively reared by genetically unrelated homosexuals—a study showing that the rates of homosexuality in such adoptees are no different from the expected rate of roughly 2 to 5 percent. That finding would at once illuminate the biological basis of the homosexual disposition and demonstrate that it is no more contagious than, say, high intelligence or extroversion. At the same time, it would be one more example of just how really superficial if not illusory parental influence can be where the inborn dispositions of any one child are especially strong—just how, despite intense social pressure, some children can develop in such an alien way that they become like strangers to their parents. . . .

Note

1. David Reimer, who had been known as "John," committed suicide on May 4, 2004. His mother reported he had been depressed following a job loss, marital separation, and death of his twin brother two years earlier. NY: *Times*, May 2004).

NO ↵

Bernice L. Hausman

Do Boys Have to Be Boys?

Introduction

Standard medical theory and practice for sex reassignment during childhood maintains that gender identity (the sense of oneself as one sex or the other) develops postnatally and is not established definitively until the child reaches about 2 years of age, that vaginas are more easily made than penises, that gender identity reflects sex assignment and rearing more than chromosomal and other physical factors, and that to be male without a penis is unthinkable in psychological or social terms. Thus, chromosomally (and often gonadally) male infants born with deformed or unspecific genitals are almost always reared as girls; throughout their childhood and adolescence, they are subject to medical and surgical treatments to bring their anatomy into conformity with typical female morphology. This protocol was first initiated by John Money and colleagues in the 1950s at Johns Hopkins Hospital and then solidified as standard practice in the 1960s and 1970s (Dreger 1998; Fausto-Sterling 2000; Hausman 1995; Kessler 1990, 1998).

According to Alice Dreger, 96 percent of intersex infants are "made into girls" (Dreger 1999). One in 1500 infants are born with genitalia so unusual that sex assignment into the standard categories of male and female is difficult, although one in 200 or 300 infants are referred to surgery because of "somewhat problematic" genital configurations, such as hypospadias, a condition in which the urethra does not exit from the tip of the penis (Dreger 1999). One particularly interesting aspect of the treatment protocols for intersex infants, however, is that they are based on an "index case" where the initial sex assignment of the child was not in question. (An index case is one that establishes treatments for a particular condition.) In the late 1990s, the status and meaning of the outcomes of the index case for intersexuality came into question.

In the spring of 1997, a number of articles in the popular press announced that the medical community was now rethinking the standard treatment protocols concerning sex reassignment during childhood as the result of a follow-up study of an early, momentous case of identical twin boys, one of whose sex was reassigned following traumatic loss of his penis during his first year of life ("Medical Community Questions Theory on Sex Reassignment"

1997; "Can an Infant's Sex Be Changed?" 1997). The case became known as the "John/Joan" case, in reference to the pseudonyms used for the subject at different stages of his/her life, and in its original form was the recognized "index case" for treatment of intersexuality in infants. John Money was a principle figure in that original case, which was itself written up in *Time* magazine in the 1970s ("Biological Imperatives" 1973). In the recent medical account, published in *Archives of Pediatrics and Adolescent Medicine,* Milton Diamond and H. Keith Sigmundson revisit the case and show that the little boy whose sex was reassigned from male to female is now living as a man. In a lengthy discussion of the experiences of this "boy" reassigned as "girl," and then assigned again as a boy, Diamond and Sigmundson claim that "The evidence seems overwhelming that normal humans are not psychosexually neutral at birth but are, in keeping with their mammalian heritage, predisposed and biased to interact with environment, familial, and social forces in either a male or female mode" (1997, 303). Thus the authors claim that this case, in its complete form, demonstrates that gender identity is not malleable before a specific age, as Money had originally asserted, but that it is innate and based on chromosomal and hormonal sex factors.

Diamond and Sigmundson's conclusion only makes sense, however, if one accepts the dichotomy that structures it: *either* gender identity is socially constructed through the individual's responses to environmental stimuli before the age of 2, *or* gender identity is innate and determined by genetics, prenatal hormones, or some other physiological force (or combination of forces) in fetal development. Yet while Money's original discussions of the case purport to demonstrate one theory, and Diamond and Sigmundson claim to show the other, the case in all its guises demonstrates that gender identity is the result of a process of self-naming that is embedded within the cultural milieu and influenced by its gender stories. . . .

Gender and Narrativity

What does it mean to claim that gender (as identity, as positionality) is, at least in part, a product of narrativity? I want to suggest that even a basic consideration of the significance of story-telling to the creation of identity and gender can reorient our thinking about what gender is and how a gender identity comes about.

Peter Brooks opens his book, *Reading for the Plot: Design and Intention in Narrative,* with the following description of narrative:

> Our lives are ceaselessly intertwined with narrative, with the stories that we tell and hear told, those we dream or imagine or would like to tell, all of which are reworked in that story of our own lives that we narrate to ourselves in an episodic, sometimes semi-conscious, but virtually uninterrupted monologue. We live immersed in narrative, recounting and reassessing the meaning of our past actions, anticipating the outcome of our future projects, situating ourselves at the intersection of several stories not yet completed. (1992, 3)

. . . An interesting discussion of narratology by Mieke Bal divides narratives into three components: the *fabula,* events causally or logically related (the "real" of what happened); the *story,* aspects of the fabula presented in an organized fashion (in other words, the plot); and *text,* what has been written down ("finite structured whole composed of linguistic signs") (1985). This structural typology of narrative is helpful in discussing the narrativity of conflicting medical accounts, as it allows us to see precisely where the accounts differ—for example, at the level of "story/plot" or of "fabula/events"—and thus the points at which the medical interpretations of the case diverge.

Further, a narrative understanding of gender reorients what we think gender is, as well as what it does. The scientific accounts of the John/Joan case depend upon routine or systematic techniques of narration that can be typified with the categories just delineated. They also depend upon a static understanding of "gender," which is most often used to signify stereotypical social behavior. Considering "gender" in relation to the idea of narrative, it becomes a dynamic category of subjectivity, rather than a static referent of known contents. This analysis also makes it possible for us to see how the concept of gender is engaged to shore up the meanings of basic scientific and medical arguments about "sex." . . .

If "we have not seriously grappled with the fact that we afflict ourselves with a need to locate a bodily basis for assertions about gender," as Suzanne Kessler puts it in *Lessons from the Intersexed,* it may be because we have been concentrating on the wrong question (1998, 132). This question—whether gender identity is innate (and the result of biology) or nurtured (and thus socially constructed)—seems legitimate but it keeps us focused on the opposition between the categories, and thus the maintenance or destruction of that opposition. Nature *versus* nurture doesn't work because both sides of the argument depend upon a loose, untheorized, and highly stereotyped category of human behavior: gender. Once we rethink gender in terms of narrativity, the important issue is how it (gender) functions as a culturally salient category of experience. And then all of the categories—gender, gender identity, and sex (etc.)—need to be treated as ideas rather than as facts. If it seems that we have left aside the nature side of the debate and entered into culture, it is because typical discussions assume simplistic and undertheorized conceptions of gender, all the while claiming to know its origins and its meanings. To subject both nature and nurture arguments to feminist and narrative analysis will not explode or do away with the binary, but will allow us to consider how its very structure has limited our thinking on the topic.

. . . Gender narratives are stories that organize life events into socially coherent plots about sex.

In the context of an epistemological approach to gender, one question that arises is whether researchers can put aside their beliefs in gender as an ontology to get at what we think of as biology at all. Investigating the twin sex reassignment case as a series of stories about gender shows that the theory of innate, biological sex identity put forth by Diamond and Sigmundson can be unsettled by attention to its own, unrecognized narrativity, and demonstrates that gendered identities are both process and product of elaborate attempts to make sense of the relationship between the body and experience (1997). As such, gender can never be just an effect of biological processes, but is always part of a dialectical engagement of interpretation and story-making—that is, of narrativity—by specific subjects in concrete biosocial circumstances.

John/Joan

Comparing accounts of the John/Joan case necessitates distinguishing the events of the fabula, some of which differ between the stories, as well as the plotted interpretations of these events, interpretations which produce the accounts we read as medical case studies. In Money's original discussions of the case, which appeared in two books, *Man and Woman, Boy and Girl* and *Sexual Signatures* (the first coauthored with Anke Ehrhardt, the second with Patricia Tucker), the case is presented with the kind of personal detail appropriate to books oriented toward lay audiences: the parents of the twins are from farm backgrounds, with little education; the mother is very observant of gender appropriate behavior, the father less so (Money and Ehrhardt 1972, 123–31; Money and Tucker 1975, 91–8). The routine report offered by Diamond and Sigmundson is very brief and lacks this level of detail concerning the family's background and ideas about gender (1997). It provides, however, other significant details, discussed below.

In all of the recountings of the case, the story goes something like this: at seven months of age, identical twin boys were taken to a local hospital for an apparently routine circumcision. The surgeon caused irreparable damage to the first twin's penis because he used excess electrical current in the cauterizing scalpel. The organ was completely ablated. The parents, understandably distraught, sought help and were eventually directed to the psychohormonal unit at Johns Hopkins Hospital, where the doctors encouraged the parents to raise the penisless twin as a girl, with appropriate medical and surgical intervention. The parents agreed, after some intervening months of indecision. When the twins were 17 months of age, the child without the penis underwent the first phase of surgical repair: orchiectomy (removal of the testes) and feminization of the external genitalia (shaping the empty scrotum to look like labia). After this, the child was dressed exclusively in girls' clothing, given a girl's name, and brought up with gender-specific behaviors and expectations. Yearly visits to the Johns Hopkins clinic monitored the development of both children.

In Money's original presentations of this case, the discussion always ends on a positive note, as if to suggest that "all's well that ends well." However, Money's early presentations of the case were published while the children were still very young, about 9 years old. Diamond and Sigmundson's work suggests that Money's original conclusions were not only wrong, but inattentive. Their later interviews with the family (in 1994 and 1995) state that even before the age of 6 the little "girl" rejected her female role (Diamond and Sigmundson 1997, 299). Of course, these later interviews may have been influenced by hindsight, since by this time the subject was living as a male and wanting to demonstrate a consistent narrative history as a male subject. Nevertheless, the story of the child's gender identity that Diamond and Sigmundson present is not of successful gender reassignment, which is the one Money told, but of the child's consistent resistance to feminization. In this organization of the fabula, at the age of 14 the child stopped living as a girl and succeeded in convincing a local team of physicians and psychiatrists (now in charge of the case) to be allowed to return to male status.

Diamond and Sigmundson's presentation and discussion of the case is illuminating, bringing out details that are embedded but somewhat obscure in the earlier publications. For example, they write that the Hopkins clinicians "enlisted male-to-female transsexuals to convince Joan [their pseudonym for the child as a girl] of the advantages of being female and having a vagina constructed" (Diamond and Sigmundson 1997, 300). This apparently bothered the child greatly, causing her to run away from the hospital on one occasion. This aspect of the treatment program is never mentioned in the original presentations of the case, although transsexuals do appear in a slightly different context. In *Sexual Signatures,* Money and Tucker write that the child's parents, originally reluctant to allow their child to be reassigned to the female sex, inadvertently saw a television program "about the work with transexuals [sic] at Johns Hopkins. On the screen was an adult male-to-female transexual who, they could see for themselves, looked and talked like a normal, attractive woman. After that they worked their way to the decision to reassign their son as a girl" (1975, 92).

Diamond and Sigmundson add further elements of the fabula in their presentation of the story, however: "At their yearly visit to johns Hopkins Hospital, the twins were made to stand naked for inspection by groups of clinicians and to inspect each other's genitalia. . . . John's brother, decades later, recalls the experience with tears" (1997, 301). In addition, as a teenager the reassigned child "rejected requests to look at pictures of nude females, which she was supposed to emulate" (301). These aspects of the case are confirmed and expanded in greater detail by Colapinto (1997).

Diamond and Sigmundson's account of the case sheds new light on the earlier, triumphant narrative of the social construction of gender identity (and hence the malleability of gender up to a certain age). Diamond and Sigmundson, of course, assert that their follow-up on the case shows that the child's *original* and *normal male* identity eventually won the day. . . . Diamond and Sigmundson assume that gender both precedes and follows from sex—the male's predisposition is to "act like a boy"—but it and the "actual behavior" of the boy need reinforcement "in daily interactions." In this use of gender-as-explanation, Diamond and Sigmundson maintain their claim about gender's innateness at the same time that they acknowledge gender as the result of social forces. This demonstrates their adherence to the natural attitude toward gender, which establishes gender as an ontology that is both origin and goal of development.

While one could hardly quibble with the preference for long-term counseling over the medical and surgical quick fix of sex reassignment, there are ways to interpret (and renarrativize) elements of the John/Joan fabula other than to conclude that males are necessarily predisposed to act as boys. My initial and continuing response to Diamond and Sigmundson's follow-up is that the child's return to a masculine identity was heavily influenced by the coercive attempts at feminization. That is, Joan resisted the heavy-handed plot to make her into a girl. In all of the accounts, appropriate behaviors (for the child) were clearly demarcated (by the adults) according to traditional gender codes: "At five, the little girl already preferred dresses to pants, enjoyed wearing her hair ribbons, bracelets and frilly blouses, and loved being her daddy's little sweetheart" (Money and Tucker 1975, 97). "Rehearsals of future roles can also be seen in girls' and boys' toy preferences. The girl in this case wanted and received for Christmas dolls, a doll house, and a doll carriage, clearly related to the maternal aspect of the female adult role, while the boy [the twin brother] wanted and obtained a garage with cars and gas pumps and tools, part of the rehearsal of the male role. His father, like many men, was very interested in cars and mechanical activities" (Money and Ehrhardt 1972, 127). "When the twins were 4 or 5 years old, they were watching their parents. Father was shaving and mother was applying makeup. Joan applied shaving cream and pretended to shave. *When Joan was corrected* and told to put on lipstick and makeup like mother, Joan said: 'No, I don't want no makeup, I want to shave'" (Diamond and Sigmundson 1997, 299; emphasis added). Indeed, it was through such gender role training that the treatment protocol of reassignment was expected to succeed psychologically. Add to this rigid set of expectations the yearly clinical experience, where the child was made to display her body to the physicians at the hospital, submit to psychological testing, and agree to the desirability of vaginal construction (a proposal reinforced through conversations with transsexual women she did not know and had little understanding of), and we can begin to see this alternative narrative more clearly. Joan's desire to be John may simply have been a desire to be free of this coercive femininity, to be able to produce her own identity in opposition to the one that everyone else in her life seemed to want her to take on.

She may also have been responding to unconscious tension in the family. In a long and well-developed article for *Rolling Stone*, John Colapinto does the best job of revealing the familial anxiety about Joan's gender identity, an important element that goes largely unexamined in all of the accounts (even his own, where its existence is palpable but not analyzed) (1997). Before deciding upon sex reassignment, the parents "sank into a state of mute depression" (58). By the time they decided on their course of action, "they had eradicated any doubts they might have had about the efficacy of the treatment," but when the mother first put a dress on Joan,

> "She was ripping at it, trying to tear it off" [the mother said] . . . "I remember thinking, 'Oh my God, she knows she's a boy and she doesn't want girls' clothing. She doesn't want to be a girl.' But then I thought, 'Well, maybe I can *teach* her to want to be a girl. Maybe I can train her so that she wants to be a girl.'"(64)

The twin brother recalled, as an adult, that "I recognized Joan as my sister . . . but she never, ever acted the part. She'd get a skipping rope for a gift, and the only thing we'd use *that* for was to tie people up, whip people with" (68). With every action and every thing in her life carrying such heavy associations, no wonder Joan had a desire to rebel, which for a girl often means acting like a boy. Colapinto writes that the parents

> were troubled by Joan's masculine behavior. But they had been told by Dr. Money that they must not entertain any doubts about their daughter, and they felt that to do so would only increase the problem. Instead, [they] seized on those moments when Joan's behavior *could* be construed as stereotypically feminine. "And she could be sort of feminine, sometimes," [the mother] says, "when she wanted to please me. She'd be less rough, keep herself clean and tidy, and help a little bit in the kitchen." (1997, 66)

In transsexuals' autobiographies, the problem of producing an identity in the face of coercive gender conditioning is a common theme. . . . This same natural attitude toward gender is evident in the statements of John's family; for them, helping in the kitchen and staying clean is not only appropriate behavior for a girl, but evidence of an appropriately gendered identity within. . . .

The transsexual autobiographies also demonstrate that becoming a man or a woman is a process of learning how to represent that identity publicly; in Judith Butler's terms, it means producing that identity though the repeated iterations of representing it as if it already existed (Butler 1990). If one can become a man by acting like one (as "Joan" was to become a girl at least in part by acting like one), then becoming a man can be understood as an antidote for coercive, enforced femininity. Becoming a man means establishing a definitive gender identity in the face of familial and medical uncertainty, as well as acquiring the cultural perks that go along with that privileged position: higher status, encouragement of active play, an allowance to get dirty while playing, greater sexual freedom, and toy trucks. Both Martino and "Joan" had brothers, and thus could observe first hand the comparative benefits of being a boy. . . .

The "natural attitude" toward gender assumes heterosexuality, thus all those who are not heterosexual are suspected of being gender transgressors as well. This aspect of gender's ontology also works the other way: to be heterosexual is to guarantee other people's assumption that one has a "normal" (and thus socially appropriate, innate) gender identity. This is why Diamond and Sigmundson can be so secure in their claim that "John" has found his true "natural" gender as a man, because he is married and has adopted his wife's children. John's narrative has a happy and logical ending; the plot worked out the right way.

In this narrative, "John's" response to his particular situation was to repudiate the identity picked out for him and go for the one his twin got. Thus, "After his return to male living he felt his attitudes, behaviors, and body were in concert in a way they had not been when living as a girl" (Diamond and Sigmundson 1997, 300). He ends up, then, as a completely "normal" man (his wife remarks that "There is no doubt who wears the pants in this family" [302]), which is understandable, of course, after the experiences of his childhood. As Colapinto writes,

> [John] speaks of his pride in his role as husband, father and sole breadwinner in the family that he never believed he would be lucky enough to have. "From what I've been taught by my father," he says, "what makes you a

man is: You treat your wife well. You put a roof over your family's head. You're a good father. Things like that add up much more to being a man than just *bang bang bang*—sex." (1997, 97)

John's own words demonstrate that "being a man" is a completely *social* designation, given that what it takes to be one must be learned. Yet for Diamond and Sigmundson, John's status as male breadwinner, head of household, family disciplinarian, husband, and father, demonstrate that his original biological make-up as a male made him the man he eventually became.

Money's original assertions were wrong, of course, but not necessarily wrong-headed, since they suggested the essential narrativity of gender. He claimed that, given the optimal window of opportunity, you can make any individual into a woman. He argued that the stories about sex identity that one tells oneself and that are told to one are crucial to the development of identity. But this case might have taught him that gender narratives don't always work in the most expected ways, and that coercive narratives can incite creative, rebellious responses. (Publications of the Intersex Society of North America, such as the newsletter *Hermaphrodites with Attitude*, are bringing to visibility precisely such stories.) While the clinicians utilized gender narratives in their attempts to feminize the penisless twin, the child fought back with his/her own arsenal of stories. If a person's gender identity is a product of story-making, then what's to stop an individual from making him or herself up?

This begs the question, of course, of how coercive the imposition of gender is for those whose anatomy presents what are considered the normal signs of sex (what Alice Dreger [1999] calls "the standard parts"), and why most individuals do not seem to resist the rather forceful feminization and masculinization endemic to culture. One reason is that most people adhere to the natural attitude toward gender, they agree with and uphold culturally accepted gender ontologies (Kessler and McKenna [1978] 1985). For those subjects whose body does not Seem to verify gender "naturally," or those who refuse the social requirements to make body and behavior match as binary gender coordinates, the coercive nature of its imposition is more salient, and thus subject to resistance in a more obvious way.

The follow-up on the twin sex reassignment case does not demonstrate that gender identity is innate, as Diamond and Sigmundson claim. Their discussion, which curiously ignores the psychological impact of the early attempts to enforce "Joan's" femininity—except insofar as "John" feels angry at the attempted enforcement—demonstrates their inability to see outside of the nature versus nurture debate concerning the origins of gender identity. In their view, feeling uncomfortable with an enforced and exhibitionistic femininity is evidence of an innate masculinity, and not a sign that the imposition of such an identity can be a problem even for genetically female women. Opening up the John/Joan case to the multiple possibilities that understanding gender as a narrative allows—and interrogating the ontology implied by that narrative—suggests another reading, in which "John's" conviction of his innate masculinity and the authors' obvious acceptance of this conviction *as fact* show how readily some will believe that, after all, boys will be boys, especially if they won't be girls.

Conclusion

. . . The John/Joan case—with its outlandish sex stereotyping, its heavy-handed interpretive gender schema, its anguished parents and distraught children—will never prove that gender identity is the result of an innate biological force, be it prenatal hormones, genetic influence, or something else. All it can prove is that the attempt to make John into Joan didn't work, and that plausible social reasons why this was the case can be argued. The oppressive plot of female gender identity presented in all printed versions of this case is enough to make anyone run screaming from the room. We need to be asking why this narrative about gender's relation to the body is so readily accepted as a seeming antidote to the "horror" of the idea that gender is a social construct. And we ought to wonder about how such simplistic views of gender were allowed to proliferate (and still do) in discourses meant to study and treat complex human behavior.

The John/Joan case resembles, but is not identical to, the intersexual cases that currently receive treatment and sex reassignment soon after birth. In both scenarios, there is a desire to "fix" the anatomical "error," as well as to "fix" the child into one sex or another. Diamond and Sigmundson recognize this when they comment that "[a]s parents will still want their children to be and look normal as soon after birth or injury as possible, physicians will have to provide the best advice and care consistent with current knowledge" (1997, 303). The current medical protocols for intersex infants certainly reveal a cultural discomfort with individuals whose bodily existence challenges categories we hold dear. These protocols also show that, at least in the realm of sexual behavior and identity, most of us suffer from a lack of imagination. Instead of enabling the creation of new narratives, both to aid these individuals in developing their identities as sexed persons and to free other people's rigid identity constructions as well, medical theory and practice enforces upon all of us tired and oppressive stories about who wears the pants, who gets to shave, and who plays with dolls, because it assumes that these stories constitute the necessary foundation for a "normal" life. But if, as the intersex activists suggest, we can resist the either/or dichotomous opposition of current gender scenarios—if we can, in other words, "unfix" identity from its current mooring in traditional, bipolar gender narratives—rereading the biological signifiers of sex can offer us the starting point for truly alternative stories of sexed identity.

The question then becomes, do there have to be boys (or girls, for that matter)?

References

Bal, Mieke. 1985. *Narratology: Introduction to the Theory of Narrative*. Toronto, Canada: University of Toronto Press.

"Biological Imperatives." 1973. *Time*, 8 January, 34.

Brooks, Peter. 1992. *Reading for the Plot: Design and Intention in Narrative*. Cambridge, MA: Harvard University Press.

Butler, Judith. 1990. *Gender Trouble: Feminism and the Subversion of Identity*. New York: Routledge.

"Can an Infant's Sex Be Changed?" 1997. *The Washington Post,* 18 March, Health Section, 7, 19.

Colapinto, John. 1997. "The True Story of John Joan." *Rolling Stone,* 11 December, 54–72, 92, 94–7.

Diamond, Milton, and Keith Sigmundson. 1997. "Sex Reassignment at Birth: Long-Term Review and Clinical Implications." *Archives of Pediatrics and Adolescent Medicine,* 151: 298–304.

Dreger, Alice Domurat. 1998. *Hermaphrodites and the Medical Invention of Sex.* Cambridge, MA: Harvard University Press.

——— 1999. "In Love with a Ruler: Phallometers and the Surgical 'Treatment' of Intersexuality." Paper presented at the annual meeting of the Society for Social Studies of Science, 29 October, San Diego, California.

Fausto-Sterling, Anne. 2000. *Sexing the Body: Gender Politics and the Construction of Sexuality.* New York: Basic Books.

Hausman, Bernice L. 1995. *Changing Sex: Transsexualism, Technology, and the idea of Gender.* Durham, NC: Duke University Press.

Kessler, Suzanne J. 1990. "The Medical Construction of Gender: Case Management of Intersexed Infants." *Signs.* 16: 3–26.

——— 1998. *Lessons from the Intersexed.* New Brunswick, NJ: Rutgers University Press.

Kessler, Suzanne J., and Wendy McKenna. (1978) 1985. *Gender: An Ethnomethodological Approach.* Reprint. Chicago, IL: University of Chicago Press.

"Medical Community Questions Theory on Sex Reassignment." 1977. *American Medical News,* 24–31 March, 48.

Money, John, and Anke Ehrhardt. 1972. *Man and Woman, Boy and Girl.* New York: New American Library—Mentor.

Money, John, and Patricia Tucker. 1975. *Sexual Signatures: On Being a Man or a Woman.* Boston: Little, Brown.

POSTSCRIPT

Is Gender Identity Innate?

What are the implications of intersexuality for psychological health? Open investigation of this question has been skirted in the medical community by the near-automatic action to surgically and hormonally repair intersexuality. Many medical professionals reason that if "normal" sexuality is restored, we will not have to be concerned about psychological consequences. Important insights are provided by case studies of unaltered intersexuals completed in the mid-1900s before the norm of surgical intervention was established. Reports document the remarkable psychological adaptability of these individuals, leading to healthy psychological and social outcomes. Just as there are few more contemporary case studies of intersexuals, there are also few follow-up studies of "corrected" intersexuals. Anecdotal accounts such as the case of John/Joan reveal emotional pain, discomfort from frequent genital examinations and invasive treatments, and destruction of sexual pleasure.

Suzanne Kessler analyzed the medical construction of sex by interviewing six medical specialists in pediatric intersexuality about the medical decision-making process. She explains that in Western culture, chromosomal and hormonal makeup determines what is defined as the real, natural, biological sex. Yet in the medical management of intersexuality, cultural factors are considered—often preempting biological factors—when assigning the sex of the infant. For example, the key consideration for the assignment of a child as a boy is the appearance of an appropriately sized penis. In fact, in her interviews, Kessler reveals great latitude in assigning sex and concludes that appearance of external genitalia, not chromosomal makeup, is often the driving force. *NO!*

Should genitalia be given primacy in determining gender? Every day, we make gender attributions without genital inspection based on outward performances that culturally define gender. To catch a revealing glimpse of this gender attribution process, ask a two- or three-year-old to determine the sex of individuals or fictitious characters; and have them indicate what makes the individual male or female. Indeed, preschool curricula often include direct instruction on gender attributions, and developmental diagnostic criteria often include the ability to make such gender attributions. *↳ well...*

Medical professionals claim that the humanitarian aim of eliminating the child's intersexuality is to enable intersexuals to "fit in" as "normal" heterosexual males or females, avoiding feelings of deviance or freakishness. Anne Fausto-Sterling identifies the assumptions behind this goal as (1) there are only two sexes; (2) heterosexuality alone is normal, and (3) there is one true model of psychological health. Kessler asks whether or not this effort is in fact to free culture from having to deal with gender ambiguity? Alternately, medical professionals may not be practicing surgical and hormonal management

31

to consciously reinforce the current social order but rather, as part of that social order, their perceptions of viable options are limited.

Fausto-Sterling argues that broadening definitions of sexuality beyond a binary to consider multiple sexualities will challenge cultural gender dictates. In contrast, Kessler suggests that challenging traditional notions of gender may serve to diminish the defining and delimiting power of biological sex characteristics.

Fausto-Sterling challenges us to imagine a culture that had overcome sexual division. What would it be like to raise children as "unabashed intersexuals"? If surgery is undertaken less often, and intersexuality acknowledged more openly, will our cultural notions of sex and gender change? What is involved in protesting a cultural norm?

Suggested Readings

J. Colapinto, *As Nature Made Him: The Boy Who Was Raised as a Girl* (HarperCollins, 2000).

A. D. Dreger, "'Amiguous Sex'—or Ambivalent Medicine?" *The Hastings Center Report* (May/June 1998).

Alice Domurat Dreger, *Hermaphrodites and the Medical Invention of Sex* (Cambridge, MA: Harvard University Press, 2000).

Judith Rich Harris, *The Nurture Assumption: Why Children Turn Out the Way They Do* (New York: Free Press, 1999).

S. Kessler, *Lessons From the Intersexed* (Rutgers University Press, 1998).

Sharon E. Preves, *Intersex and Identity: The Contested Self* (Piscataway, NJ: Rutgers University Press, 2003).

- Biological make-up is important
- So are social gender norms
- Being different isnt bad, but I would not want to live where some peo
  I don't know if I'm talking to a boy or a girl

ISSUE 3

Is the Motive to Rape Biological?

YES: Randy Thornhill and Craig T. Palmer, from *A Natural History of Rape: Biological Bases of Sexual Coercion* (2000)

NO: Mary P. Koss, from "Evolutionary Models of Why Men Rape: Acknowledging the Complexities," *Trauma, Violence, and Abuse* (April 2000)

ISSUE SUMMARY

YES: Randy Thornhill and Craig T. Palmer use evolutionary biology to explain the biological causes of rape.

NO: Clinical psychologist Mary P. Koss highlights the complexity of any causal analysis of rape and concludes that no theory emphasizing a single cause is adequate.

Sexual assault, sexual coercion, and sexual aggression are all terms used to refer to instances in which one person engages in sexual behavior against another's will. These terms encompass acts that range from unwanted sexual contact, such as forced kissing or the fondling of breasts and/or genitals, to attempted rape and rape. The criminal justice system distinguishes rape from less severe forms of sexual coercion. The *Uniform Crime Reports* produced by the FBI defines forcible rape as "the carnal knowledge of a female forcibly and against her will. Assaults or attempts to commit rape by force or threat of force are also included; however, statutory rape (without force) and other sex offenses are excluded." The definition of rape varies by jurisdiction, as does the specific elements of the definition: gaining carnal knowledge (which may include oral and anal, as well as vaginal penetration by the penis or other objects), threatening or using force, and lack of consent are included in most legal definitions of rape. According to Amnesty International rape includes any kind of unwanted genital contact related to cultural rituals (such as genital mutilation—see Issue 14), child rapes occurring as part of arranged marriages, and forced female genital examinations, as well as forced prostitution, sexual slavery, rape of refugees, rape in war and genocidal rape. Although the legal definition of rape appears straightforward, people are often reluctant to apply the term when acquaintances are involved, particularly if any of the following circumstances were present: the man initiated the date; he spent a great deal of money; the couple went to his place; there had been drinking, kissing and petting; the couple had been sexually intimate on previous occasions; the woman had sex with other men. Furthermore, the term rape often has different meanings for women and men. Issues of women raping men and same-sex sexual assault add to the complexity.

The *Uniform Crime Reports* and National Incident-Based Reporting System reflect only instances of *reported* forcible rape and other sexual offenses, and only the most serious offense charged to a perpetrator. Approximately 45.4 percent of arrests for forcible rape in 2001 were of persons under 25 years of age. These reports do not reflect unreported instances of sexual assault, and rape is known to be the least reported and least prosecuted crime. Large-scale surveys consistently find higher estimates than official crime statistics. Based on survey data the percentage of women who have experienced some form of sexual victimization is over 50 percent, and about 25 percent have had experiences that met the legal definition of rape or attempted rape. Surveys also find that about 33 percent of men will admit to some form of sexually coercive behavior.

Few questions stir as much heated discussion than those of who rapes and why. The etiology and prevalence of sexual violence have been heavily debated topics with little consensus. Theoretical development regarding rape has evolved within the multiple disciplines. However, within each discipline, theory development typically has taken the form of singular explanations. One such single-factor theory, put forth by Thornhill and Palmer, argues that rape can be understood in an evolutionary framework as a behavioral adaptation molded by sexual selection; this is, rape is a biological phenomenon with a reproductive agenda. Rape, although not the most advantageous reproductive strategy for men, nevertheless increases their reproductive likelihood. They even argue that culture can ultimately be explained in biological terms. In contrast, for over two decades, since Susan Brownmiller's groundbreaking book *Against Our Will* (1975), feminists and other social scientists have argued that rape is a nonbiologically based event. Rather, it is a cultural phenomenon with a political agenda and a significant social problem. Consistent with this perspective Koss's research, as well as her critique of Thornhill and Palmer, has made important contributions regarding the pervasiveness of rape in American society. She argues that although it is possible to consider rape as having some biological foundation, Thornhill and Palmer present more of an ideological basis for their theory rather than one grounded in empirical evidence. Additionally, she suggests that their work neglects over 25 years of literature in the field of evolutionary psychology, as well as in social psychology and sociology. Rather, rape is a complex and multiply determined phenomenon.

YES ⬅

**Randy Thornhill and
Craig T. Palmer**

A Natural History of Rape:
Biological Bases of Sexual Coercion

Conclusion

Why are males the rapists and females (usually) the victims?   This question can
be answered at each of the two complementary levels of causation in biology:
the ultimate and the proximate. We will begin with the ultimate, which is the
more general and encompassing level of causation.

Males and females, both juvenile and adult, faced many sex-specific obstacles to reproductive success during human evolutionary history. As a result,
selection favored different adaptations in the two sexes. Sexual selection—the
primary kind of selection that explains the sex differences that lead to rape—is
the differential reproductive success of individuals due to their trait differences
that affect mating success (measured by mates' survival, parental investment,
and reproductive capacity, and, in males, also by number of mates and by
successful fertilization of eggs in competition with the sperm of other
males). Sexual selection's action on each sex is governed by the relative
parental investment of the sexes. Parental investment consists of the parental
materials and services that determine the number and the survival of offspring; thus, it is the commodity for which each sex competes in the competition for mates. In humans, the parental investments of the two sexes may
sometimes be nearly equal; however, the minimum parental investment for
offspring production by a male is trivial: a few minutes of mating and the small
amount of energy needed to place an ejaculate in a female's reproductive tract.
The female must invest all the time and energy required for gestation, birth,
and lactation.

The sex difference in the minimum parental investment is the key to
understanding the sex-specific historical selection that gave rise to rape. Given
the small investment of males and thus the low cost of each male mating, sexual selection favored males who achieved high mate number. As a result, men
show greater interest than women in variety of sex partners and in casual sex
without investment or commitment. Selection on females favored careful mate
choice that allowed them to expend their precious parental investment under
the circumstances most conducive to the production of viable offspring.

Female adaptations for mate selection fall into two categories: (1) preference for males with status and resources, which evolved because such males provided material benefits to females and their offspring, and (2) preferences for males with physical markers in behavior and body of genetic benefits, which evolved because they increased the survival chances of a female's offspring.

Human rape arises from men's evolved machinery for obtaining a high number of mates in an environment where females choose mates. If men pursued mating only within committed relationships, or if women did not discriminate among potential mates, there would be no rape. The two leading evolutionary hypotheses for the existence of human rape behavior are (1) that rape is an incidental effect (a by-product) of men's adaptation for pursuit of casual sex with multiple partners and (2) that rape is an adaptation in and of itself. According to the first hypothesis, rape was indirectly sexually selected. According to the second, rape was directly selected because rape itself promoted success in competition for mates. Mutation-selection balance, drift, and other ultimate causes other than selection are not consistent with the data on rape's common occurrence and its high cost to rapists. Data also disconfirm general explanations of rape that are based solely on evolutionarily novel environments.

Ultimate explanations pertain to evolutionary agents that account for the existence of biological traits. Distinguishing the two leading ultimate hypotheses for rape empirically would require additional research. . . . Existing data do not allow a strong conclusion one way or another. It is entirely clear, however, that rape is centered in men's evolved *sexuality*.

The proximate causes of rape include genes, environmental cues, ontogeny, learning, physiology, and psychological and behavioral responses to environmental stimuli. The importance of evolutionary theory for reducing rape lies in its ability to identify likely proximate causes, which may enable individuals to eliminate the immediate factors that bring about rape. Therefore, we have emphasized the importance of identifying the developmental cues that construct the adaptation responsible for rape as well as the cues that activate this adaptation after its ontogenetic construction.

Why is rape a horrendous experience for the victim?   Mate choice was a fundamental means of reproductive success for females in human evolutionary history. Thus, rapists' circumvention of mate choice has had extremely negative consequences for female reproductive success throughout human evolutionary history. The psychological pain that rape victims experience appears to be an evolved defense against rape. The pain focuses the victim on the rape and on the negative changes it has brought about in her life, thus helping her to solve current problems (e.g., her mate's divestment and suspicions) and to avoid being raped again. Women also appear to have psychological adaptations other than mental pain that also defend against rape, such as avoiding contexts with elevated risk of rape when at the point of maximum fertility in the menstrual cycle.

The females who outreproduced others and thus became our ancestors were individuals who were highly distressed by rape.

Why does the mental trauma of rape vary with the victim's age and marital status?
From biological (evolutionary) theory, we can predict that the negative
reproductive consequences faced by rape victims in evolutionary history
depended on their age and on their pair-bond status. Since only reproductive-
age females can get pregnant from rape, females of reproductive age and those
with investing mates are predicted to have experienced the greatest negative
consequences. Males of species in which males engage in parental effort
have been selected to invest in their own offspring because cuckoldry was, in
human evolutionary history, a persistent problem that lowered or eliminated a
male's offspring production. A female with an investing mate faced the prospect of losing some or all of the mate's investment as a result of his concern
about rape's effect on his paternity. Research shows that females of reproductive age and married women indeed exhibit more psychological pain after rape
than other females. That mental pain is a variable response rather than an
invariant one is predicted on the ground that mental pain historically entailed
costs to reproductive success (such as distraction from other important life
events) as well as reproductive benefits.

Why does the mental trauma of rape vary with the sex acts? The epitome of circumvention of female mate choice is insemination by an unwanted mate. If
such insemination results in pregnancy, it leads the female to expend her limited parental investment in a maladaptive manner. Research indicates that
rapes that include copulation give rise to more psychological pain in female
victims than non-copulatory sexual assaults. This pattern is driven by the
greater pain of reproductive-age females, who during human evolutionary
history had the most to lose (in terms of lowered reproductive success) from
insemination by rapists.

Why does the mental trauma of rape decrease as physical injuries increase?
The answer to this question is related to men's evolved desire to invest in
offspring they have sired rather than in offspring born to their mates but sired
by other men. A rape is less threatening to a man's paternity than a consensual
affair. That a partner has indeed been raped is less ambiguous if there are visible
signs that she resisted. Thus, evolutionary theory predicts that raped women
with visible signs of having resisted will experience less post-rape mental
anguish, and indeed this is a strong pattern in women's response to rape trauma.

Why do young males rape more often than older males? Sexual selection on males
for mate number has endowed boys and men with a much greater risk proneness than is seen in human females. The risk proneness of male humans peaks in
young adulthood. So does that of females, but they are much less risk prone than
males. Both peaks stem from sexual selection's favoring maximal risk taking
when the competition for entering the breeding population is most intense: at
the onset of adulthood. Males have been strongly sexually selected to pursue
resources and climb the social ladder at this stage because success in these pursuits positively affected male reproductive success in human evolutionary history.
That men's sexual interest and impulsiveness peak early in adulthood is also due

to past sexual selection. The combination of the two peaks—that of risk taking and that of sexual desire—accounts for the fact that young men rape more.

Why are young women more often the victims of rape than older women or girls? Fertility is strongly related to age in women but not in men. In Western countries, menarche usually occurs between the ages of 10 and 13. Women's fertility declines markedly after age 30 and drops to zero at menopause. Men's fertility begins at puberty and remains high into the fifties or even later, with no abrupt cessation comparable to menopause. The sex difference in fertility schedules gives women a narrow window of opportunity for offspring production. This had tremendous evolutionary consequences in humans, and it led to selection on males for preferring young women as mates. This preference is manifested in men's pursuit of consensual and non-consensual sex. Young women are the focus of men's sexual interest, whether the context is prostitution, pornography, marriage, romantic affairs, or rape. Men's focus on visual indicators of youth is due to the fact that a female's mate value is largely manifested in her bodily signals of fertility. A male's mate value, in contrast, is spread across bodily features, resources, and status.

Why is rape more frequent in some situations, such as war, than in others? Humans (including rapists), like all animals, pay attention to costs and benefits when making decisions. Rape by conquering soldiers is common because the benefits are high (many young women are available) and because the costs are low (the women are vulnerable; the rapists are anonymous and relatively free from sanctions against rape). Cost-benefit considerations also go part of the way toward explaining why modern societies have relatively high rape rates. In such societies, young women rarely are chaperoned and often encounter social circumstances that make them vulnerable to rape. Moreover, anonymity is more prevalent, and the sanctions against rape are less effective deterrents, in modern societies than in traditional human environments, where individuals are more likely to be known to others.

Why does rape occur in all known cultures? The capacity to rape is attributable ultimately to selection and proximately to ontogeny and adaptation. Rape behavior arises from elements of men's sexual nature—their sexual psychology. This psychology is characteristic of men in general, but not of pre-pubescent boys. It is reliably generated during development across a wide range of rearing environments.

Why are some instances of rape punished in all known cultures? Rape within the rapist's own social group (known as *in-group* rape and usually defined by kinship in traditional societies) is punished across human societies because it has negative consequences for the reproductive success of all whose reproductive interests overlap with those of the victim, including her relatives, her mate, and her mate's relatives. Sanctions against in-group rape take the form of codified rules (law) and unwritten rules that protect the interests of those who make and enforce them. The rules and other forms of teaching are directed at controlling men's sexual desires.

Why are people (especially husbands) often suspicious of the victim's claim to have been raped? The husband of the victim is looking for evidence of an unambiguous rape that the woman tried to avoid to the best of her ability—an act that is less threatening to his paternity than either a consensual affair or a rape that the woman did not resist strongly. In his suspicions, the husband is unconsciously assessing the cost of the rape to him and whether he should desert the mate or continue to invest in her and her offspring. Significant social allies of the victim other than her husband are also gaining information about the rape's impact on their reproductive interests through their suspicions. On theoretical grounds, they are expected to adjust their investment in the victim according to the same criteria that her husband uses.

Intuition that some women use false accusations, gossip, rumor, and ostracism of others to obtain resources and other social benefits may also play a part in suspicion toward claims of rape. Indeed, women do use these tactics more than men. Men rely more on direct forms of competition, such as intimidation and aggression. Humans are socially astute because of past selection for analysis of social behavior, which contains many predictive elements that are also products of past selection.

Why is rape often treated as a crime against the victim's husband? Men are selected to control the sexual behavior of their mates and of their sisters and daughters. Control of mates serves the purpose of protecting paternity; control of female relatives is intended to make them more attractive to discriminating men with resources. Because in human evolutionary history only males could be cuckolded, a female's mate value depended greatly on how much paternity reliability she could provide. Rape of a woman, therefore, is viewed as a cost to the men whose reproductive interests she is expected to serve.

Why have attempts to reform rape laws met with only limited success? To date, attempts to reform rape laws have not taken into account various evolved human intuitions about human behavior. This is true of all aspects of the reform movement, including expanding the definition of rape, eliminating the requirements that rape be corroborated by other persons and that proof of the victim's resistance be provided, and disallowing consideration of the victim's sexual history.

Humans are selected to define rape in a specific way because, as discussed just above, the events involved in the sexual act affect the woman's value to her male and female social allies. Much the same is true of rape corroboration, victim resistance, and victim sexual history. Furthermore, intuition about women's use of sexual allegations for self-gain may tend to block reform of the laws.

Why does rape exist in many, but not all, other species? The vast majority of species show the same sex differences in sexuality that humans show: relative to females, males are more eager to mate, show less discrimination about mating partners, and pursue sexual variety without commitment. Females, on the other hand, are very choosy about mates. All these species have an evolutionary history of a high degree of polygyny. A very small percentage of species practice monogamy, but even in these species the stronger sexual selection for high mate number (attributable to the trivial minimum investment by males) creates virtually the same male sexual features seen in highly polygynous species, with "monogamous" males seeking extra-pair copulation. (A fraction of species show sex-role reversal, the males choosing mates and the females competing for multiple mates. Sex-role reversal arises out of the rare circumstance in which males contribute more parental investment than do females.)

Although males of essentially all species exhibit sexual psychological adaptations for obtaining a high number of mates, rape is not universal across animal species. It is, however, common. Most of the attempts to theorize about the ecological variation that creates selection for rape are very recent. Recent research by biologists examining selection for and against rape focuses on ecological factors that affect rape's benefits and costs, such as whether or not females are distributed spatially in ways that make them vulnerable to males (for example, whether they form female-female social alliances against coercive males, and whether they live within range of protective relatives). Also, how well adapted females are against rape in the coevolutionary race with rapist males appears to be relevant to the selection on males to rape. Another factor is the cost of rape to females and to rapist males when the degree of force used lowers female survival.

Some of the same factors that select for or against rape across species may be relevant to the conditional use of rape by men across human societies. Protection of women by family members and husbands may be especially important in inhibiting rape; structural barriers such as chaperoning may also help.

Why does rape still occur among humans?   . . . [T]wo reasons [have been given] for why it has not yet proved possible to eliminate rape: First, social scientists and people in general have such a limited understanding of ultimate causation that they fail to see how evolutionary theory can contribute to an understanding of rape's proximate causes. [Several theories] have discussed some possible reasons for this difficulty, including ideological biases and the fact that thinking about ultimate causation requires us to envision vast stretches of historical time when we are designed only to understand short-term causal factors. We have emphasized the role of ideological bias, but certainly there is reason to think that other factors often play important roles. Second, most attempts to eliminate rape have been based on the social science explanation, which is fundamentally ideological rather than empirical and which hence contains many fundamental inaccuracies.

Biologists are in a position to inform others about how evolution applies to humans. Biologists have deep understanding of ontogeny and of the theory of evolution, both of which deny the dichotomies for traits of individuals (e.g., learned vs. genetic) that have misinformed and misguided social scientists' research on rape. In addition, the existence of rape across many animal species is one of the many evidentiary blows biology has dealt to the social science explanation, which insists that rape is not natural, not evolved, not biological, uniquely human, and attributable to "culture" (a non-biological entity that works its magic through children's arbitrary socialization). The existence of the same differences between the sexes in humans and in most other animals is another blow to the notion that rape is just about cultural causation, since relatively few of the non-human species have any socialization of offspring at all, much less sex-differentiated socialization.

Recently some social scientists have asserted that the entire "animal literature" does not count. . . . In a few sentences they discount all evidence for rape in nonhuman species and dismiss all the data on the evolution of sexual differences—findings that, in fact, are clearly relevant to an understanding of human behavior, as we have explained. [T]he evolutionary view of rape [has been criticized] on the ground that men's strong desire for partner number is cultural rather than biological. This too reflects a fundamental misunderstanding of the fact that culture is biology. We would not be surprised to hear social scientists suggest, next, that insects, other arthropods, other invertebrates, and most vertebrates are somehow being influenced during development by music videos, television, and movies.

How can rape be prevented? Among the important implications of the biological understanding of rape is that programs meant to educate people about rape should be revised so as to stop spreading the notion that rape is not sex but violence. Both young men and young women should be taught about male and female sexuality (particularly male sexuality) and about risk factors for rape. Men should be informed of the penalties for rape. Structural barriers to rape should be considered, and efforts to change evolved biases about rape accusations should be considered. Finally, changes in the law with regard to rape and related matters should be based on scientific knowledge.

Though we have not advocated specific methods of punishing rapists, we have stressed the value of punishment for changing human behavior, keeping in mind that some claims of rape are false and that false conviction is possible. Voters must decide what is a suitable punishment for rape. Science has nothing to say about what is right or wrong in the ethical sense. Biology provides understanding, not justification, of human behavior. Biological knowledge is useful to a democratic society to the extent that it can be used to achieve goals that people decide are appropriate. These goals are typically based on ideological considerations. Whereas many ideological issues (e.g., abortion, conservation, taxation) involve a great deal of disagreement, it is safe to say that the vast majority of people are against rape. This being the case, it is our hope that concerned people will begin making use of the knowledge that evolutionary biology provides in order to reduce the incidence of rape and to better deal with this horrendous crime's effects on its victims and their significant others.

Mary P. Koss

NO

Evolutionary Models of Why Men Rape: Acknowledging the Complexities

Randy Thornhill and Craig Palmer's new book *A Natural History of Rape: Biological Bases of Sexual Coercion* (2000) sets up a stark contrast between evolutionary theory and feminist theory that performed perfectly in its intended role as a media hook. The authors have appeared on CNN, *Dateline,* and other television programs, and on National Public Radio disseminating their position. Victim advocates, National Organization of Women officers, experts on evolutionary biology, and Susan Brownmiller herself rebutted these authors. This media phenomenon was a sad incident for rape prevention advocates, evolutionary biology, and science itself. The framing of the issues by Thornhill and Palmer increased the resistance to evolutionary analysis, ill represented the process of science, and encouraged harmful prevention suggestions. This commentary examines in more depth than permitted in the public media their thesis, supporting evidence, and recommendations for rape prevention. The complexity of the causal analysis of rape is highlighted, including the consensus of expert panels on violence against women that no theory emphasizing a single cause is adequate to explaining why men rape, no matter what its ideology is.

The Evolutionary Thesis

Not only do Thornhill and Palmer have some evolutionary ideas to advance, they want to do so on a battlefield. The authors frame their presentation as a battle of evolution versus the social sciences, likening those who reject a reproductive explanation for rape to right-wing fundamentalists. As Thornhill and Palmer see it, evolutionary biology is armed with a knowledge-based approach to the issues, whereas social science mounts only an ideologically driven advance. They repeatedly put on the armor of science. The battle cries that are echoed include the following: "Science is value free," "Science is the only road to the truth," "Science has the answers," "Science solves diseases and can solve social problems," and "Science will win." Most of these sentiments are

From *Trauma, Violence, and Abuse,* vol. 1, no. 2, April 2000, pp. 182–193. Copyright © 2000 by Sage Publications. Reprinted by permission.

naive from the perspective of the social construction of science—no theory or measurement is free from being shaped by the human mind. Paradigms guiding designs of studies are human creations and are well known for their resistance to change, even in the face of compelling empirical data. In addition, as soon as statements about the meaning of results are made, numbers become subject to interpretation. As Moore and Travis (2000) note, "Biologically based science has the nice quality of disguising politics" (p. 36). By cloaking themselves in science talk ("bio-proof"), Thornhill and Palmer aim to camouflage their unstated ideological agenda, deflect attention away from the obvious flaws in their logic and supporting evidence, and inflate the importance of their own work. They succeeded only in diminishing the stature of science and fueling the public's anti-intellectualism.

Now that we have examined the framing of the issues, let us inspect the evolutionary arguments themselves. Thornhill and Palmer's primary aim is to challenge the idea that rape is an expression of power, which they correctly identify as the prevailing view in the advocate community. The book actually presents two alternative hypotheses of human rape. The first is the idea that rape is a special adaptive strategy that human males have developed because it helps them to sire more offspring. The second is that rape is a by-product of male sexual desire and a preference for higher numbers of sexual partners. The latter alternative is totally undeveloped, and the entire text is designed to describe, support, and consider the implications of rape as a special adaptation. In so doing, Thornhill and Palmer commit the same error for which their work has already been taken to task by numerous published commentaries. The peer review process is the best system yet devised to ensure that science moves forward and that bad ideas are separated from good ideas. Given the mantle of science that the authors have gathered around them, it is surprising to see so little attention devoted to acknowledging and responding to the peer criticism of which they have long been aware. Elaborating the by-product model would have been more palatable to the general public because its links with reproduction are more indirect and would have provided a basis for the integration of feminist thought about rape. However, in the media world, controversy sells, and some scholars fall prey to its lures. In the field of sexual violence, we have seen this all before.

Grasping the gist of rape as a reproductive strategy involves a short overview of the principles of Darwinian natural selection. As Moore and Travis succinctly summarize (2000),

> The general principles of natural selection are not inherently sexist and simply stated propose that individuals vary; some variations are more favorable than others; some of this variation is heritable; differential reproductive success may occur; and differing gene frequencies may result. (p. 44)

The special adaptation model views rape as one of three strategies that have ostensibly evolved to help males find mates, gain sexual access, and produce offspring bearing their genes. These strategies are possessing physical attractiveness, being a powerful warrior, and when all else fails, raping. Thornhill and

Palmer argue that men resort to rape when they cannot gain access to women through looks, wealth, or status. To the extent that offspring have been conceived by rape, any genes associated with raping are passed along.

A cornerstone of Thornhill and Palmer's treatise is their interpretation of the old concept of differential parental investment. It states that male and female animals differ in their potential to reach maximum breeding potential. Females are choosy about their mates because raising offspring, especially a higher primate or human baby, is a lengthy and effortful investment that is most likely to reach a successful conclusion when the father contributes emotionally and materially to their care. Because the male's minimum investment in children is limited to fertilizing the egg, the parental investment theory states that they best ensure their genes will be represented in future generations by mating with a large number of females. From this viewpoint, if they cannot obtain mates through other strategies, rape is better than leaving no offspring.

To support their model, Thornhill and Palmer follow a confirmatory strategy, listing the predictions that logically flow from it and providing purported supportive evidence. The major predictions that Thornhill and Palmer make about rape as a special adaptation include the following:

1. Most rape victims will be women of childbearing age.
2. Rapists will not seriously injure their victims.
3. Rape victims who experience more violence will suffer less emotional distress.
4. Vaginal penetration will be more distressing than other forms.
5. Married women and women of childbearing age will experience more psychological distress over rape than single women or menopausal women.

The logic behind Predictions 1 and 2 is that, for rape to be a special adaptation, you need to show that it has reproductive consequences, in this case, by demonstrating that it is done primarily to women who could bear children as a result and who were not so seriously injured by the forced impregnation that they died, miscarried, or gave birth to defective offspring. Predictions 3 through 5 are based on Palmer's work with his former wife Nancy Thornhill. Her thinking was that women's emotional distress should be greater the more rape affected their reproductive interests. The link of these hypotheses to the special adaptation model is never explained, and they appear tangential.

Although most of the documentation provided by Thornhill and Palmer concerns insects and birds, they also used standard social science data. They tested their deductions with a secondary analysis of a data set originally presented by McCahill, Meyer, and Fischman in the pioneering work *The Aftermath of Rape* (1979). The data came from rape survivors seeking services at a Philadelphia emergency room. The authors fail to address the potential concerns with these data, such as validity: How well were the constructs assessed given that the data collection predated the formulation of the theory? Was the measurement of the constructs reliable and valid? In addition, the generalizability to the universe of rape survivors was not examined. The validity is certainly questionable given that only 5% of them sought emergency room care, according to the national survey conducted for the U.S. Department of Justice.

The presentation concludes with suggestions for rape prevention activities. Thornhill and Palmer confidently predict that any prevention effort will fail unless based on an understanding that rape evolved as a form of male reproductive behavior. Their recommendations include the following:

- Educating youths that all men are potential rapists who must learn to inhibit their natural impulses
- Sensitizing women to the biological proclivities of men and to the role that women's apparel plays in triggering rape
- Recommending that women exert more control over the circumstances of dating, socializing only in public places
- Providing a Darwinian perspective to women undergoing counseling to help them understand why they are distressed about being raped

The Evidence

Disputing the facts.   Had each of the deductions been the subject of a peer-reviewed, empirical paper, they would have been examined in the context of related findings from the existing literature. Thornhill and Palmer make virtually no reference to other empirical findings on sexual assault. The bulk of the available data makes fiction of the facts, thus eliminating all the data that the authors purport to be supportive of their theory, except for their observations of insect and bird behavior.

Many rape victims are children, not women of reproductive age.   Contrary to the assertion that rapists favor reproductive-age women, the Rape in America national survey reported that exactly one third of victims were younger than 11 years old when first raped and that a total of two thirds were younger than 17 years old. The National Violence Against Women Survey reported that 22% of rape victims were younger than 12 years old when first sexually assaulted and that 32% were between 12 and 17 years old. Even without taking into account the data on rapes of postmenopausal women, men, and boys, these figures establish that a sizable number of rapes are lacking in reproductive consequences.

Women of childbearing age do not experience the most distress.   The literature of the impact of sexual trauma fails to support the linkage of childbearing potential to distress. Instead, child sexual abuse is consistently associated with the most severe, broad, and long-lasting effects, including lifelong elevated risks of physical problems, emotional distress, and more unsafe health behaviors like smoking, excessive drinking, and lack of physical activity. In terms of the greatest fear, the elderly suffer from rape the most.

Distress does not vary inversely with the rapist's violence.   The idea that less violence causes more distress is not only contraintuitive, it is also at odds with the bulk of trauma literature. Recent nationwide studies established that the major predictors of post-traumatic stress disorder were the objective severity of the violence inflicted, the subjective fear of death or serious injury, and whether penetration of the body occurred. Also important were how much a woman blamed herself for what happened and how threatening the rape was to her worldview. Most people intuitively understand these findings because they support the obvious: The harder you are hit, the more it hurts.

All unwanted penetration is traumatic in women of all ages.   Is vaginal rape, because of its potential for impregnation, more traumatic than other forms of penetration? This hypothesis is faulty on its face because it overlooks the invention of modern methods of birth control, including postconception interventions that restore to women control over reproduction and render moot any selective advantage for rape. Even if this issue had the importance attributed to it by Thornhill and Palmer, there are several methodological obstacles that raise questions as to whether they or anyone else could establish that vaginal penetration is most distressing. The following are some barriers to establishing a clear-cut relationship:

- The meaning of different forms of penetration is culturally conditioned, precluding universal statements about how they would be viewed by the survivor.
- Many rapes may involve multiple forms of penetration, thereby resisting categorization.
- The amount of injury caused by rape is highly significant and would need to be measured and controlled for before the relationship between distress and the form of penetration could be disentangled.

Current literature establishes that all unwanted penetration is traumatic. It may not really matter if a Chevy truck or a Ford truck hits you; in either case, you are seriously harmed.

Although rapists rarely kill, life threat is high.   Thornhill and Palmer conclude that rapists rarely harm their victims. This statement is somewhat true for half the picture. According to the Rape in America study, 28% of rapes involved some degree of physical injury. However, as we saw earlier, postassault impact is predicted not just by objective severity but also by subjective severity. Half of all women feared that they would be seriously harmed or killed during their rape.

Prevention Recommendations Are Naive and Harmful

Although good scientific practice dictates not generalizing beyond the capability of the data, Thornhill and Palmer move from the consideration of insects and lower animals to making recommendations for preventing human rape and treating rape survivors. They address prevention at the individual level of causation. They ignored the need for prevention initiatives at broader societal levels. Even from their biological perspective, several societal-level strategies would be helpful, such as revamping the legal system to better deter rape by enforcing penalties for men who fail to restrain themselves or advocating legislation that would continue to guaranteewomenaccess to the means to control the outcomes of forced sexual contact. Bioprevention based on the flawed assumptions listed below will not solve the rape problem.

Men as potential rapists. One of the critical problems faced by those who design rape prevention education is the backlash that results in male attendees leaving even more resentful and angry at women than before the program. Thornhill and Palmer suggest that prevention programs for young men teach them about their biological propensities to rape and warn them of the need to inhibit these impulses. In short, men should be taught that they are all potential rapists. Years of experience in rape prevention have taught me that this approach is not productive. Men vociferously challenge any presenter who fails to distinguish between rapists and regular guys who want emotional relationships with women who they will eventually end up with, raising kids who they love and invest in. In addition, the recommendation is not grounded in established fact. The jury is still out on men's potential to rape, even among evolutionary psychologists. When pushed, many who assert that all men are potential rapists limit their assertion only to the moment of birth. From there on, the potential is shaped by social and environmental influences that render most men incapable of raping. This is similar to saying that all humans are potential killers at birth. Men differ greatly in the extent to which they are aroused by sexual aggression and in their self-reported likelihood that they would force sex on a woman. Few men say that they would rape even if they were guaranteed not to be caught or punished, and even with a softer wording about forcing a woman to have sex, only a minority indicate any likelihood of sexual coercion.

Thornhill and Palmer's suggestion that time in rape prevention should be spent explaining Darwinian theory is laughable from the practical perspective. Even when rape seminars are marketed as how-to-be-a-better-lover workshops, attendance by men is low and limited to the already converted. What would attendance be for a lecture on Darwin? In addition, presenting such material takes away precious time from more critical prevention targets for men, such as teaching them how to get affirmative consent from a woman so that they are certain their advances are reciprocated and educating them about what acts constitute rape. For example, young men need to know that having sex with a drunken woman, something commonly seen as a stroke of good luck, is actually rape under the law. They need to know that adding a little speck of a party drug to her drink elevates the crime to an aggravated level with the harsh sentences typical of the country's war on drugs.

Women should dress to avoid rape. . . . How? How would you advise women to dress to avoid rape? There have been rapists who were acquitted because the victims dressed provocatively in a turtle neck sweater and a midcalf skirt.

Where would it end? The mind-set behind this advice is the same as that of countries where women are required by law to dress in shapeless, head-to-toe, black bags with a mask and two slits for the eyes so as not to provoke sexual attacks.

As Thornhill and Palmer see it, the capacity for women to avoid rape has been selected because those female ancestors who reproduced most successfully were very distressed about rape and learned how to identify the circumstances that resulted in rape and avoided them. The implication is that many women today know how to avoid rape, but prevention programs are needed for those poor souls who do not know. We are not told how these highly vulnerable women would be identified.

The entire premise is based on an empirically unfounded assumption that women can protect themselves from rape. In fact, there has been no success in separating those women who have and who have not been raped on the basis of routine activities, personality, or beliefs. Although there have been isolated reports that women who drink in bars have a high rape rate, a longitudinal study demonstrated that alcohol use is triggered by past victimization and does not predict future victimization. Furthermore, sexual assault is an exception to the rule in criminology that routine activities have some power to predict vulnerability to crime. To the extent that rape can be predicted, a history of sexual abuse in childhood is the most prominent factor. However, even sexual abuse fails the test of practical significance. Chance would allow for 15% of rape victims to be predicted correctly, whereas child abuse increases that figure only to 19%. Thus, it has not been for the lack of study that no powerful correlates of vulnerability are known.

It is also hard to see how formulating an acquaintanceship would be protection against rape. Fully 86% of rape victims knew the man who raped them, and 20% of married women have been raped by a spouse. Furthermore, socializing in public places is not going to eliminate rape. Among women raped by nonstrangers, the U.S. Department of Justice reported that 32% of rapes occurred in the street or in a restaurant or bar, commercial building, parking lot, school, park, or playground (these figures are virtually identical to those for women raped by strangers). Giving up going out at night would not help either—30% of rapes happened in the daytime. The most scientifically appropriate reading of the data is that rape is most predictable on the grounds of being female, and the best protection would be avoiding all men, including family members.

Advice on women's dress and conduct should be rejected not only because it is unscientific but also because of its tacit assumption that women have a responsibility to act reasonably and live their lives in fear of men. This thinking is absolutely unacceptable in a democratic society. Because rape is a gendered crime, such recommendations harm equality by infringing more on women's liberties than on men's. "Women citizens have a legal entitlement to act on a day-to-day basis on the premise that others will not intentionally rape them." The U.S. Constitution guarantees freedom of movement, a right to travel, a right of locomotion, and a right to associate with others. In other words, women have the right to use public transportation, travel geographically, socialize with whom they choose, and express themselves through their dress in anyway they find comfortable that does not violate public decency laws. If, as a society, we are to have a citizen duty to take reasonable steps to avoid crime, the steps should be the same for sex crimes as other crimes and, by extension, be the same for men as for women.

Problems With Bioprevention

From a public policy perspective, conceptualizing rape largely as a biological issue reframes it as "a problem to be punished but still expected in certain unavoidable numbers of occurrences, rather than as social problem with the possibility of social remediation" (Moore & Travis, 2000, p. 47). The work becomes misguided "when the biology of sexual reproduction is taken as a general template or justification for a wide range of stereotypic gender role behaviors, often producing prescriptions for behavior that limit individual opportunity and choice" (Moore & Travis, 2000, p. 50). Biologically based public policy recommendations in the area of rape are downright scary. Jones (1999) moved beyond calls for restrictions in women dress and activities. He advocates consideration of

- implementing chemical castration as the penalty for rape;
- varying punishments for rape by the age of the victim, with lesser penalties for older women as they are purportedly less traumatized by rape;
- having male judges refrain from making judgments on rape due to inherent sex differences that render them incapable of making assessments of female psychology;
- repealing the Violence Against Women Act of 1994 on the grounds that gender animus as a motivation for rape is inconsistent with biological models;
- legalizing prostitution to make voluntary sex partners available to men;
- and using evolutionary material on relative harm by form of penetration, amount of violence, and age of victim to set damages in civil trials.

Conceptualizing rape as a sex act alone ignores that it is a serious crime in which the penis is used as a weapon. Clearly, a man is not engaging in a sex act when he screams "You know you like this, bitch" while penetrating a woman and forcefully restraining her. The force behind the criminal act of rape is a mixture of sexual motives and motives to control, dominate, or punish that vary in degree from case to case. My example would be low in sexual motives. Some date rapes might provide scenarios for rapes in which sexual motives appear more prominently. The important semantic distinction is that rape is not a sex act, it is a crime that can be impelled by sexual motives. [It has been] concluded that rape is best defined as an integration of both components and that learning how sex and aggressive elements interact will advance the field.

Dismissing One-Factor Theories

As a one-factor, one-level theory, rape as a special adaptation model implicates a single set of causes that reside within individuals. Rape long ago proved itself to be too complex to yield to such simplistic thinking. Although it is cloaked in biology, individual-level evolutionary analysis is also out of step with modern biology's focus on more complex issues, such as the evolution of a successful adaptation between the species and its environment and the survival of the group and the species. It is widely accepted that sexual assault is influenced by causes at multiple levels that range from the broader society to institutions such as the media and religion, family, peer group, intimate relationships, and ultimately, features that are interior to each individual.

Researchers have demonstrated the links of sexual aggression to heredity; physiology; neurophysiology; social learning; gender schemas; sexual scripts; personality traits; attitudes about rape, power, and sex motives; and alcohol as causes of rape that are interior to the individual. At the dyadic level, studies have examined contextual features of relationships such as communication styles, the type and stages of relationships, and features that may render women more vulnerable to sexual predation. Institutional influences that have been linked to rape include family, school, athletic teams, religion, and media promotion of sex role stereotypes that teach or reinforce female and male role imbalances, favor impersonal sex, downplay the seriousness of violence against women, and fail to present successful alternatives to male aggression.

Evolutionary influences have been acknowledged as part of a comprehensive model of rape by panels of experts such as the National Academy of Science Panel on Violence Against Women and the American Psychological Association Taskforce on Male Violence Against Women. Those who wish to learn about how evolutionary concepts can be integrated in a model that also addresses environmental and social causation are referred to the work of Neil Malamuth and colleagues. Alone, biological explanations will not solve social problems because people cannot change their evolutionary history. However, the conceptualization of biological influences, not as hardwiring but as potential pathways that are shaped by the environment, can lead to research with practical implications. Viewing men as inherently rapacious is hopeless. On the other hand, knowing how harsh environments, the lack of secure attachments, or social learning favor the development of promiscuous male sexuality sets the prevention agenda.

Conclusions

Evolutionary psychologists must be pulling their hair out over this book. Having recently changed their name from sociobiology, this is a perfect time to show the public the new face of evolutionary psychology. Instead, they find the spotlight grabbed by a work that is offensive, scientifically flawed, misguided, reckless, and unreflective of the field's contributions to knowledge. It will be much harder now in many quarters to advocate for the explanatory role of evolutionary factors in violence against women. This is unfortunate because scholars on sexual assault, like most scientifically oriented people, place themselves somewhere in the evolutionary camp with regard to the origins of human behavior, confining their contemplation of creationist themes to their spiritual life.

References

Jones, O. D. (1999). Sex, culture, and the biology of rape: Toward explanation and prevention. *California Law Review, 87,* 827–941.

McCahill, T. W., Meyer, L. C., & Fischman, A. M. (1979). *The aftermath of rape.* Lexington, MA: D.C. Health.

Moore, D. S., & Travis, C. B. (2000). Biological models and sexual politics. In J. G. White & C. B. Travis (Eds.), *Sexuality, society, and feminism* (pp. 35–56). Washington, DC: American Psychological Press.

Thornhill, R., & Palmer, C. T. (2000). *A natural history of rape: Biological bases of sexual coercion.* Cambridge, MA: MIT Press.

POSTSCRIPT

Is the Motive to Rape Biological?

To understand rape it is probably useful to recognize that it occurs at different rates in different cultures, at different points in time, and is more likely to occur during adolescence and young adulthood than at other points in one's life cycle. It is also useful to remind ourselves that not all women are equally likely to be victims nor are all men equally likely to be perpetrators. What is the relative contribution of biological and sociocultural factors? Discussions of men's motives for sexual assault look at attitudes and values, but also consider potential biological factors. Taking a sociobiological perspective, Ellis has argued that only men whose sex drive and need to control others surpass some threshold have any likelihood of committing sexually aggressive acts. Once that biological threshold is surpassed, the actual commission of the acts will be influenced by the strength of the drive and by various environmental factors, including opportunity and societal sanctions. The stronger the drives, the less effective environmental restraints will be. Some theories have suggested that men who perpetrate violent acts against women have some underlying deviant physiological arousal pattern or intrapsychic pathology. For instance, researchers have found that sexually coercive men display more penile tumescence than sexually noncoercive men when exposed to audiotape and slide presentations depicting forced sex or when asked to read a story about a rape. However, other researchers find more similarities than differences between sexual perpetrators and nonperpetrators. For example, no single "typical" profile of sex offenders has been found, and incestuous and pedophilic men resemble community volunteers in levels of some, although not all, sex hormones. Similarly, arousal patterns to rape depictions only inconsistently distinguish college-aged men who perpetrate acquaintance rape from those who do not.

To understand rape we must also recognize that culturally based socialization practices encourage men to be aggressors and women to be victims. In societies where there is no formal hierarchy that privileges one group over another and in which women and men exercise relatively equal power, general levels of aggression, male violence against women, and rape are low. Data demonstrate that not all women are victims of rape nor are all men rapists. Inequality in relationships, coupled with cultural values that embrace domination of the weaker by the stronger, creates the potential for rape. Both men and women learn that violence is a method people use to get their way. When individuals use force and are successful, they are reinforced and thus more likely to use it in the future; however, men have historically received greater rewards for aggression and violence than have women. White and Felson (see Issue 6) have suggested a model that can account for the complexities associated with sexual assault and rape. The model can better account for why some men rape and why some women are raped than a singular explanation, such as an evolutionary theory. The model suggests that a fuller understanding of rape can be achieved by examining it systematically at several levels, cultural, social, interpersonal, situational, and intrapersonal, in addition to biological. Dynamic factors at each level operate to affect the likelihood of who will rape, who will be raped, and when rape is most likely to occur.

Suggested Readings

Howard E. Barbaree and William L. Marshall, eds., *The Juvenile Sex Offender,* 2nd ed. (New York: Guilford Press, 2005).

Raquel Kennedy Bergen, *Issues in Intimate Violence* (Thousand Oaks, CA: Sage Publications, 1998).

Mary Koss, Lisa Goodman, Louise Fitzgerald, Nancy Russo, Gwendolyn Keita, and Angela Browne, *No Safe Haven* (Washington, DC: American Psychological Association, 1994).

Neil M. Malamuth, Mark Huppin, and Bryant Paul, "Sexual Coercion," in D. M. Buss, ed., *The Handbook of Evolutionary Psychology* (pp. 394–418) (Hoboken, NJ: John Wiley & Sons, 2005).

Danny S. Moore and Cheryl B. Travis, "Biological Models and Sexual Politics," in J. W. White and C. B. Travis, eds., *Sexuality, Society, and Feminism* (pp. 35–56) (Washington, DC: American Psychological Association, 2000).

Diana E. H. Russell, *Making Violence Sexy: Feminist Views on Pornography* (New York: Teachers College Press, 1993).

C. M. Renzetti, J. L. Edelson, and R. K. Bergen, eds., *Sourcebook on Violence Against Women* (Thousand Oaks, CA: Sage Publications, 2001).

Schewe, P., *Preventing Violence in Relationships: Interventions Across the Life Span* (Washington DC: American Psychological Association, 2002).

On the Internet . . .

Cultural Psychology Meets Evolutionary Psychology

This Web site by the Nijmegen Cultural Psychology Group (NCPG) contains a paper by Paul Voestermans and Cor Baerveldt that was presented at the 8th conference of the International Society for Theoretical Psychology (ISTP) in Sydney, Australia. The paper is entitled "Cultural Psychology Meets Evolutionary Psychology: Toward a New Role of Biology in the Study of Culture and Experience," and is a rich overview of evolutionary psychological thought. {follow these links: Voestermans, select Voestermans & Baerveldt; select Sydney; select cultural psychology meets evolutionary psychology}

http://www.cultpsy.org/

Genderlect Styles of Deborah Tannen

This Web site on the genderlect styles of Deborah Tannen provides an overview of Deborah Tannen's popular work on gender and communication.

http://www.usm.maine.edu/com/genderlect/

Men, Women, and Sex Differences: The Attitudes of Three Feminists—Gloria Steinem, Gloria Allred, and Bella Abzug

A paper by Russell Eisenman entitled "Men, Women, and Sex Differences: The Attitudes of Three Feminists—Gloria Steinmen, Gloria Allred, and Bella Abzug" is presented on this Web site. This paper is a case study of perspectives on sex differences of three prominent feminists.

http://www.theabsolute.net/misogyny/eisenman.html

The Web site for Life Positive describes different life stressors women and men might experience and offers suggestions for coping.

http://www.lifepositive.com/Mind/psychology/
stress/male-depression.asp

Website 101 is designed to help businesses expand to the Web. This link discusses a recently commissioned study, which looked at gender-based values and stress in the workplace.

http://www.website101.com/Health_Insurance/
gender-health-issues.htm

PART 2

The Question of Difference

*W*hat is the most fruitful approach for better understanding sex and gender? For decades, the dominant approach in social scientific research on sex and gender is studying sex differences, termed a difference model. The goal is to examine whether or not sex differences exist and to describe the differing group tendencies. In this research, sex differences are identified from a comparison of the average tendency of a group of males to the average tendency of a group of females. The result is typically expressed in the form of generalizations of ways in which males and females differ, presuming within-sex homogeneity (i.e., all females are alike). Although most of the research is descriptive, assumptions and theories of what causes these sex differences abound. The three aims of this section are to:

(1) explore some ways in which the difference model has shaped our understanding of gender in various domains of human functioning, including communication, responses to stress, and aggression.

(2) examine critically whether it is more useful to ask the question "Are there sex differences?" or to ask the question "How does the cultural construction of gender lead to apparent differences between females and males?"

(3) examine the possibility that differences in social context, which include differences in status and power lead to apparent sex differences; that is, is sex confounded with status and power?

- Do Women and Men Communicate Differently?

- Do Women and Men Respond Differently to Stress?

- Are Differences in Aggressive Behavior Between Women and Men Due to Gender-related Factors?

ISSUE 4

Do Women and Men Communicate Differently?

YES: Julia T. Wood, from *Gendered Lives: Communication, Gender and Culture* (2001)

NO: Laura L. Winn and Donald L. Rubin, from "Enacting Gender Identity in Writing Discourse: Responding to Gender Role in Personal Ads," *Journal of Language and Social Psychology* (2001)

ISSUE SUMMARY

YES: Julia T. Wood examines how gender images of masculinity and femininity result in different communication styles in women and men.

NO: Laura L. Winn and Donald L. Rubin report on a study that demonstrated that contextual factors were more important than biological sex in stylistic features of writing.

Feminists view the study of communication and gender as very important since language is a powerful agent in the creation and maintenance of the gender system. In 1978, a major review of the scientific literature on gender and language by Cheris Kramer, Barrie Thorne, and Nancy Henley entitled, "Perspectives on Language and Communication," *Signs: Journal of Women in Culture and Society* (vol. 3, 1978) was published. This review summarized the three central research questions: 1) Do men and women use language in different ways? 2) In what ways does language—in structure, content, and daily usage—reflect and help constitute sexual inequality? 3) How can sexist language be changed?

Twenty-five years later, these three questions continue to dominate the field, but they have been reframed in more contemporary work because of an interest in *specificity* and *complexity*. Rather than studying "generic" groups of males and females, we must study particular men and women in particular settings and examine the interactions of gender and other identity categories and power relations.

In a recent issue of *Ladies Home Journal* (June 2005) an article on "Why Communication Counts" declared "Over and over again, communication problems are targeted as the number-one cause of marital strife. In many cases, couples think they're communicating, but the messages aren't getting through. Communication problems stem from differences in conversational styles between men and women." The article then proceeded to give readers (presumably mostly women) tips on how to communicate more effectively with their partner. The popular press is quick to agree with assertions such as these. In fact, most of these claims are based on the widely cited work on gender and language by author Deborah Tannen. Following up on her classic *You Just Don't Understand: Women and Men in Conversation* (1991), she has recently examined women and men's "conversational rituals" in the workplace in *Talking from 9 to 5: Women and Men at Work (2001).* In her writings she argues that "men and women live in different worlds . . . made of different words," and that how women and men converse determines who gets heard and who gets ahead in the workplace, via a verbal power game.

Tannen parallels male-female difference to cultural difference and regards males and females as different but equal. She explores how this cultural difference manifests itself in male-female (mis)communication. Her aim in her popular publications is to reassure women and men that they are not alone in experiencing miscommunication and communication problems because of sex-differentiated communication styles. Moreover, she says that she does not value one style over the other. If anything, she praises women's communication styles. Tannen urges that males and females need to respect each other's differences so that they understand why they misunderstand each other.

Similarly, Julia Wood suggests that gendered communication is a result of masculine and feminine socialization. She agrees with Tannen that women and men live in different worlds, and these worlds differ beginning in childhood with the games children play. The sex-segregated nature of children's play encourages girls to cooperate and boys to compete.

Critics, such as Mary Crawford, claim that analyses such as Tannen's and Wood's universalize and generalize, thereby creating generic individuals. She asserts that questions of difference are misguided and counterproductive not only because they are invariably marked by a political agenda but also because sex comparisons locate gender in the individual rather than in social relations and processes. Thus, she observes, responses to claims of sex difference in communication styles frequently involve blaming women for deficiencies or minimizing conflicts between men and women by reframing them as miscommunication for which we must develop tolerance. Sociocultural inequalities are not addressed.

What do we *know* about differences between males' and females' communication styles? In the following selections, Julia Wood draws on research to test Tannen's claims. Regarding the question of sex differentiation in communication styles, Wood indicates unequivocally yes. In contrast, Winn and Rubin conducted a study examining writing style in response to personal ads. They found that various contextual factors better accounted for writers' use of various gender-typed language features than their biological sex per se. In particular they noted an audience effect. Writers adjusted their presentations of themselves (as more instrumental or expressive) depending on the type of person to whom they believed they were responding.

Julia T. Wood  **YES**

Gendered Lives: Communication, Gender, and Culture

Gendered Interaction: Masculine and Feminine Styles of Verbal Communication

Language not only expresses cultural views of gender but also constitutes individuals' gender identities. The communication practices we use define us as masculine or feminine; in large measure, we create our own gender through talk. Because language constitutes masculinity and femininity, we should find generalizable differences in how women and men communicate. Research bears out this expectation by documenting rather systematic differences in the ways men and women typically use language. . . .

Studies of gender and communication convincingly show that in many ways women and men operate from dissimilar assumptions about the goals and strategies of communication. [M]en and women live in two different worlds and that this is evident in the disparate forms of communication they use. Given this, it seems appropriate to consider masculine and feminine styles of communicating as embodying two distinct speech communities. To understand these different communities and the validity of each, we will first consider how we are socialized into feminine and masculine speech communities. After this, we will explore divergencies in how women and men typically communicate. Please note the importance of the word *typically* and others that indicate we are discussing generalizable differences, not absolute ones. Some women are not socialized into feminine speech, or they are and later reject it; likewise, some men do not learn or choose not to adopt a masculine style of communication. What follows describes gendered speech communities into which *most* women and men are socialized.

The Lessons of Childplay

. . . One way to gain insight into how boys and girls learn norms of communication is to observe young children at play. In interactions with peers, boys and girls learn how to talk and how to interpret what each other says; they discover how to signal their intentions with words and how to respond appropriately to others' communication; and they learn codes to demonstrate involvement and interest. In short, interacting with peers teaches children rules of communication. . . .

Boys' games.   Boys' games usually involve fairly large groups—nine individuals for each baseball team, for instance. Most boys' games are competitive, have clear goals, and are organized by rules and roles that specify who does what and how to play. Because these games are structured by goals, rules, and roles, there is little need to discuss how to play, although there may be talk about strategies to reach goals. [In] boys' games, an individual's status depends on standing out, being better, and often dominating other players. In their games, boys engage in more heckling, storytelling, interrupting, and commanding than girls typically do. From these games, boys learn how to interact in their communities. Specifically, boys' games cultivate three communication rules:

1. Use communication to assert yourself and your ideas; use talk to achieve something.
2. Use communication to attract and maintain an audience.
3. Use communication to compete with others for the "talk stage," so that they don't gain more attention than you; learn to wrest the focus from others and onto yourself.

These communication rules are consistent with other aspects of masculine socialization. . . . For instance, notice the emphasis on individuality and competition. Also, we see that these rules accent achievement—doing something, accomplishing a goal. Boys learn they must *do things* to be valued members of the team. It's also the case that intensely close, personal relationships are unlikely to be formed in large groups. Finally, we see the undercurrent of masculinity's emphasis on being invulnerable and guarded: If others are the competition from whom you must seize center stage, then you cannot let them know too much about yourself and your weaknesses.

Girls' games.   Turning now to girls' games, we find that quite different patterns exist, and they lead to distinctive understandings of communication. Girls tend to play in pairs or in very small groups rather than large ones. Also, games like house and school do not have preset, clear-cut goals, rules, and roles. There is no analogy for the touchdown in playing house. Because girls' games are not structured externally, players have to talk among themselves to decide what they're doing and what roles they have. Playing house, for instance, typically begins with a discussion about who is going to be the daddy and who the mommy. This is typical of the patterns girls use to generate rules and roles for their games. The lack of stipulated goals for the games is also important, because it tends to cultivate in girls an interest in the process of interaction more than its products. For their games to work, girls have to cooperate and work out problems by talking: No external rules exist to settle disputes. From these games, . . . girls learn normative communication patterns of their speech communities. Specifically, girls' games teach three basic rules for communication:

1. Use collaborative, cooperative talk to create and maintain relationships. The *process* of communication, not its content, is the heart of relationships.

2. Avoid criticizing, outdoing, or putting others down; if criticism is necessary, make it gentle; never exclude others.
3. Pay attention to others and to relationships; interpret and respond to others' feelings sensitively.

[T]he typically smaller size of girls' play groups fosters cooperative discussion and an open-ended process of talking to organize activity, whereas the larger groups in which boys usually play encourage competition and external rules to structure activity. [B]oys used talk to exert control and give orders, whereas girls were more likely to make requests. . . . Girls in the groups typically used inclusive and nondirective language, whereas boys tended to issue commands, used talk to compete, and worked to establish status hierarchies in their groups.

These basic patterns in communication echo and reinforce other aspects of gender socialization. Girls' games stress cooperation, collaboration, and sensitivity to others' feelings. Also notice the focus on process encouraged in girls' games. Rather than interacting to achieve some outcome, girls learn that communication itself is the goal. Whereas boys learn they have to do something to be valuable, the lesson for girls is *to be*. Their worth depends on being good people, which is defined by being cooperative, inclusive, and sensitive. The lessons of child's play are carried forward. In fact, the basic rules of communication that adult women and men employ turn out to be only refined and elaborated versions of the very same ones evident in girls' and boys' childhood games.

Gendered Communication Practices

In her popular book *You Just Don't Understand: Women and Men in Communication,* linguist Deborah Tannen declares that "communication between men and women can be like cross cultural communication, prey to a clash of conversational styles." Her study of men's and women's talk led her to identify distinctions between the speech communities typical of women and men. Not surprisingly, Tannen traces gendered communication patterns to differences in boys' and girls' communication with parents and peers. Like other scholars, Tannen believes that women and men typically engage in distinctive styles of communication with different purposes, rules, and understandings of how to interpret talk. . . .

Women's speech.   For most women, communication is a primary way to establish and maintain relationships with others. They engage in conversation to share themselves and to learn about others. This is an important point: For women, talk *is* the essence of relationships. Consistent with this primary goal, women's speech tends to display identifiable features that foster connections, support, closeness, and understanding.

Equality between people is generally important in women's communication. To achieve symmetry, women often match experiences to indicate "You're not alone in how you feel." Typical ways to communicate equality would be saying, "I've done the same thing many times," "I've felt the same way," or "Something like that happened to me too and I felt like you do." Growing out of the quest for equality is a participatory mode of interaction in which communicators respond to and build on each other's ideas in the process of conversing. Rather than a rigid "You tell your ideas then I'll tell mine" sequence, women's speech more characteristically follows an interactive pattern in which different voices weave together to create conversations.

Also important in women's speech is showing support for others. To demonstrate support, women often express understanding and sympathy with a friend's situation or feelings. "Oh, you must feel terrible," "I really hear what you are saying," or "I think you did the right thing" are communicative clues that we understand and support how another feels. Related to these first two features is women's typical attention to the relationship level of communication. You will recall that the relationship level of talk focuses on feelings and the relationship between communicators rather than on the content of messages. . . .

A fourth feature of women's speech style is conversational "maintenance work." This involves efforts to sustain conversation by inviting others to speak and by prompting them to elaborate their experiences. Women, for instance, ask a number of questions that initiate topics for others: . . . Communication of this sort opens the conversational door to others and maintains interaction.

Inclusivity also surfaces in a fifth quality of women's talk, which is responsiveness. Women usually respond in some fashion to what others say. A women might say "Tell me more" or "That's interesting"; perhaps she will nod and use eye contact to signal she is engaged; perhaps she will ask a question such as "Can you explain what you mean?" Responsiveness reflects learned tendencies to care about others and to make them feel valued and included. It affirms another person and encourages elaboration by showing interest in what was said.

A sixth quality of women's talk is personal, concrete style. Typical of women's conversation are details, personal disclosures, anecdotes, and concrete reasoning. These features cultivate a personal tone in women's communication, and they facilitate feelings of closeness by connecting communicators' lives. . . .

A final feature of women's speech is tentativeness. This may be expressed in a number of forms. Sometimes women use verbal hedges such as "I kind of feel you may be overreacting." In other situations they qualify statements by saying "I'm probably not the best judge of this, but . . ." Another way to keep talk provisional is to tag a question onto a statement in a way that invites another to respond: "That was a pretty good movie, wasn't it?" "We should get out this weekend, don't you think?" Tentative communication leaves open the door for others to respond and express their opinions. . . .

Men's speech.   Masculine speech communities tend to regard talk as a way to exert control, preserve independence, entertain, and enhance status. Conversation is often seen as an arena for proving oneself and negotiating prestige. This leads to two general tendencies in men's communication. First, men often use talk to establish and defend their personal status and their ideas, by asserting themselves, telling jokes and stories, or by challenging others.

Second, when they wish to comfort or support another, they typically do so by respecting the other's independence and avoiding communication they regard as condescending.

To establish their status and value, men often speak to exhibit knowledge, skill, or ability. Equally typical is the tendency to avoid disclosing personal information that might make a man appear weak or vulnerable. For instance, if someone expresses a problem, a man might say "The way you should handle that is . . . ," "Don't let him get to you," or "You ought to just tell him . . ." On the relationship level of communication, giving advice does two things. First, it focuses on instrumental activity—what another should do or be—and does not acknowledge feelings. Second, it expresses superiority and maintains control. It says "I know what you should do" or "I would know how to handle that." The message may be perceived as implying the speaker is superior to the other person. Between men, advice giving seems understood as a give-and-take, but it may be interpreted as unfeeling and condescending by women whose rules for communicating differ.

A second prominent feature of men's talk is instrumentality—the use of speech to accomplish instrumental objectives. In conversation, this is often expressed through problem-solving efforts to get information, discover facts, and suggest solution. Again, between men this is usually a comfortable orientation, because both speakers have typically been socialized to value instrumentality. However, conversations between women and men are often derailed by the lack of agreement on what this informational, instrumental focus means. To many women it feels as if men don't care about their feelings. When a man focuses on the content level of meaning after a woman has disclosed a problem, she may feel he is disregarding her emotions and concerns. He, on the other hand, may well be trying to support her in the way that he has learned to show support—suggesting ways to solve the problem.

A third feature of men's communication is conversational command. Despite jokes about women's talkativeness, research indicates that in most contexts, men talk more than women. This tendency, although not present in infancy, is evident in preschoolers. Compared with girls and women, boys and men talk more frequently and for longer periods of time. Further, men engage in other verbal behaviors that sustain prominence in interaction. They may reroute conversations by using what another said as a jump-off point for their own topic, or they may interrupt. Although both sexes engage in interruptions, most research suggests that men do it more frequently. Not only do men seem to interrupt more than women, but they may do so for different reasons. [M]en use interruptions to control conversation by challenging other speakers or wresting the talk stage from them, whereas women interrupt to indicate interest and to respond. . . . A different explanation is that men generally interrupt more than women because interruptions are considered normal and good-natured within the norms of masculine speech communities. Whereas interruptions that reroute conversation might be viewed as impolite and intrusive within feminine speech communities, the outgoing, give-and-take character of masculine speech may render interruptions just part of normal conversation.

Fourth, men tend to express themselves in fairly direct, assertive ways. Compared with women, their language is typically more forceful and authoritative. Tentative speech such as hedges and disclaimers is used less frequently by men than by women. This is consistent with gender socialization in which men learn to use talk to assert themselves and to take and hold positions. When another person does not share that understanding of communication, however, speech that is absolute and directive may seem to close off conversation and leave no room for others to speak.

Fifth, compared with women, men communicate more abstractly. They frequently speak in general terms that are removed from concrete experiences and distanced from personal feelings. The abstract style typical of men's speech reflects the public and impersonal contexts in which they often operate and the less personal emphasis in their speech communities. Within public environments, norms for speaking call for theoretical, conceptual, and general thought and communication. Yet, within more personal relationships, abstract talk sometimes creates barriers to knowing another intimately.

Finally, men's speech tends not to be highly responsive, especially not on the relationship level of communication. Men, more than women, give what are called "minimal response cues," which are verbalizations such as "yeah" or "umhmm." In interaction with women, who have learned to demonstrate interest more vigorously, minimal response cues generally inhibit conversation because they are perceived as indicating lack of involvement. Men's conversation also often lacks expressed sympathy, understanding, and self-disclosures. Within the rules of men's speech communities, sympathy is a sign of condescension, and revealing personal problems is seen as making one vulnerable. Yet women's speech rules count sympathy and disclosure as demonstrations of equality and support. This creates potential for misunderstanding between women and men.

Misinterpretations Between Women and Men

Showing support. The scene is a private conversation between Martha and George. She tells him she is worried about her friend. George gives a minimum response cue, saying only "Oh." To Martha this suggests he isn't interested, because women make and expect more . . . "listening noises" to signal interest. . . . George is probably thinking if she wants to tell him something she will, because his rules of speech emphasize using talk to assert oneself. Even without much encouragement, Martha continues by describing the tension in her friend's marriage and her own concern about how she can help. She says, "I feel so bad for Barbara, and I want to help her, but I don't know what to do." George then says, "It's their problem, not yours. Just butt out and let them settle their own relationship." At this, Martha explodes: "Who asked for your advice?" George is now completely frustrated and confused. He thought Martha wanted advice, so he gave it. She is hurt that George didn't tune into her feelings and comfort her about her worries. Each is annoyed and unhappy.

The problem here is not so much what George and Martha say and don't say. Rather, it's how they interpret each other's communication—actually, how they *misinterpret* it, because each relies on rules that are not familiar to the other. They fail to understand that each is operating by different rules of talk. George is respecting Martha's independence by not pushing her to talk. When he thinks she directly requests advice, he offers it in an effort to help. Martha, on the other hand, wants comfort and a connection with George— that is her purpose in talking with him. She finds his advice unwelcome and dismissive of her feelings. He doesn't offer sympathy, because his rules for communication define this as condescending. Yet within Martha's speech community, not to show sympathy is to be unfeeling and unresponsive.

"Troubles talk."   [T]alk about troubles, or personal problems, [is] a kind of interaction in which hurt feelings may result from the contrast between most men's and women's rules of communication. A woman might tell her partner that she is feeling down because she did not get a job she wanted. In an effort to be supportive, he might respond by saying, "You shouldn't feel bad. Lots of people don't get jobs they want." To her this seems to dismiss her feelings—to be-little them by saying lots of people experience her situation. Yet within masculine speech communities, this is a way of showing respect for another by not assuming that she or he needs sympathy.

Now let's turn the tables and see what happens when a man feels troubled. When he meets Nancy, Craig is unusually quiet because he feels down about not getting a job offer. Sensing that something is wrong, Nancy tries to show interest by asking, "Are you okay? What's bothering you?" Craig feels she is imposing and trying to get him to show a vulnerability he prefers to keep to himself. Nancy probes further to show she cares. As a result, he feels intruded on and withdraws further. Then Nancy feels shut out.

But perhaps Craig does decide to tell Nancy why he feels down. After hearing about his rejection letter, Nancy says, "I know how you feel. I felt so low when I didn't get that position at Datanet." She is matching experiences to show Craig that she understands his feelings and that he's not alone. Within his communication rules, however, this is demeaning his situation by focusing on her, not him. When Nancy mentions her own experience, Craig thinks she is trying to steal the center stage for herself. Within his speech community, that is one way men vie for dominance and attention. Yet Nancy has learned to share similar experiences as a way to build connections with others.

The point of the story.   Another instance in which feminine and masculine communication rules often clash and cause problems is in relating experiences. Typically, men have learned to speak in a linear manner in which they move sequentially through major points in a story to get to the climax. Their talk tends to be straight-forward without a great many details. The rules of feminine speech, however, call for more detailed and less linear storytelling. Whereas a man is likely to provide rather bare information about what happened, a woman is more likely to embed the information within a larger context of the people involved and other things going on. Women include details not because all of the specifics are important in themselves but because recounting them shows involvement and allows a conversational partner to be more fully part of the situation being described.

Because feminine and masculine rules about details differ, men often find women's way of telling stories wandering and unfocused. Conversely, men's style of storytelling may strike women as leaving out all of the interesting details. Many a discussion between women and men has ended either with his exasperated demand, "Can't you get to the point?" or with her frustrated question, "Why don't you tell me how you were feeling and what else was going on?" She wants more details than his rules call for; he is interested in fewer details than she has learned to supply.

Relationship talk. "Can we talk about us?" is the opening of innumerable conversations that end in misunderstanding and hurt. . . . [M]en and women tend to have very different ideas about what it means to talk about relationships. In general, men are inclined to think a relationship is going fine as long as there is no need to talk about it. They are interested in discussing the relationship only if there are particular problems to be addressed. In contrast, women generally think a relationship is working well as long as they can talk about it with partners. The difference here grows out of the fact that men tend to use communication to do things and solve problems, whereas women generally regard the *process* of communicating as a primary way to create and sustain relationships with others. For many women, conversation is a way to be with another person—to affirm and enhance closeness. Men's different rules stipulate that communication is to achieve some goal or fix some problem. No wonder men often duck when their partners want to "discuss the relationship," and women often feel a relationship is in trouble when their partners are unwilling to talk about it. . . .

Public speaking.   Differences in women's and men's communication patterns also surface in public contexts. In Western society, the public sphere traditionally has been considered men's domain. . . . [O]ne of the constraints on women's efforts to gain legal rights in the 1800s was the proscription against women speaking in public. Although many women are now active and vocal in public life, feminine forms of communication are still devalued. The assertive, dominant, confident masculine style is the standard for public speaking, whereas the more collaborative, inclusive feminine style of communicating is considered less effective. This male generic standard for public speaking places feminine speakers at a disadvantage in public life. Their style of speaking is judged by a standard that neither reflects nor respects their communication goals and values. Women such as former Texas governor Ann Richards who are considered effective public speakers manage to combine the traditionally feminine communication style (which includes personal compassion and use of anecdotal information) with more masculine qualities such as assertiveness and instrumentality. Even today, a conventionally feminine communication style is usually devalued, because masculine standards of public speaking still prevail.

Summary

. . . [L]anguage reflects and sustains cultural views of masculinity and femininity. By defining, classifying, and evaluating gender, language reinforces social views of men as the standard and women as marginal and men and masculinity as more valuable than women and femininity. From generic male terms to language that demeans and diminishes women, verbal communication is a powerful agent of cultural expression. . . .

. . . [W]omen and men constitute their gender identities through their styles of communication. Because males and females tend to be socialized into distinct speech communities, they learn different rules about the purposes of communication and ways to indicate support, interest, and involvement. Because women and men have some dissimilar rules for talk, they often misread each other's meanings and misunderstand each other's motives. This frequently leads to frustration, hurt, and tension between people who care about each other and misjudgments of people speaking in public settings. Appreciating and respecting the distinctive validity of each style of communication is a foundation for better understanding between people. Further, learning to use different styles of communication allows women and men to be more flexible and effective in their interactions with each other. . . .

NO ↩

**Laura L. Winn and
Donald L. Rubin**

Enacting Gender Identity in Written Discourse: Responding to Gender Role Bidding in Personal Ads

Recent theories depict social identity as enacted or constructed within interactions. Individuals may choose to either emphasize or de-emphasize aspects of their identities in response to the characteristics of a situation. Communication adaptation theory (CAT) holds that individuals vary their language choices within interactions, depending on their social goals. Thus, speakers may choose to emphasize (or de-emphasize) particular aspects of their identities as a way of aligning with (or distancing from) interaction partners. In this manner, situational influences may have a profound effect on discourse. . . . [T]he primary value of CAT is that it is designed to address the interactive nature of identity construction. . . .

Gender schematic information is a particularly influential aspect of social identity formation. Of particular interest to the current study was the way participants might use language to frame gendered identities within their writing. . . . Studies on gender-related linguistic markers demonstrate that . . . goals . . . [may] often override the sex of the message sender as potential influences on language style. . . .

. . . [T]he use of gender-linked linguistic markers may be subject to considerable situational influence. In fact, although gender differences in speech often occur, these are just as likely to be indicators of gender-related role behaviors as markers of biological sex. . . . [S]peech accommodation theory . . . predict[s] that there would be both biological gender–related and gender role–related differences in speakers' behavior. . . .

. . . [F]emale speakers [have been shown to] use more "masculine" (i.e., instrumental) terms and fewer "feminine" (i.e., expressive) terms in heterogeneous group situations than when they [speak] in all-female dyads. In dyads, both men and women adapt their speech to the more affiliative context of the situation, whereas in groups, both men and women use more instrumental speech, indicating an awareness of the different needs of this context. . . .

The current study was conducted as a means of further investigating gender-linked use of linguistic markers in managing written identity presentation. We

From *Journal of Language and Social Psychology*, vol. 20, no. 4, December 2001, pp. 393–418. Copyright © 2001 by Sage Publications. Reprinted by permission.

chose the heterosexual personal ad context as a way of obtaining cross-sex targeted discourse. . . .

[A discussion of gender and spoken and written language is provided before the study is described.]

Gender and Language

Early studies of gender and language associate female speakers with features that hedge or blunt assertions (e.g., "maybe," "sort of," "I guess") and avoid conflict with listeners by the use of politeness formulas (e.g., "if you don't mind" or the use of question forms rather than bald requests). Other "markers" commonly associated with female language include the use of double-sided arguments (e.g., "It was probably Shakespeare's sister, but then again, some people believe it was Marlowe"), expressions of uncertainty (e.g., "I don't know, but . . ."), and the use of certain vocabulary likely to be judged as trivial (e.g., fine-grained color terms such as *fuchsia*).

Curiously, research on language and gender remains vulnerable to criticism for failing to take into account more dynamic models of identity. . . . [Some researchers have] argued that across the literature, men's and women's language is more similar than different and that apparent differences are quite context specific. Rather than enumerating superficial sex differences, it would be more productive for researchers to examine features of interaction contexts that lead speakers to enact gender roles in particular ways. . . .

. . . [Findings] that male and female speakers were more similar than different in their use of previously gender-linked linguistic markers of tag questions, hedges, and interruptions [Challenges the "dual cultures" model of gender]. . . . Because language use is socioculturally conditioned, where gender differences do exist, they are more likely due to differences in gender role schemata than to biological sex.

Within oral discourse, if women are found to use more standard dialect features than men, the reason may be that women are more often compelled by the terms of their employment to function in contexts demanding linguistic propriety, whereas men may be less subject to those particular workplace demands on language. On the other hand, if women use "you know" more often than men, the reason may be that they are failing to receive the back-channel cues from their listeners, affirming that they still have their listeners' attention. This view receives support from studies on men's language as well. Men who by happenstance find themselves occupying interaction roles more typically occupied by women (e.g., a powerless witness in a trial) are likely to enact those roles using language that is stereotypically associated with women's speech. Consequently, there is considerable support for a view of gender identity as dynamically constructed through language choice rather than as a static label.

Studies of gender and written language have proliferated. . . .

To be sure, some of these studies are guilty of a "sex difference" approach to simply cataloguing stylistic features of men's and women's writing. However, others do look at gendered writing as a function of the interaction context from which it emerges. . . .

[In many studies,] gender typicality was difficult to establish. . . . [C]ontext seemed to have the greatest effect on some aspects of gender performance. . . .

Personal Ads

Most studies of personal ads consider only the writers' and readers' biological sex, failing to consider more theory-driven issues of gender role identity. However, the findings of a few studies suggest that gender identity (as opposed to biological sex alone) can be an important factor for the process of identity bargaining within the context of mate selection. . . . [In an analysis of] over 800 personal ads placed in newspapers. . . . [T]hose ads preferred mainly by men (i.e., rated lowest by women) and those preferred mainly by women (i.e., rated lowest by men) were labeled "sexually dimorphic," meaning that the content of the ads was likely to appeal to only one gender. Those that were preferred by both men and women were considered to be more androgynous by the authors. The ads that appeared to "target" opposite gender readers (by emphasizing the writers' own gender traits) were more likely to be successful. Thus, it appears that within this context, individuals privilege more stereotypical gender identity bids. . . .

[An examination of] the instrumental and expressive content within personal ads collected from local newspapers [revealed/that] instrumental traits tend to be more "male valued" (e.g., assertive, independent, and goal oriented), whereas expressive traits tend to be more "female valued" (e.g., warm, caring, and family oriented). Ads that referenced educational and professional status were coded as instrumental. . . . [B]oth women and men were likely to write ads that offered what they apparently believed the other preferred. Women shaped their social identities in more instrumental terms, whereas men emphasized more expressive traits. At the same time, women were more likely to describe their desired partners in expressive terms, whereas men listed more instrumental qualities in describing their ideal mates.

Consequently, the findings suggest that within the discourse of personal ads, individuals are likely to base their descriptions of both themselves and their ideal partners on their beliefs about what their readers may prefer. . . .

The present study was designed to examine adaptation in the gender identity of individuals as portrayed in their written discourse. As suggested by CAT, we predicted that characteristics of the hypothetical audience would influence writers' self-presentations. Therefore, we manipulated the gender role orientation (instrumentality or expressivity) of the hypothetical target audience. To maximize the chance that writers would indeed attempt to attract readers, writers were given instructions to this effect for [two] letter-writing tasks. Much of the research conducted within the frame of CAT indicates that attraction, or solidarity, in interpersonal relationships is often accomplished via converging language styles. Alternatively a complementary language style may occur when there is reason to believe that attraction or solidarity may best be expressed by adopting a slightly divergent language style. . . .

Method

Participants

A total of 84 undergraduate college students attending a large, southeastern U.S. university participated in the study. Participants were recruited from introductory communication courses and received course credit for their involvement. Participants' ages ranged between 18 and 34, with a mean age of 21.4 years. . . .

Stimulus Materials

Two personal ads were constructed for each of the two study conditions. The first ad was intended as a bid for an expressive gender role schema companion (enjoys walking in the woods, attending art shows, and seeking a meaningful relationship). The other ad bid for a prototypical instrumental gender role schema companion (enjoys fitness training and NASCAR races and seeks a mate to "walk on the wild side"). The ad texts were otherwise comparable (equal length, physical layout, etc.). The ad texts were constructed from portions of personal ads appearing in the local newspaper. They were presented to participants in a format designed to simulate an actual newspaper ad.

Participants also completed a 20-item adaptation of the Bem Sex Role Inventory (BSRI). This scale asks participants to rate themselves according to whether they tend to exhibit 10 expressive traits (e.g., caring) and 10 instrumental traits (e.g., assertiveness). . . .

Procedure

Participants engaged in two writing tasks. For the first, they wrote self-descriptions that could hypothetically be submitted to a dating service. Participants were instructed to represent themselves as honestly as possible so that the dating service could match them with companions who would be truly compatible. This first writing sample was intended to assess each participant's "baseline" gender self-presentation before exposure to the stimulus ads. Participants were instructed to write letters that described themselves realistically and yet that would be most likely to attract someone to whom they would be compatible.

Following this first writing episode, participants read one of the two simulated personal ads (either instrumental or expressive). Participants were instructed to produce a second writing sample, intended to be a letter of response to the personal ad. For this second writing task, participants were asked to assume that they had chosen the particular ad and were interested in meeting this person. They were also told to "try to present yourself in a way that this person would find appealing" to maximize the chance that they would write letters designed to attract (rather than repel) the hypothetical other. . . .

Discussion

Our goal was to consider the joint effects of two contextual factors, (a) audience-related gender role bidding and (b) type of writing task, on the written language of men and women in light of communication adaptation and communication accommodation theories. In addition to considering the biological gender of the language users, we also took into account their instrumental and expressive gender role schemata. For some language features associated with gendered language (e.g., nonessentials, hedges, connectives), either biological gender or psychological gender schemata exerted independent effects. In general, however, the results support previous notions that the writing context plays at least as much of a role in shaping gender-typed language use as the gender of the writer. . . .

Gender Effects

Our first research question focused on effects of the biological gender of the writer, in contrast with psychological gender role orientation, on the production of gender-typed written language. Given that linguistic style is socioculturally rather than biologically conditioned, and given previous findings that biological sex is not the dominant determinant of female-typed language, we surmised that we would find few effects of biological sex after covarying for gender role schemata. The results, however, were mixed on this score. Two language features, syntactic complexity and first-person pronouns, showed no effects for either the writer's own biological gender or gender role orientation.

Simple main effects for biological sex, but no covariate effects for gender role schema, did emerge for two variables. . . . [W]omen as compared with men in this study did produce a higher relative frequency of nonessentials (e.g., parenthetical expressions). . . . Women also expressed more markers of excitability (e.g., exclamations), postulated as tokens of emotionality. Consequently, for these two language features at least, the results show some support for the prevalent idea that women tend to use more female-typed language features in their writing. . . .

Connectives (e.g., "because," "unless," "then," "and") were associated not only with biological sex but also with psychological gender roles. For connectives, women and low instrumentals tended to produce more connectives than men and high instrumentals. This finding runs contrary to previous suppositions, which attribute more hierarchically organized discourse rich in explicit connections to men. . . .

A number of gender-related effects also emerged for the category of hedges (e.g., "kinda," "I think," "probably," "might have"). People who reported high levels of expressive gender role orientation used hedges infrequently. Although hedges have been stereotypically associated with women's speech, empirical research has generally not borne out any such association. In the present study, . . . personality traits such as nurturing and cooperativeness can actually depress expressions of tentativeness.

Nor was there any main effect of biological sex on use of hedges once the effects of psychological gender had been partialed out. On the other hand, the analysis of interaction effects suggested that women did use hedges more adaptively than men, for example, deploying a higher frequency of hedges when responding to an expressive gender role bid compared with an instrumental gender role bid. Indeed, a similar result emerged for connectives. For these two language features, then, it appears that women were more responsive to the perceived nature of the audience than men. Similarly, Hogg found that women engaged in more adaptive use of gender-typed features than men. . . .

Audience Effects

The . . . most central research question concerned the effects of the gender role bid (instrumental or expressive) issued by the hypothetical target audience's personal ads. No main effects for this factor emerged, but we were especially interested in any interactions that may have emerged between writing task and gender role bid of the advertisement. It is within those interactions that one would find the most direct evidence of communication adaptation. . . .

Two language variables in these data did evince . . . a complementary pattern. First, there was . . . a statistically significant interaction between writing task and gender role bid of the personal ad for markers of excitability. In responding to the instrumental gender role bid (traditional masculine values), participants increased their use of this female-typed feature. The instrumental ad thus appeared to elicit a complementary adaptation from writers (an increase in excitability markers relative to baseline self-descriptions). In a parallel fashion, the interaction for first-person pronouns showed similar evidence of complementary adaptation. In the face of an expressive gender role bid (traditionally feminine), writers reduced their output of these female-typed markers from their baseline output.

Thus, this study provides at least some evidence of a complementary type of communication adaptation in the context of responding to personal ads. If the person who places the ad expresses an instrumental gender role identity himself or herself, the linguistic response is to emphasize the responder's expressive gender role identity by increasing the output of subjectivity markers. Conversely, if the ad appears to express an instrumental gender role identity, the responder may use excitability markers to emphasize his or her expressive traits. . . .

In sum, we conclude that contextual influences need to be accounted for when analyzing gender and language use in written discourse. The findings of the present study, though modest, do offer some concrete illustration of ways in which people enact varying gender identities in the face of an interlocutor's bid for one or another gender role. These identities are enacted by modulating the use of socially meaningful language features, for example, in a manner that complements the interlocutor's apparent gender identity.

POSTSCRIPT

Do Women and Men Communicate Differently?

It is important to situate discourse about sex differences in communication (indeed in any domain) in a sociopolitical context. Beliefs that the sexes differ, whether supported by empirical evidence or not, are deeply entranched in our society. Indeed, while academic critics signal the lack of a scientific basis to Tannen's sweeping claims, her popular works have shot to the top of the bestseller list. We, the consumers, have to be very careful about scrutinizing how knowledge has been constructed and used. There is no such thing as a "simple" yes or no answer to a question of sex difference.

Scholarly and popular writing on sex differences is impacted greatly by what can be called the "hall of mirrors" effect. As described by Deborah Cameron in "Gender and Language: Gender, Language, and Discourse: A Review Essay," *Signs: Journal of Women in Culture and Society* (1998), "in the course of being cited, discussed, and popularized over time, originally modest claims have been progressively represented as more and more absolute, while hypotheses have been given the status of facts." Thus, for example, the originally modest claim made by researchers Don Zimmerman and Candace West in "Sex Roles, Interruptions and Silences in Conversation," in Barrie Thorne and Nancy Henley, eds., *In Language and Sex: Differences and Dominance* (Newbury House, 1975), that men interrupt women more than the reverse may have been exaggerated by constant repetition and then critiqued for being overstated (much like the "telephone" game played by children).

Currently there is less interest in examining sex differences in language and more emphasis on how people use language in everyday life to create and maintain social realities. Mary Crawford points out that feminists have worked to create a more gender-balanced language through the coining of new words and putting old words to new uses. She notes that language is power.

Suggested Readings

Daniel J. Canary and Kathryn Dindia, Eds., *Sex Differences and Similarities in Communication: Critical Essays and Empirical Investigations of Sex and Gender in Interaction,* (2nd ed. New York: Lawrence Erlbaum, 2006).

Mary Crawford, "Gender and Language," in R. K. Unger, ed., *Psychology of Women and Gender* (pp. 228–244), (New York: John Wiley & Son, 2001).

Diana Ivy and Phil Backlund, *Gender Speak: Personal Effectiveness in Gender Communication* (New York: McGraw-Hill, 2003).

H. Kotthoff and R. Wodak, eds., *Communicating Gender in Context* (John Benjamins, 1997).

Charlotte Krolokke and Anne Scott Sorenson, *Gender Communication Theories and Analyses: From Silence to Performance* (Thousand Oaks, CA: Sage, 2005).

Deborah Tannen, *Talking from 9 to 5: Women and Men at Work* (San Francisco: HarperCollins, 2001).

ISSUE 5

Do Women and Men Respond Differently to Stress?

YES: Shelley Taylor, L. C. Klein, B. P. Lewis, T. L. Gruenewald, R. A. R. Gurung, and J. A. Updegraff, from "Biobehavioral Responses to Stress in Females: Tend-and-Befriend, not Flight-or-Fight," *Psychological Review* (2000)

NO: John T. Cacioppo, G. G. Berntson, J. F. Sheridan, and M. K. McClintock, from "Multilevel Integrative Analyses of Human Behavior: Social Neuroscience and the Complementing Nature of Social and Biological Approaches," *Psychological Bulletin* (2000)

ISSUE SUMMARY

YES: Social psychologist Shelley Taylor and her colleagues, in a review of the literature, conclude that there is an evolutionarily based biobehavioral mechanism that underlies women's tend-and-befriend response to stress.

NO: Social psychologist John T. Cacioppo and his colleagues argue for the value of examining the influence of social influences on biological processes rather than vice versa. In numerous examples they document the effects of the context on fundamental biological processes.

Women's caring and nurturing nature is often contrasted with the stereotype of men as aggressive and competitive (see Issue 6). In numerous theories it has been assumed that women's reproductive role as childbearers and caregivers is foundational and at the root of their affiliative nature. There is substantial empirical evidence that supports the idea that women can more reliably be depended on for meeting the long-term needs of family and friends. Women have been shown to, on average, have deeper and more intimate friendships, more extensive social networks, be more likely to discuss personal problems with friends, be more likely to seek treatment for psychological problems, and be more person-oriented rather than task-oriented in work situations. What is in dispute is the reason for these observed differences. Such generalizations oversimplify very complex patterns of gender-related patterns across cultures, at different ages, and in different contexts.

The selections here alert us to the dangers of confusing correlation with causation, an especially easy error to make when one of the correlates is biological. Shelly Taylor's writings have made a valuable contribution by noting that classic research on stress and coping relied exclusively on studies of males (animal and human research). These classic theories proposed that there are two responses to stress: flight or fight. She pondered the relevance of these two possibilities for females (animal and human). She subsequently concluded that there may be a different possible response to stress for females: tend-and-befriend, and built a new theoretical model based on this possibility. Cacioppo and his colleagues provide the counterpoint argument, showing the power of social context in numerous cases, from genetic constitution and genetic expression to cardiovascular functioning and immune-system responses. Their review of the research, especially experimental studies with animals, show that within males and females of different species it is the social context that is relevant. This is illustrated in research that has shown that socially dominant female monkeys have less coronary artery atherosclerosis (i.e., hardening of the arteries) than subordinate females housed in similar conditions. In research with human males it was found that although hypertension runs in families, it was the men who were in the top quartile in cardiovascular reactivity who showed the greatest increases in blood pressure in responses to daily stressors, and social stressors were more strongly associated with cardiovascular reactivity than other factors such as exercise. Also consider a few key findings from a recent study by Katie Kivlighan, Douglas Granger, and Alan Booth (2005). They examined gender-related patterns of hormone-behavior relationships in novice and experienced varsity rowers in a particular stressful situation, a competition. They found a complex set of interactions based on level of experience and time (pre-event, during the event, and post-event), as well as gender and type of measure. For example, higher cortisol levels pre-event in men were associated with more bonding and social affiliation with teammates. In contrast, HPA axis (i.e., "stress system") elevation pre-event was associated with social bonding in women but social withdrawal in men. During the competition, higher testosterone levels were associated with slower race times and poorer finishes in both novice female and male rowers. After the competition, novice rowers "recovered" more quickly than experienced rowers, who tended to focus their thoughts and feelings on the events, even after their hormonal levels declined. Novice male rowers showed the most rapid decline in cortisol and female rowers the slowest. They concluded that there is a "need for more sophisticated measurement of social behavior and cognitions involved in affiliation and bonding with teammates such as the timing of the behavior in relation to competitive event, the role an individual plays as a giver or receiver of social support, and the means through which bonding occurs," and in attempting to integrate their findings with Taylor's model they conclude "the model provides little guidance regarding the possibility of gender differences."

YES ↵

Shelley E. Taylor et al.

Biobehavioral Responses to Stress in Females: Tend-and-Befriend, Not Fight-or-Flight

Survival depends on the ability to mount a successful response to threat. The human stress response has been characterized as fight-or-flight and has been represented as an essential mechanism in the survival process. We propose that human female responses to stress (as well as those of some animal species) are not well characterized by fight-or-flight, as research has implicitly assumed, but rather are more typically characterized by a pattern we term "tend-and-befriend." Specifically, we suggest that, by virtue of differential parental invest-ment, female stress responses have selectively evolved to maximize the survival of self and offspring. We suggest that females respond to stress by nurturing offspring, exhibiting behaviors that protect them from harm and reduce neuroendocrine responses that may compromise offspring health (the tending pattern), and by befriending, namely, affiliating with social groups to reduce risk. We hypothesize and consider evidence from humans and other species to suggest that females create, maintain, and utilize these social groups, especially relations with other females, to manage stressful conditions. We suggest that female responses to stress may build on attachment–caregiving processes that downregulate sympathetic and hypothalamic-pituitary-adrenocortical (HPA) responses to stress. In support of this biobehavioral theory, we consider a large animal and human literature on neuroendocrine responses to stress, suggesting that the tend-and-befriend pattern may be oxytocin mediated and moderated by sex hormones and endogenous opioid peptide mechanisms.

Background

The fight-or-flight response is generally regarded as the prototypic human response to stress. . . .

A coordinated biobehavioral stress response is believed to be at the core of reactions to threats of all kinds, including attacks by predators; assaults by members of the same species; dangerous conditions such as fire, earthquake,

From *Psychological Review*, vol. 107, no. 3, 2000, excerpts from 411–429. Copyright © 2000 by American Psychological Association. Reprinted by permission.

tornado, or flooding; and other threatening events. As such, an appropriate and modulated stress response is at he core of survival.

A little-known fact about the fight-or-flight response is that the preponderance of research exploring its parameters has been conducted on males, especially on male rats. Until recently, the gender distribution in the human literature was inequitable as well. . . .

Theoretical Model

An empirical gap such as the identified gender bias in stress studies provides a striking opportunity to build theory. From a metatheoretical perspective, we reasoned that a viable theoretical framework for understanding female responses to stress may be derived by making a few conservative evolutionary assumptions and then building parallel and mutually constraining biological and behavioral models.

We propose, first, that successful responses to stress have been passed on to subsequent generations through principles of natural selection: Those without successful responses to threat are disproportionately unlikely to reach an age when reproduction is possible. An additional assumption is that, because females have typically borne a greater role in the care of young offspring, responses to threat that were successfully passed on would have been those that protected offspring as well as the self. The female of the species makes a greater investment initially in pregnancy and nursing and typically plays the primary role in activities designed to bring the offspring to maturity. High maternal investment should lead to selection for female stress responses that do not jeopardize the health of the mother and her offspring and that maximize the likelihood that they will survive. "Tending," that is, quieting and caring for offspring and blending into the environment, may be effective for addressing a broad array of threats. . . .

We propose that the biobehavorial mechanism underlying the tend-and-befriend pattern is the attachment–caregiving system, a stress-related system that has been previously explored largely for its role in maternal bonding and child development. In certain respects, the female tending response under stressful conditions may represent the counterpart of the infant attachment mechanism that appears to be so critical for the development of normal biological regulatory systems in offspring. . . .

In essence, then, we are proposing the existence of an endogenous stress regulatory system that has heretofore been largely ignored in the biological and behavioral literatures on stress, especially in humans. . . .

Females and the Fight-or-Flight Response

The basic neuroendocrine core of stress responses does not seem to vary substantially between human males and females. Both sexes experience a cascade of hormonal responses to threat that appears to begin with the rapid release of oxytocin, vasopressin, corticotropin-releasing factor (CRF), and possibly other hormones produced in the paraventricular nucleus of the hypothalamus. . . .

As already noted, however, a stress response geared toward aggressing or fleeing may be somewhat adaptive for males but it may not address the different challenges faced by females, especially those challenges that arise from maternal investment in offspring. The demands of pregnancy, nursing, and infant care render females extremely vulnerable to external threats. Should a threat present itself during this time, a mother's attack on a predator or flight could render offspring fatally unprotected. Instead, behaviors that involve getting offspring out of the way, retrieving them from threatening circumstances, calming them down and quieting them, protecting them from further threat, and anticipating protective measures against stressors that are imminent may increase the likelihood of survival of offspring. Given the adaptiveness of such behaviors for females, neuroendocrine mechanisms may have evolved to facilitate these behaviors and inhibit behavioral tendencies to fight or flee. . . .

Tending Under Stress

Tending

As we previously stated, the basic neuroendocrine core of stress responses does not seem to vary substantially between human males and females. In both sexes, threat triggers sympathetic-adrenal-medullary (SAM) and hypothalamic-pituitary-adrenal (HPA) activation, as well as the release of other neuroendocrine responses that operate to prepare the organism to respond to the stressor. How would a female responding to stress with sympathetic arousal nonetheless quiet and calm down offspring? We propose that the biobehavioral mechanism for the tending process builds on the attachment–caregiving system. . . .

Attachment was originally conceived as a stress-related biobehavioral system that is the mainstay of maternal bonding and of child socialization. This largely innate caregiving system is thought to be especially activated in response to threat and to signs of offspring distress (such as "distress vocalization"). The caregiving system has been heavily explored through animal studies, with parallels in human developmental investigations . . .

Oxytocin and endogenous opioid mechanisms may be at the core of the tending response. Evidence from a broad array of animal studies involving rats, prairie voles, monkeys, and sheep show that central administration of oxytocin reduces anxiety and has mildly sedative properties in both males and females. . . . [T]his response appears to be stronger in females than in males, and oxytocin may play two roles with regard to the female stress response. It may serve both to calm the female who is physiologically aroused by a stressor and also to promote affiliative behaviors, including maternal behavior toward offspring. . . .

Nurturing behavior under stressful conditions may not only quiet and soothe offspring but it may also have discernible effects on health-related outcomes, directly affecting the likelihood that offspring will survive and mature properly. . . .

If mothers in particular exhibit nurturing behavior under conditions of stress, it should also be possible to see behavioral evidence for this prediction in parenting behaviors. Such evidence is provided by Repetti's studies of the effects of stressful workdays on parenting behavior. Repetti gave question-naires to both fathers and mothers about their workdays and their behaviors at home on those days and to children regarding their experiences with their parents on those days. She found that fathers who had experienced an inter-personally conflictual day at work were more likely to be interpersonally con-flictual in the home after work. Fathers who had highly stressful workdays, but not involving interpersonal conflict, were more likely to withdraw from their families. A very different pattern was found for mothers. Specifically, women were more nurturant and caring toward their children on their stress-ful work days. In particular, on days when women reported that their stress levels at work had been the highest, their children reported that their mothers had shown them more love and nurturance. . . .

In summary, whereas male responses to stress may be tied to sympa-thetic arousal and to a fight-or-flight pattern that is, at least in part, organized and activated by androgens, female stress responses do not show these andro-gen links and, instead, may be tied, at least in part, to the release of oxytocin and its biobehavioral links to caregiving behavior. Oxytocin is believed not only to underlie attachment processes between mothers and offspring but it may also be implicated in other close social bonds. We extend this analysis . . . by arguing that female responses to stress are also characterized by affiliation with social groups because group living provides special benefits for females.

Befriending Among Females

Group living is generally regarded as an evolutionary adaptation among many species that benefits both males and females. Groups provide more eyes for the detection of predators, and most predators are reluctant to attack potential prey if they believe there are others who may come to that prey's rescue. Moreover, groups can create confusion in a predator. If a predator charges a large group, the group may disband in many directions, which may confuse the predator long enough to reduce the likelihood that any one member of the group can be taken down. Group life, then, is fundamental to primate existence, making it an important evolutionary strategy by which primates have survived. As we have noted, female stress responses have likely evolved in ways that not only protect the female herself but also protect her offspring. As such, group life is likely to have been an especially important adaptation for females and offspring, because of the limitations of fight-or-flight as a female response to stress. Like human males, human females once required successful defense against external predators, such as tigers, leopards, hyenas, packs of hunting dogs, and other primates. In addition, human females have much to fear from human males, including rape, assault, homicide, and abuse of offspring. The pairing of human females with human males may be, in part, an evolutionary adaptation that protects females and offspring against random assault by males. However, under some conditions, human females also have reason to fear their own male partners. In North America, estimates of the percentage of women who have been assaulted by their partners range from 20% to 50% and statistical analyses of assault and homicide data reveal that human females are most likely to be assaulted or killed by their own partners. There is no reason to believe that this is a particularly modern phenomenon. Thus, evolved mechanisms of female survival likely protected against a broad array of threats, including those from males of her own species. . . .

Research on human males and females shows that, under conditions of stress, the desire to affiliate with others is substantially more marked among females than among males. In fact, it is one of the most robust gender differences in adult human behavior, other than those directly tied to pregnancy and lactation, and it is the primary gender difference in adult human behavioral responses to stress. . . .

Across the entire life cycle, females are more likely to mobilize social support, especially from other females, in times of stress. They seek it out more, they receive more support, and they are more satisfied with the support they receive. Adolescent girls report more informal sources of support than do boys, and they are more likely to turn to their same-sex peers for support than are boys. Female college students report more available helpers and report receiving more support than do males. Adult women maintain more same-sex close relationships than do men, they mobilize more social support in times of stress than do men, they rely less heavily than do men on their spouses for social support, they turn to female friends more often, they report more benefits from contact with their female friends and relatives (although they are also more vulnerable to network events as a cause of psychological distress), and they provide more frequent and more effective social support to others than do men. Although females give help to both males and females in their support networks, they are more likely to seek help and social support from other female relatives and female friends than from males.

Women are also more engaged in their social networks than are men. They are significantly better at reporting most types of social network events than men, such as major illnesses of children, and they are more likely to report being involved if there is a crisis event in the network. . . . So consistent and strong are these findings that theorists have argued for basic gender differences in orientation toward others, with women maintaining a collectivist orientation or connectedness and males, a more individualistic orientation. . . .

The preceding analysis is not intended to suggest that males are not benefitted by social group living or that they do not form social groups in response to external threats or stress. However, anthropological accounts, as well as survey literature, suggest that the functions of the groups that men and women form and turn to under stress are somewhat different. . . .

Conclusions, Implications, and Limitations

We propose a theory of female responses to stress characterized by a pattern termed "tend-and-befriend." Specifically, we propose that women's responses to stress are characterized by patterns that involve caring for offspring under stressful circumstances, joining social groups to reduce vulnerability, and contributing to the development of social groupings, especially those involving female networks, for the exchange of resources and responsibilities. We maintain that aspects of these responses, both maternal and affiliative, may have built on the biobehavioral attachment–caregiving system that depends, in part, on oxytocin, estrogen, and endogenous opioid mechanisms, among other neuroendocrine underpinnings. We suggest that these patterns may have evolved according to principles of natural selection and by virtue of differential parental investment. We propose this theory as a biobehavioral alternative to the flight-or-flight response which has dominated stress research of the past 5 decades and has been disproportionately based on studies of males. . . .

Social and Political Implications

The issue arises as to whether sex differences in human behavior would be better understood as differences in social roles rather than as evolved biobehavioral responses. For example, given substantial human behavioral flexibility, one can question whether maternal investment in offspring continues to be higher than that of fathers. In response, we note that current differences between men and women in parental investment do not matter as much as differential parental investment during the period of time that stress responses evolved. An evolutionary biobehavioral argument does not constrain current human behavior but neither is it necessarily challenged by current human behavioral flexibility. We also note that, although human social roles vary substantially across cultures and may, in some cases, prescribe behavioral patterns for women similar to the tend-and-befriend pattern, social roles alone are unlikely to account for it. A social role position neither addresses the cross-species similarities we have identified nor accounts for the underlying biological evidence for our position. Nonetheless, it will be important for future research to detail the parts of our biobehavioral model that are sensitive to environmental input.

An analysis that posits biological bases for gender differences in behavior raises important political concerns as well. Many women feel, with some justification, that such models can be used to justify patterns of discrimination and social oppression. To head off any such effort, we emphatically point out that our analysis makes no prescriptive assumptions about the social roles that women occupy. Our analysis should not be construed to imply that women should be mothers, will be good mothers, or will be better parents than men by virtue of these mechanisms. Similarly, this analysis should not be construed as evidence that women are naturally more social than men or that they should shoulder disproportionate responsibility for the ties and activities that create and maintain the social fabric.

Other political concerns, however, may be based on false assumptions about what biological underpinnings signify. Biological analyses of human behavior are sometimes misconstrued by social scientists as implying inflexibility or inevitability in human behavior or as reductionist efforts that posit behavioral uniformity. These perceptions constitute unwarranted concerns about biological bases of behavior. Biology is not so much destiny as it is a central tendency, but a central tendency that influences and interacts with social, cultural, cognitive, and emotional factors, resulting in substantial behavioral flexibility. The last few decades of biological research have shown that, just as biology affects behavior, so behavior affects biology, in ways ranging from genetic expression to acute responses to stressful circumstances. Rather than viewing social roles and biology as alternative accounts of human behavior, a more productive theoretical and empirical strategy will be to recognize how biology and social roles are inextricably interwoven to account for the remarkable flexibility of human behavior.

Multilevel Integrative Analyses of Human Behavior: Social Neuroscience and the Complementing Nature of Social and Biological Approaches

Social and biological explanations traditionally have been cast as incompatible, but advances in recent years have revealed a new view synthesized from these 2 very different levels of analysis. The authors review evidence underscoring the complementing nature of social and biological levels of analysis and how the 2 together can foster understanding of the mechanisms underlying complex behavior and the mind. Specifically, they review *the utility of considering social influences on biological processes* that are often viewed as outside the social domain including genetic constitution, gene expression, disease, and autonomic, neuroendocrine, and immune activity. This research underscores the unity of psychology and the importance of retaining multilevel integrative research that spans molar and molecular levels of analysis. Especially needed in the coming years is more research on the mechanisms linking social and biological events and processes.

Social and biological approaches to human behavior have traditionally been contrasted as if the two were antagonistic or mutually exclusive. . . . The thesis of this article is that the mechanisms underlying mind and behavior are not fully explicable by a biological or a social approach alone but rather that a multilevel integrative analysis may be required. . . .

Within the discipline of psychology, the tensions between biological and social approaches surface in biopsychology/behavioral neuroscience and social psychology. Biopsychology focuses on neural substrates and production mechanisms for behavior, whereas social psychology emphasizes multivariate systems and situational influences in studies of the impact of human association on mind and behavior. . . .

The nervous, endocrine, and immune systems were also once thought to function independently, outside the reach of the personal ties and cultural influences. . . .

From *Psychological Bulletin*, vol. 126, no. 6, 2000, excerpts from 829–843. Copyright © 2000 by American Psychological Association. Reprinted by permission.

Research that considers contextual and social factors has uncovered new effects that challenge some of the existing conceptualizations in the neurosciences. . . . As discussed below, the effects of social context also appear to be powerful determinants of the expression of autonomic, neuroendocrine, and immune reactions. . . .

The Centrality of Personal Ties and Social Interactions

Evolution has sculpted the human genome to be sensitive to and succoring of contact and relationships with others. People form associations and connections with others from the moment they are born. The very survival of newborns depends on their attachment to and nurturance by others over an extended period of time. . . .

The need to belong does not stop at infancy; rather, affiliation and nurturant social relationships are essential for physical and for psychological well-being across the life span. . . .

In humans, hormonal and neurophysiological substrates of caregiving and attachment have been identified. Consistent with animal research, the restriction of social contact during infancy and childhood has dramatic effects on psychopathology across the life span. People who report having contact with intimate friends not only are more likely to report that their lives are very happy as compared with those who do not report such contact but also tend to have lower blood pressure. Disruptions of personal ties, whether through ridicule, discrimination, separation, divorce, or bereavement, are among the most stressful events people must endure.

The motivational potency of the absence of personal ties and social acceptance is reminiscent of more basic needs such as hunger. Solitary confinement is one of humankind's most severe punishments. Ostracism, the exclusion by general consent from common privileges or social acceptance, is universal in its aversive and deleterious effects. Positively, tactile contact is a stronger determinant of mother–infant attachment than feeding. Subtle cultural influences can also rival more basic drives in governing feeding behavior and body weight.

Social and cultural influences not only cause behavior but alter biological processes as well. In such instances, a strictly physiological (or social) analysis is not sufficient to reveal the orderly relationships that exist, regardless of the sophistication of the measurement technology. For example, when Haber and Barchas investigated the effects of amphetamine on male Rhesus macaques, no clear contrast between the drug and placebo conditions was detected until each male's role in the social group was considered. When this social factor was taken into account, amphetamines were found to increase dominant behavior in males high in the social rank and to increase submissive behavior in low-ranking animals. . . .

[The authors identify five ways social factor influence biological processes.]

[1] Social Influences on Genetic Constitution

In biology, the environment is seen as the agent of natural selection. The notion that physical and social forces modulate gene frequency may therefore be regarded as uncontroversial. Mechanisms of selection may help explain otherwise perplexing demographic differences. For instance, the prevalence and incidence rates of hypertension, obesity, and Type 2 diabetes in immigrants from developing countries are substantially higher than in the majority population. . . . [T]he "thrifty gene" hypothesis [states] that across generations, individuals who were most likely to survive the hardship and food and water deprivation of developing countries inherited a gene (or set of genes) that conserved energy. Those who were constitutionally characterized by high insulin levels, low metabolism, high fat storage, and insulin resistance were more likely to survive these severe conditions. Migration from traditional lifestyles and environments to more sedentary lifestyles and calorie-dense environments has, therefore, been posited to increase the likelihood of obesity, Type 2 diabetes, and related diseases. . . .

. . . [Examination of] the historical record of the transatlantic slave trade and New World slavery from the 16th to 19th centuries to determine the circumstantial evidence for this reasoning. More than 12 million young men and women were imported to the western hemisphere from Africa during the centuries of slave trade. Wilson and Grim estimated that the average mortality from capture to delivery on the West African coast was about 10%, mortality during confinement on the coast was about 12%, and mortality during the transatlantic passage was about 12%–15%. Of those who made it to the western hemisphere, 10%–30% were estimated to not have survived the first 3 years of slavery, and mortality rates remained high thereafter. Fertility rates of the survivors were low, and infant mortality rates may have been as high as 50%. It is at least plausible, therefore, that the transatlantic slave trade, which continued for centuries, imposed a strong selection pressure favoring specific biological mechanisms enabling survival and reproduction under the harsh conditions of slave trading. . . .

[2] Social Influences on Cardiovascular Function

Animal studies provide among the best experimental evidence for social influences on autonomic function and cardiovascular disease. In a series of studies in cynomolgus monkeys, . . . social disruptions and instability promote coronary atherogenesis. . . .

In both males and females in this research, high cardiovascular reactivity has been associated with increased risk for atherosclerosis.

. . . [A] handful of intervention studies [with humans have attempted] to foster social support in an attempt to lower blood pressure in hypertensives. . . . In [a] family support intervention, for instance, patients identified an individual with whom they had frequent contact (e.g., spouse), and these individuals were trained to increase understanding, support, and reinforcement about the positive management of the patient's hypertension. Assessment at an 18-month follow-up indicated that family support was associated with an 11% decrease in diastolic blood pressure, and all of the interventions combined produced a 28% decrease. Subsequent follow-ups revealed that there were long-term benefits in blood pressure regulation as well. Meta-analyses of this and related studies confirmed that increases in social support resulted in decreased blood pressure in hypertensive patients. . . .

[3] Social Influences on Genetic Expression

. . . Our thesis in this article is that the social world, as well as the organization and operation of the brain, shapes and modulates genetic and biological processes, and accordingly, knowledge of biological and social domains is necessary to develop comprehensive theories in either domain. In this section, we review evidence that some aspects of genetic expression that had been thought to be encapsulated within each living cell far from the reach of personal ties or social influences are in fact subject to modulation by the social environment. . . .

The social influence on phenotypic expression is also illustrated in recent research on early nurturance. Suomi selectively bred Rhesus monkeys to produce offspring who, on the basis of their genetic pedigree, were either normally or highly reactive to stressors. These selectively bred infants were then cross-fostered to unrelated multiparous females who were either normally or unusually nurturant with respect to attachment-related behavior. The infants were reared by their foster mothers for the first 6 months of life and were then placed in a larger social group containing age-mates who were cross-fostered or were raised by their biological mothers. Genetically high-reactive infants raised by normal (i.e., highly reactive) females showed the typical deficits in early exploration and accentuated responses to mild stressors, relative to genetically high-reactive infants raised by especially nurturant females. These latter infants explored their environments more and showed as little disturbance to mild stressors as, or lower levels than, their genetically high-reactive counterparts who were fostered by normal rather than nurturant mothers. Behavioral differences among these groups persisted when these monkeys were permanently separated from their foster mothers and were placed into a larger social group at 6 months of age. . . .

[4] Social Influences on Immune Activity

Empirical observations of social influences on autonomic activity date back more than 2,000 years. . . . It is now clear that the immune system is tightly regulated and integrated with the nervous and endocrine systems and that social events influence immune function through these systems. . . . Studies of the effects of psychosocial stress on vaccine responses have . . . found that the response to vaccination was diminished in high- compared with low-stress conditions. . . .

[A relationship has been found between] wound healing and the immunological responses contributing to this end point in spousal caregivers of patients with Alzheimer's disease and age- and gender-matched controls and in dental school students when they were or were not undergoing exams. . . . [H]igher levels of stress were associated with delayed wound healing. . . .

The social ordering within social hierarchies may also play a role in the individual responses to psychosocial stress and susceptibility to infectious disease. For instance, in the social disruption paradigm, dominant male mice, when latently infected in the trigeminal ganglia with herpes simplex virus (HSV; a model for recurrent herpes labialis in humans), were twice as likely as subordinate animals to reactivate and shed infectious virus when their social environment was disrupted by reorganization. . . .

[5] Social Influences on Disease

One implication of the research reviewed thus far is that the development and progression of disease, once bastions of the biological approach, may be influenced dramatically by social factors. Epidemiological research has indeed marshaled evidence for a strong relationship between health and various social circumstances. In a classic study, Berkman and Syme operationalized social connections as marriage, contacts with friends and extended family members, church membership, and other group affiliations. They found that adults with fewer social connections suffered higher rates of mortality over the succeeding 9 years even after accounting for self-reports of physical health, socioeconomic status, smoking, alcohol consumption, obesity, race, life satisfaction, physical activity, and preventive health-service usage.

A using physical examinations to assess health status. A review of five prospective studies, concluded that social isolation was a major risk factor for morbidity and mortality from widely varying causes. This relationship was evident even after statistically controlling for known biological risk factors, social status, and baseline measures of health. The negative health consequences of social isolation were particularly strong among some of the fastest growing segments of the population: the elderly, the poor, and minorities such as African Americans. The strength of social isolation as a risk factor was comparable to high blood pressure, obesity, sedentary lifestyles, and possibly even smoking. . . .

. . . People's perceptions of others in light of their desire for affiliation appear to be important, too, as subjective indices of social isolation/support have been found to be more powerful predictors of stress and health than objective indices. . . .

The research by Cohen and colleagues also suggests that close relationships are not uniformly positive or salubrious. Indeed, results from the Terman Life Cycle Study indicate that past negative behaviors in social relationships are associated with greater mortality. Laboratory research has found that negative or hostile behaviors during a marital conflict produce greater and/or more persistent alterations in autonomic activation. Moreover, couples characterized by high, relative to low, negative behaviors during a marital conflict also showed greater decrements in cellular immune function over the 24 hours of study. . . .

In writing about unhealthy environments, Taylor, Repetti, and Seeman articulated a general framework for thinking about how social factors penetrate the skin. [They identified seven routes that] are applicable generally to the question of how social factors get under the skin.

1. the cumulative effects of chronic or repeated stressors.
2. the impact on affective processes.
3. impact on beliefs and attitudes about oneself (e.g., self-esteem), one's life (e.g., life satisfaction), one's future (e.g., hopefulness), or one's purpose in life (e.g., religiosity).
4. effects of coping strategies.
5. influence on health habits and behaviors.
6. individual differences.
7. social isolation.

POSTSCRIPT

Do Women and Men Respond Differently to Stress?

Feminist theorists have been reluctant to consider biologically based explanations of women's and men's behavior, such as Taylor's tend-and-befriend model. These explanations essentialize the nature of women's and men's behaviors. Such thinking provides the justification for the various inequalities in our society based on one's sex. It absolves society of the responsibility of seeing the inequalities as social problems. Shelley's model assumes that there is an evolutionarily based biobehavioral mechanism that underlies the tend-and-befriend response to stress. She suggests that it is an attachment-caregiving system based on women's mothering role. However, when her model is considered in light of Cacioppo's social neurosciences approach, we can begin to reconsider Taylor's claims. In example after example, he shows how social context can be a powerful determinant of a host of biological systems, even genetic constitution. Typically, social scientists have viewed biological approaches to be too reductionistic to be useful; the accusation is that in search of the ultimate cause these approaches have ignored the realities of an organism's real-life context. On the other hand, proponents of the biological approach often question the scientific rigor of social scientists' methods for establishing a knowledge base. Cacioppo's social neurosciences approach argues that perhaps neither approach is preferable to the other. Rather, they represent different levels of analyses and that "multilevel integrative analyses may contribute to the empirical data and theoretical insight needed for a comprehensive understanding of human behavior."

Perhaps there is really no place for sex differences per se in such debates. It might be more useful to entertain the view that biological organisms exist in differential social contextual factors that result in different biobehavioral responses to stress in a dynamic interplay of influences across time; that is, biology and social context are both cause and effect. Thus, when males and females find themselves in different social contexts, different biobehavioral responses to stress occur. Cacioppo and colleagues review evidence for numerous social contextual factors, such as migratory versus sedentary lifestyles. They discuss hardship, such as difficulty finding food and water. From this purview, we might think about the number of women who are poor, who are the victims of abuse beginning in early childhood, who are dependent on men for their well-being, as well as that of their children, who are sexually harassed at work and fear losing their jobs if they complain, or who are denied access to the highest levels of power at work and in the community, including the faith community. Do such social contexts increase the likelihood of tending-and-befriending rather than flight-or-fight? What would be the social consequences for the woman who stands to fight, or where would the woman who wants to flee go? And think of the numbers of boys and men who have been expected, and even taunted, to stand and take it like a man, whether on the football field or the battlefield. So, are the hormonal and neuro-endocrinological differences seen in women and men the result of evolutionarily hard-wired systems or logical consequences of different positions in the status hierarchy? What is the role of power? Society gives the weaker, women, children, the elderly, permission to ask for help, but the stronger are expected to give help, to be the "hero."

Suggested Readings

Roy Baumeister and Mark Leary, "The Need to Belong: Desire for Interpersonal Attachment as a Fundamental Human Motivation," *Psychological Bulletin* (vol. *117*, 1995) 497–529.

D. C. Geary and M. V. Flinn, "Sex Differences in Behavioral and Hormonal Response to Social Threat: Commentary on Taylor et al. (2000)," *Psychology Review* (vol. *109*, 2002) 745–750.

Debra L. Nelson and Ronald J. Burke, eds., *Gender, Work Stress, and Health,* Washington, DC: American Psychological Association, 2002.

Jerry Suls and Kenneth A. Wallston, *Social Psychological Foundations of Health and Illness.* Malden, MA: Blackwell Publishing, 2003.

ISSUE 6

Are Differences in Aggressive Behavior Between Women and Men Due to Gender-related Factors?

YES: Jacquelyn W. White, Patricia L. N. Donat, and Barrie Bondurant, from "A Developmental Examination of Violence Against Girls and Women," in R. Unger, ed., *Handbook of the Psychology of Women and Gender* (John Wiley & Sons, 2001)

NO: Richard B. Felson, from *Violence and Gender Reexamined* (American Psychological Association, 2002)

ISSUE SUMMARY

YES: Social psychologist Jacquelyn W. White and her colleagues conclude, based on a review of the literature, that girls and women are highly likely to be the targets of male aggression and are less likely to use physical aggression than men due to different developmental experiences.

NO: Social psychologist Richard B. Felson argues that aggression is related to physical strength and a general tendency toward violence, not male domination, and that there is not an epidemic of violence against women.

One of the most pervasive gender-related stereotypes is that of sex differences between women and men. The view that males are physically more aggressive and women are more verbally aggressive persists in spite of inconsistent findings. American society is thought by many to be a violent culture, marked by the high prevalence of family and school violence, as well as high rates of aggression and violence in the media. A host of factors likely contribute to the rise of violence in the USA, including alcohol and drug consumption, increased access to guns, and gender expectations. Are youth, especially males, learning to model the violence they see on TV and in the family? Some lament that "boys will be boys," believing that boys are aggressive by nature, while others argue that boys' aggression results from societal rules and expectations tied to masculinity. One result of these expectations is that any feminine characteristics or behaviors (e.g., emotional expression, gentleness) in males lead to rejection and ridicule. Social desirability restricts boys' public display of emotions to anger, resulting in aggressive and violent behaviors. Boys face a Catch-22; expressing their fears and frustrations is unacceptable for "real men," but such expression is what they so desperately need. As noted in the Postscript to Issue 3, "culturally based socialization practices encourage men to be aggressors and women to be victims. In societies where there is no formal hierarchy that privileges one group over another and in which women and men exercise relatively equal power, general levels of aggression, male violence against women, and rape are low." In contrast, the one emotion women are not supposed to display is anger. Just as many people assume that males are by nature aggressive they likewise assume that females are by nature nonaggressive. Thus, what do girls do with their anger? Evidence suggest that there are no sex differences in level of anger experiences, but there are gendered patterns in what leads to anger and the form and function of the behavior that follows from the anger. Research on intimate partner violence and child abuse documents that women can be just as aggressive and sometimes more so than men, but the aggression is manifested differently. Recent research on relational aggression has also established a number of ways in which girls are more relationally aggressive than boys. Thus, rather than asking the question of whether men are more aggressive than women is to ask how do men and women differ in their expression of aggression and what role does gender play. Most feminist scholars, especially those in the behavioral sciences, use the principles of social learning theory to account for how sociocultural values are transmitted and learned at the individual level and to describe how individual women and men come to behave in gender typical as well as atypical ways.

White and her colleagues argue that the childhood experiences of girls and boys provide the roots for the gendered nature of aggression and violence. Gendered in this context means that the who, how, and why of violence cannot be understood without consideration of the sex of the perpetrator, the victim, their relationship, and the context of the violence. Their review of the literature leads to the conclusion that gendered aggression can be observed in childhood, adolescence, and adulthood, including the elder years. Gender role expectations, socialization, and power inequalities are central to understanding aggression and violence in both women and men. Felson in contrast argues that aggression has to do with size and strength and not gendered constructs such as status, power, and dominance.

Jacquelyn W. White, Patricia L. N. Donat, and Barrie Bondurant

YES

A Developmental Examination of Violence against Girls and Women

In spite of images of loving, supportive families and caring, protective lovers, intimate relationships may be plagued by alarming levels of aggression and violence. Although men are usually the victims of nonintimate crimes, girls and women are much more likely than men to be the victims of violence in intimate relationships. Physical violence against women takes many forms, including childhood sexual abuse, dating violence, acquaintance rape, battering and wife abuse; nonphysical forms of violence include sexual harassment, stalking, and pornography. All these forms of violence share in common the fact that they frequently are committed by men known to the girls and women. Unlike other crimes, they are crimes in which others, as well as the victim herself, tend to blame the victim for what happened. By blaming the individual victims, attention and responsibility are shifted away from the perpetrators and from the social context that contributes to violence against women. The present chapter suggests that the roots of violence against women can be found in the childhood experiences of girls and boys, and that the messages learned in and the consequences of these early experiences are repeated and reinforced in adolescence and young adulthood. In this chapter, we discuss these experiences from a developmental perspective and conclude with a model for examining the commonalities among the various forms of violence against women. . . .

Gendered Violence in Childhood

The gendered nature of violence is evident early in childhood and establishes a framework for patterns of interactions between adult women and men. Children are at great risk for victimization because of their small physical stature and dependency on adults; they have little choice over whom they live with and few opportunities to leave an abusive home. From the beginning, they learn the major lesson of patriarchy: The more powerful control the less powerful. Furthermore, children learn that power is gendered and associate men and masculinity with power and dominance. Victimization is also gendered. During childhood, boys experience more physical aggression and girls experience more sexual aggression. Among adolescents, girls are at a greater risk than boys for both physical and sexual victimization. . . .

Gender and Parental Punishment

In both normal and abusive homes, children receive gendered messages about aggression and violence. Children, especially those from abusive homes, have many opportunities to learn that the more powerful person in a relationship can use aggression to successfully control the less powerful person. The majority of parents in American homes use verbal and physical aggression as disciplinary tactics. . . . [O]ver 90% of children are spanked sometime in their youth, with many parents (62%) reporting physical aggression against their children; this aggression includes pushing, shoving, and slapping. Fewer parents (11%) report using severe aggression, including hitting, kicking, beating, threatening, and using weapons against their children.

Punishment does not appear to be uniform, however; the sex of the child and the parent affect the pattern and outcome. During early childhood, boys are at greater risk than girls for severe abusive punishment, whereas during preadolescence and adolescence, girls' risk increases. This is presumably because of boys' increased ability to inflict harm on others as they physically mature. Although parents do not differ in the frequency with which they spank girls and boys, the effects of the spanking are different. Paternal spanking leads to reactive (angry) aggression in both girls and boys, but only boys show unprovoked bullying aggression against others when spanked by their fathers. . . . [F]athers' spanking of boys communicates a "gender-based approach to interpersonal disagreements, that of physical dominance, . . . explicitly transmitting gender-stereotypic notions" (p. 457). Moreover, parents' reactions to their children's aggressive behavior differs. Although parents generally see aggression as an undesirable attribute for children, they view it as a tolerated *masculine* behavior. Thus, boys expect less parental disapproval than girls for aggression directed toward peers although they are punished more harshly for aggression than are girls.

Childhood Sexual Abuse

The message that the more powerful can control the less powerful is also learned in a sexual context for a minority of girls and boys. . . .

The sexual victimization of children is an abuse of interpersonal power and a violation of trust. What makes the statistics even more tragic is the fact that most children are victimized by people they know and trust to protect them. Almost 90% of children who are raped are victimized by someone known to them. Boys are more likely to be sexually abused by someone outside the family, whereas girls are more likely to be sexually abused by a family member or a quasi–family member (e.g., mother's boyfriend). Betrayal of the trust vested in those who have power is central to understanding childhood sexual abuse, its consequences, and the systems that sustain it. . . .

Characteristics of Abusive Families

. . . The family system in which parent-child incest typically occurs is headed by a father who is authoritarian, punitive, and threatening. Children who are victimized often feel powerless to stop the abuse and feel they have nowhere to turn for help, comfort, and support. The child's ability to confront and refuse sexual contact is overwhelmed by the feelings of loyalty and trust that the child may have developed for the perpetrator. The adult is in a position of authority (and often one of trust as well) and communicates to the child that the behavior is part of an exclusive, secretive, and special relationship. The perpetrator may even come to believe and attempt to convince the child that the relationship is a mutually loving and caring one. For children who may otherwise be neglected and emotionally isolated, the special attention and inappropriate sexual contact with the adult may be confusing and may complicate the coping process.

Ethnicity and Childhood Sexual Abuse

The relationship between racial ethnicity and victimization is currently being studied. No statistical differences between the percentages of Black (57%) and White (67%) women reporting childhood sexual victimization have been reported. Similarly, 49% of the women in a Southwestern American Indian tribal community reported childhood sexual victimization. . . . [N]o significant differences in the prevalence of childhood sexual abuse among Hispanic and non-Hispanic women [have been found,] with 27.1% of Hispanic women and 33.1% of non-Hispanic White women reporting victimization as children. Thus, girls from several ethnic groups appear to be at risk for becoming a victim of sexual abuse. . . .

Gendered Violence in Adolescence

During adolescence, young men and women experience extreme pressure to conform to traditional gender roles. Unfortunately, part of establishing a masculine identity for young men often involves distancing oneself socially and psychologically from anything feminine. "Thus, to turn away and distance oneself from a woman is what a man does because he is a man, and what boys do in relation to girls because they are boys. Such behavior is expected, is tacitly approved, often goes unnoticed, and contributes to the implicit definition or understanding of manliness in a sexist society." Young men seek out companionship from other men and distance themselves from women except in social contexts involving "power-enhancing" or sexual opportunities. . . .

Dating Violence

The gender-related patterns learned in childhood are played out in adolescent dating and committed relationships. Young people usually begin dating in high school, although children as young as kindergartners talk about having boyfriends and girlfriends. The idea of being paired with a member of the other sex is pervasive in our society. Traditionally, it has been assumed that children's "playing house" and, later, dating provide a context for socialization into later roles, including husband, wife, lover, and confidante. Dating also offers opportunities for companionship, status, sexual experimentation, and conflict resolution. However, courtship has different meanings for young women and men. Whereas for men, courtship involves themes of "staying in control," for women, themes involve "dependence on the relationship." Violence is one of the tactics used to gain control in a relationship.

Dating and Sexual Scripts

It appears that dating violence and sexual assault among adolescents and college students is so prevalent, in part, because of the overall structure and meaning of dating in our culture, which give men greater power. Adolescent dating patterns follow a fairly well-defined script that has not changed much over several decades. A dating script is a set of rules to be followed by girls and boys that affords men greater power relative to women because they are expected to initiate and pay for dates, and because relationships generally are perceived as more important to women than to men. Women are assumed to be responsible for "how far things go," and if things "get out of hand," it is their fault.

Relationship Traps for Women

Romantic relationships may become "destructive traps" for women when they feel they must put maintenance of the relationship above their own self-interests. Violence is more likely to occur in serious than in casual relationships. Women who experience ongoing victimization often report more commitment to and love for their partner; they are less likely to end the relationship because of abuse and they allow their partner to control them. These women also report more traditional attitudes toward women's roles, justify their abuse, and tend to romanticize relationships and love. Many students believe dating violence is more acceptable in serious relationships and is not sufficient grounds for ending the relationship. . . .

Incidence and Prevalence of Dating Violence

Studies indicate that dating violence during the teen years is pervasive, with as many as 35% of female and male students surveyed reporting at least one episode, with fewer experiencing recurring violence. A national survey of approximately 2,600 college women and 2,100 college men revealed that within the year prior to the survey, 81% of the men and 88% of the women had engaged in some form of verbal aggression, either as perpetrator or victim. Approximately 37% of the men and 35% of the women inflicted some form of physical aggression, and about 39% of the men and 32% of the women sustained some physical aggression. In this survey, all types of heterosexual relationships were included, from the most casual to the most serious, thus providing a comprehensive estimate of the scope of courtship violence. The measures of verbal aggression included arguing heatedly, yelling, sulking, and stomping. Physical aggression included throwing something at someone, pushing, grabbing, shoving, or hitting. The ubiquity of courtship violence among college students is apparent in that comparable rates of violence have been observed across gender, ethnic group, and type of institution of higher learning, such as private or public, religious or secular. All the evidence to date suggests that it would be unusual to find a high school or college student who had not been involved in some form of verbal aggression and a substantial number who have not been involved in physical aggression. Also, it appears that the same people who report inflicting some form of violence are the ones who report experiencing violence.

Motives for Dating Violence

Some studies suggest that women and men do not appear to differ in the frequency with which they report engaging in aggressive acts. However, this cannot be taken to mean there are no gender-related differences in aggression. On the contrary, studies have shown that the motives and consequences for such behavior are different for women and men. Most data suggest that women are more likely to engage in aggression for self-defense, whereas men report that they aggress to instill fear and to intimidate.

Predictors of Dating Violence

The underlying processes involved in courtship violence for women and for men appear different. The results of studies are quite consistent. Although the best predictor of being aggressive is having an aggressive partner, other predictors are different for women and men. Men who are quick to react to anger, believe that violence will aid in winning an argument, and have successfully used violence in other situations are likely to do so again. Similarities between men who engage in courtship violence and wife batterers have been found. Drug use, divorced parents, stressful life events, beliefs that violence between intimates is justifiable, and less traditional sex-role attitudes also have been identified as predictors.

For women, on the other hand, a history of parent-child abuse, as well as anxiety, depression, and drug use, have been related to courtship violence. It is likely that these latter factors are reactions to childhood experiences with violence, rendering women more vulnerable to being the target of a violent partner, which in turn increases the likelihood of being violent. Learning about violence in the home and associating with peers who endorse the use of violence may provide a backdrop of social norms that legitimate violence. Violence is learned as a tactic of dealing with interpersonal conflict.

However, women may be the initiator of aggression in dating relationships. [Others] have shown that prior experience with sexual victimization as well as physical victimization in a dating context during adolescence predicts being physically aggressive in dating situations during the first year of college. Prior experience with violence may disinhibit aggression, thus enabling women to overcome gender-related constraints on aggressive expression. A recently developed theory proposes that threat and perceptions of threat underlie relational violence. Past victimization experiences, including witnessing and experiencing parental aggression, may increase women's expectations of harm from male partners. Thus, offensive aggression may actually be preemptive aggression. Feelings of isolation resulting from prior victimization (reflected in passivity) may contribute to a greater awareness of threat associated with the intimidating behaviors of their male partners, resulting in the perceived need not only for self-defensive efforts, but for offensive (or initiating acts) as well.

Sexual Violence

As men and women establish intimate relationships, dominance and violence also surface in the form of sexual aggression. Although the legal definition of rape appears straightforward, both the social meaning of the term rape and the circumstances surrounding an act of forced sexual intercourse make some reluctant to use the label. The term rape has been shown to have different meanings for women and men. College students in general, and sexually aggressive men in particular, believe that sexual precedence (i.e., a past history of sexual intercourse) reduces the legitimacy of sexual refusal. Moreover, some people are hesitant to label forced sex as rape if consent was not explicitly verbalized, even if threats, intimidation, or incapacitation are present. Although a woman may not realize that forced sexual intercourse by an acquaintance during a date is rape, this does not change the legal definition of the act as rape, nor does it reduce the culpability of the perpetrator. Furthermore, whether a sexual assault is labeled rape does not alter the consequences for the victim.

Frequency of Sexual Victimization

A comprehensive survey asked over 3,000 college women from 32 institutions of higher education across the United States about sexual experiences since the age of 14. Of those surveyed, over half of the women (53.7%) had experienced some form of sexual victimization; 15.4% had experienced acts by a man that met the legal definition of rape (though only 27% labeled the experience rape), and 12.1% had experienced attempted rape. An additional 11.9% had been verbally pressured into sexual intercourse, and the remaining 14.4% had experienced some other form of unwanted sexual contact, such as forced kissing or fondling with no attempted penetration. More recent studies confirm these high numbers among college students in the United States and among Canadians, as well as among a probability sample of 8,000 women in the United States.

High school women also appear to be at greater risk for rape than previously thought. A recent survey of 834 entering college students found that 13% reported being raped between the ages of 14 and 18, and an additional 16% reported being victims of an attempted rape (Humphrey & White, in press). Most victims knew the perpetrator, and the assaults frequently occurred in a dating context. Similar rates of reported sexual assault have been found among adolescents, indicating that sexual assault is not just a problem for college campuses. It is a frequent experience during the high school years as well.

The . . . survey described earlier also examined the sexual experiences of over 2,900 college men. Of this group, 4.4% admitted to behaviors meeting the legal definition of rape, 3.3% admitted to attempted rape, 7.2% to sexual coercion, and 10.2% to forced or coerced sexual contact; thus, 25.1% of the college men admitted to some form of sexual aggression. Similar rates have been reported in college samples and in a community college sample. . . .

Risk Factors for Perpetration

The typical acquaintance rapist appears to be a "normal" guy. He is not a crazed psychopath, although he may display psychopathy-related traits. Among college students, alcohol use, athletic affiliation, and fraternity membership have been associated with sexual aggression toward women. Other significant correlates of sexual assault include a history of family violence; an early and varied sexual history, including many sexual partners; a history of delinquency; acceptance of rape myths; an impulsive personality; hedonistic and dominance motives for sex; lower than average sense of self-worth; and lower religiosity; as well as peers who condone and encourage sexual conquests. Finally, sexually aggressive men are more likely to perceive a wider range of behaviors as indicative of sexual interest than do nonsexually aggressive men and are attracted to sexual aggression.

It appears that sexual promiscuity and hostile attitudes combine to characterize sexually aggressive men, particularly in men who tend to be self-centered and have little regard for others (i.e., low in empathy). Sexually aggressive men tend to be more domineering with women, using "one-up" messages aimed at "gaining control of the exchange" (e.g., bragging about oneself and criticizing the other person). Domineeringness in conversation may be a test sexually aggressive men use to identify vulnerable targets. A woman who resists the domination may be seen as unavailable, but a subordinate response from a woman may indicate that she is a potential target. Furthermore, it is likely that a woman experiencing the helplessness and powerlessness associated with a previous victimization will be less likely to resist the man's domineering behavior than women without a victimization history. This may help us understand why and how perpetrators target vulnerable women.

Ethnicity and Sexual Assault

Dating violence and sexual assault pose additional problems among adolescents who are not White, middle class, and heterosexual. Although it is difficult for any young person to admit being victimized by a dating partner, it is especially so for ethnic minorities. The legacy of slavery and distrust of White authority figures have made it difficult for African American teens to report abusive dating relationships. Asian/Pacific women, too, are reluctant to disclose abuse because of cultural traditions of male dominance and reticence to discuss private relationships in public. For lesbian teens, the problem is complicated by the fact that, in reporting abuse, they may have to reveal their sexual orientation, something they may not be psychologically ready to do. . . .

Violence in Marriage and Other Committed Relationships

The patterns established during adolescence may continue in adulthood. The greatest threat of violence to adult women is from their intimate partners; for men, the greatest threat is from other men. Women are more likely to be physically or sexually assaulted by an intimate partner than by a stranger. It is estimated that 2 to 3 million women are assaulted by male partners in the United States each year and that at least half of these women are severely assaulted (i.e., punched, kicked, choked, beaten, threatened with a knife or gun, or had a knife or gun used on them). As many as 21% to 34% of women will be assaulted by an intimate partner during adulthood. Further, it is estimated that 33% to 50% of all battered wives are also the victim of partner rape. Studies have shown that 22% to 40% of the women who seek health care at clinics or emergency rooms are victims of battering.

Intimate violence may escalate, resulting in homicide. Approximately 66% of family violence deaths are women killed by their male partners; over 50% of all murders of women are committed by current or former partners. In contrast, only 6% of male murder victims are killed by wives or girlfriends. Murder-suicides are almost always cases where the man kills his partner or estranged partner and then kills himself. He also may kill his children or other family members before he kills himself. Although there are instances where a woman murders a partner who has been abusing her, this happens less frequently than men killing partners they have abused chronically.

When women kill their partners, they are often reacting to abuse rather than initiating it. A study of women who killed partners found several common factors. The women were in abusive relationships and the abuse was increasing in frequency and severity. The increased violence was associated with a rise in the number and seriousness of the women's injuries. It was common for these men to have raped their spouses, forced them into other sexual acts, and made threats against their lives. The men typically used excessive alcohol daily and used recreational drugs. The effects of this intense and repeated abuse has prompted attorneys to use "the battered-woman syndrome" in court cases to describe the psychological state of battered women who kill. . . .

Ethnicity and Intimate Partner Violence

Community-based surveys have found that 25% of African American women and 8% of Hispanic women reported at least one physical sexual assault experience in their lifetime. However, when norms regarding violence approval, age, and economic stressors are held constant, . . . [no] differences between Hispanic Americans and Americans [have been found] in the odds of wife abuse. However, . . . that being born in the United States increases the risk of wife assaults by Mexican and Puerto Rican American husbands. Importantly, . . . in any group, regardless of SES, the presence of norms sanctioning wife assaults is a risk factor for wife abuse. . . .

Violence in Lesbian Relationships

Relationship abuse is not limited to heterosexual relationships. Although there have been no prevalence studies, research with convenience samples indicates that partner abuse is a significant problem for lesbian women and gay men. Gay male couples report slightly less sexual abuse than lesbian couples, but more severe physical violence. Apparently, violence in committed relationships is not simply a gender issue. Issues of power and control arise in all relationships, and provide the basis for abuse. Partner abuse has been associated with issues of power and dependency in both lesbian and heterosexual couples. For lesbians and gay men, the internalization of societal homophobic attitudes may, in part, lead to aggression against partners and reduce reporting due to threats that they may be "outed" by their partner. For gay men, the fear of AIDS or the stress of having AIDS or caring for a partner with AIDS may be associated with abuse. Fortunately, shelters and organizations are slowly beginning to assimilate information on the issue. For gay men, there are still few resources.

Elder Abuse: Violence Toward Elderly Women

Power inequalities between women and men continue into the later years and result in the continued victimization of older women by men. . . . [E]lder abuse is often spouse abuse that has continued for years. Although most data on elder abuse do not look specifically at spouse abuse or sexual assault, some patterns do emerge from the available data. In one of the only random-sample-based surveys examining elder abuse, . . . that in the over-65 population of Boston, 2% were the victims of physical abuse, with 58% of those being abused by a spouse and 24% by an adult child. Victimization by adult children reflects the change in relationship dynamics as parents age. Adult children gain power and the aging lose power in a social context that values youth and devalues maturity. Although half the victims were men, women were much more severely injured than men. . . . [S]ubmissiveness, self-blame, self-doubt, and lack of social support mediate the effects of older woman abuse.

Even less in known about the sexual abuse of older women. This remains a taboo topic, although there is growing recognition that the problem needs attention. Clinical evidence suggests that older women may be raped in their homes as well as in institutions (such as residential treatment facilities and nursing homes). . . . [E]xamples of the sexual abuse of women in nursing homes [are difficult to verify] because of dementia and other memory-related problems among this group. . . . [A] study of elder sexual abuse in Great Britain [found] a ratio of 6:1 female:male victims; . . . the perpetrators were more likely to be sons than husbands. . . . [In a comparison of] the rape experiences of a group of older women (age 55 to 87) with those of a younger group . . . greater injury [was found in the older women.] Additionally, one study suggests that men who sexually assault older women may suffer from more severe psychopathological processes and that their assaults are more brutal and motivated by anger and a need for power. . . .

The American Association of Retired Persons produced a report identifying similarities between elder abuse and other forms of violence against women. The report identified power imbalances, secrecy and isolation, personal harm to victims, social expectations and sex roles, inadequate resources to protect victims, and the control perpetrators have over their actions. The report further suggested that life span factors pose unique problems for elder abuse. . . .

Understanding Violence against Girls and Women

The pattern of intimate violence, where women are the victims and men are the perpetrators, is not due to biological destiny. Women are not born victims and men are not biologically predetermined to be aggressors. Rather, stereotypes of how women and men are supposed to behave, experiences that reinforce stereotypical behaviors, and a social structure that supports power inequities between women and men all contribute to violence against women.

To understand violence against girls and women we must first recognize that culturally based socialization practices encourage men to be aggressors and women to be victims. In societies where there is no formal hierarchy that privileges one group over another and in which women and men exercise relatively equal power, general levels of aggression and male violence against women are low. As this chapter has described, gendered violence is learned early in life and continues in our different relationships as we age. Statistics allow us to examine larger social influences and overall patterns found in society. They reveal that women are the victims of intimate violence more often than men at every stage of development, with the exception of early childhood physical abuse.

Although women also may be the perpetrators of aggression, this does not destroy the argument that intimate violence is related to gender and social roles. The reason is that patriarchy as a social system carries with it the message that the more powerful are entitled to dominate the less powerful. Aggression and violence are inherently gendered; even when girls and women act aggressively, they are responding to and enacting male models of behavior and control, models our culture has endorsed. Because men more often hold higher-status positions than women, it follows that men will abuse more than women; because adults are more powerful than children, children will be victimized more than adults; and because the young are more powerful than the elderly, the aged are more at risk.

Inequality in relationships, coupled with cultural values that embrace domination of the weaker by the stronger, creates the potential for violence. The more powerful partner can control money, resources, activities, and decisions. Partner abuse has been associated with issues of power and dependency in both lesbians and heterosexual couples. Both men and women learn that violence is a method people use to get their way. When individuals use violence and get their way, they are reinforced and thus more likely to use aggression in the future; however, men have historically received greater rewards for aggression and violence than have women. Women are as likely as men to aggress in situations that are congruent with their gender identities and where they hold relatively more power.

Traditionally, secrecy and myths regarding male-female relationships trivialized and/or justified male violence against women. The women's movement has done much to bring to public awareness the extent of the harm done to women by men and has prompted redefinitions that acknowledge the violence. Thus, for example, no longer is rape defined as a sexual act, sexual harassment as standard working conditions, and wife abuse as a legitimate way to "show the little woman who is boss"; rather, each are seen as acts by men intended to dominate and control women.

Violence against women, in its various forms, is now recognized as a public health and social problem. Hence, research has moved from focusing on individual psychopathology to identifying the sociocultural factors that contribute to such violence. Also, communities, institutions, and organizations are combating violence against women by developing interventions that not only help individuals but also promote change in values and attitudes at the societal level.

NO ↩

Richard B. Felson

Violence and Gender Reexamined

Violence involving women is special, according to the feminist perspective and current conventional wisdom. Academic feminism includes different strands, but most feminists would agree with the following assertions about violence involving women:

1. Sexism plays an important role in male violence against women.
2. Because sexism is pervasive, male violence against women is at epidemic levels, or at least occurs with enough frequency to be considered a special social problem.
3. Violence involving women typically has special motives—sexist men use violence to control women or to demonstrate their power, whereas women use violence to defend themselves.
4. Patriarchal societies support violence against women by blaming the victim and by treating offenders leniently.

I have argued and provided evidence that each of these statements is misleading or false. There is not an epidemic of violence against women: Its frequency reflects the frequency of violence generally. Men are more likely than women to injure their partners, but the pattern reflects gender differences in strength and the tendency to engage in violence, not male domination. The frequency of partner violence reflects the inevitable conflict that exists in intimate relationships, not sexism. Finally, societies are no more likely to blame female victims than male victims or to treat those who attack women more leniently. In fact, societies make a special attempt to protect women and generally treat those who offend against them more severely. . . .

Comparative Approach

I have used a comparative approach to examine whether men's violence against women or wives is special. The approach is useful in disentangling the effects of gender of perpetrator, gender of target, and whether the perpetrator is an intimate partner of the target. It enables one to convert loosely stated arguments into clear, testable hypotheses. . . .

The comparisons should apply to both sexual and nonsexual violence. In the case of sexual coercion and partner violence, comparisons must control for the fact that there are many more heterosexual than homosexual people. For example, in computing the frequency of homosexual partner violence, the denominator might be the number of gay men. The hypotheses implied by the feminist approach and the corresponding evidence are presented and critiqued a follows:

Hypothesis 1

The highest frequency of violence should occur [(for men aggressing against women)] because there is an epidemic of male violence against women. This hypothesis is not supported: Violence against women is much less frequent than violence against men. The most frequent type of violence involves men.

Hypothesis 2

The rate of male violence against women should vary across cultures and over time independently of other rates of violence. This hypothesis is not supported: Temporal and cross-national variation in homicide victimization rates are similar for men and women. When rates of violence against women are high, rates of violence against men are also high. Cross-national comparisons also reveal that male victimization rates dominate homicide statistics: There is much less variation in rates of homicide against women than in rates in homicide against men. Evidence from international crime victimization surveys does not support the idea that U.S. rape rates are particularly high or that they are high relative to the rate of general violence. American students do report more sexual coercion than Swedish students, but they report more violence generally.

Hypothesis 3

Men who use violence against women should be more likely to have sexist attitudes than men who commit violence against men. This hypothesis is not supported: The gender-related attitudes of men who use violence against women are similar to the attitudes of other criminals. Male criminal offenders are more likely than other men to have negative attitudes toward women, but the interpretation is unclear: Offenders express more antisocial attitudes generally.

Hypothesis 4

Men who have committed a violent act against a woman should be more likely to have a history of violence against women than men who have committed a violent act against a man. This hypothesis is not supported: Most men who commit violence against women are generalists who target both men and women. Their histories of violence against women are therefore similar to those of men who use violence against men.

Hypothesis 5

Men's violence (and other behavior) directed at female partners should be more likely to involve a control motive than similar behavior involving other gender-relationship combinations. This hypothesis has mixed support: Male assaults on female partners are more likely to be preceded by threats than assaults involving other gender-relationship combinations, suggesting a more important role for the control motive. However, studies that examine gender differences in the use of nonviolent means of control cast doubt on the idea that men have a greater desire to control their partners than women. Women are just as likely as men (and perhaps more likely) to attempt to control their partner's activities, and this behavior is just as highly related to women's violence as men's violence. In addition, women are more likely than men to complain—a verbal means of control—when they have grievances with their partners. This evidence suggests that when men use violence to control their partners, it is because of their greater coercive power—they are bigger, not bossier.

Hypothesis 6

Men involved in verbal conflicts with their female partners should be particularly likely to use violence, because many men believe that violence is a legitimate method of domination. This hypothesis is not supported: Both men and women show greater reluctance to use violence with their partners. Verbal conflicts are less, not more, likely to become physical when the antagonists are partners than when they are strangers. Only minor violence against children is legitimated according to evidence on the relative frequency of violence and verbal aggression.

Hypotheses 7a and 7b

Men should be more likely than women to engage in violence against their heterosexual partners due to sexism and men's desire for control over these partners. This difference should exceed gender differences in violence against other target. This hypothesis is not supported: Survey research of minor violence involving heterosexual couples has found that men and women have similar rates. Men are more likely than women to engage in serious violence against their partners, probably because of their greater coercive power. However, the gender difference in partner violence is not as large as the gender difference in stranger violence. The evidence suggests that men are inhibited about using violence against female partners, not specially motivated to use it.

Hypothesis 8

Love triangles should be more likely to motivate men's violence than women's violence, particularly men's violence toward their partners, given the strong male desire to control partners. This hypothesis is not supported: When men commit homicide it is less likely to stem from love triangles than when women commit homicide. When men kill their partners, it is no more likely to stem from love triangles then when women kill their partners. The evidence suggests that women are just as angry with unfaithful partners; they just are not as violent as men. In addition, male protagonists are much more likely to kill their rivals than their partners. In love triangles involving college students, men are more likely than women to attempt to intimidate or control male rivals than to intimidate or control female partners.

Hypothesis 9

Heterosexual men should be more likely than homosexual men to engage in violence against their partners. This hypothesis is not supported. In fact, data from the [National Crime Victimization Survey] suggests that gay men are *more* likely to be violent toward their partners than are heterosexual men. In addition, there is some evidence that homosexual men are just as likely as heterosexual men to use sexual coercion. The evidence suggests that violence against women is not a function of male dominance or special attitudes toward women. Rather, men are more violent than women and they sometimes use violence with their partners or those with whom they desire sexual relations, whether the target is a man or woman.

Hypothesis 10

Men's violence against women, particularly their wives, should be less likely to be reported to the police than other violence and less likely to lead to arrest, prosecution, and punishment. Authorities and other third parties should be less likely to believe the charges of female victims and more likely to blame them for the crime. This hypothesis is not supported: No statistical interactions between gender and social relationship on reporting and legal treatment were observed. Male violence against female partners is not less likely to be reported, and the reaction of the criminal justice system is not special. There is evidence of gender discrimination in the criminal justice system, but it favors women. In general, violence against women is more likely to be reported than violence against men, and it is more likely to lead to arrest, prosecution, and punishment.

Women are less likely to report sexual assaults to the police than other crimes, particularly sexual assaults committed by acquaintances. However, evidence suggests that the underreporting of sexual assaults by acquaintances is the result of greater privacy concerns, not lack of confidence that the case will be successfully prosecuted. Research has not examined whether female victims are more or less likely than male victims to report sexual assaults to the police. However, women are probably more likely to report sexual assaults than men; research shows that they are more likely to report other crimes, and sexual assault victimization is probably more stigmatizing for male victims.

There is no evidence that the police are more skeptical when women charge their husbands with assault than when men charge their wives; the opposite may occur because of (valid) stereotypes about male violence. Anecdotal evidence suggests that the police are often skeptical of female charges of rape, but we do not know whether the police are more skeptical of female charges of rape than male charges of rape, or of male and female charges of other crimes. If the police are more skeptical about rape charges, there may a good reason for it. Evidence suggests that rape charges are more likely to be false than charges for other crimes. We also know from DNA evidence that there are many cases of misidentification in rape.

Finally, there is evidence that female victims of rape are assigned less, not more, blame than male victims of rape. Observers assign blame to rape victims when they think victims have engaged in irresponsible behavior;

however, they assign the bulk of blame to offenders. Finally, prosecution and conviction rates for rape are similar to other violent crimes, and convicted rapists are punished severely relative to most other crimes.

Hypothesis 11

Legal authorities and other observers are more tolerant of violence against women who violate gender roles than violence against men who violate gender roles, and they treat offenders more leniently. This hypothesis is not supported: There is some evidence that we judge men more harshly than women for violations of gender roles. In addition, the criminal justice system does not punish women more for violations of gender roles (e.g., sexual violations) than for other criminal behavior, and it generally punishes women less severely than men for the same crime.

Hypothesis 12

Women's violence against their male partners is more likely to be motivated by self-defense and victim-precipitated than other violence. This hypothesis is not supported: Neither victim precipitation nor self-defense is especially prevalent when women kill their male partners. Gender does have additive effects, however: Men are more likely to initiate violence in serious incidents (although not in minor incidents).

In sum, the comparative method is useful for testing theoretical claims that a particular type of violence is special. None of the hypotheses about the distinctiveness of violence against women or wives suggested by a feminist approach are supported. Many are in the opposite direction to the one predicted. The results suggest that the study of partner violence and violence against women she incorporated into the study of violence. Until future evidence suggests otherwise, the parsimony principle suggests that social scientists should prefer more general theories of violence. . . .

Race and Class

I have not said much about the role of race and social class in violence against women. Some scholars would criticize the neglect of these demographic variables, suggesting that it is critical that one study the intersection of "race, class, and gender." The comparative approach and standard statistical language are useful in considering the issue empirically and resolving the problem. We must be concerned with the intersection of race, class, and gender if we observe a three-way statistical interaction between these variables. If the effects of gender on violence depend on both race and socioeconomic status, then we must incorporate interaction terms in our equations and qualifications in our theoretical discussion. If the effects of gender depend on race alone or social class alone, then we need to incorporate two-way interaction terms. . . .

It is clear that there are class and race differences in violent behavior generally. Higher rates of violence among poor people and among African

Americans are typically attributed to discrimination and lack of economic opportunity. It is therefore interesting that this same treatment does not lead women to have higher rates of violence than men—the gender difference is strong and in the opposite direction. The pattern suggests that either women are not subject to much discrimination or that discrimination does not lead to violent crime or that discrimination leads to violent crime only under as yet unspecified conditions. For example, some commentators believe that race and class effects are mediated by neighborhood effects. . . .

Both feminism and chivalry lead those who study violence involving women to attempt to protect the image of women. Scholars avoid ideas that might cast women in a negative light, because such ideas might support stereotypes and encourage sexism. For example, although we can talk about gender differences in violence, it is controversial to mention gender differences in complaining; it sounds like a negative stereotype about women. It is ironic that so many sociologists and other social scientists condemn stereotyping, when they are in the stereotype business. Any discussion of gender differences involves generalizations about men and women. Science suffers when hypotheses about group differences are evaluated according to the image they project for protected groups. The scientific analysis of group differences is often in conflict with the promotion of tolerance and diversity. In the study of human behavior, no group comes out unscathed. . . .

One could argue that, overall, feminist influence has been positive because it drew attention to a social problem. Even if their methods were inadequate and their conclusions erroneous, they influenced the public to devote attention and resources to helping female victims. I do not agree that the end justifies the means in this instance for three reasons: (1) There is no evidence that the feminist approach has had any effect on reducing rates of violence against women, (2) bad research produces bad public policy, and (3) social scientists lose credibility when they generate information on social problems that is later revealed to be false.

POSTSCRIPT

Are Differences in Aggressive Behavior Between Women and Men Due to Gender-related Factors?

Because of the notion that aggression is a predominantly male attribute, researchers have disproportionately used male as opposed to female participants in their research studies. Even when female aggression has been the research focus, the conceptualization of aggression has stemmed from the "male" perspective on aggression. For example, much of the research on aggression has focused specifically on physical aggression using the teacher-learner paradigm. In this paradigm, the participant, acting as teacher, punishes the "learner" with electric shocks for incorrect responses. Research has shown, however, that women perceive electric shock more negatively and a less-effective deterrent than do men; thus, they are more reluctant than men to administer it. Research demonstrating gender differences in aggression might be reflecting gender differences in a willingness to behave physically aggressively rather than the potential for aggression.

A continued focus on types of aggression in which men consistently emerge as more aggressive than women fails to examine those situations in which women might aggress and the modes of aggression they might adopt. Cross-cultural analyses suggest that despite tremendous cross-cultural variation, men tend to be more physically aggressive but women may use more indirect aggression. Men are more likely to use aggression that produces pain or physical harm, whereas women are more likely to use aggression that produces psychological or social harm. Because the majority of researchers have been male, they may have chosen questions and contexts regarding aggression of greatest personal relevance.

Thus, when asking questions about gender and aggression, aggression should be defined as any behavior directed toward another person or a person's property with the intent to do harm, even if the aggressor was unsuccessful. The behavior could be physical or verbal, active or passive, direct or indirect (i.e., aggressor may remain anonymous), and the consequence for the target could be physical or psychological. All forms of harm-doing behavior, including self-defense, should be considered because in some cases, such as domestic violence, it is difficult to distinguish retaliative from self-defense motives. Also, aggression, broadly defined, allows us to examine more fully the broad range of harm-doing behaviors available to human beings. Thus, whether than asking who is more aggressive, it might be more productive to ask what are the forms and functions of aggression for women and men, and to what degree is the expression of aggression shaped by cultural expectations regarding masculinity (power, dominance, strength) and femininity (nurturing, passive, weak).

Suggested Readings

Lyn Mikel Brown, *Raising Their Voices: The Politics of Girls' Anger* (Cambridge, MA: Harvard University Press, 1998).

Lyn Mikel Brown, *Girlfighting: Betrayal and Rejection Among Girls* (New York: New York University Press, 2005).

Jonathan L Freedman, *Media Violence and Its Effect on Aggression* (Toronto: University of Toronto Press, 2002).

Sharon Lamb, *The Secret Lives of Girls: What Good Girls Really Do—Sex Play, Aggression, and their Guilt* (New York: The Free Press (Simon and Schuster, 2002).

Myriam Miedzian, *Boys Will Be Boys: Breaking the Link Between Masculinity and Violence* (New York: Lantern Books, 2002).

The Swearer Center for Public Services at Brown University

This website from the Swearer Center for Public Service at Brown University is part of a public education campaign to challenge misconceptions about welfare and contain links to resources and statistics related to welfare, welfare reform, legislation and related information.

```
http://www.brown.edu/Departments/Swearer_
     Center/Literacy_Resources/welfare.html
```

Religious Tolerance Organization

Religious Tolerance is a multi-faith group that promotes religious freedom and diversity as positive cultural values. It presents all viewpoints on controversial religious topics objectively and fairly. It covers numerous "hot topics" including equal rights and protections for homosexuals and bisexuals, including same-sex marriage.

```
www.religioustolerance.org
```

FatherWork

FatherWork is a Web page on "generative fathering" and was developed by family science professors David Dollahite and Alan Hawkins and their students at Brigham Young University. Start with the conceptual framework for generative fathering. Included in the site are insightful personal stories about fatherhood across the life span, and ideas and activities to encourage generative fathering. Many useful discussion questions are provided.

```
http://fatherwork.byu.edu
```

Work and Family: National Partnership for Women and Families

This public education and advocacy site by the National Partnership for Women and Families aims "to promote fairness in the workplace, quality health care, and policies that help women and men meet the dual demands of work and family." This site includes a wealth of information about relevant public policy issues, including the Family Medical Leave Act. See the research report entitled "Family Matters: A National Survey of Women and Men" for some interesting national statistics.

```
http://www.nationalpartnership.org
```

The Family Economic Strategies

This website from The Family Economic Self-Sufficiency Project, describes six strategies that families., especially women, can follow as they move from welfare to self-sufficiency.

```
http://www.sixstrategies.org/
   sixstrategies/sixstrategies.cfm
```

PART 3

From Ozzie to Harriet to My Two Dads: Gender in Childhood

*I*n contemporary America, the "ideal" family continues to be defined as one in which mother and father are married, father is the breadwinner, and mother maintains the home and cares for the children. This ideal is no longer matched by actual family structure, with more and more alternative family structures, including families with same-sex parents and single-parent families being developed to meet personal desires and needs and to cope with societal pressures and changes. Nonetheless, traditional family ideology remains dominant in America. Traditional family ideology institutionalizes conventional gender roles, so much so that many gender scholars view the family as a "gender factory." The institutionalization of gender roles also extends to parental desires regarding the sex of one's children.

In this section, we examine issues surrounding what constitutes a "normal" family, from the perspective of couples themselves. Are same-sex couples just as well adjusted as heterosexual couples? What are the effects on children of being raised by same-sex parents or heterosexual parents? What does it mean when expectant parents say they are hoping for a girl or boy? What does it mean to say one wants family balance, that is, a girl and a boy?

- Is Fetal Sex Selection Harmful to Society?

- Are Fathers Essential for Children's Well-Being?

- Should Same-Sex Couples Be Able to Marry?

- Can Lesbian and Gay Couples Be Appropriate Parents for Children?

ISSUE 7

Is Fetal Sex Selection Harmful to Society?

YES: Dena S. Davis, from *Genetic Dilemmas: Reproductive Technology, Parental Choices, and Children's Futures* (Routledge, 2001)

NO: Rosamond Rhodes, from "Ethical Issues in Selecting Embryos," *Annals of the New York Academy of Sciences* (2001)

ISSUE SUMMARY

YES: Dena S. Davis argues that fetal sex selection is an ethical issue because it is really about gender selection that promotes traditional stereotypes and can interfere with a child's right to an open future.

NO: Rosamond Rhodes describes the acceptable scope of fetal sex selection, as well as professional responsibilities of practitioners of reproductive medicine

Gender is influenced before conception, in making decisions to carry a fetus to term. The potency of sex and gender as explanations for differences between males and females escalates early in life. By early childhood, a host of differences are observed between boys and girls as children internalize a sense of themselves and others as gendered. Concern has been raised about inequities and deficits resulting from the effects of sex and gender.

Research has consistently documented the preference and desire for sons in twentieth-century America and in other cultures. In many cultures, such as India and China, maleness means social, political, and economic entitlement. Men are expected to support their parents in their old age. Moreover, men remain with their family throughout life; women, upon marriage, become part of the husband's family. Thus, women are traditionally seen as a continuing economic burden on the family—particularly in the custom of large dowry payments at weddings. In some cultures if a bride's family cannot pay the demanded dowry, the brides are often killed (usually by burning). Although dowries and dowry deaths are illegal, the laws are rarely enforced.

In such cultures, there is an expressed desire for male children and an urgency to select fetal sex. Recently, sex-determination technology is most commonly used to assay the sex of fetuses, although in many cultures the use of such technology has been banned. When the fetus is determined to be female, abortion often follows because of cultural pressures to have sons. Such sex-determination practices have led to many more male than female infants being born. The gap grows even wider because of a high childhood death rate of girls, often from neglect or killing by strangulation, suffocation, or poisoning. Furthermore, women are blamed for the birth of a female child and are often punished for it (even though, biologically, it is the male's sperm, carrying either X or Y chromosomes, that determines sex).

Research shows that in contemporary America, 78 percent of adults prefer their firstborn to be a boy. Moreover, parents are more likely to continue having children if they have all girls versus if they have all boys. Faced with having only one child, many Americans prefer a boy. But there is also a high preference for a "sex-balanced" family—the "perfect" family having a firstborn son and a second-born daughter. The availability of sex-selection technology in the last quarter of the twentieth century was met with growing interest and widespread willingness to make use of the technology.

Available technologies for sex selection include preconception, preimplantation, and postconception techniques. Preconception selection techniques include folkloric approaches like intercourse timing, administering an acid or alkaline douche, and enriching maternal diets with potassium or calcium/magnesium, all thought to create a uterine environment conducive to producing male or female fetuses. There are also sperm-separating technologies whereby X- and Y-bearing sperm are separated, and the desired sperm are artificially inseminated into the woman, increasing the chance of having a child of the chosen sex.

Preimplantation technologies identify the sex of embryos as early as three days after fertilization. For sex-selection purposes, the choice of an embryo for implantation is based on sex. Postconception approaches use prenatal diagnostic technologies to determine the sex of the fetus. The three most common technologies are amniocentesis (available after the 20th week of pregnancy), chorionic villi sampling (available earlier but riskier), and ultrasound (which can determine sex as early as 12 weeks but is not 100 percent accurate).

The American demand for social acceptance of sex-selection technologies have increased in the last decade. Preconception selection techniques are becoming quite popular in the United States, and preimplantation technologies (though more expensive) are also more frequently used. It has become more and more socially accepted to use prenatal diagnostic technologies to determine fetal sex. But incidence rates for sex-selective abortions are difficult to obtain. There is mixed opinion about the frequency of sex-selective abortions, tinged by political controversy.

In the following selections Dena Davis asserts that fetal sex selection is always unethical, that parents are really not interested in the genitalia that their infants are born with. What they are really choosing is an "ideal," defined by gender role expectations: a boy dad can play ball with or a girl who can wear mom's wedding gown when she marries. In contrast, Rosamond Rhodes argues that there are conditions under which fetal sex selection is ethical; gender imbalance in the population is one such condition. There are cases in which a genetic disease is sex-linked, in which case sex-selection to avoid the disease is acceptable.

Dena S. Davis  **YES**

Genetic Dilemmas: Reproductive Technology, Parental Choices, and Children's Futures

Sex Selection and Reproductive Choice

A common argument asserts that, whatever the causes and consequences of sex selection, choosing the sex of one's baby with available technology is part of a couple's basic right to reproductive choice. In a 1985 study two researchers presented 295 American geneticists with the case of a couple who have four daughters and requested prenatal diagnosis so that they could abort a fifth pregnancy if the fetus was a girl. Sixty-two percent of the geneticists surveyed responded that they would accede to the couple's request. When asked why, the geneticists stated that they perceived sex choice as a "logical extension of parents' rights to control the number, timing, spacing, and quality of their offspring."

In the case of arguments that rest on parental choice, the most common opposition focuses on the dangers of turning children into commodities. Parents become consumers whose goal is the perfect child, with the assumed corollary that children who are considered to be less than perfect will be devalued. Thus just as yuppie consumers purchase the perfect house, the perfect sport utility vehicle, and the perfect bottled water, they may also purchase the perfect baby. Maura Ryan, in a feminist critique of unlimited parental choice, points out that assisted reproduction is expensive and burdensome and wonders "how parents might look upon offspring when they enter the process with the belief that a certain kind of child is *owed* to them and after they have paid a high price for that child." Some ethicists worry that if sex selection is accepted, the next step will be selection to avoid short children, nearsighted children, or children whose intelligence is merely average. Like the inhabitants of Garrison Keillor's mythical Lake Wobegon, we want to believe that "all our children are above average." The result could be a return to the excesses of the eugenics movement. . . .

As I said earlier, the challenge I have set myself is to argue against sex selection in the absence of abortion, and even in the instance where girls are as desired as boys. In the United States, where genetic counseling embodies a culture of autonomy and where population control is not a pressing issue, a subtle but powerful argument can still be made that sex selection is wrong because it abrogates the child's right to an open future. Why, after all, do parents have strong preferences for girls or boys, even if those preferences are merely in the context of "family balance," the one rationale that some ethicists are willing to find blameless if not compelling?

In a 1990 study of 281 American undergraduates, only 18 percent indicated a willingness to use sex selection technology if it was "an inexpensive device or pill" that would allow them to select the sex of their first child. (However, of those who would use the technology, 73 percent preferred boys. It is also possible that if the question had been posed in terms of willingness to use the technology to select their *second* child, more people would have said yes.) In a 1989 study Nan Chico surveyed 2,505 letters to Ronald Ericsson, a Montana physician who patented an early version of the sperm-sorting technique. Chico found that most couples interested in the process already had at least one child and were seeking "mixed" families. There was almost a fifty-fifty split in requests for girls and boys. Ten years later Ericsson reports a larger number of requests for girls than for boys, despite the fact that his process has a higher success rate for producing boys. Microsort, the Virginia company that sorts sperm by a process that first dyes them and then "zaps" them with an ultraviolet laser, reports that many more couples are interested in having girls than boys. (Microsort accepts only couples who are trying to "balance" their familes, that is, they already have at least one child and are attempting to have a child of the sex underrepresented in their family.)

Parents whose preference for one sex or the other is compelling enough for them to take active steps to control the outcome must, I submit, be committed to certain strong gender-role expectations of the children they will raise. As Rothman points out, the genetic test selects for *sex*, that is, for a child with XX or XY chromosomes, but what the parents are really selecting for is *gender*, the social role of being a boy, girl, man, woman. When people go out of their way to choose, they don't want just the right chromosomes and the attendant anatomical characteristics, they want a set of characteristics that go with "girl-ness" or "boyness." Rothman says, "I've heard women say that they want the kind of relationship that they had with their mothers; they think they can't have that kind of relationship with a son. I've heard women talk about wanting to have the frills, the clothes, the manicures together, the pretty mother-daughter outfits, the fun of a prom gown and a wedding gown, that come with girls." Lisa Belkin, who surfed the Web sites devoted to discussions of gender choice, said that women who want girls "speak of Barbies and ballet and butterfly barrettes. They also describe the desire to rear strong young women." If parents want a girl badly enough to go to all the trouble of sperm sorting and artificial insemination, they are likely to make it more difficult for the actual child to resist their expectations and follow her own bent. Rothman says, "[W]hen you start from the premise that one can 'determine' fetal sex in the sense that it can be chosen, then the stereotypes predict the choice: people who want an active, vigorous, achieving child will have boys. And when they want a sweeter, quieter, more loving child, they will have girls." Of course, it is probably impossible to raise children without some gender stereotyping, but the more we can manage to do so, the more we can give our children the gift of the most open possible future, the one least trammeled by notions of how girls and boys (and women and men) are "supposed" to behave. As feminist activist Letty Cottin Pogrebin says, "Instead of dividing human experience in half, locking each child in the prison of either 'masculine' or 'feminine' correctness, and creating two separate definitions of human integrity, the nonsexist parent celebrates the *full* humanity of each girl or boy."

This point holds even for those who would argue that gender stereotypes have been breaking down dramatically in the years since Rothman and Pogrebin wrote. For example, the 1996 Olympics exhibited exhilarating performances by women athletes, the U.S. Supreme Court has required the Virginia Military Institute and the Citadel to admit women, and the current administration in Washington includes our first female attorney general and our first female secretary of state. But such optimism does not invalidate Rothman's point. If stereotypes are breaking down, why is it so important to have a child of the "desired" sex? If someone wants a daughter so that she can be groomed to be the first female navy admiral, that is still perceiving her primarily in terms of gender.

Because gender is only one among many characteristics, but one that carries very heavy baggage in our society, to view a child primarily through its gender narrows the child's ability to choose his or her own path through life. The same would be true if we could choose a child's height, musical ability, or aptitude for nuclear physics. At present, however, the one thing we can pinpoint and control is gender. Maura Ryan, arguing more generally against unfettered procreative liberty, challenges a framework where a desire

> for a particular type of child . . . is seldom weighed appropriately against the reality of the child-to-be as a potential autonomous human being. At what point does a being, who has been conceived, gestated, and born according to someone's specifications, become himself or herself? And if a child comes into the world primarily to fulfill parental need, are there limits to what a parent may do to ensure that the child will continue to meet the specific expectations?

Knowledge of Fetal Sex and the Child's Right to an Open Future

In the process of doing a chromosomal analysis to rule out Down syndrome and other problems, or in the course of a routine ultrasound, it is impossible for a lab technician *not* to determine the fetus's sex. The custom in the United States at this time is for this piece of information to be transmitted from the lab to the physician, who typically asks the couple if they wish to know the sex of their baby-to-be. Although women have reported mixed feelings on this subject, the vast majority of women who have had amniocentesis, CVS, or ultrasound do end up learning the sex of their fetus. Because all women over thirty-five are counseled to consider amniocentesis, as well as younger women with medical indications or family histories of genetic disease, this means that a great many women in America today know their baby's sex before it is born. In fact, it is quite common for people to ask a pregnant woman if she is carrying a boy or girl, or for parents to announce their baby's name when he or she is still months away from making an appearance.

Few commentators see this practice as an ethical issue (at least when parents have no plans to act upon this knowledge to abort a fetus of the undesired sex). It is certainly a strange development, in that it calls into question many common customs. Of course, friends and relatives will still be delighted to get that dramatic phone call from the happy parents telling them that mother and baby are healthy, but without the news that it is a girl or a boy, the announcement lacks a certain something. And the obstetrician does not say, as she holds the baby up for the mother to see, "It's a baby!" However odd these issues seem, we will leave them for anthropologists (and marketers of infant goods) to worry about.

In my view, there *is* an ethical issue here, albeit a very subtle one. There is some evidence to show that for parents who know the sex of their fetus, sexual stereotyping begins even before birth. Joan Callahan describes a conversation with a woman whose daughter had recently learned that the baby she was carrying was a boy:

> The woman had no discernible preference for a boy grandchild over a girl grandchild, but she was delighted to know that her grandchild would be a boy because, she said, she could now "begin getting ready for him." When asked what that meant, she saw immediately that it meant certain colors for blankets and sweaters, certain sorts of toys and room decorations. Long before he was even born, this child would be started on a "boy track," surrounded by blues and trains, never pinks and dolls.

Pregnancy, perhaps especially when amniocentesis has freed one from at least some of the attendant anxieties, is a time rich with dreaming. If the fetus is quiet while one is listening to Bach, that shows great musical talent, while every fetal kick means that an Olympic soccer player is in the making. Just as the early developing embryo is totipotent, which is to say that each of its cells has an unlimited capacity to differentiate into different tissues and organs, so too the very early developing parent entertains a vast range of possibilities. In our heavily gendered culture, many of those dreams are lost and others become locked in the minute the baby is born and the sex is known.

Most social scientists agree that gender socialization begins at birth. Studies show that adults treat babies they think are male or female very differently from the first day of life. Experiments with babies from birth to a year show adults (men and women) interacting quite differently with the exact same baby, depending on whether or not they have been told that the (diapered) baby is a girl or a boy. Based on the baby's supposed sex, they offered it different toys, spoke in a different tone of voice, and interpreted the baby's behaviors quite differently. (When "boy" babies cried, for example, they were thought to be angry, while "girl" babies who cried were thought to be scared.)

These new techniques make it possible for gender socialization to begin *before* birth. Barbara Katz Rothman, in an ingenious study, asked women to decribe the movements of their fetus during the final trimester. Women who did not know their baby's sex before birth used a variety of adjectives, without any pattern connected to the sex of their baby. However, when women knew their fetus's sex, a distinct pattern emerged. The movements of female fetuses were much less likely to be described as "strong" and "vigorous." The word *lively* was used often to describe females, but never males, although parents who did not know the sex of their fetus were equally likely to describe male or female fetuses as strong or lively. Some masculine-sounding descriptions were used for female fetuses, but feminine-sounding descriptions were never used for males. This is in keeping with our culture, where tomboys are more acceptable than sissies and a girl in boy's pajamas looks cute, while a boy in a girl's nightgown sets off alarm signals.

Thus it seems that knowing the baby's sex before it is born encourages the kind of gender stereotyping that threatens to limit the child's right to an open future. This is such a subtle argument that it hardly justifies frustrating parents' right to know should they demand access to the information. However, Rothman points out that the urge to know the fetus's sex often arises from the parents' awareness that the doctor or lab technician already knows. Rothman comments:

> It is not simply that the information is now knowable. It is also that it is known. It is known to the medical personnel, and once the sex of the fetus becomes part of the medical record, it makes sense to treat it just as one would other information on that record. Nancy said she asked the sex because: "I want all the information available to the physician to be available to me."

One way to discourage the practice of reporting fetal sex while still respecting the rights of parents who insist on knowing is to adopt a policy suggested by Wertz and Fletcher in the context of discouraging actual sex selection. They propose that information about fetal sex remain in the lab and not be routinely reported to the doctor. Therefore the doctor also would not know, and few patients would be prompted to ask for the information. The information would be available for parents who ask, but reporting it to parents would no longer be routine. This would also avoid the now rather common occurrence of parents who have asked not to know accidentally being told by overenthusiastic nurses and physicians.

Conclusion

Sex selection, even in the absence of abortion, raises serious concerns of justice in the context of developing countries and societies in which there is a dramatic preference for boys. But even in countries such as ours, where preference for boys may soon be a nonissue, I believe that sex selection presents an ethical problem because it promotes gender role stereotyping and encourages parents to invest heavily in having certain types of children. This combination of investment and stereotyping makes it more difficult for the child to grow and develop in ways that are different than, perhaps even in conflict with, parental expectations. Just *knowing* the fetus's sex, even outside of any attempt to predetermine it, may exacerbate gender stereotyping by allowing parents to begin the tracking process before the baby is born. Thus policies that encourage sex selection or predetermination should be discouraged.

Rosamond Rhodes

← NO

Ethical Issues in Selecting Embryos

Introduction

People involved in assisted reproduction frequently make decisions about which of several embryos to implant or which of several embryos to reduce from a multiple pregnancy. Physicians involved in embryo transfers or pregnancy reductions have to choose which embryos will have a chance of developing into a baby and which will not. Currently, the embryos that look healthiest are most often the ones to be implanted and the ones that appear unhealthy or are conveniently positioned are the ones that are most commonly discarded or reduced.

Developing technology will enable doctors to know more about the embryos among which they are selecting. Embryos can already be selected because of their gender or because they do not have some specific genetic anomaly. But, being able to do something does not mean that it should be done. In the case of selecting embryos, people have already raised questions about the ethical acceptability of using sex as a selection criterion. Disabilities activists have challenged the morality of using criteria related to illness, disease, or disability. And fiction writers and others with vivid imaginations have raised questions about possible future uses of diagnostic technology in fashioning future human beings. They spark reflection about whether it is acceptable to select an embryo because its genes promise great intelligence, aggressiveness, physical prowess, and blue eyes. These issues also change significantly when we consider them from the perspective of different decision makers. Is the selection of embryos a choice for physicians to make or should it be left to government, to insurance providers, or to parents? If the choice is to be made by persons other than the physician, when should a physician cooperate with their choice and when should a physician refuse to act on their grounds for embryo selection?

With the possibility of selecting against kinds of humans, people worry about the morality of using the new technology. They are anxious about the ethical borders that might be crossed, they are apprehensive about eugenics, concerned about reinforcing negative social attitudes about gender and disability, and uneasy about producing humans without intending to allow them to live and to develop. The religiously inclined are concerned about meddling with the "sanctity of life." As Paul Ramsey explained, "the value of human life is ultimately grounded in the value God is placing on it. . . . [The] essence [of human life] is [its] existence before God and to God, and it is from Him." For believers, selecting embryos sounds dangerously close to playing God, trespassing in His domain, or treading on the sanctity of life.

In response to such concerns from so many disparate perspectives, specialists in assisted reproduction have been hesitant in making their techniques available on request, because of uncertainty about making decisions on the ethical frontier and concerns about their moral reputation. Nevertheless, this paper will argue that, for the most part, we must resist the movement to proscribe or prohibit embryo selection. Our society's commitment to liberty requires that we allow individuals to make choices according to their own lights, and in the absence of actual substantial evidence that such practices cause serious harm or at least a demonstration of a significant likelihood of untoward repercussions, we are not justified in denying individuals the option.

In this presentation, I review some of the important considerations for allowing embryo selection and arguments that have been put forward for rejecting embryo selection criteria based on sex or genetic characteristics. I discuss the subject of choosing our offspring in terms of the centrality to ethics of liberty and autonomous choice and in terms of well accepted ideas about limiting liberty because of harm to others. In light of these remarks, I shall present a position on the acceptable scope of embryo selection, on who should be making the choices, and on the professional responsibilities of those who practice reproductive medicine.

Liberty

From its inception, our society has embraced the value of liberty. Freedom has been our creed and the foundation for building our government both because of its inherent value and because it is such a crucial component of happiness. In particular, reproductive freedom is a very important human value. Through reproductive choice people are allowed to act on their own values and to try to create their own image of happiness. For the most part, people want the liberty to choose their own reproductive partners, the timing of their reproduction, and their rate of reproduction.

While there has been a great deal of discussion about the concept of liberty, John Stuart Mill's account has been given significant weight in moral and political philosophy, and in this discussion, because of the strength of his arguments and their analytic power, I will follow his account. As Mill has explained, for people who extol liberty, "the sole end for which mankind are warranted, individually or collectively, in interfering with the liberty of action of any of their number is self-protection." This principle for limiting legislative and policy intervention with liberty has become known as the "harm principle." It demands that no action be forbidden unless it can be shown to cause harm to others in the enjoyment of their rights. . . .

Although anything one person does may give another affront, upset, or sadness and thereby cause some harm, only those actions that "violate a distinct and assignable obligation to any person or persons" may be proscribed by legislation. . . .

Embryo Selection, Rights, and Harms

Rights.   With respect to embryo selection, the question relevant to Mill's criterion is whether someone's use of the technology would violate anyone else's rights? To answer, we must consider all of those who we could anticipate might have rights violated. As far as I can foresee, those who might be harmed by the production of selected offspring would include the perspective children, their peers, and those in the community who would be upset by people overstepping the line into God's domain. Under any circumstances of implanting only a few of several embryos or reducing a pregnancy of one or more of several embryos, only some of the possible embryos will actually become children. Without invoking a theological argument about fertilized eggs having a right to life, it is hard to imagine that the destruction of a non-selected embryo would involve a violation of rights. None of the others who might claim some harm would suffer any violation of rights.

Devaluation and discrimination.   Some disabilities activists worry that by selecting against embryos with genetic abnormalities we would diminish our appreciation of people with disabilities. Similarly, some feminists worry that by allowing people to select against females we would encourage sexist attitudes and support gender discrimination. These concerns do not meet Mill's standard for prohibiting individual choice. First, it is not at all clear that the imagined untoward affects will actually occur, and if the attitudes did arise in a few instances, it is not clear that their limited social impact could justify limiting reproductive liberty. These are empirical matters, and a significant amount of evidence would have to be amassed before the concern reached the level of meriting a restrictive social policy. Second, it seems that no one has a right to prevent the existence of the selected others who might, in some way, be preferred or superior to themselves and, just by living, make the less desired or inferior feel unappreciated. That embryo selection technology might be the means to enable fewer females or fewer individuals with disabilities to be born does not, therefore, violate the rights of women, or people with disabilities, or anyone else.

Religious concerns.   The religious concern over interfering with the sanctity of life also fails to meet Mill's criterion for legislating against a practice. While liberty allows individuals the freedom to choose a religious perspective and the freedom to live according to the religious views they embrace, it limits individuals' infringement on the similar rights of others. In other words, no one may impose his own religious views on others. So while no one has the right to interfere with anyone else's religious practice, the others who he respects have no right to intervene in his living by his own religious or non-religious standards. The religious liberty guaranteed by the harm principle does not extend rights to control the lives of others, and so those whose religious sensitivities are upset by the prospect of other people meddling with the creation of human life cannot claim that harm as grounds for limiting others' procreative practice.

Justification.   Some people base their objections to embryo selection on the particular moral justification that people may offer for their choice. Yet, while we may consider some reasons better than others, efforts to constrain peoples' moral judgments are rejected by Mill as illegitimate "moral legalism." Many people consider the medical reason of wanting to avoid having a child with a serious genetic disease and the nonmedical reason of family balance as good reasons for embryo selection. Putting these "good" reasons aside, it is important to point out that we do not question the reasoning that motivates nontechnology-assisted reproduction. The ordinary desire to have biologically related offspring is not challenged even in the face of overpopulation and the large numbers of orphaned children around the world. Without aid and without society's interference people have children in order to pass along their genes, or to pressure a partner into marriage, or to get an apartment, or to keep a marriage together, or to get an inheritance, or to have a real live doll to play with, or to have some body to love. It is not even clear which reasons are "good" reasons and which are not. But it is clear that privacy and respect for autonomy require that people be allowed to follow their own reasons. So reasons for procreation should be irrelevant to policy makers. And, at least since Hobbes's writings in the seventeenth century, it has been understood that law could only govern action and not thought or belief.

Further Considerations

In sum, I find no persuasive argument for restricting embryo selection (or, similarly, preconception sex selection) as long as there is no empirical evidence of significant social harm from allowing the technology to be freely available. Yet, I would like to press this conclusion in several directions to show what more might be said in defense of sex selection or selecting embryos for other reasons, such as to avoid having a child with a serious genetic disease.

Impact.   Significant social harms from resulting gender imbalance in the population would count against allowing access to embryo selection technology. Yet, in an environment resembling contemporary U.S. society, it is hard to imagine that the number of births that employed the technology could be large enough to have a demographic effect. Since the cost, inconvenience, discomfort, risks, and loss of privacy entailed by the procedure would be likely to make embryo selection a rarely employed technology, and since there would be a variety of motivations and procreators, the numbers of individuals produced by the technology in our society (or an other that was sufficiently similar to ours) would not be great enough or similar enough to have any significant impact on demographics or on social attitudes towards females or people with disabilities. While studies show that people have preferences about gender and birth order, in actual decisions about using embryo selection those considerations will have to be balanced against the others that mitigate against it. Only those for whom gender or avoiding a genetic disease is extremely important are likely to avail themselves of the technology.

Consequences.   Any conclusion about the social impact of a practice has to take all of its effects into account. While my guess is that embryo selection is likely to have only a negligible societal impact, nevertheless, if we were to evaluate that effect we would have to assess all of its consequences, those that count as harms as well as those that count as benefits. Although gender imbalance in the population may turn out to be a harm at some point, other effects of embryo selection are likely to be beneficial. (1) Embryo selection for gender is likely to be used by parents who want an additional child to be of a different gender than other children in the family. Without assisted reproductive technology, "try again" has been the method to achieve that goal. Embryo selection (and preconception sex selection [PSS], if it should be effective) has the social advantage of not adding to society's overpopulation problems. (2) By helping couples achieve the gender balance they want with fewer children, embryo selection (or PSS) can benefit families by easing the economic and human burdens of providing for a large family. Today, when few enjoy the support of an extended family to help with the chores of everyday life and when both parents are typically employed outside the home, additional children tax a family's limited resources. (3) Potential parents, that is, autonomous adults, are in the best position to assess the kind of rearing and companionship experience that would be valuable to them. For those to whom gender or the avoidance of a child with disabilities makes a significant enough difference to justify embryo selection (or PSS), the gender- or genetic-selected child is likely to provide a more rewarding experience. (4) Children produced by embryo selection (or PSS) are also more likely to be attentively reared and to have a good childhood because their parents have chosen the kind of child who they are more likely to nurture well.

Context.   Some objectors to embryo selection find the idea of choosing one's offspring, rather that accepting whichever ones happen to arrive, to be immoral *per se* or to support discrimination and therein be immoral. Sympathetic moral imagination can, however, help us to appreciate that embryo selection (or PSS) can be moral or, in some cases, may be obligatory. Consider the hypothetical case of George and Katherine. Many years ago, George had engaged in pederastic behavior. He was apprehended for his assaults on young boys, tried, convicted, and punished for his crimes. After years of psychotherapy he now understands and deeply regrets his previous behavior. He no longer experiences any sexual attraction for young boys. In fact, he has fallen in love with Katherine and they want very much to have a family. After fully discussing George's past and considering their options, they decide that they don't want to chance having a boy. The risk of triggering some old feelings would be far too costly for both George and a son, and George and Katherine would both be very happy as parents to a girl. Because of age-related factors, Katherine needs to use assisted reproductive technology and her obstetrician discusses the option of embryo selection with the couple. They opt for selecting only female embryos for implantation.

As I see it, the behavior of George and Katherine is morally responsible. They consider the value of a child in their lives, the conceivable danger to themselves and their future offspring, and how to minimize the possibility of related harms. Their choice exemplifies far-sighted prudence, appropriate care and concern, and ethical responsibility. It would be immoral for people in their situation to ignore the risks or to eschew embryo selection out of concern for appearing to display sexism. This case makes the point that sex selection is not necessarily immoral and it is not necessarily an act of unacceptable sex discrimination. The circumstances and the reasons for choosing selection can make a significant difference, and there is likely to be a broad array of situations in which embryo selection is ethically acceptable.

Prohibition. Moral imagination can also be used to make a further point. There is a significant difference between judging that a particular act is unethical and deciding that the practice should be legally prohibited. If we could know enough about the situations and reasons involved in other people's procreative decisions, we might decide that some were ethically unacceptable. While that information could be sufficient for our judgment about a particular case, it would not be sufficient to justify legislation that would limit the liberty of everyone. Allowing people to live their lives by their own lights and to make some bad or even unethical decisions is inherent in our valuing liberty. A demonstration of actual overriding harms is the only legitimate justification for constraining liberty.

Selfishness. Finally, we should consider the place of personal satisfaction in moral decisions, particularly in reproductive decisions. The most obvious social problem of serious gender imbalance is that those in the gender majority will be less likely than otherwise of having a heterosexual mating with all its attendant promise of personal satisfaction. And the reason most people want to have children involves the promise of personal satisfaction associated with being a parent. Such pleasure motivate us. They are importantly constitutive of well-being, and the pleasure associated with securing such basic goods is typically taken into account in moral and political philosophy. In the context of recognizing the importance of personal satisfaction as a moral consideration, we should notice that demeaning the pleasure that some people associate with having a child of a particular gender or devaluing the pain that some people associate with having a child with a genetic disease as unethically selfish requires justification. Those who want to decry embryo selection have to explain why the desire to have a child of a particular gender or a child without a genetic disease is unethical while the selfish desire to have any child is ethically acceptable.

Who Makes the Choice

My argument, so far, has focused on the unacceptability of government or policy restrictions on embryo selection. The questions that remain involve the proper scope for patient and physician choice. The answers require an understanding of physician professional responsibility and the doctor-patient relationship, subjects that may be even more controversial than the ones addressed so far.

The uncontroversial features of physician professional responsibility involve the doctor's commitment to: (1) using the scientific method and guiding practice by the knowledge provided by science, (2) relying on the cooperative model of practice involving a team of health care providers, and (3) pursuing the moral goal of acting for the patient's good. But, as soon as we recognize that a physician and a patient could have very different views of the good, we confront the controversial problem of whose view of the good should rule? When the doctor cares most about avoiding risks of physical harm and the patient cares more about some other component of her well-being, the doctor's and the patient's values are likely to clash. The issue raised by such conflict involves decisions about the appropriate goals and scope of medicine. These are lofty abstract philosophical questions. But the answers have very practical implications when it comes to embryo selection.

A physician may feel comfortable in going along with some patient requests for embryo selection and also be inclined to refuse the service in other cases. Taking personal comfort as the standard suggests that different obstetricians can each have their own personal standard for providing embryo selection and that there are no professional criteria to be used as a guide in these decisions. While physicians may be comfortable with this Lone Ranger approach to bioethics, recognizing that there are standards for professional behavior points us in another direction.

When we consider a patient's abortion decision or a patient's decision to undergo assisted reproduction with its attendant risks and harms, we can appreciate that a patient's values and goals play an important role and often rightly determine the course of treatment. Some people take a narrow and rigid view of the appropriate goals of medicine as promoting health, curing disease, or preserving life. However, thinking about abortion, assisted reproduction, or even plastic surgery provides a different view of the appropriate goals of medicine, something akin to the use of medicine's special knowledge, skills, and privileges to help promote a set of socially defined goods. This view allows a significant place for the patient's conception of the good in medical decision making. In other words, as long as the treatment requested provides an accepted good, and so long as it is likely to achieve the patient's goals without causing significant harm, the requested treatment should be provided and the patient's view of the good should rule.

Obstetrics has been called upon to promote reproductive choice as a socially accepted good and as an appropriate use of medicine's special knowledge, skills, and privileges. Embryo selection certainly fits within that widely appreciated class of goods. As such, patients should expect access to the technology and cooperation from their physicians in offering and providing the option. Regardless of whether the physician shares the patient's conception of the good and regardless of whether the physician feels comfortable with the decision, the patient's choice should rule, at least in most cases, and the physician would not be justified in withholding the technology.

While the reasons I have offered leave me "comfortable" with this conclusion for cooperating with gender selection and selection against genetic disease, I am inclined to give the opposite answer when it comes to genetic selection for dwarfism or deafness. In those cases, because such disabilities are so widely seen as harms, disabilities, and disadvantages, I think physicians would have good reason for not cooperating with a parental request for embryo selection.

Conclusion

In these remarks I have put forward a framework for thinking about the ethics of embryo selection. I have argued that the reasons for restricting the use of the technology are not sufficiently compelling to overcome our commitment to protecting liberty and reproductive liberty in particular. Furthermore, I have urged a view of the doctor-patient relationship that takes the values of patients very seriously and, therefore, accepts patient choice as ruling almost always in reproductive decisions. I suggest that the limitation on this freedom is the traditional stand against doing harm. In the case of embryo selection even though a resulting deaf child or dwarf would not be harmed in the sense that the particular resulting child would not be made worse off, I have broadly interpreted the concept of doing harm to include deliberately selecting a child who is likely to be impaired as creating a harmful outcome.

While a number of my conclusions may invite disagreement, my further agenda in this paper was to suggest that disputes in bioethics are to be settled by giving reasons that other reasonable people could accept. I see this view of morality as preferable to an attitude that accepts moral matters as settled on the grounds of claims about personal comfort or uneasiness. Recalling that the practice of medicine involves the cooperation of a team of physicians and other health care providers, forging a moral consensus among those who will be called upon to act becomes a significant concern. Understanding ethics in terms of reasons invites us to share our concerns and to reason together in defining moral positions in reproductive medicine.

POSTSCRIPT

Is Fetal Sex Selection Harmful to Society?

A primary focus of critics' concern about sex-selection technologies (and cultural biases toward males) is their impact on population sex ratios. A skewed sex ratio, they fear, will cause dire consequences for a society, particularly for heterosexual mating (although it is ironic that the same class of reproductive technological advances not only facilitate sex selection but also make reproduction less reliant on conventional heterosexual mating). But what about social concerns about sex selection? How will the increasing frequency of the use of sex-selection technologies impact families? How will it affect gender assumptions and sex discrimination?

Is the acceptability of sex-selection conditional? If Americans were not as biased toward having just boys or just girls, and therefore the population sex ratio would not be threatened, would sex selection be acceptable to control the birth order of the sexes, to ensure a mixture of boys and girls, or to have an only child of a certain desired sex? Sex-selection technology might reduce overpopulation by helping families who already have a child of one sex "balance" their family with a second child of the other sex, rather than continue to have children "naturally" until they get the sex they want. Is using sex selection as a "small family planning tool" an acceptable use of sex-selection technologies? Many feel that using sex selection to balance a family is not sexist. But others argue that it is sexist because it promotes gender stereotyping, which undermines equality between the sexes.

Some feminists argue that sex selection for any reason, even family-balancing perpetuates gender roles and thus the devaluation of women. Some people in the disabilities right movement have joined with this perspective suggesting that if it is permissible to select against female embryos (is sex per se a genetic "abnormality?"), then so it permissible to select against embryos with genetic abnormalities of all types; and who is to define what is "abnormal"—height, IQ? Then the door is open to increasing discrimination against people with disabilities.

Should abortions solely for the purpose of sex selection be allowed? This is a profound dilemma for many pro-choice feminists for whom a woman's right to choose an abortion for any reason is opposed to gross sex discrimination in the form of sex-selective abortions (usually of female fetuses). It is interesting to note that when parents choose to abort based on fetal sex in an effort to "balance" their family, sex selection is regarded as more acceptable than when only female fetuses are aborted because of a preference for males. What assumptions about sex and gender underlie this judgment?"In these selections the effects of sex and gender on fetuses, children, and adolescents are examined. Is fetal sex selection ethical? Are sex differences located in biology and/or culture? Can children's gender roles be redefined?

Suggested Readings

K. M. Boyd, "Medical Ethics: Principles, Persons, and Perspectives: From Controversy to Conversation," *Journal of Medical Ethics, 31* (Year): 481–486.

John Harris, "Sex Selection and Regulated Hatred," *Journal of Medical Ethics, 31* (2005): 291–294.

S. Matthew Liao, "The Ethics of Using Genetic Engineering for Sex Selection," *Journal of Medical Ethics, 31* (2005): 116–118.

Rosamond Rhodes, "Acceptable Sex Selection," *American Journal of Bioethics, 1* (2001): 31–32.

Susan M. Wolf, *Feminism and Bioethics: Beyond Reproductions* (New York: Oxford University Press, 1996).

See also the following organizations' statements on sex selection:

1. The American College of Obstetricians and Gynecologists Committee on Ethics, "*Committee Opinion: Sex Selection*," Number 177 (November 1996).

2. FIGO [International Federation of Gynecology and Obstetrics], "Recommendations on Ethical Issues in Obstetrics and Gynecology by the FIGO Committee for the Study of Ethical Aspects of Human Reproduction, July 1997.

3. The Ethics Committee of the ASRM [American Society for Reproductive Medicine], "Sex Selection and Preimplantation Genetic Diagnosis," *Fertility and Sterility,* Volume 72, Number 4 (October 1999).

4. The Ethics Committee of the ASRM, "Preconception Gender Selection for Nonmedical Reasons," *Fertility and Sterility,* Volume 75, Number 5 (May 2001).

ISSUE 8

Are Fathers Essential for Children's Well-Being?

YES: Sarah S. McLanahan and Marcia J. Carlson, from "Welfare Reform, Fertility, and Father Involvement," *Future of Children* (2002)

NO: Louise B. Silverstein and Carl F. Auerbach, from "Deconstructing the Essential Father," *American Psychologist* (June 1999)

ISSUE SUMMARY

YES: Sarah S. McLanahan and Marcia J. Carlson examine the negative effects of father-absence in children's lives and offer suggestions for how to increase father involvement.

NO: Louise B. Silverstein and Carl F. Auerbach are the founders and co-directors of the Yeshiva Fatherhood Project. They conclude that neither mothers nor fathers are essential to children's well-being; rather, children can thrive in a number of different family structures.

For decades there has been active debate about parenting roles and responsibilities. What does it mean to be a responsible parent? Is one sex naturally better at parenting than the other? Are there essential characteristics of fathering versus mothering? Is having parents of two sexes necessary for the well-being of children? Should mothers work or engage in other activities outside the family? Should fathers move beyond the provider or breadwinner role and become more involved in the physical and emotional care of their children? Should fathers emulate mothers' traditional nurturing activities? Or, should fathers uphold their role as masculine role models for their children? Are fathers essential?

The twentieth century saw significant changes in the American family. Well over half of mothers are currently in the paid workforce. More than half of all new marriages end in divorce. One-third of all births are to single women. The traditional family ideal in which fathers work and mothers care for children and the household characterizes less than 10 percent of American families with children under the age of 18.

Mothers' increased labor force participation has been a central catalyst of change in the culture of fatherhood. Mothers began to spend less time with children, and fathers began to spend more time. Thus, the cultural interest in fatherhood increased, and it was assumed that fathers were becoming more nurturant, and more essential. The history of the ideals of fatherhood reveals that fathers have progressed from distant breadwinner to masculine sex-role model to equal coparent.

Despite changes in the *ideals* of fatherhood, some family scholars observe that fathers' behavior has not changed. Rather, it appears that mothers' behavioral change may be responsible for the change in the culture of fatherhood. A recent review of comparisons of fathers' and mothers' involvement with their children (in "intact" two-parent families) reveals a gap: fathers' engagement with their children is about 40 percent that of mothers'; fathers' accessibility is about two-thirds that of mothers. Fathers' lesser involvement is even more characteristic of divorced and never-married families. Nearly 90 percent of all children of divorce live with their mothers. Most single-parent fathers are "occasional" fathers. More than one-third of children in divorced families will not see their fathers at all after the first year of separation. Only 10 percent of children will have contact with fathers 10 years after divorce. Yet at the same time, research has documented the important ways in which fathers influence their children. But does this mean that fathers are essential?

Some contend that fathers are not mothers; fathers are essential and unique. Many reject a gender-neutral model of parenting, arguing that mothers and fathers have specific roles that are complementary; both parents are essential to meet children's needs. Proponents of this model assert that fatherhood is an essential role for men and pivotal to society. They maintain that fathers offer unique contributions to their children as male role models, thereby privileging their children. Moreover, fathers' unique abilities are necessary for children's successful development.

The following selections advance two models. McLanahan and Carlson's paper suggests that father-absence plays an essential role in the economic welfare of children and their mothers. They contend that fathers serve as not only a financial resource but an emotional resource as well for children. They conclude that welfare policy reform is necessary and make several policy recommendations to increase the presence of fathers in children's lives. Their arguments are premised on the assumption that men bring something special to the parent-child relationship. In contrast, Louise Silverstein and Carol Auerbach suggest that traditional views of fathering are essentialist; that is, the biological differences between women and men automatically translate into different parenting behaviors. Their analyses suggest that neither mothers nor fathers are essential to a child's well-being. Rather, that responsible parenting can occur in a variety of family structures, including single parents and same-sex parents. With appropriate government policies that do not privilege fathers over mothers and discriminate against single mothers, the quality of life for children will improve.

Sara S. McLanahan and
Marcia J. Carlson

YES

Welfare Reform, Fertility, and Father Involvement

The Personal Responsibility and Work Opportunity Reconciliation Act of 1996 represented a historic shift in U.S. policy toward poor families and children. In addition to requiring that low-income parents assume greater responsibility for their own economic well-being through increased work, the reform legislation included provisions to discourage births outside of marriage, to promote and strengthen two-parent families, and to encourage father involvement (at least with respect to financial support). These provisions reflect—and contribute to—a growing awareness of the importance of fathers for children.

Until recently, discussions about welfare policy have largely excluded fathers, except with respect to their frequent failure to pay child support. Despite rising concerns since the 1980s about the negative consequences of out-of-wedlock childbearing and single-parenthood (particularly for children, but also for society), most policy and research about families on welfare have focused only on single mothers. However, recent research on fatherhood has pointed to the range of contributions that fathers can make in their children's lives, as well as to the barriers that some fathers face in providing economic and emotional support for their children.

Recent Trends and Effects on Children

Several major demographic trends in the latter half of the twentieth century have affected the composition of families in the United States, especially low-income families. In particular, declining marriage rates, increasing divorce rates, and increasing rates of births to unmarried women have combined to increase the likelihood that children will spend time living away from their fathers. Although many unmarried parents work together to raise their children by cohabiting or maintaining frequent contact, father involvement for most low-income families in this situation is not necessarily stable. . . .

From *The Future of Children Journal,* vol. 12, no. 1, 2002, excerpts from 148, 150, 152–156, 159–160. A publication of the David and Lucile Packard Foundation. Reprinted by permission.

. . . [T]rends suggest the emergence of a new family type—the "fragile family," comprised of unmarried parents who are working together to raise their children either by cohabiting or maintaining frequent contact. Such families are deemed fragile because of the multiple risks associated with non-marital childbearing, including poverty, and to signify the vulnerability of the parents' relationship. Union dissolution rates are much higher among cohabiting couples than among married couples; this is true particularly in the United States, but also in Western European countries, where cohabitation is even more prevalent.

Fathers as Resources for Children

The consequences of not having a father have been a source of long-standing concern to society, but the focus of research on fathers has evolved as the larger cultural meaning of fatherhood has changed over time. Only in the last several decades have scholars begun to examine father involvement more broadly. Early studies focused on the effects of *father absence,* defined as the father not living with the child. In this "deficit model," children in mother-only (or "father-absent") families were compared to children in two-parent ("father-present") families without directly measuring what fathers—whether living with their children or not—were actually contributing to their children's lives. . . .

In the 1980s, with the emergence of a "new" fatherhood model (particularly among the middle class) in which there were greater expectations for fathers' emotional investment and active participation in parenting, studies began to investigate the potential *positive* effects of father involvement. The first studies in this area focused on fathers' financial support and found that the payment of child support is positively associated with children's well-being. . . .

A growing literature in sociology and child development has investigated the effects of fathers' nonmonetary involvement as well, such as participating in shared activities with the child and developing a close, high-quality relationship with the child. Positive father involvement, particularly by fathers who live with their children, has been linked to less-frequent child and adolescent behavioral problems, including delinquency, substance use, anxiety, and depression. . . .

Not surprisingly, fathers who do not live with their children see them less often, which decreases the likelihood that the father and child will develop a close relationship. Also, fathers who do not share the child's household are less likely to contribute financial resources to support their child, as they have less ability than a father living with the child has to monitor the allocation of resources by the mother. Particularly following divorce, absent fathers may become less altruistic toward their children over time. Divorced parents also may be less able to reinforce one another in child rearing, further diminishing the father's role. Although these findings refer to formerly married couples, the consequences are likely similar for unmarried couples following a separation. . . .

Policies Designed to Promote Father Involvement

As family demographics and the social environment have changed, public policy also has evolved in an attempt to mitigate the consequences of family instability and, in some cases, to reshape the demographic trends themselves. Most recently, the 1996 federal welfare reform law gave new emphasis to two primary categories of programmatic interventions intended to promote father involvement: 1) programs designed to discourage nonmarital fertility and thus decrease the formation of "father-absent" families; and 2) programs intended to increase nonresident fathers' support for and involvement with their children.

Programs to Discourage the Formation of Father-Absent Families

Efforts to reduce the rising number of father-absent families have focused primarily on preventing unwanted pregnancy among unmarried women, especially teenage girls. This approach is guided by the awareness that when a pregnancy is unintended, the father is less likely to live with the child and provide "positive parenting." In contrast, when a pregnancy is intended and births are spaced appropriately, better maternal and child health outcomes are likely, and assurance is greater that the child will be loved and nurtured by both the mother and the father. Most births to unmarried couples, however, are unintended. . . . Therefore, reducing the incidence of unintended pregnancy among unmarried couples represents a promising strategy to reduce the likelihood that a child will grow up without a father's involvement in his or her life. Pregnancy prevention efforts fall into three main categories: family planning, teen programs, and family caps. . . .

Overall, though pregnancy prevention programs have met with some success, they have not fundamentally abated the high levels of nonmarital fertility and the formation of father-absent families. This is because nonmarital fertility has risen for reasons that reflect larger cultural shifts in attitudes, values, and practices—simply because couples lack information about sex or access to contraceptive technology. As described in the section on demographic trends, consensual unions other than marriage have become more accepted and prevalent, increasing the likelihood that children will be born outside of marriage.

Programs to Encourage Greater Father Involvement

Because "father absence" is the defining characteristic of most single-parent families, public policy has attempted to compensate for the resources that children lose when the father is not in the household. The most obvious resource deficit is economic—without fathers' income, female-headed families are much more likely to be poor. Initially, policies were designed to compensate for the loss of the father's income directly with cash assistance and in-kind benefits such as food stamps and Medicaid. Then, as single mothers increasingly were women who were separated and divorced from their partners, as opposed to being widowed, policymakers began to consider seeking resources from fathers. Programs were initiated to collect child support from unmarried fathers and, more recently, to increase their earnings so that they can pay child support. Only recently has policy attention to fathers broadened beyond financial support to incorporate nonmonetary investments in children as well. . . .

Until very recently, poor noncustodial fathers of children on welfare were largely ignored by social policymakers and disconnected from resources that might help them become more involved in their children's lives. The child support system has operated solely as an enforcement agency collecting money from fathers (and punishing those who fail to pay) rather than as a social service organization attempting to balance responsibility with appropriate services and supports (and providing incentives to pay). This is changing as the confluence of three factors—demographic changes that have increased the number of fragile families; growing awareness of the difficulties faced by low-income fathers and families; and greater understanding of the benefits to children of father involvement—has led to the development of programs that more effectively promote fathers' financial and emotional involvement with their children.

Representing an important first step toward developing such programs, in March 2000 the U.S. Department of Health and Human Services approved 10 state demonstration projects to "improve the opportunities of young, unmarried fathers to support their children both financially and emotionally." These new programs serve both divorced fathers and new fathers in fragile families. They have varied emphases, but they generally are designed to improve fathers' parenting skills and employment capabilities, and to ensure that fathers have access to their children. Initial assessments of these new programs have found that enrolling fathers and sustaining their participation over time present particular challenges. More rigorous evaluations have yet to determine the nature and magnitude of the impacts across various program types. . . .

Conclusion

This article has highlighted the changing composition of families in the United States, particularly the fact that many children will spend some time living away from their father during childhood. Because fathers offer important financial and emotional resources to children, it is important to encourage greater father involvement, especially among fathers who do not live with their children. Recent trends and concern for such children have stimulated a variety of new public policies and programs to promote fathers' involvement with their children, both financially and emotionally.

Public policy, supported by sound research, can improve the likelihood that fathers will be involved with their children, both by discouraging the formation of father-absent families in the first place, and by increasing incentives and supports for positive father involvement. For example, programs designed to reduce the rising number of father-absent families by focusing on preventing unwanted pregnancies, especially among teens, appear to be most successful when they seek to alter adolescents' life opportunities in addition to providing family planning education or services. Also, although early efforts to encourage father involvement yielded disappointing results, newer programs that are better targeted and timed to the birth of a child appear to hold greater promise for improving the circumstances of low-income fathers and families.

NO ↩

**Louise B. Silverstein and
Carl F. Auerbach**

Deconstructing the Essential Father

*Neoconservative social scientists have claimed that fathers are essential to positive
child development and that responsible fathering is most likely to occur within the
context of heterosexual marriage. This perspective is generating a range of governmental initiatives designed to provide social support preferences to fathers over
mothers and to heterosexual married couples over alternative family forms. The
authors propose that the neoconservative position is an incorrect or oversimplified
interpretation of empirical research. Using a wide range of cross-species, cross-
cultural, and social science research, the authors argue that neither mothers nor
fathers are essential to child development and that responsible fathering can occur
within a variety of family structures. The authors conclude with alternative recommendations for encouraging responsible fathering that do not discriminate against
mothers and diverse family forms.*

In the past two decades, there has been an explosion of research on fathers.
There is now a broad consensus that fathers are important contributors to both
normal and abnormal child outcomes. Infants and toddlers can be as attached
to fathers as they are to mothers. In addition, even when fathers are not physically present, they may play an important role in their children's psychological
lives. Other important issues about fathers and families remain controversial.
For example, scholars continue to debate the extent to which paternal involvement has increased over the past 20 years. Similarly, researchers are only beginning to study the ways that fathering identities vary across subcultures, and the
effects of divorce on fathers and their children are not yet clearly understood.

Overall, this explosion of research on fathering has increased the complexity of scholarly thinking about parenting and child development. However,
one group of social scientists has emerged that is offering a more simplistic
view of the role of fathers in families. These neoconservative social scientists
have replaced the earlier "essentializing" of mothers with a claim about the
essential importance of fathers. These authors have proposed that the roots of a
wide range of social problems (i.e., child poverty, urban decay, societal violence,
teenage pregnancy, and poor school performance) can be traced to the absence
of fathers in the lives of their children. . . . In our view, the essentialist framework represents a dramatic oversimplification of the complex relations between
father presence and social problems.

From *American Psychologist*, vol. 54, no. 6, 1999, excerpts from 397–405. Copyright © 1999 by
American Psychological Association. Reprinted by permission.

We characterize this perspective as essentialist because it assumes that the biologically different reproductive functions of men and women automatically construct essential differences in parenting behaviors. The essentialist perspective defines mothering and fathering as distinct social roles that are not interchangeable. Marriage is seen as the social institution within which responsible fathering and positive child adjustment are most likely to occur. Fathers are understood as having a unique and essential role to play in child development, especially for boys who need a male role model to establish a masculine gender identity.

Our research experience has led us to conceptualize fathering in a way that is very different from the neoconservative perspective. Over the past six years, we have studied the fathering identities of men who are actively involved with their children. To date, approximately 200 men from 10 different subcultures within U.S. society have participated in this qualitative research. Our research participants include Haitian Christian fathers; Promise Keeper fathers; gay fathers; Latino fathers; White, nongay divorced fathers; Modern Orthodox Jewish fathers; and Greek grandfathers.

In contrast to the neoconservative perspective, our data on gay fathering couples have convinced us that neither a mother nor a father is essential. Similarly, our research with divorced, never-married, and remarried fathers has taught us that a wide variety of family structures can support positive child outcomes. We have concluded that children need at least one responsible, caretaking adult who has a positive emotional connection to them and with whom they have a consistent relationship. Because of the emotional and practical stress involved in child rearing, a family structure that includes more than one such adult is more likely to contribute to positive child outcomes. Neither the sex of the adult(s) nor the biological relationship to the child has emerged as a significant variable in predicting positive development. One, none, or both of those adults could be a father (or mother). We have found that the stability of the emotional connection and the predictability of the caretaking relationship are the significant variables that predict positive child adjustment.

We agree with the neoconservative perspective that it is preferable for responsible fathers (and mothers) to be actively involved with their children. We share the concern that many men in U.S. society do not have a feeling of emotional connection or a sense of responsibility toward their children. However, we do not believe that the data support the conclusion that fathers are essential to child well-being and that heterosexual marriage is the social context in which responsible fathering is most likely to occur.

Many social scientists believe that it is possible to draw a sharp distinction between scientific fact and political values. From our perspective, science is always structured by values, both in the research questions that are generated and in the interpretation of data. For example, if one considers the heterosexual nuclear family to be the optimal family structure for child development, then one is likely to design research that looks for negative consequences associated with growing up in a gay or lesbian parented family. If, in contrast, one assumes that gay and lesbian parents can create a positive family context, then one is likely to initiate research that investigates the strengths of children raised in these families.

The essentialist theoretical framework has already generated a series of social policy initiatives. For example, a 1998 congressional seminar recommended a series of revisions to the tax code that would reward couples who marry, and end taxes altogether for married couples with three or more children. Other federal legislation has emerged with a similar emphasis on the advantages of marriage. The 1996 welfare reform law begins by stating, "Marriage is the foundation of a successful society." Similarly, a housing project in Hartford, Connecticut now provides economic supports to married couples and special opportunities for job training to men (but not to women) who live with their families. In 1997, Louisiana passed a Covenant Marriage Act that declared marriage a lifelong relationship and stipulated more stringent requirements for separation and divorce. The social policy emerging out of the neoconservative framework is of grave concern to us because it discriminates against cohabiting couples, single mothers, and gay and lesbian parents. . . .

The Essentialist Position

[1] Biological Sex Differences Construct Gender Differences in Parenting

[Claim:] One of the cornerstones of the essentialist position is that biological differences in reproduction construct gender differences in parenting behaviors. This theoretical framework proposes that the biological experiences of pregnancy and lactation generate a strong instinctual drive in women to nurture. This perspective assumes that men do not have an instinctual drive to nurture infants and children. . . .

. . . [Critique:] Cross-species and cross-cultural data indicate that fathering can vary from a high level of involvement to a total lack of involvement. Given these wide variations in paternal behaviors, it is more accurate to conclude that both men and women have the same biological potential for nurturing and that the sexual division of labor in any culture is defined by the requirements of that culture's specific bioecological context.

[2] Marriage Matters

[Claim:] The neoconservative perspective has argued that without a biological basis for nurturing in men, the best way to ensure that men will behave responsibly toward their offspring is to provide a social structure in which men can be assured of paternity (i.e., the traditional nuclear family). . . .

. . . [Critique:] Data on human parenting behaviors conform to the predictions of the reciprocity hypothesis. In social contexts where either the fathers or the mothers have few benefits to exchange, paternal involvement is low. When both fathers and mothers have benefits that contribute to family well-being, paternal involvement is relatively high. Thus, improving employment opportunities for women, as well as men, is crucial to increasing father involvement. These findings suggest that in our current cultural context, it is economics, not marriage, that matters.

[3] The Civilizing Effects of Marriage

[Claim:] The essentialist position has also proposed that marriage has a civilizing effect on men, that marriage protects women and children from domestic violence. . . .

. . . [Critique:] Multiple variables lead to abuse. These include personality of the perpetrator (such as low self-esteem or poor impulse control), characteristics of the immediate family context (such as job loss), and qualities of the broader ecological context (such as poverty or high levels of violence in the community). Stepchildren, unplanned children, and children in large families are all at greater risk for abuse. Thus, high levels of child abuse are associated with a broad array of biopsychosocial variables. In summary, we do not find any empirical support that marriage enhances fathering or that marriage civilizes men and protects children.

[4] Fathers Make a Unique and Essential Contribution to Child Development

[Claim:] The neoconservative perspective has proposed that if men can be induced to take care of young children, their unique, masculine contribution significantly improves the developmental outcomes for children. . . .

. . . [Critique:] Father absence covaries with other relevant family characteristics (i.e., the lack of an income from a male adult, the absence of a second adult, and the lack of support from a second extended family system). . . . [B]ecause single-mother families are overrepresented among poor families, it is difficult to differentiate the effects of father absence from the effects of low income.

. . . [F]ather involvement exists on a continuum, whether or not fathers live with their children. Fathers can be absent even when they reside with their children and can be present despite nonresident status.

The essentialist position also fails to acknowledge the potential costs of father presence. . . . [S]ome fathers' consumption of family resources in terms of gambling, purchasing alcohol, cigarettes, or other nonessential commodities, actually increased women's workload and stress level.

[5] The Importance of a Male Role Model

[Claim:] Another aspect of the neoconservative perspective is the argument that . . . [f]athers are . . . essential role models for boys, relationship models for girls, and "protectors" of their families. . . . The essentialist perspective assumes that boys need a heterosexual male parent to establish a masculine gender identity.

. . . [Critique:] Empirical research does not support this assumption. A significant amount of research on the children of lesbian and gay parents has shown that children raised by lesbian mothers (and gay fathers) are as likely as children raised in heterosexual, two-parent families to achieve a heterosexual gender orientation. Other aspects of personal development and social relationships were also found to be within the normal range for children raised in lesbian and gay families. . . .

Taken as a whole, the empirical research does not support the idea that fathers make a unique and essential contribution to child development. From our perspective, it is not the decline of marriage that is discouraging responsible fathering. Rather, various social conditions inhibit involved parenting by unmarried and divorced men. For example, unmarried teen fathers typically have low levels of education and job training. Thus, they lack the ability to contribute significantly to the economic security of their offspring. Similarly, many divorced fathers cannot sustain a positive emotional connection to their children after the legal system redefines their role from parenting to visitation. . . .

Change and the Change-Back Reaction

If the essentialist paradigm is not supported by empirical data, why has it been so widely accepted? We believe that the appeal of the essentialist position reflects a reaction against the rapid changes in family life that have taken place in the past three decades. Since the 1960s, family-formation strategies have changed dramatically in Western, industrialized cultures. The cultural norm of early and universal marriage has been reversed. Fertility rates have declined overall, and age at the birth of a first child has risen across all cohorts. More couples are choosing to live together outside the context of marriage, and a first pregnancy more frequently precedes rather than follows marriage. Previously rare family types (e.g., single mothers by choice, dual career families, and gay or lesbian parents) are increasingly more common.

Industrialized cultures are in the process of changing from a context in which child development could flourish with fathers as the sole or primary provider to a context in which two providers are now necessary in the vast majority of families. In a survey of 1,502 U.S. families, 48% of married women reported that they provided half or more of the family income. Given this commitment to breadwinning, women can no longer shoulder the sole responsibility for raising children.

In this context of rapid change, the neoconservative position reflects a widespread societal anxiety about who will raise the children. Mothers are no longer at home, and society has not embraced other-than-mother care. The United States, in contrast to other Western countries, has not yet developed a social policy agenda designed to help women and men integrate their work and family responsibilities. Thus, many people believe that a return to the traditional nuclear family structure with its gendered division of labor would be preferable to large numbers of neglected and unsupervised children.

In addition to an authentic concern about the welfare of children, we believe that the appeal of the essential father also reflects a backlash against the gay rights and feminist movements. In the past two decades, the employment of women has dramatically increased, whereas the employment of men has declined significantly. Many more women than in past historical periods can now choose to leave unsatisfactory marriages or to have children on their own, outside of the context of a traditional marriage. Two of three divorces are now initiated by women.

Just as the feminist movement created new opportunities for women, the gay rights movement has encouraged many more gay men and lesbians to live an openly homosexual lifestyle. Many gay men and women who would previously have entered into a heterosexual marriage to have children, now see a gay family structure as a viable alternative for raising children. Parallel to these changes is the tendency emerging among heterosexual couples to live together and delay marriage until after a first pregnancy. Thus, the distinctions between marital and cohabiting unions and between marital and nonmarital childbearing are losing their normative force.

These social changes require heterosexual men to relinquish certain aspects of power and privilege that they enjoyed in the context of the traditional nuclear family. Most men no longer have sole economic power over their families. Similarly, most men must accept some degree of responsibility for child care and household tasks. The majority of heterosexual men no longer have full-time wives to buffer the stress of balancing work and family roles. Within this new context of power sharing and role sharing, heterosexual men have been moved from the center to the margins of many versions of family life. In our view, the societal debate about gender differences in parenting is, in part, a reaction to this loss of male power and privilege. We see the argument that fathers are essential as an attempt to reinstate male dominance by restoring the dominance of the traditional nuclear family with its contrasting masculine and feminine gender roles. . . .

An Alternative Blueprint for Social Change

We have argued that the neoconservative paradigm is based on an oversimplification of empirical research. Thus, we believe that the social policy emanating from this perspective cannot ultimately be successful in encouraging responsible fathering. Pressuring men and women to enter into or maintain unsatisfactory marriages is unlikely to enhance paternal involvement. We now present an alternative framework that we believe more accurately fits the data. Our framework has three main recommendations: reconstructing traditional masculinity ideology, restructuring societal institutions, and providing a comprehensive program of governmental subsidies to all families with children.

Because we believe that ideology defines both social policy and individual behavior, our first recommendation speaks to the necessity of reconstructing cultural ideology about gender roles. . . . Our goal . . . is to create an ideology that defines the father–child bond as independent of the father–mother relationship.

If the father–child bond were accorded the same importance as the mother–child bond, then young boys would be socialized to assume equal responsibility for the care and nurturing of their children. A father's relationship with his children could then develop and remain independent of his relationship with the child's mother. This ideological shift would encourage the development of diverse models of responsible fatherhood. . . .

We believe that this change in cultural gender ideology would be effective in maintaining a high level of paternal involvement for resident as well as nonresident fathers. Divorce and nonmarital childbirth would then be less likely to be characterized by father absence, because cultural norms would prescribe that never-married and divorced fathers remain actively involved with their children.

This ideological enhancement of the father–child bond is also necessary for restructuring societal institutions so that father involvement is encouraged, rather than inhibited. Maintaining the sacred status of the mother–child dyad continues the myth of separate (i.e., gendered) spheres of life. The cultural assumption of separate spheres links public/work/masculine and private/family/feminine. This cultural linking of family and feminine is reflected in the assumption that women, but not men, will decrease their involvement in paid work to balance the competing demands of work and family life.

[M]en are reluctant to take advantage of family-supportive policies because they fear that they will be perceived as uncommitted to their job or unmasculine. Until workplace norms acknowledge that men have equivalent responsibility for child care, it is unlikely that most men will feel comfortable restructuring their commitment to work in a manner that allows more family involvement. . . . Governmental policy must acknowledge the link between father absence and job absence. Men who can contribute substantially to family finances are more likely to get married and to assume financial responsibility for their children.

Our final recommendation relates to an overall governmental family policy. The United States cultural ideology of rugged individualism continues to assume that individual families can and should balance the stress of work and family without the benefits of large-scale government supports. The United States remains one of the few industrialized countries without a comprehensive family policy that provides paid parental leave, governmentally financed day care, and economic subsidies for all families with children. Without these benefits, the responsibility for child care continues to fall largely on women.

Because women continue to bear the bulk of the responsibility for the welfare of children, the goal of economic equality remains elusive. Providing families with governmental supports would not only alleviate many of the stresses of working families, it would also free women from the unequal burden of making major accommodations in their involvement in paid work. This shift would then decrease gender inequalities in the workplace, provide women with more resources to exchange, and thus contribute to higher paternal involvement.

?'s • What is a "fragile family" as described
by M + C? pg 137.
• What are the three main recommendatio
of A and S that would provide a
framework for more/better parental
involvement?

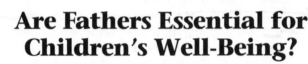

POSTSCRIPT

Are Fathers Essential for Children's Well-Being?

Researchers have explored under what conditions optimal father involvement is possible. Some state that the three necessary conditions are: (1) when a father is highly motivated to parent, (2) when a father has adequate parenting skills and receives social support for parenting, and (3) when a father is not undermined by work and other institutional settings. The reconstruction of fathering, whatever the redefinition, has proven to be very difficult, contested by many cultural forces.

At issue is the assumption that there is something natural and thus rooted in the basic nature of women and men that makes a two-parent family, with a mother and father, essential and ideal for children's well-being. The fundamental assumption of different parenting styles and roles of men and women have led to debates about whether "fathers can mother." That is, can men and should they begin to fill the role of nurturer? The result is that (men's "job description" . . .) men's "job description" as fathers is less clear than expectations of women as mothers. Therefore, fathering is very sensitive to context (including the marital or coparental relationship, children, extended family, and cultural institutions). The role of mother is especially delimiting. Mothers often serve as gatekeepers in the father-child relationship. Father involvement is often contingent on mothers' attitudes toward, expectations of, and support for the father.

Many mothers are ambivalent about active father involvement with their children. The mothering role has been a central feature of adult women's identity, so it is no wonder that some women feel threatened by paternal involvement in their domain, which affects their identity and sense of control. In the absence of social consensus on fathering and counterarguments about the deficits of many fathers, many mothers are restrictive of father involvement. However, some maintain that responsible mothering will have to evolve to include support of the father-child bond.

In addition, with increasing latitude for commitment to and identification with their parental role, men are increasingly confused about how to exercise their roles as fathers. This also makes them sensitive to contextual factors such as others' attitudes and expectations. Worse yet, they frequently encounter disagreement among different individuals and institutions in their surrounding context, further complicating their role choices and enactment.

Four other contextual forces challenge a redefinition of fathering. (1) Legal notions of fatherhood disregard nurturing. Adequate fathering is primarily equated with financial responsibility. (2) Concepts of masculinity conflict with nurturant parenting. Nurturant fathers risk condemnation as being "unmanly." How can nurturant fatherhood fit into notions of maleness and masculinity? (3) Homophobic attitudes further obstruct nurturant fatherhood. Ironically, active legal debate about sexual orientation and parenting might be influential in reconstructing fatherhood. Is there a model of shared parenting within the gay community? (4) Nurturing by fathers and mothers has typically functioned in a single-parent model, whether with a two-parent marriage or with parents living in separate households. One parent usually does most, if not all, of the nurturing. Gender neutrality and equality in parenting is undefined. How would you conceptualize a model of shared parenting (taking care not to discriminate against single-parent families)? What would parental equality look like in practice? Is it essential that children be exposed to both female and male role models? If so, why? If women and men were not expected to conform to a specific set of expectations associated with their sex would the sex of the people raising children matter? Which benefits the child more, a heterosexual set of parents who are bound by strict gender-related conventions which results in an over-bearing, abusive father, or a loving single father or loving, nurturing gay parents?

Suggested Readings

W. D. Allen and M. Connor, "An African American Perspective on Generative Fathering," in A. J. Hawkins and D. C. Dollahite, eds., *Generative-Fathering: Beyond Deficit Perspectives* (Sage Publications, 1997).

D. Blankenhorn, *Fatherless America: Confronting Our Most Urgent Social Problem* (Basic Books, 1995).

S. Coltrane, *Family Man: Fatherhood, Housework, and Gender Equity* (Oxford University Press, 1996).

Cynthia R. Daniels, *The Unexpected Legacy of Divorce: The 25 Year Landmark Study* (New York: Hyperion, 1998).

Lucia Albino Gilbert and Jill Rader, "Current Perspectives on Women's Adult Roles: Work, Family, and Life," in Rhoda K. Unger, ed., *Handbook of the Psychology of Women and Gender* (Hoboken, NJ: John Wiley & Sons, Inc., 2001), pp. 156–169.

F. Daniel McClure and Jerry B. Saffer, *Wednesday Evenings and Every Other Weekend: From Divorced Dad to Competent Co-Parent. A Guide for the Noncustodial Father* (Charlottesville, VA: The Van Doren Company, 2001).

Ross Parke and Armin Brott, *Throwaway Dads: The Myths and Barriers That Keep Men from Being the Fathers They Want to Be* (New York: Houghton Mifflin, 1999).

Janice M. Steil, "Family Forms and Member Well-Being: A Research Agenda for the Decade of Behavior," *Psychology of Women Quarterly, 25* (2001): 344–363.

ISSUE 9

Should Same-Sex Couples Be Able to Marry?

YES: Larry A. Kurdek, from "Are Gay and Lesbian Cohabiting Couples *Really* Different from Heterosexual Married Couples?" *Journal of Marriage and Family* (November 2004)

NO: Peter Sprigg, from *Questions and Answers: What's Wrong with Letting Same-Sex Couples 'Marry'?* (Family Research Council, 2004)

ISSUE SUMMARY

YES: Psychology professor Lawrence A. Kurdek reports on a longitudinal study comparing gay and lesbian partners with partners from heterosexual married couples with children. For half of the comparisons there were no differences and for 78% of the comparisons for which differences were found, gay or lesbian partners functioned better than heterosexual partners.

NO: Peter Sprigg, director of the Center for Marriage and Family Studies at the Family Research Council, outlines why non-heterosexual relationships do not carry with them the same validity as heterosexual relationships, and therefore should not be allowed to marry legally. He states that the rights same-sex couples maintain that they would get by being able to marry are rights that are already available to them.

Many people believe that a person should have the same rights as anyone else, regardless of their race, age, gender—or sexual orientation. When this discussion moves into the arena of same-sex marriage, however, those beliefs start to waiver a bit. The past few years have seen the topic of same-sex marriage rush into the forefront of the news and other media.

Vermont became the first state to make civil unions legal between two people of the same sex. Although a same-sex couple cannot have a marriage license or refer to their union as a marriage, the benefits are the same as they would be for a heterosexual marriage. These unions are not, however, recognized in any other state. This is due in great part to the Defense of Marriage Act, which was signed into law in 1996 by President Bill Clinton. This Act says that no state is required to recognize a same-sex union, and defines marriage as being between a man and a woman only. Therefore, same-sex unions that are legal in one state do not have to be recognized as legal in another. In anticipation of efforts to have state recognition of civil unions, over 30 states have passed legislation saying they would not recognize a same-sex union that took place in another state.

In the 2004 national election few issues were more hotly debated than same-sex marriage. In that election 11 states passed constitutional amendments that effectively banned same-sex marriage. President Bush was quoted as saying "The union of a man and a woman is the most enduring human institution, honored and encouraged in all cultures and by every religious faith." Political conservatives claimed that the election results indicated that the country generally rejects same-sex marriage. However, beneath the political rhetoric are questions about what is really wrong with gays and lesbians being granted the same legal rights of heterosexual couples.

Those who oppose same-sex marriage believe that marriage is, and always has been, between a man and a woman. They believe that a key part of marriage for many heterosexual couples is reproduction or another type of parenting arrangement, such as adoption. In those case, they believe that any child should have two parents, one male and one female (see Issue 8). Many do not oppose granting domestic partner benefits to same-sex partners, or even, in some cases, civil unions. They do, however, believe that if lesbian and gay couples were allowed to marry and to receive the legal and social benefits thereof, it would serve only to further erode the institution of marriage as it is currently defined, which, in the United States, boasts one divorce for every two marriages.

Supporters of same-sex marriage believe that if lesbian and gay couples wish to make a lifetime commitment, they should be afforded the same rights, privileges, and vocabulary as heterosexual couples. While some would be as happy with the term "civil union," accompanied by equal rights, others believe that making marriage available to all is the only way to go.   *nonsense that is silly!*

An argument that is raised in this debate is that granting same-sex couples the right to marry would open the door for adult pedophiles to petition to marry the children with whom they engage in their sexual relationships. Most lesbian and gay individuals and their supporters find this offensive, as well as an invalid comparison. What do you think?

As you read, consider what is at the base of each argument. Consider the assertions pertaining to the effects of same-sex couples or their unions on different-sex couples. Do you agree? What effect do you think the relationship status, choices, and behaviors of heterosexual couples have on lesbian and gay individuals and couples?

In the following selections, both Larry Kurdek and Peter Sprigg raise the most common questions pertaining to same-sex marriage. Kurdek's research challenges assumptions that there is something inherently "wrong" with same-sex couples. The concerns Peter Sprigg raises pertains to the expectation of heterosexual marriage to raise children, and that a same-sex couple is a harmful setting in which to do that.

Lawrence A. Kurdek

 **YES**

Are Gay and Lesbian Cohabiting Couples *Really* Different from Heterosexual Married Couples?

Despite the current controversy surrounding same-sex marriage in the United States, there are no reliable estimates of the number of American gay and lesbian couples. Survey data indicate that between 40% and 60% of gay men and between 45% and 80% of lesbians are currently involved in a romantic relationship. Data from the 2000 United States Census indicate that of the 5.5 million couples who were living together but not married, about 1 in 9 (594,391) involved same-sex couples. Other survey data indicate that between 18% and 28% of gay couples and between 8% and 21% of lesbian couples have lived together 10 or more years. Because presenting oneself publicly as part of a gay or lesbian couple opens the door for discrimination, abuse, and even violence, these numbers are likely to be underestimates. Nonetheless, it is clear that despite a general social climate of prejudice against gay men and lesbians, being part of a couple is integral to the lives of many gay men and lesbians.

As one indication of the importance of identifying oneself as part of a couple, some gay and lesbian citizens of the United States are currently arguing that they, just like heterosexual citizens, are entitled to the privileges associated with having their relationships legalized as marriages. These privileges include access to spousal benefits from Social Security; veterans', health, and life insurance programs; hospital visitation rights; the ability to make medical decisions for partners; and exemption from state inheritance taxes. They also argue that being deprived of these privileges is unjust because it involves discriminating against a defined class of individuals. In response, some legislators have counterargued that same-sex marriages violate the sanctity of marriage as a union between a man and a woman, and that legal steps are needed to protect that sanctity. In that vein, 38 states to date have approved Defense of Marriage Acts ensuring that those states need not recognize the legality of same-sex unions effected by other states, and support is growing for an amendment to the Constitution that will define marriage as the legal union of a man and a woman.

From *Journal of Marriage and Family*, vol. 66, November 2004, excerpts from 880–883, 895–897. Copyright © 2004 by National Council on Family Relations. Reprinted by permission.

Despite extensive media coverage of the same-sex marriage issue, the voice of relevant research is rarely heard. Consequently, my premise is that the complex controversy surrounding same-sex marriage can be examined, in part, as an *empirical* question of the extent to which gay and lesbian partners differ from heterosexual spouses on variables that matter to long-term relationships. I make no claims that answers to this question will provide a definitive resolution to the controversy, but I do submit that answers to this question will help to inform reasoned discussion of the controversy. If marriage is to be reserved for only unions of a man and a woman, it seems reasonable to assume that opposite-sex relationships work in ways that are radically different from the way that same-sex relationships work. Comparing partners from gay and lesbian couples to spouses from heterosexual couples on variables already known to be relevant for relationship health affords one way of testing this assumption.

Addressing the same-sex marriage issue on empirical grounds is complicated, however. Despite an increased scientific interest in gay and lesbian couples, systematic comparisons of partners from gay or lesbian couples to spouses from heterosexual couples have been characterized by several methodological and statistical problems. These include studying only one partner from the couple; averaging individual scores from both partners; using measures with unknown psychometric properties; not taking into account whether the couples had children living with them; not quantifying the size of any differences found among couples; comparing couples without first ensuring that the members of these couples were equivalent on demographic characteristics such as age, education, income, and length of relationship; and treating members of the couples as independent units of analysis.

These problems are redressed in this article by my reporting of findings from a longitudinal project involving psychometrically sound measures completed by both members of gay cohabiting, lesbian cohabiting, and heterosexual married couples. Further, I conducted comparisons between partners from both gay and lesbian couples and heterosexual couples with controls for potentially key demographic variables (i.e., age, education, income, and years living together). I assessed the size of the effects associated with type-of-couple differences, and I employed statistical analyses that took partner interdependence into account.

In the samples I recruited, partners from gay and lesbian cohabiting couples did not live with children. Because children are known to affect marital functioning, partners from heterosexual married couples were divided into those with children and those without children. In view of the complexities associated with living with stepchildren, the group of heterosexual couples identified as having children was restricted to those who lived only with their biological children.

I defend the selection of childless gay and lesbian couples on the basis of reports that the majority of gay and lesbian couples do *not* live with children. Using data from the 2000 Census, . . . [it has been] estimated that 33% of female same-sex householders and 22% of male same-sex householders lived with their own children who were under the age of 18. By extension, one can assume that the majority of gay and lesbian couples wanting to get married also would be childless. Indeed, . . . of 212 lesbians and 123 gay men who obtained same-sex civil unions in Vermont, only 30% and 18%, respectively, had children. . . . [S]uch percentages are likely to be lower than the percentages of lesbians and gay men who have children.

I conducted type-of-couple comparisons using married couples with children as the reference group for four reasons. First, an important topic in the study of cohabitation among heterosexual couples is whether such cohabitation provides a lasting arrangement in which to raise children. Second, some scholars have argued that married couples—including, potentially, gay and lesbian couples—should receive state-funded services only if they are raising children. Third, based on the 2000 Census, 46% of married householders had at least one biological child, adopted child, or stepchild living with them. It is safe to assume that the number of married householders who have *ever* had children is well over 50%. Finally, legislators who have lobbied for constitutional amendments to ban same-sex marriage have done so to promote the best interests of children. For example, in calling for a constitutional amendment protecting marriage, President Bush stated that "Ages of experience have taught humanity that the commitment of a husband and wife to love and to serve one another promotes the welfare of children and the stability of society." In sum, I compared typical partners from gay and lesbian couples not living with children to typical partners from married heterosexual couples living with their own children. For reviews of literature regarding children raised by gay, lesbian, or heterosexual parents.

Participants in the Project

Participants were drawn from two separate longitudinal studies, one in which heterosexual married couples were participants, and the other in which gay and lesbian cohabiting couples were participants. In both studies, annual assessments were obtained by mailed surveys. Up to 11 assessments were available for heterosexual couples, whereas up to 14 assessments were available for gay and lesbian couples. Heterosexual couples were initially recruited as newlyweds from marriage licenses published in the *Dayton Daily News*. Partners from gay and lesbian couples were recruited through requests for participants published in periodicals for gay men and lesbians, and from couples who had already participated in the survey. At the sixth and eighth assessments, additional couples (recommended by couples already participating) were added to the sample. Unlike the heterosexual couples who were first studied shortly after their wedding, gay and lesbian couples were first studied at different points in their relationship careers. There were no requirements for how long gay and lesbian partners had to be cohabiting, and none of the couples lived with children. . . .

Conclusion

My major premise in this article is that the complex controversy surrounding same-sex marriage can be examined, in part, as an empirical issue. I asked whether and the extent to which partners from the most likely type of gay and lesbian cohabiting couples—those without children—differ from partners from the most likely type of heterosexual married couples—those with children. My findings are of note because both partners from gay cohabiting, lesbian cohabiting, and heterosexual married couples were assessed repeatedly with psychometrically sound measures. Further, I employed statistical techniques appropriate for analyzing data obtained from both partners of the same couple. Finally, I examined the critical issue of the extent to which gay and lesbian partners differ from heterosexual parents over a range of issues. I studied average levels of variables known to be linked to relationship health, concurrent predictors of relationship quality, and predictors of relationship stability. These issues rarely have been addressed together, even in prospective longitudinal studies of married heterosexual couples.

Despite these positive features, the data I collected were limited. I make no claim that the samples of couples are representative, all measures were open to the biases associated with self-report, partners from the different types of couples were not matched on demographic variables, and gay and lesbian partners who were also parents were not studied. Further, had I selected different variables either from the domains of interest or from different domains (e.g., sexual behavior) and used different methodologies (e.g., interviews and direct observations), I might have obtained different findings. In the context of the current controversy over same-sex marriage, however, the nonrepresentative nature of the samples in particular may not be problematic. Opponents of same-sex marriage have not indicated that marriage should be denied to only *some* types of gay and lesbian couples (such as those in short-term relationships or those living with children). Rather, opponents have objected to marriage for *any and all* same-sex couples. Because opponents of same-sex marriage have targeted gay and lesbian partners as a class of individuals, the data reported here are relevant because the gay and lesbian partners studied are members of that class.

The overall pattern of findings across the range of issues studied here is clear: Relative to heterosexual parents, partners from gay couples and partners from lesbian couples do not function in ways that place their relationships at risk for distress. In particular, there is no evidence that gay partners and lesbian partners were psychologically maladjusted, that they had high levels of personality traits that predisposed them to relationship problems, that they had dysfunctional working models of their relationships, and that they used ineffective strategies to resolve conflict. The only area in which gay and lesbian partners fared worse than heterosexual parents was in the area of social support: Gay partners and lesbian partners received less support for their relationships from family members than heterosexual parents did.

Although the rates of relationship dissolution for the heterosexual couples and gay and lesbian couples were not directly comparable, it is safe to conclude that gay and lesbian couples dissolve their relationships more frequently than heterosexual couples, especially heterosexual couples with children. Perhaps a positive side of *not* having same-sex marriage is that gay and lesbian partners confront no *formal* institutionalized barriers and obstacles to leaving unhappy relationships. Lawyers need not be consulted, court action is not required, religious vows are not broken, and no recognized kin-by-marriage ties are severed. As a result, the relatively high rate of dissolution for gay and lesbian couples might indicate that gay and lesbian cohabiting partners are less likely than heterosexual married partners to find themselves trapped in empty relationships. Nonetheless, the absence of formal institutionalized barriers for members of gay and lesbian couples does not mean that partners from gay and lesbian couples do not perceive barriers to leaving their relationships, and that gay and lesbian partners easily exit from their relationships. To the contrary, I have reported elsewhere that partners from gay and lesbian cohabiting couples are similar to partners from heterosexual married couples in both appraisals of barriers to leaving their relationships and in the personal emotional turmoil experienced subsequent to dissolution.

Given the current lack of formal institutionalized barriers to leaving a same-sex relationship, perhaps the most remarkable finding from this project is that gay men and lesbians nonetheless build and sustain durable relationships. At the time of the last available assessment, 52% of the 125 gay stable couples and 37% of the 100 lesbian stable couples had been together for more than 10 years. Further, 14% of the 125 gay stable couples and 10% of the 100 lesbian stable couples had been together for more than 20 years. To the extent that marriage is regarded as a social and legal institution, conferring the right of marriage to gay men and lesbians might actually defend their relationships against the stresses that plague any couple in the early critical stages of the relationship, stresses that may lead to premature dissolution. Because involvement in a close relationship is linked to overall well-being, protecting same-sex relationships is tantamount to protecting the well-being of the partners involved in those relationships.

That concurrent relationship quality was predicted with variables from the psychological adjustment, personality traits, relationship styles, conflict resolution, and social support domains equally well for heterosexual parents as compared to gay partners and lesbian partners is strong evidence that the processes regulating close personal relationships are robust. . . . Further, that change in relationship quality discriminated unstable couples from stable couples for both heterosexual and gay and lesbian couples is additional evidence that models of marriage and marriagelike unions should recognize change as a core relationship process.

The findings reported here should not be taken to mean that gay and lesbian cohabiting couples and heterosexual married couples do not differ from each other *in any regard*. Indeed, the findings regarding social support from family members signify that gay and lesbian couples function in a social context that is very different from that of heterosexual couples. Further, because gay men and lesbians cannot use the gender of the partner to fashion the content of their relationships, they must negotiate common couple-level issues such as household labor and family rituals in creative ways that do not involve gender. The findings reported here *can* be taken as one basis for claiming that gay men and lesbians are entitled to legal recognition of their relationships not only because, as gay and lesbian citizens, they deserve the same rights and privileges as heterosexual citizens, but also because the processes that regulate their relationships are the same as those that regulate the relationships of heterosexual partners.

weak
I don't feel
like that was well
displayed

Peter Sprigg  **NO**

Questions and Answers: What's Wrong with Letting Same-Sex Couples "Marry?"

What's Wrong With Letting Same-Sex Couples Legally "Marry?"
There are two key reasons why the legal rights, benefits, and responsibilities of civil marriage should not be extended to same-sex couples.

The first is that homosexual relationships are not marriage. That is, they simply do not fit the minimum necessary condition for a marriage to exist—namely, the union of a man and a woman.

The second is that homosexual relationships are harmful. Not only do they not provide the same benefits to society as heterosexual marriages, but their consequences are far more negative than positive.

Either argument, standing alone, is sufficient to reject the claim that same-sex unions should be granted the legal status of marriage.

Let's Look at the First Argument. Isn't Marriage Whatever the Law Says It Is?
No. Marriage is not a creation of the law. Marriage is a fundamental human institution that predates the law and the Constitution. At its heart, it is an anthropological and sociological reality, not a legal one. Laws relating to marriage merely recognize and regulate an institution that already exists.

But Isn't Marriage Just a Way of Recognizing People Who Love Each Other and Want to Spend Their Lives Together?
If love and companionship were sufficient to define marriage, then there would be no reason to deny "marriage" to unions of a child and an adult, or an adult child and his or her aging parent, or to roommates who have no sexual relationship, or to groups rather than couples. Love and companionship are usually considered integral to marriage in our culture, but they are not sufficient to define it as an institution. . . .

Why Should Homosexuals Be Denied the Right to Marry Like Anyone Else?
The fundamental "right to marry" is a right that rests with *individuals*, not with *couples*. Homosexual *individuals* already have exactly the same "right" to marry

as anyone else. Marriage license applications do not inquire as to a person's "sexual orientation.". . .

However, while every individual person is free to get married, *no* person, whether heterosexual or homosexual, has ever had a legal right to marry simply any willing partner. Every person, whether heterosexual or homosexual, is subject to legal restrictions as to whom they may marry. To be specific, every person, regardless of sexual preference, is legally barred from marrying a child, a close blood relative, a person who is already married, or a person of the same sex. There is no discrimination here, nor does such a policy deny anyone the "equal protection of the laws" (as guaranteed by the Constitution), since these restrictions apply equally to every individual.

Some people may wish to do away with one or more of these longstanding restrictions upon one's choice of marital partner. However, the fact that a tiny but vocal minority of Americans desire to have someone of the same sex as a partner does not mean that they have a "right" to do so, any more than the desires of other tiny (but less vocal) minorities of Americans give them a "right" to choose a child, their own brother or sister, or a group of two or more as their marital partners.

Isn't Prohibiting Homosexual "Marriage" Just as Discriminatory as Prohibiting Interracial Marriage, Like Some States Used to Do?

This analogy is not valid at all. Bridging the divide of the sexes by uniting men and women is both a worthy goal and a part of the fundamental purpose of marriage, common to all human civilizations.

Laws against interracial marriage, on the other hand, served only the purpose of preserving a social system of racial segregation. This was both an unworthy goal and one utterly irrelevant to the fundamental nature of marriage.

Allowing a black woman to marry a white man does not change the definition of marriage, which requires one man and one woman. Allowing two men or two women to marry would change that fundamental definition. Banning the "marriage" of same-sex couples is therefore essential to preserve the nature and purpose of marriage itself. . . .

How Would Allowing Same-Sex Couples to Marry Change Society's Concept of Marriage?

As an example, marriage will open wide the door to homosexual adoption, which will simply lead to more children suffering the negative consequences of growing up without both a mother and a father.

Among homosexual men in particular, casual sex, rather than committed relationships, is the rule and not the exception. And even when they do enter into a more committed relationship, it is usually of relatively short duration. For example, a study of homosexual men in the Netherlands (the first country in the world to legalize "marriage" for same-sex couples), published in the journal *AIDS* in 2003, found that the average length of "steady partnerships" was not more than 2 < years (Maria Xiridou et al., in *AIDS* 2003, 17:1029–1038).

In addition, studies have shown that even homosexual men who are in "committed" relationships are not sexually faithful to each other. While infidelity among heterosexuals is much too common, it does not begin to compare to the rates among homosexual men. The 1994 National Health and Social Life Survey, which remains the most comprehensive study of Americans' sexual practices ever undertaken, found that 75 percent of married men and 90 percent of married women had been sexually faithful to their spouse. On the other hand, a major study of homosexual men in "committed" relationships found that only seven out of 156 had been sexually faithful, or 4.5 percent. The Dutch study cited above found that even homosexual men in "steady partnerships" had an average of eight "casual" sex partners per year.

So if same-sex relationships are legally recognized as "marriage," the idea of marriage as a sexually exclusive and faithful relationship will be dealt a serious blow. Adding monogamy and faithfulness to the other pillars of marriage that have already fallen will have overwhelmingly negative consequences for Americans' physical and mental health. . . .

Don't Homosexuals Need Marriage Rights So That They Will Be Able to Visit Their Partners in the Hospital?

The idea that homosexuals are routinely denied the right to visit their partners in the hospital is nonsense. When this issue was raised during debate over the Defense of Marriage Act in 1996, the Family Research Council did an informal survey of nine hospitals in four states and the District of Columbia. None of the administrators surveyed could recall a single case in which a visitor was barred because of their homosexuality, and they were incredulous that this would even be considered an issue.

Except when a doctor limits visitation for medical reasons, final authority over who may visit an adult patient rests with that patient. This is and should be the case regardless of the sexual orientation or marital status of the patient or the visitor.

The only situation in which there would be a possibility that the blood relatives of a patient might attempt to exclude the patient's homosexual partner is if the patient is unable to express his or her wishes due to unconsciousness or mental incapacity. Homosexual partners concerned about this (remote) possibility can effectively preclude it by granting to one another a health care proxy (the legal right to make medical decisions for the patient) and a power of attorney (the right to make all legal decisions for another person). Marriage is not necessary for this. It is inconceivable that a hospital would exclude someone who holds the health care proxy and power of attorney for a patient from visiting that patient, except for medical reasons.

The hypothetical "hospital visitation hardship" is nothing but an emotional smokescreen to distract people from the more serious implications of radically redefining marriage.

Don't Homosexuals Need the Right to Marry Each Other in Order to Ensure That They Will Be Able to Leave Their Estates to Their Partner When They Die?

As with the hospital visitation issue, the concern over inheritance rights is something that simply does not require marriage to resolve it. Nothing in current law prevents homosexual partners from being joint owners of property such as a home or a car, in which case the survivor would automatically become the owner if the partner dies.

An individual may leave the remainder of his estate to whomever he wishes—again, without regard to sexual orientation or marital status—simply by writing a will. As with the hospital visitation issue, blood relatives would only be able to overrule the surviving homosexual partner in the event that the deceased had failed to record his wishes in a common, inexpensive legal document. Changing the definition of a fundamental social institution like marriage is a rather extreme way of addressing this issue. Preparing a will is a much simpler solution.

Don't Homosexuals Need Marriage Rights So That They Can Get Social Security Survivor Benefits When a Partner Dies?

... Social Security survivor benefits were designed to recognize the non-monetary contribution made to a family by the homemaking and child-rearing activities of a wife and mother, and to ensure that a woman and her children would not become destitute if the husband and father were to die.

The Supreme Court ruled in the 1970s that such benefits must be gender-neutral. However, they still are largely based on the premise of a division of roles within a couple between a breadwinner who works to raise money and a homemaker who stays home to raise children.

Very few homosexual couples organize their lives along the lines of such a "traditional" division of labor and roles. They are far more likely to consist of two earners, each of whom can be supported in old age by their own personal Social Security pension.

Furthermore, far fewer homosexual couples than heterosexual ones are raising children at all, for the obvious reason that they are incapable of natural reproduction with each other. This, too, reduces the likelihood of a traditional division of labor among them.

Survivor benefits for the legal (biological or adopted) *children* of homosexual parents (as opposed to their partners) are already available under current law, so "marriage" rights for homosexual couples are unnecessary to protect the interests of these children themselves. ...

Even If "Marriage" Itself Is Uniquely Heterosexual, Doesn't Fairness Require That the Legal and Financial Benefits of Marriage Be Granted to Same-Sex Couples—Perhaps Through "Civil Unions" or "Domestic Partnerships?"

No. The legal and financial benefits of marriage are not an entitlement to be distributed equally to all (if they were, single people would have as much reason to consider them "discriminatory" as same-sex couples). Society grants benefits to marriage because marriage has benefits for society—including, but not limited to, the reproduction of the species in households with the optimal household structure (i.e., the presence of both a mother and a father).

Homosexual relationships, on the other hand, have no comparable benefit for society, and in fact impose substantial costs on society. The fact that AIDS is at least ten times more common among men who have sex with men than among the general population is but one example. ...

harsh

Isn't It Possible That Allowing Homosexuals to "Marry" Each Other Would Allow Them to Participate in Those Benefits as Well?

Opening the gates of "marriage" to homosexuals is far more likely to change the attitudes and behavior of heterosexuals for the worse than it is to change the lifestyles of homosexuals for the better. . . .

What About the Argument That Homosexual Relations Are Harmful? What Do You Mean by That?

Homosexual men experience higher rates of many diseases, including:

- Human Papillomavirus (HPV), which causes most cases of cervical cancer in women and anal cancer in men
- Hepatitis A, B, and C
- Gonorrhea
- Syphilis
- "Gay Bowel Syndrome," a set of sexually transmitted gastrointestinal problems such as proctitis, proctocolitis, and enteritis
- HIV/AIDS (One Canadian study found that as a result of HIV alone, "life expectancy for gay and bisexual men is eight to twenty years less than for all men.")

Lesbian women, meanwhile, have a higher prevalence of:

- Bacterial vaginosis
- Hepatitis C
- HIV risk behaviors
- Cancer risk factors such as smoking, alcohol use, poor diet, and being overweight . . .

Do Homosexuals Have More Mental Health Problems as Well?

Yes. Various research studies have found that homosexuals have higher rates of:

- Alcohol abuse
- Drug abuse
- Nicotine dependence
- Depression
- Suicide

Isn't It Possible That These Problems Result From Society's "Discrimination" Against Homosexuals?

This is the argument usually put forward by pro-homosexual activists. However, there is a simple way to test this hypothesis. If "discrimination" were the cause of homosexuals' mental health problems, then one would expect those problems to be much less common in cities or countries, like San Francisco or the Netherlands, where homosexuality has achieved the highest levels of acceptance.

In fact, the opposite is the case. In places where homosexuality is widely accepted, the physical and mental health problems of homosexuals are greater, not less. This suggests that the real problem lies in the homosexual lifestyle itself, not in society's response to it. In fact, it suggests that increasing the level of social support *for* homosexual behavior (by, for instance, allowing same-sex couples to "marry") would only increase these problems, not reduce them. . . .

Haven't Studies Shown That Children Raised by Homosexual Parents Are No Different From Other Children?

No. This claim is often put forward, even by professional organizations. The truth is that most research on "homosexual parents" thus far has been marred by serious methodological problems. However, even pro-homosexual sociologists Judith Stacey and Timothy Biblarz report that the actual data from key studies show the "no differences" claim to be false.

Surveying the research (primarily regarding lesbians) in an *American Sociological Review* article in 2001, they found that:

- Children of lesbians are less likely to conform to traditional gender norms.
- Children of lesbians are more likely to engage in homosexual behavior.
- Daughters of lesbians are "more sexually adventurous and less chaste."
- Lesbian "co-parent relationships" are more likely to end than heterosexual ones.

A 1996 study by an Australian sociologist compared children raised by heterosexual married couples, heterosexual cohabiting couples, and homosexual cohabiting couples. It found that the children of heterosexual married couples did the best, and children of homosexual couples the worst, in nine of the thirteen academic and social categories measured. . . .

Do the American People Want to See "Marriages" Between Same-Sex Couples Recognized by Law?

No—and in the wake of the June 2003 court decisions to legalize such "marriages" in the Canadian province of Ontario and to legalize homosexual sodomy in the United States, the nation's opposition to such a radical social experiment has actually grown.

Five separate national opinion polls taken between June 24 and July 27, 2003 showed opponents of civil "marriage" for same-sex couples outnumbering supporters by not less than fifteen percentage points in every poll. The wording of poll questions can make a significant difference, and in this case, the poll with the most straightforward language (a Harris/CNN/Time poll asking "Do you think marriages between homosexual men or homosexual women should be recognized as legal by the law?") resulted in the strongest opposition, with 60 percent saying "No" and only 33 percent saying "Yes."

Even where pollsters drop the word "marriage" itself and use one of the euphemisms to describe a counterfeit institution parallel to marriage, we see a decline in public support for the homosexual agenda. The Gallup Poll, for instance, has asked, "Would you favor or oppose a law that would allow homosexual couples to legally form civil unions, giving them some of the legal rights of married couples?"

This question itself is misleading, in that it downplays the legal impact of "civil unions." Vermont, the only U.S. state to adopt "civil unions" (under coercion of a state court), actually gives *all* "of the legal rights of married couples" available under state law to people in a same-sex "civil union"—not just "some." But despite this distortion, a 49-percent-to-49-percent split on this question in May 2003 had changed to opposition by a margin of 58 percent to 37 percent when the *Washington Post* asked the identical question in August 2003.

Even the percentage of Americans willing to declare that "homosexual relations between consenting adults" (never mind homosexual civil "marriage") "should be legal" dropped from 60 percent to only 48 percent between May and July of 2003. The biggest drop in support, a stunning 23 percentage points (from 58 percent to 35 percent), came among African Americans—despite the rhetoric of pro-homosexual activists who seek to frame the issues of "gay rights" and same-sex unions as a matter of "civil rights." . . .

POSTSCRIPT

Should Same-Sex Couples Be Able to Marry?

Part of this discussion is that marriage is a civil right, not an inherent or moral one. Those supporting marriage rights for lesbian and gay couples cite the struggles of the civil rights movement of the 1960s in their current quest for equality for all couples. Among the points they make is that up until 1967, it was still illegal in some states for people of different races to marry. Many opponents find the idea of comparing same-sex marriage to the civil rights struggles of the 1960s and earlier is offensive, that it is like comparing apples and oranges. Many of these individuals believe that sexual orientation is chosen, rather than an inherent part of who one is—unlike race, which is predetermined. Most sexuality experts, however, agree that while we do not know for sure what "causes" a person to be heterosexual, bisexual, or homosexual, it is clear that it is determined very early in life, perhaps even before we are born. Regardless, is marriage a civil right? A legal right? An inherent right?

A final concern deals with mental health issues. What if Kurdek's research had found a different pattern of results indicative of more mental health and relationship issues among same-sex couples than heterosexual couples? Would such findings be a reasonable basis for arguing against same-sex marriage? Currently no heterosexual has to pass a "mental health test" in order to marry. Additionally, heterosexual couples do not have to demonstrate a "healthy" relationship in order to either marry or remain married. Finally, given that on at least some dimensions Kurdek found that same-sex couples actually functioned better than heterosexual couples. Is it possible that heterosexual couples could learn something from same-sex couples?

Suggested Readings

George Chauncey, *Why Marriage? The History Shaping Today's Debate over Gay Equality* (Basic Books, 2004).

Linda Hollingdale, *Creating Civil Union: Opening Hearts and Minds* (Common Humanity Press, 2002).

Jonathan Rauch, *Gay Marriage: Why It Is Good for Gays, Good for Straights, and Good for America* (Owl Books, 2004).

A. Sullivan and J. Landau, *Same-Sex Marriage: Pro and Con* (Vintage Books, 1997).

ISSUE 10

Can Lesbian and Gay Couples Be Appropriate Parents for Children?

YES: American Psychological Association, from *APA Policy Statement on Sexual Orientation, Parents, & Children.* Adopted July, 2004.

NO: Timothy J. Dailey, from "State of the States: Update on Homosexual Adoption in the U.S." *Family Research Council* (no. 243)

ISSUE SUMMARY

YES: The American Psychological Associations Council of Representatives adopted this resolution that was drafted by a task force of expert psychologists. The resolution, based on a thorough review of the literature, opposes any discrimination based on sexual orientation and concludes that children reared by same-sex parents benefit from legal ties to each parent.

NO: Timothy J. Dailey, senior research fellow at the Center for Marriage and Family Studies, provides an overview of state laws pertaining to adoption by lesbian or gay parents. He points to studies showing that children do much better in family settings that include both a mother and a father, and that the sexual behaviors same-sex parents engage in make them, by definition, inappropriate role models for children.

Currently, there are thousands of children awaiting adoption. In many cases, there are strict requirements as to who can and cannot adopt. In one country, for example, a heterosexual couple must be married for at least four years—and if they already have one child, they can only adopt a child of a different. Most countries do not allow same-sex couples or openly lesbian or gay individuals to adopt children.

In the United States, same-sex couples can adopt in a number of ways. Some will adopt as single parents, even though they are in a long-term, committed relationship with another person, because the state or agency does not permit same-sex couples to adopt together. Others will do what is called "second parent" adoption—where one partner is the biological parent of the child, and the other can become the other legal parent by going through the court system. In other cases, the biological parent must terminate her or his own rights so that there can be a "joint adoption." Both parents jointly adopt the child and become equal, legal parents. This applies to unmarried different-sex couples, too.

There are a range of feelings about who should or should not parent children. Some individuals feel that children should be raised by a man and a woman who are married, not by a gay or lesbian individual or couple. Starting with the premise that homosexuality is wrong, they feel that such a relationship is an inappropriate context in which to raise children. For some of these opponents of lesbian and gay parenting, homosexuality is defined by behaviors. Opponents believe that children would be harmed if they grew up in gay or lesbian families, in part because they would grow up without a mother figure if raised by gay men or without a father figure if raised by lesbians. Additionally, because they fear that sexual orientation and behaviors can be learned, they also fear that a child raised by a lesbian or gay couple will be more likely to come out as lesbian or gay her or himself.

Other people do not believe that a person's sexual orientation determines her or his ability to parent. Whether a person is raised by one parent, two men, two women, or a man and a woman is less important than any individual's or couple's ability to love, support, and care for a child. They oppose the concept that a heterosexual couple in which there is abuse or where there are inappropriate sexual boundaries would be considered preferable to a lesbian or gay couple in a long-term, committed relationship who care for each other and their children. They point to the fact that most lesbian, gay, and bisexual adults were raised by heterosexual parents. Therefore, they believe, being raised by a lesbian or gay couple will not create lesbian, gay, or bisexual children, any more than being raised by a heterosexual, married couple would guarantee heterosexuality.

Some state laws support same-sex couples' right to adopt children, and some do not. In New Jersey, California, Connecticut, and Massachusetts, for example, joint or second parent adoption is currently available. In Utah, married heterosexual couples are given priority for foster or adoptive children, and in Mississippi, there is a law that outright bans a same-sex couple from being able to adopt children.

As you read this issue, think about what you think the characteristics of a good parent are. Can these characteristics be found only in heterosexual relationships, or can they be fulfilled by a same-sex relationship? Does the gender of a same-sex relationship affect your feelings on the subject? For example, do you find two women raising a child more or less threatening than two men?

In the following selections, the American Psychological Association's resolution concludes that there is no empirical evidence to support the claim that children raised by same-sex parents are harmed psychologically and that all children benefit from legal ties to both parents. Timothy J. Dailey asserts that gay men are sexually promiscuous, and are therefore poor role models and parents for children. Lesbians, he believes, are ineffective parents because they are raising a child without the presence and influence of a father figure, which theorists, he maintains, argue is vital to the psychosocial development of children, male and female.

American Psychological
Association

 **YES**

APA Policy Statement on Sexual Orientation, Parents, & Children

Research Summary

Lesbian and Gay Parents

Many lesbians and gay men are parents. In the 2000 U.S. Census, 33% of female same-sex couple households and 22% of male same-sex couple households reported at least one child under the age of 18 living in the home. Despite the significant presence of at least 163,879 households headed by lesbian or gay parents in U.S. society, three major concerns about lesbian and gay parents are commonly voiced (Falk, 1994; Patterson, Fulcher & Wainright, 2002). These include concerns that lesbians and gay men are mentally ill, that lesbians are less maternal than heterosexual women, and that lesbians' and gay men's relationships with their sexual partners leave little time for their relationships with their children. In general, research has failed to provide a basis for any of these concerns (Patterson, 2002, 2004a; Perrin, 2002; Tasker, 1999; Tasker & Golombok, 1997). First, homosexuality is not a psychological disorder (Conger, 1975). Although exposure to prejudice and discrimination based on sexual orientation may cause acute distress (Mays & Cochran, 2001; Meyer, 2003), there is no reliable evidence that homosexual orientation per se impairs psychological functioning. Second, beliefs that lesbian and gay adults are not fit parents have no empirical foundation (Patterson, 2000, 2004a; Perrin, 2002). Lesbian and heterosexual women have not been found to differ markedly in their approaches to child rearing (Patterson, 2002; Tasker, 1999). Members of gay and lesbian couples with children have been found to divide the work involved in childcare evenly, and to be satisfied with their relationships with their partners (Patterson, 2000, 2004a). The results of some studies suggest that lesbian mothers' and gay fathers' parenting skills may be superior to those of matched heterosexual parents. There is no scientific basis for concluding that lesbian mothers or gay fathers are unfit parents on the basis of their sexual orientation (Armesto, 2002; Patterson, 2000; Tasker & Golombok, 1997). On the contrary, results of research suggest that lesbian and gay parents are as likely as heterosexual parents to provide supportive and healthy environments for their children.

Paige, R. U. (2005). Proceedings of the American Psychological Association, Incorporated, for the legislative year 2004. Minutes of the meeting of the Council of Representatives July 28 & 30, 2004, Honolulu, HI. Retrieved November 18, 2004, from the World Wide Web http://www.apa.org/governance/.

Children of Lesbian and Gay Parents

As the social visibility and legal status of lesbian and gay parents has increased, three major concerns about the influence of lesbian and gay parents on children have been often voiced (Falk; 1994; Patterson, Fulcher & Wainright, 2002). One is that the children of lesbian and gay parents will experience more difficulties in the area of sexual identity than children of heterosexual parents. For instance, one such concern is that children brought up by lesbian mothers or gay fathers will show disturbances in gender identity and/or in gender role behavior. A second category of concerns involves aspects of children's personal development other than sexual identity. For example, some observers have expressed fears that children in the custody of gay or lesbian parents would be more vulnerable to mental breakdown, would exhibit more adjustment difficulties and behavior problems, or would be less psychologically healthy than other children. A third category of concerns is that children of lesbian and gay parents will experience difficulty in social relationships. For example, some observers have expressed concern that children living with lesbian mothers or gay fathers will be stigmatized, teased, or otherwise victimized by peers. Another common fear is that children living with gay or lesbian parents will be more likely to be sexually abused by the parent or by the parent's friends or acquaintances.

Results of social science research have failed to confirm any of these concerns about children of lesbian and gay parents (Patterson, 2000, 2004a; Perrin, 2002; Tasker, 1999). Research suggests that sexual identities (including gender identity, gender-role behavior, and sexual orientation) develop in much the same ways among children of lesbian mothers as they do among children of heterosexual parents (Patterson, 2004a). Studies of other aspects of personal development (including personality, self-concept, and conduct) similarly reveal few differences between children of lesbian mothers and children of heterosexual parents (Perrin, 2002; Stacey & Biblarz, 2001; Tasker, 1999). However, few data regarding these concerns are available for children of gay fathers (Patterson, 2004b). Evidence also suggests that children of lesbian and gay parents have normal social relationships with peers and adults (Patterson, 2000, 2004a; Perrin, 2002; Stacey & Biblarz, 2001; Tasker, 1999; Tasker & Golombok, 1997). The picture that emerges from research is one of general engagement in social life with peers, parents, family members, and friends. Fears about children of lesbian or gay parents being sexually abused by adults, ostracized by peers, or isolated in single-sex lesbian or gay communities have received no scientific support. Overall, results of research suggest that the development, adjustment, and well-being of children with lesbian and gay parents do not differ markedly from that of children with heterosexual parents. *what ages?*

Resolution

WHEREAS APA supports policy and legislation that promote safe, secure, and nurturing environments for all children (DeLeon, 1993, 1995; Fox, 1991; Levant, 2000);

WHEREAS APA has a long-established policy to deplore "all public and private discrimination against gay men and lesbians" and urges "the repeal of all discriminatory legislation against lesbians and gay men" (Conger, 1975);

WHEREAS the APA adopted the Resolution on Child Custody and Placement in 1976 (Conger, 1977, p. 432);

WHEREAS Discrimination against lesbian and gay parents deprives their children of benefits, rights, and privileges enjoyed by children of heterosexual married couples;

WHEREAS some jurisdictions prohibit gay and lesbian individuals and same-sex couples from adopting children, notwithstanding the great need for adoptive parents (Lofton v. Secretary, 2004);

WHEREAS There is no scientific evidence that parenting effectiveness is related to parental sexual orientation: lesbian and gay parents are as likely as heterosexual parents to provide supportive and healthy environments for their children (Patterson, 2000, 2004; Perrin, 2002; Tasker, 1999);

WHEREAS Research has shown that the adjustment, development, and psychological well-being of children is unrelated to parental sexual orientation and that the children of lesbian and gay parents are as likely as those of heterosexual parents to flourish (Patterson, 2004; Perrin, 2002; Stacey & Biblarz, 2001);

THEREFORE BE IT RESOLVED That the APA opposes any discrimination based on sexual orientation in matters of adoption, child custody and visitation, foster care, and reproductive health services;

THEREFORE BE IT FURTHER RESOLVED That the APA believes that children reared by a same-sex couple benefit from legal ties to each parent;

THEREFORE BE IT FURTHER RESOLVED That the APA supports the protection of parent-child relationships through the legalization of joint adoptions and second parent adoptions of children being reared by same-sex couples;

THEREFORE BE IT FURTHER RESOLVED That APA shall take a leadership role in opposing all discrimination based on sexual orientation in matters of adoption, child custody and visitation, foster care, and reproductive health services;

THEREFORE BE IT FURTHER RESOLVED That APA encourages psychologists to act to eliminate all discrimination based on sexual orientation in matters of adoption, child custody and Visitation, foster care, and reproductive health services in their practice, research, education and training ("Ethical Principles," 2002, p. 1063);

THEREFORE BE IT FURTHER RESOLVED That the APA shall provide scientific and educational resources that inform public discussion and public policy development regarding discrimination based on sexual orientation in matters of adoption, child custody and visitation, foster care, and reproductive health services and that assist its members, divisions, and affiliated state, provincial, and territorial psychological associations.

References

Armesto, J. C. (2002). Developmental and contextual factors that influence gay fathers' parental competence: A review of the literature. *Psychology of Men and Masculinity, 3,* 67–78.

Conger, J. J. (1975). Proceedings of the American Psychological Association, Incorporated, for the year 1974: Minutes of the Annual meeting of the Council of Representatives. *American Psychologists, 30,* 620–651.

Conger, J. J. (1977). Proceedings of the American Psychological Association, Incorporated, for the legislative year 1976: Minutes of the Annual Meeting of the Council of Representatives. *American Psychologist, 32,* 408–438.

Fox, R. E. (1991). Proceedings of the American Psychological Association, Incorporated, for the year 1990: Minutes of the annual meeting of the Council of Representatives August 9 and 12, 1990, Boston, MA, and February 8–9, 1991, Washington, DC. *American Psychologist, 45,* 845.

DeLeon, P. H. (1993). Proceedings of the American Psychological Association, Incorporated, for the year 1992: Minutes of the annual meeting of the Council of Representatives August 13 and 16, 1992, and February 26–28, 1993, Washington, DC. *American Psychologist, 48,* 782.

DeLeon, P. H. (1995). Proceedings of the American Psychological Association, Incorporated, for the year 1994: Minutes of the annual meeting of the Council of Representatives August 11 and 14, 1994, Los Angeles, CA, and February 17–19, 1995, Washington, DC. *American Psychologist, 49,* 627–628.

Ethical Principles of Psychologists and Code of Conduct. (2002). *American Psychologists, 57,* 1060–1073.

Levant, R. F. (2000). Proceedings of the American Psychological Association, Incorporated, for the Legislative Year 1999: Minutes of the Annual Meeting of the Council of Representatives February 19–21, 1999, Washington, DC, and August 19 and 22, 1999, Boston, MA, and Minutes of the February, June, August, and December 1999 Meetings of the Board of Directors. *American Psychologist, 55,* 832–890.

Lofton v. Secretary of Department of Children & Family Services, 358 F.3d 804 (11th Cir. 2004).

Mays, V. M. & Cochran, S. D. (2001). Mental health correlates of perceived discrimination among lesbian, gay, and bisexual adults in the United States. *American Journal of Public Health, 91,* 1869–1876.

Meyer, I. H. (2003). Prejudice, social stress, and mental health in lesbian, gay, and bisexual populations: Conceptual issues and research evidence. *Psychological Bulletin, 129,* 674–697.

Patterson, C. J. (2000). Family relationships of lesbians and gay men. *Journal of Marriage and Family, 62,* 1052–1069.

Patterson, C. J. (2004a). Lesbian and gay parents and their children: Summary of research findings. In *Lesbian and gay parenting: A resource for psychologists.* Washington, DC: American Psychological Association.

Patterson, C. J. (2004b). Gay fathers. In M. E. Lamb (Ed.), *The role of the father in child development* (4th Ed.). New York: John Wiley.

Patterson, C. J., Fulcher, M., & Wainright, J. (2002). Children of lesbian and gay parents: Research, law, and policy. In B. L. Bottoms, M. B. Kovera, and B. D. McAuliff (Eds.), *Children, social science and the law* (pp. 176–199). New York: Cambridge University Press.

Perrin, E. C., and the Committee on Psychosocial Aspects of Child and Family Health (2002). Technical Report: Coparent or second-parent adoption by same-sex parents. *Pediatrics, 109,* 341–344.

Stacey, J. & Biblarz, T. J. (2001). (How) Does sexual orientation of parents matter? *American Sociological Review, 65,* 159–183.

Tasker, F. (1999). Children in lesbian-led families—A review. *Clinical Child Psychology and Psychiatry, 4,* 153–166.

Tasker, F., & Golombok, S. (1997). *Growing up in a lesbian family.* New York: Guilford Press.

NO ↩

Timothy J. Dailey

State of the States: Update on Homosexual Adoption in the U.S.

The legal status of homosexual adoption varies from state to state, and is constantly changing due to court decisions and new state laws addressing the issue. Further complicating the issue are gay activist organizations that present misleading accounts of court rulings and laws reflecting unfavorably on homosexual parenting.

States that Specifically Prohibit Gay Adoption

Three states, Florida, Mississippi, and Utah, have passed statutes specifically prohibiting homosexual adoption. The advocates of gay adoption downplay the Utah statute, asserting that it was not intended to prevent adoption by homosexuals. Liz Winfeld, writing in the *Denver Post,* discusses claims that the Utah law was aimed squarely at homosexuals: "Not true. Utah disallows any unmarried person from adopting regardless of gender or orientation."[1] . . .

In fact, the Utah law was enacted specifically to close loopholes in Utah adoption laws that were being taken advantage of by homosexual couples seeking to adopt children. . . .

The ensuing fight led to the legislature passing a statute barring homosexual adoptions. . . .

States that Specifically Permit Gay Adoption

USA Today reports that seven states, including California, Connecticut, Illinois, Massachusetts, New Jersey, New York, Vermont, and the District of Columbia permit homosexuals to adopt.[2] However, at present the inclusion of California on this list is inaccurate.

States that Permit Second-Parent Adoption

Homosexual couples have adopted children through "second-parent" adoption policies in at least twenty states. There is no evidence that homosexuals in the remaining states are permitted to adopt children, a fact admitted by the gay activist Human Rights Campaign (HRC): "In the remaining 24 states, our research has not revealed any second-parent adoptions."[3]

At least one state has reversed its policy of permitting second-parent adoptions. In November 2000, the Superior Court of Pennsylvania ruled that same-sex couples cannot adopt children.[4] In addition, a court decision in California has reversed that state's policy of permitting homosexuals to adopt children. On October 25, 2001, the 4th District Court of Appeal (San Diego) ruled that there was no legal authority under California law permitting second-parent adoptions.[5] . . .

Homosexual Households in the United States

There are widely varying and unsubstantiated claims about the numbers of children being raised in gay and lesbian households. . . .

- The U.S. Census Bureau reports that there are 601,209 (304,148 male homosexual and 297,061 lesbian) same-sex unmarried partner households, for a total of 1,202,418 individuals, in the United States.[6] If one million children were living in households headed by homosexual couples, this would mean that, on average, *every* homosexual household has at least one child.
- However, a survey in *Demography* indicates that 95 percent of partnered male homosexual and 78 percent of partnered lesbian households do *not* have children.[7] This would mean that the one million children presumed to be living in homosexual households would be divided among the 15,000 (five percent of 304,148) male homosexual and 65,000 (22 percent of 297,061) lesbian households that actually have children. This would result in an astounding 12.5 children per gay and lesbian family.

The cases highlighted by the media to generate sympathy for homosexual adoption typically feature "two-parent" homosexual households. Of course, some children are also being raised by a natural parent who identifies himself or herself as homosexual and live alone. Nevertheless, the hypothetical calculations above give some indication of how absurdly inflated most of the estimates are concerning the number of children being raised by homosexuals. Far from being the proven success that some claim, homosexual parenting remains a relatively rare phenomenon.

Implications for Homosexual Parenting

Demands that homosexuals be accorded the right to . . . adopt children fit into the gay agenda by minimizing the differences between homosexual and heterosexual behavior in order to make homosexuality look as normal as possible. However, as already shown, only a small minority of gay and lesbian households have children. Beyond that, the evidence also indicates that comparatively few homosexuals choose to establish households together—the type of setting that is a prerequisite for the rearing of children. Consider the following:

- HRC claims that the U.S. population of gays and lesbians is 10,456,405, or 5 percent of the total U.S. population over 18 years of age.[8] The best available data supports a much lower estimate for those who engage in same-sex sexual relations.[9] However, assuming the higher estimate for the purposes of argument, this would indicate that *only 8.6 percent* of homosexuals (1,202,418 out of 10,456,405) choose to live in a household with a person of the same sex.

- HRC asserts that "30 percent of gay and lesbian people are living in a committed relationship in the same residence."[10] Assuming HRC's own figures, that would mean over three million gays and lesbians are living in such households, which, as shown above, is a wildly inflated estimate over the census figures. It is worth noting that the HRC claim amounts to a tacit admission that 70 percent of gays and lesbians choose not to live in committed relationships and establish households together.
- HRC claims that the numbers of gay and lesbian households were "undercounted" by the census. However, if true, it would represent an unprecedented, massive undercount of 260 percent on the part of the U.S. Census Bureau.

The census figures indicate that only a small minority of gays and lesbians have made the lifestyle choice that is considered a fundamental requisite in any consideration regarding adoption, and only a small percentage of those households actually have children. The evidence thus does not support the claim that significant numbers of homosexuals desire to provide a stable family setting for children.

The Nature of Homosexual "Committed Relationships"

Gay activists admit that the ultimate goal of the drive to legitimize homosexual marriage and adoption is to change the essential character of marriage, removing precisely the aspects of fidelity and chastity that promote stability in the home. They pursue their goal heedless of the fact that such households are unsuitable for the raising of children:

- Paula Ettelbrick, former legal director of the Lambda Legal Defense and Education Fund, has stated, "Being queer is more than setting up house, sleeping with a person of the same gender, and seeking state approval for doing so. . . . Being queer means pushing the parameters of sex, sexuality, and family, and in the process transforming the very fabric of society."[11]
- According to homosexual writer and activist Michelangelo Signorile, the goal of homosexuals is to redefine the term *monogamy.*

For these men the term 'monogamy' simply doesn't necessarily mean sexual exclusivity. . . . The term 'open relationship' has for a great many gay men come to have one specific definition: A relationship in which the partners have sex on the outside often, put away their resentment and jealousy, and discuss their outside sex with each other, or share sex partners.[12]

- The views of Signorile and Ettelbrick regarding marriage are widespread in the homosexual community. According to the *Mendola Report,* a mere 26 percent of homosexuals believe that commitment is most important in a marriage relationship.[13] . . .

Even those who support the concept of homosexual "families" admit to their unsuitability for children:

- In their study in *Family Relations,* L. Koepke et al. observed, "Even individuals who believe that same-sex relationships are a legitimate choice for adults may feel that children will suffer from being reared in such families."[14]
- Pro-homosexual researchers, J. J. Bigner and R. B. Jacobson describe the homosexual father as "socioculturally unique," trying to take on "two apparently opposing roles: that of a father (with all its usual connotations) and that of a homosexual man." They describe the homosexual father as "both structurally and psychologically at social odds with his interest in keeping one foot in both worlds: parenting and homosexuality."[15]

In truth, the two roles are fundamentally incompatible. The instability, susceptibility to disease, and domestic violence that is disproportionate in homosexual relationships would normally render such households unfit to be granted custody of children. However, in the current social imperative to grant legitimacy to the practice of homosexuality in every conceivable area of life, such considerations are often ignored.

But children are not guinea pigs to be used in social experiments in redefining the institutions of marriage and family. They are vulnerable individuals with vital emotional and developmental needs. The great harm done by denying them both a mother and a father in a committed marriage will not easily be reversed, and society will pay a grievous price for its ill-advised adventurism.

Notes

1. Liz Winfeld, "In a Family Way," *Denver Post,* November 28, 2001.

2. Marilyn Elias, "Doctor's Back Gay "Co-Parents," *USA Today,* February 3, 2002.

3. "Chapter 4: Second-Parent Adoption," in *The Family* (Human Rights Campaign, 2002): available at: www.hrc.org/familynet/documents/SoTF_Chapter_4.pdf

4. Ibid.

5. Bob Egelko, "Court Clarifies Decision on Adoptions," *San Francisco Chronicle,* November 22, 2001. The decision is under review by the California Supreme Court.

6. "PCT 14: Unmarried-Partner Households by Sex of Partners" (U.S. Census Bureau: Census 2000 Summary File 1).

7. Dan Black et al., "Demographics of the Gay and Lesbian Population in the United States: Evidence from Available Systematic Data Sources," *Demography* 37 (May 2000): 150.

8. David M. Smith and Gary J. Gates, "Gay and Lesbian Families in the United States: Same-Sex Unmarried Partner Households," *Human Rights Campaign* (August 22, 2001): 2.

9. Dan Black et al., "Demographics of the Gay and Lesbian Population," "4.7 percent of men in the combined samples have had at least one same-sex experience since age 18, but only 2.5 percent of men have engaged in exclusively same-sex sex over the year preceding the survey. Similarly, 3.5 percent of women have had

at least one same-sex sexual experience, but only 1.4 percent have had exclusively same-sex sex over the year preceding the survey." (p. 141.)

10. Ibid.

11. Paula Ettelbrick, quoted in William B. Rubenstein, "Since When Is Marriage a Path to Liberation?" *Lesbians, Gay Men, and the Law,* (New York: The New Press, 1993), pp. 398, 400.

12. Michelangelo Signorile, *Life Outside* (New York: HarperCollins, 1997), p. 213.

13. Mary Mendola, *The Mendola Report* (New York: Crown, 1980), p. 53.

14. L. Koepke et al., "Relationship Quality in a Sample of Lesbian Couples with Children and Child-free Lesbian Couples," *Family Relations* 41 (1992): 228.

15. Bigner and Jacobson, "Adult Responses to Child Behavior and Attitudes Toward Fathering," Frederick W. Bozett, ed., *Homosexuality and the Family* (New York: Harrington Park Press, 1989), pp. 174, 175.

POSTSCRIPT

Can Lesbian and Gay Couples Be Appropriate Parents for Children?

Parenting is an area that has so many unknown factors, influences, and outcomes. Two-parent, high-income families sometimes have children who grow up with emotional and/or behavioral problems. Single parents can raise healthy, well-adjusted children. Some heterosexual couples raise children effectively and some do not; some lesbian or gay couples raise children effectively, and some do not. Some parents abuse their children; most do not.

While there is much research exploring correlations between economic health, number of parents, and other factors, literature reviewing the connections between a parent's sexual orientation and her or his ability to parent remains inconclusive. There are studies maintaining that children need to be raised by a married, heterosexual couple, and there are studies asserting that a same-sex couple can do just as effective a job.

There is also insufficient information about sexual orientation itself, and the effects that having a lesbian, gay, or bisexual parent may or may not have on a child. The lack of information and plethora of misinformation breed fear. When people are afraid, they want to protect—in this case, people who do not understand the bases of sexual orientation feel they need to protect children. In doing so, they sometimes make decisions that are not always in the best interest of the child. For example, in 1996, a divorced heterosexual couple living in Florida was battling over custody of their 11-year-old daughter. The male partner had recently completed an eight-year prison sentence for the murder of his first wife, and had married his third. His ex-wife, however, had since met and partnered with a woman. A judge determined that the man and his new wife would provide a more appropriate home for the child than the child's mother because she was in a relationship with another woman. In the end, the judge believed that the child would do best in a home with a mother and a father, even though the father was convicted of second-degree murder and accused of sexually molesting his daughter from his first marriage.

How do you feel about this? If you feel that heterosexual couples are more appropriate parents than same-sex couples, how would the fact that one of the heterosexual partners had committed a capital crime affect your opinion?

Sometimes, we argue for what we think "should be" in a given situation. A challenge arises when comparing the "should be" to the "is"—what we think is best as opposed to the reality. If you feel that heterosexual married couples make the best parents, what should be done with those same-sex couples who are providing a loving, stable home for their children? Would it be best to leave the child where she or he is, or do you think the child would be better off removed from her or his existing family structure and placed with a heterosexual couple? Clearly, this is a discussion and debate that will continue as more and more same-sex couples not only adopt, but also have biological children of their own.

Suggested Readings

Jane Drucker (2001). *Lesbian and Gay Families Speak Out: Understanding the Joys and Challenges of Diverse Family Life*. HarperCollins: New York.

Noelle Howey, Ellen Samuels, Margarethe Cammermeyer, & Dan Savage (2000). *Out of the Ordinary: Essays on Growing Up with Gay, Lesbian, and Transgender Parents*. St. Martin's Press: New York.

Patricia Morgan (2002). *Children as trophies? Examining the evidence on same-sex parenting*. The Christian Institute: Newcastle upon Tyne, NE, UK.

On the Internet . . .

About Women's Issues

This Web site addresses a number of issues related to gender and the world of work.

http://womensissues.about.com/od/
genderdiscrimination/i/isgendergap.htm

International Labour Organization

This Web site provides a comprehensive bibliography of materials related to gender issues and women at work.

http://www.ilo.org/public/english/
support/publ/textww.htm

World Alliance for Citizen Participation

CIVICUS: World Alliance for Citizen Participation is an international alliance of over 1000 members from 105 countries that has worked for over a decade to strengthen citizen action and civil society throughout the world, especially in areas where participatory democracy and citizens' freedom of association are threatened.

http://www.civicus.org/new/default.asp

Gender at Work

The Web site for Gender at Work was created in June 2001 by AWID (Association for Women's Rights in Development), WLP (Women's Learning Partnership), CIVICUS (World Alliance for Citizen Participation), and UNIFEM (United Nations Fund for Women). They state "We aim to develop new theory and practice on how organizations can change gender-biased institutional rules (the distribution of power, privileges and rights), values (norms and attitudes), and practices. We also aim to change the political, accountability, cultural and knowledge systems of organizations to challenge social norms and gender inequity."

http://www.genderatwork.org/index.php/
about/genderquotes

The New York Times

Read an article in the *New York Times* by Cornelia Dean that discusses the problems girls who are good at math encounter. People who encounter girls and women who are good at math and science treat them as though there is something wrong with them.

http://www/nytimes.com/2005/02/01/
science/01math.html

PART 4

From 9 to 5: Gender in the World of Work

*T*here are few places other than the workplace where gendered patterns are more apparent. There are sex-segregated jobs: "pink" collar jobs for women and "blue" collar jobs for men. Within occupational categories there is sex-stratification, with men more often holding the higher, more prestigious and better-paying positions, such as anesthesiologist versus pediatrician, or corporate lawyer versus family lawyer. Women on average make $ .75 for each man's dollar; this holds across race, ethnicity, social class, educational level, and work status (full-time or part-time). Such disparities provoke heated discussion. Are they the result of discrimination against women in the workplace or are they justifiable differences based on natural talents, such as purported differences in mathematical, reasoning and spatial abilities, and women's greater likelihood than men of moving in and out of the workplace due to parenting responsibilities? In what ways does gender influence women's efforts to balance work and family interests and responsibilities? Why do we ask the question about the impact on children of mothers working outside the home but never the question of the impact of fathers working? What are the ramifications of this question for poor people, especially women? Are these women to be blamed for their status as single mothers on welfare? As you explore the issues raised in this section consider the competing, or perhaps complementary, explanations for gender differences in the workplace: biologically based differences that lead to differences in interests, motivations, and achievement level and/or culturally based differences, such as discrimination in hiring and promotion practices, the devaluing of women's work, the social rejection of competent women, and the lack or role models and mentors.

- Do Sex Differences in Careers in Mathematics and Sciences Have a Biological Basis?

- Is the Gender Wage Gap Justified?

- Are Gender Inequalities Primarily Responsible for the Increased Number of Low-Wage Single-Mother Families?

ISSUE 11

Do Sex Differences in Careers in Mathematics and Sciences Have a Biological Basis?

YES: Steven Pinker, from "The Science of Gender and Science: Pinker vs. Spelke Debate," *Edge: The Third Culture*, 2005

NO: Elizabeth Spelke, from "The Science of Gender and Science: Pinker vs. Spelke Debate," *Edge: The Third Culture*, 2005

ISSUE SUMMARY

YES: Steven Pinker reviews arguments supporting the claim that there is a biological basis for gender differences in math and science.

NO: Elizabeth Spelke argues that the underrepresentation of women in the sciences is due to environmental factors.

Cognition represents a complex system of skills that enable the processing of different types of information. Cognitive processes underlie our intellectual activities and many other daily tasks. For three decades, researchers have actively explored whether or not males and females differ in their cognitive abilities. The most common taxonomy of cognitive processes used in cognitive sex differences research is based on the type of information used in a cognitive task: verbal (words), quantitative (numbers), and visual-spatial (figural representations).

The study of cognitive sex differences became especially active after the publication of Eleanor Emmons Maccoby and Carol Nagy Jacklin's now famous book entitled *The Psychology of Sex Differences* (Stanford University Press, 1974). While concluding with a generally skeptical perspective on the existence of sex difference, the authors maintained that one area in which the sexes did appear to differ was intellectual ability and functioning. Specifically, the sexes appeared to differ in verbal, quantitative, and spatial abilities.

This compilation and synthesis of sex comparison findings spawned extensive research on sex differences in numerous areas of functioning but especially in the domain of cognitive abilities. Researchers began to use the quantitative technique of meta-analysis, which has been used to explore whether or not any sex differences change in magnitude over the life cycle or over time, whether or not there is cross-cultural consistency in any sex differences, and whether or not cognitive sex differences are found across various ethnic groups.

At an academic conference in January, 2005 Harvard's president Lawrence Summers gave a talk in which he suggested that innate differences in the math ability of women and men help explain why so few women are found at the highest levels in careers in mathematics and sciences. His speech has generated a huge outcry from feminists and numerous scholars who dispute such claims.

Summers's comments have refueled the ongoing debate regarding the biological basis of math and science abilities. We know that in careers in mathematics and the sciences women tend to earn 25 percent less than men. They are twice as likely to be out of a job. Consider as well that only 2.5 percent of Nobel Prize winners are female and only 3 percent of the members of the U.S. National Academy of Sciences are women.

There has been contradiction among findings. Some researchers document what they describe as important sex differences; others report negligible sex differences that have become smaller over time. When sex differences are described, males show better visual-spatial ability, especially the ability to mentally rotate three-dimensional figures. Males are also found to have greater mathematical ability. Females show better verbal fluency.

This is a politically charged area of research because the stakes are high for the more and less cognitively able. Cognitive abilities relate to valued and "marketable" occupational and societal skills, often putting males at an advantage for higher social status and advancement. This "cognitive ability hierarchy" is not determined by findings of sex differences but reflect differential societal valuation of different cognitive abilities. Critical questions are, What causes cognitive sex differences? Must cognitive ability differences between the sexes, and thus societal inequalities, continue?

A criticism of explanatory research (including both biological and sociocultural studies) is the lack of direct testing of causal links. For example, sex differences in brain structure may exist, as might sex differences in spatial test performance. But do sex differences in brain structure *cause* sex-differentiated performance on spatial tests? Evidence is lacking for such causal claims. Observers caution that we must discriminate between causal theory and scientific evidence when evaluating causal claims.

The debate falls into the classic concern that correlation does not mean causation. Consider a study that was done examining visual-spatial skills in children. Boys on average outperformed girls. However, the sex disparity was eliminated after girls had been given training in the requisite skills. In these selections you will be reading a debate that was held at Harvard between two professors. Steven Pinker summarizes the mass of evidence supporting the claim that there is a biological basis for sex differences in math and science and believes that "social forces are over-rated as the causes of gender differences." Elizabeth Spelke could not disagree more. For her, social factors are by major forces causing the gap between the sexes in careers in math and science.

183

The Science of Gender and Science: Pinker vs. Spelke, A Debate

(STEVEN PINKER:) . . . For those of you who just arrived from Mars, there has been a certain amount of discussion here at Harvard on a particular datum, namely the under-representation of women among tenure-track faculty in elite universities in physical science, math, and engineering. Here are some recent numbers:

As with many issues in psychology, there are three broad ways to explain this phenomenon. One can imagine an extreme "nature" position: that males but not females have the talents and temperaments necessary for science. Needless to say, only a madman could take that view. The extreme nature position has no serious proponents.

There is an extreme "nurture" position: that males and females are biologically indistinguishable, and all relevant sex differences are products of socialization and bias.

Then there are various intermediate positions: that the difference is explainable by some combination of biological differences in average temperaments and talents interacting with socialization and bias.

Liz [Elizabeth Spelke] has embraced the extreme nurture position. There is an irony here, because in most discussions in cognitive science she and I are put in the same camp, namely the "innatists," when it comes to explaining the mind. But in this case Liz has said that there is "not a shred of evidence" for the biological factor, that "the evidence against there being an advantage for males in intrinsic aptitude is so overwhelming that it is hard for me to see how one can make a case at this point on the other side," and that "it seems to me as conclusive as any finding I know of in science."

Well we certainly aren't seeing the stereotypical gender difference in *confidence* here! Now, I'm a controversial guy. I've taken many controversial positions over the years, and, as a member of *Homo sapiens,* I think I am right on all of them. But I don't think that in any of them I would say there is "not a shred of evidence" for the other side, even if I think that the evidence *favors* one side. I would not say that the other side "can't even make a case" for their position, even if I think that their case is not as *good as* the one I favor. And as for saying that a position is "as conclusive as any finding in science"—well, we're talking about social science here! . . .

These are extreme statements—especially in light of the fact that an enormous amount of research, summarized in these and many other literature reviews, in fact points to a very different conclusion. I'll quote from one of them, a book called *Sex Differences in Cognitive Ability* by Diane Halpern. She is a respected psychologist, recently elected as president of the American Psychological Association, and someone with no theoretical axe to grind. She does not subscribe to any particular theory, and has been a critic, for example, of evolutionary psychology. And here what she wrote in the preface to her book:

> At the time I started writing this book it seemed clear to me that any between sex differences in thinking abilities were due to socialization practices, artifacts, and mistakes in the research. After reviewing a pile of journal articles that stood several feet high, and numerous books and book chapters that dwarfed the stack of journal articles, I changed my mind. The literature on sex differences in cognitive abilities is filled with inconsistent findings, contradictory theories, and emotional claims that are unsupported by the research. Yet despite all the noise in the data, clear and consistent messages could be heard. There are real and in some cases sizable sex differences with respect to some cognitive abilities. Socialization practices are undoubtedly important, but there is also good evidence that biological sex differences play a role in establishing and maintaining cognitive sex differences, a conclusion I wasn't prepared to make when I began reviewing the relevant literature.

This captures my assessment perfectly.

Again for the benefit of the Martians in this room: This isn't just any old issue in empirical psychology. There are obvious political colorings to it, and I want to begin with a confession of my own politics. I am a feminist. I believe that women have been oppressed, discriminated against, and harassed for thousands of years. I believe that the two waves of the feminist movement in the 20th century are among the proudest achievements of our species, and I am proud to have lived through one of them, including the effort to increase the representation of women in the sciences.

But it is crucial to distinguish the *moral* proposition that people should not be discriminated against on account of their sex—which I take to be the core of feminism—and the *empirical* claim that males and females are biologically indistinguishable. They are not the same thing. Indeed, distinguishing them is essential to protecting the core of feminism. Anyone who takes an honest interest in science has to be prepared for the facts on a given issue to come out either way. And that makes it essential that we not hold the ideals of feminism hostage to the latest findings from the lab or field. Otherwise, if the findings come out as showing a sex difference, one would either have to say, "I guess sex discrimination wasn't so bad after all," or else furiously suppress or distort the findings so as to preserve the ideal. The truth cannot be sexist. Whatever the facts turn out to be, they should not be taken to compromise the core of feminism.

Why study sex differences? Believe me, being the Bobby Riggs of cognitive science is not my idea of a good time. So should I care about them, especially since they are not the focus of my own research?

First, differences between the sexes are part of the human condition. We all have a mother and a father. Most of us are attracted to members of the opposite sex, and the rest of us notice the difference from those who do. And we can't help but notice the sex of our children, friends, and our colleagues, in every aspect of life.

Also, the topic of possible sex differences is of great scientific interest. Sex is a fundamental problem in biology, and sexual reproduction and sex differences go back a billion years. . . .

The nature and source of sex differences are also of practical importance. Most of us agree that there are aspects of the world, including gender disparities, that we want to change. But if we want to *change* the world we must first *understand* it, and that includes understanding the sources of sex differences.

Let's get back to the datum to be explained. In many ways this is an *exotic* phenomenon. It involves biologically unprepared talents and temperaments: evolution certainly did not shape any part of the mind to do the work of a professor of mechanical engineering at MIT, for example. The datum has nothing to do with basic cognitive processes, or with those we use in our everyday lives, in school, or even in most college courses, where indeed there are few sex differences.

Also, we are talking about extremes of achievement. Most women are not qualified to be math professors at Harvard because most *men* aren't qualified to be math professors at Harvard. These are extremes in the population.

And we're talking about a subset of fields. Women are not under-represented to nearly the same extent in all academic fields, and certainly not in all prestigious professions.

Finally, we are talking about a statistical effect. This is such a crucial point that I have to discuss it in some detail.

Women are nowhere near absent even from the field in which they are most under-represented. The explanations for sex differences must be statistical as well. And here is a touchstone for the entire discussion:

These are two Gaussian or normal distributions: two bell curves. The X axis stands for any ability you want to measure. The Yaxis stands for the proportion of people having that ability. The overlapping curves are what you get whenever you compare the sexes on any measure in which they differ. In this example, if we say that this is the male curve and this is the female curve, the means may be different, but at any particular ability level there are always representatives of both genders.

So right away a number of public statements that have been made in the last couple of months can be seen as red herrings, and should never have been made by anyone who understands the nature of statistical distributions. This includes the accusation that President Summers implied that "50% of the brightest minds in America do not have the right aptitude for science," that "women just can't cut it," and so on. These statements are statistically illiterate, and have nothing to do with the phenomena we are discussing.

There are some important corollaries of having two overlapping normal distributions. . . . [E]ven when there is only a small difference in the means of two distributions, the more extreme a score, the greater the disparity there will be in the two kinds of individuals having such a score. That is, the ratios get more extreme as you go farther out along the tail. If we hold a magnifying glass to the tail of the distribution, we see that even though the distributions overlap in the bulk of the curves, when you get out to the extremes the difference between the two curves gets larger and larger. . . .

A second important corollary is that tail ratios are affected by differences in variance. And biologists since Darwin have noted that for many traits and many species, males are the more variable gender. So even in cases where the mean for women and the mean for men are the same, the fact that men are more variable implies that the proportion of men would be higher at one tail, and also higher at the other. As it's sometimes summarized: more prodigies, more idiots.

With these statistical points in mind, let me begin the substance of my presentation by connecting the political issue with the scientific one. Economists who study patterns of discrimination have long argued (generally to no avail) that there is a crucial conceptual difference between *difference* and *discrimination*. A departure from a 50-50 sex ratio in any profession does not, by itself, imply that we are seeing discrimination, unless the interests and aptitudes of the two groups are equated. Let me illustrate the point with an example, involving myself.

I work in a scientific field—the study of language acquisition in children—that is in fact dominated by women. Seventy-five percent of the members the main professional association are female, as are a majority of the keynote speakers at our main conference. I'm here to tell you that it's not because men like me have been discriminated against. I decided to study language development, as opposed to, say, mechanical engineering, for many reasons. . . .

Now, all we need to do to explain sex differences without invoking the discrimination or invidious sexist comparisons is to suppose that whatever traits *I* have that predispose *me* to choose (say) child language over (say) mechanical engineering are not exactly equally distributed statistically among men and women. For those of you out there—of either gender—who also are not mechanical engineers, you should understand what I'm talking about.

Okay, so what *are* the similarities and differences between the sexes? There certainly are many similarities. Men and women show no differences in general intelligence or g—on average, they are exactly the same, right on the money. Also, when it comes to the basic categories of cognition—how we negotiate the world and live our lives; our concept of objects, of numbers, of people, of living things, and so on—there are no differences.

Indeed, in cases where there *are* differences, there are as many instances in which women do slightly better than men as ones in which men do slightly better than women. For example, men are better at throwing, but women are more dexterous. Men are better at mentally rotating shapes; women are better at visual memory. Men are better at mathematical problem-solving; women are better at mathematical calculation. And so on.

But there are at least six differences that are relevant to the datum we have been discussing. The literature on these differences is so enormous that I can only touch on a fraction of it. . . .

1. The first difference, long noted by economists studying employment practices, is that men and women differ in what they state are their priorities in life. To sum it up: men, on average, are more likely to chase status at the expense of their families; women give a more balanced weighting. Once again: Think statistics! The finding is not that women value family and don't value status. It is not that men value status and don't value family. Nor does the finding imply that every last woman has the asymmetry that women show on average or that every last man has the asymmetry that men show on average. But in large data sets, on average, an asymmetry is what you find. . . .

2. Second, interest in people versus things and abstract rule systems. There is a *staggering* amount of data on this trait, because there is an entire field that studies people's vocational interests. . . . [T]here are consistent differences in the kinds of activities that appeal to men and women in their ideal jobs. I'll just discuss one of them: the desire to work with people versus things. There is an enormous average difference between women and men in this dimension, about one standard deviation.

   And this difference in interests will tend to cause people to gravitate in slightly different directions in their choice of career. The occupation that fits best with the "people" end of the continuum is "director of a community services organization." The occupations that fit best with the "things" end are physicist, chemist, mathematician, computer programmer, and biologist. . . .

3. Third, risk. Men are by far the more reckless sex. In a large meta-analysis involving 150 studies and 100,000 participants, in 14 out of 16 categories of risk-taking, men were over-represented. The two sexes were equally represented in the other two categories, one of which was smoking, for obvious reasons. And two of the largest sex differences were in "intellectual risk taking" and "participation in a risky experiment." . . .

4. Fourth, three-dimensional mental transformations: the ability to determine whether the drawings in each of these pairs the same 3-dimensional shape. Again I'll appeal to a meta-analysis, this one containing 286 data sets and 100,000 subjects. The authors conclude, "we have specified a number of tests that show highly significant sex differences that are stable across age, at least after puberty, and have not decreased in recent years." Now, as I mentioned, for some kinds of spatial ability, the advantage goes to women, but in "mental rotation, spatial perception," and "spatial visualization" the advantage goes to men.

   Now, does this have any relevance to scientific achievement? We don't know for sure, but there's some reason to think that it does. In psychometric studies, three-dimensional spatial visualization is correlated with mathematical problem-solving. And mental manipulation of objects in three dimensions figures prominently in the memoirs and introspections of most creative physicists and chemists, including Faraday, Maxwell, Tesla, Kéekulé, and Lawrence, all of whom claim to have hit upon their discoveries by dynamic visual imagery and only later set them down in equations. . . .

5. Fifth, mathematical reasoning. Girls and women get better school grades in mathematics and pretty much everything else these days. And women are better at mathematical calculation. But consistently, men score better on mathematical word problems and on tests of mathematical reasoning, at least statistically. Again, here is a meta analysis, with 254 data sets and 3 million subjects. It shows no significant difference in childhood; this is a difference that emerges around puberty, like many secondary sexual characteristics. But there are sizable differences in adolescence and adulthood, especially in high-end samples. . . .

Now why is there a discrepancy with grades? Do SATs and other tests of mathematical reasoning aptitude underpredict grades, or do grades overpredict high-end aptitude? At the Radical Forum Liz [Elizabeth Spelke] was completely explicit in which side she takes, saying that "the tests are no good," unquote. But if the tests are really so useless, why does every major graduate program in science still use them—including the very departments at Harvard and MIT in which Liz and I have selected our own graduate students?

I think the reason is that school grades are affected by homework and by the ability to solve the kinds of problems that have already been presented in lecture and textbooks. Whereas the aptitude tests are designed to test the application of mathematical knowledge to unfamiliar problems. And this, of course, is closer to the way that math is used in actually *doing* math and science.

Indeed, contrary to . . . the popular opinion of many intellectuals, the tests are *surprisingly* good. There is an enormous amount of data on the predictive power of the SAT. . . . [T]he tests predict earnings, occupational choice, doctoral degrees, the prestige of one's degree, the probability of having a tenure-track position, and the number of patents. Moreover this predictive power is the same for men and for women. . . .

6. Finally there's a sex difference in variability. It's crucial here to look at the right samples. Estimates of variance depend highly on the tails of the distribution, which by definition contain smaller numbers of people. Since people at the tails of the distribution in many surveys are likely to be weeded out for various reasons, it's important to have large representative samples from national populations. In this regard the gold standard is the *Science* paper by Novell and Hedges, which reported six large stratified probability samples. They found that in 35 out of 37 tests, including all of the tests in math, space, and science, the male variance was greater than the female variance. . . .

Now the fact that these six gender differences exist does not mean that they are innate. This of course is a much more difficult issue to resolve. A necessary preamble to this discussion is that nature and nurture are not alternatives; it is possible that the explanation for a given sex difference involves some of each. The only issue is whether the contribution of biology is greater than zero. I think that there are ten kinds of evidence that the contribution of biology *is* greater than zero, though of course it is nowhere near 100 percent.

1. First, there are many biological mechanisms by which a sex difference *could* occur. There are large differences between males and females in levels of sex hormones, especially prenatally, in the first six months of life, and in adolescence. There are receptors for hormones all over the brain, including the cerebral cortex. There are many small differences in men's and women's brains, including the overall size of the brain (even correcting for body size), the density of cortical neurons, the degree of cortical asymmetry, the size of hypothalamic nuclei, and several others.

2. Second, many of the major sex differences—certainly some of them, maybe all of them, are universal. The idea that there are cultures out there somewhere in which everything is the reverse of here turns out to be an academic legend. In his survey of the anthropological literature called *Human Universals,* the anthropologist Donald Brown points out that in all cultures men and women are seen as having different natures; that there is a greater involvement of women in direct child care; more competitiveness in various measures for men than for women; and a greater spatial range traveled by men compared to by women.

   In personality, we have a cross-national survey (if not a true cross-cultural one) in Feingold's meta-analysis, which noted that gender differences in personality are consistent across ages, years of data collection, educational levels, and nations. When it comes to spatial manipulation and mathematical reasoning, we have fewer relevant data, and we honestly don't have true cross-cultural surveys, but we do have cross-national surveys. David Geary and Catherine Desoto found the expected sex difference in mental rotation in ten European countries and in Ghana, Turkey, and China. Similarly, Diane Halpern, analyzing results from ten countries, said that "the majority of the findings show amazing cross-cultural consistency when comparing males and females on cognitive tests."

3. Third, stability over time. Surveys of life interests and personality have shown little or no change in the two generations that have come of age since the second wave of feminism. There is also, famously, *resistance* to change in communities that, for various ideological reasons, were dedicated to stamping out sex differences, and found they were unable to do so. These include the Israeli kibbutz, various American Utopian communes a century ago, and contemporary androgynous academic couples. . . .

4. Fourth, many sex differences can be seen in other mammals. It would be an amazing coincidence if these differences just happened to be replicated in the arbitrary choices made by human cultures at the dawn of time. There are large differences between males and females in many mammals in aggression, in investment in offspring, in play aggression play versus play parenting, and in the range size, which predicts a species' sex differences in spatial ability (such as in solving mazes), at least in polygynous species, which is how the human species is classified. Many primate species even show a sex difference in their interest in physical objects versus conspecifics, a difference seen their patterns of juvenile play. . . .

5. Fifth, many of these differences emerge in early childhood. It is said that there is a technical term for people who believe that little boys

and little girls are born indistinguishable and are molded into their natures by parental socialization. The term is "childless."

Some sex differences seem to emerge even in the first week of life. Girls respond more to sounds of distress, and girls make more eye contact than boys. And in [one] study . . . , newborn boys were shown to be more interested in looking at a physical object than a face, whereas newborn girls were shown to be more interested in looking at a face than a physical object.

A bit later in development there are vast and robust differences between boys and girls, seen all over the world. Boys far more often than girls engage in rough-and-tumble play, which involves aggression, physical activity, and competition. Girls spend a lot more often in cooperative play. Girls engage much more often in play parenting. . . . There are sex differences in intuitive psychology, that is, how well children can read one another's minds. For instance, several large studies show that girls are better than boys in solving the "false belief task," and in interpreting the mental states of characters in stories.

6. Sixth, genetic boys brought up as girls. In a famous 1970s incident called the John/Joan case, one member of a pair of identical twin boys lost his penis in a botched circumcision. . . . Following advice from the leading gender expert of the time, the parents agreed to have the boy castrated, given female-specific hormones, and brought up as a girl. All this was hidden from him throughout his childhood.

When I was an undergraduate the case was taught to me as proof of how gender roles are socially acquired. But it turned out that the facts had been suppressed. When "Joan" and her family were interviewed years later, it turned out that from the youngest ages he exhibited boy-typical patterns of aggression and rough-and-tumble play, rejected girl-typical activities, and showed a greater interest in things than in people. At age 14, suffering from depression, his father finally told him the truth. . . .

7. Seventh, a lack of differential treatment by parents and teachers. These conclusions come as a shock to many people. One comes from Lytton and Romney's meta-analysis of sex-specific socialization involving 172 studies and 28,000 children, in which they looked both at parents' reports and at direct observations of how parents treat their sons and daughters—and found few or no differences among contemporary Americans. In particular, there was no difference in the categories "Encouraging Achievement" and "Encouraging Achievement in Mathematics."

There is a widespread myth that teachers (who of course are disproportionately female) are dupes who perpetuate gender inequities by failing to call on girls in class, and who otherwise having low expectations of girls' performance. In fact Jussim and Eccles, in a study of 100 teachers and 1,800 students, concluded that teachers seemed to be basing their perceptions of students on those students' actual performances and motivation.

8. Eighth, studies of prenatal sex hormones: the mechanism that makes boys boys and girls girls in the first place. There is evidence, admittedly squishy in parts, that differences in prenatal hormones make a difference in later thought and behavior even within a given sex. In the

condition called congenital adrenal hyperplasia, girls in utero are subjected to an increased dose of androgens, which is neutralized postnatally. But when they grow up they have male-typical toy preferences—trucks and guns—compared to other girls, male-typical play patterns, more competitiveness, less cooperativeness, and male-typical occupational preferences. However, research on their spatial abilities is inconclusive, and I cannot honestly say that there are replicable demonstrations that CAH women have male-typical patterns of spatial cognition.

Similarly, variations in fetal testosterone, studied in various ways, show that fetal testosterone has a nonmonotic relationship to reduced eye contact and face perception at 12 months, to reduced vocabulary at 18 months, to reduced social skills and greater narrowness of interest at 48 months, and to enhanced mental rotation abilities in the school-age years.

9. Ninth, circulating sex hormones. . . . Though it's possible that all claims of the effects of hormones on cognition will turn out to be bogus, I suspect something will be salvaged from this somewhat contradictory literature. There are, in any case, many studies showing that testosterone levels in the low-normal male range are associated with better abilities in spatial manipulation. And in a variety of studies in which estrogens are compared or manipulated, there is evidence, admittedly disputed, for statistical changes in the strengths and weaknesses in women's cognition during the menstrual cycle, possibly a counterpart to the changes in men's abilities during their daily and seasonal cycles of testosterone.

My last kind of evidence: imprinted X chromosomes. In the past fifteen years an entirely separate genetic system capable of implementing sex differences has been discovered. In the phenomenon called genetic imprinting, studied by David Haig and others, a chromosome such as the X chromosome can be altered depending on whether it was passed on from one's mother or from one's father. This makes a difference in the condition called Turner syndrome, in which a child has just one X chromosome, but can get it either from her mother or her father. When she inherits an X that is specific to girls, on average she has a better vocabulary and better social skills, and is better at reading emotions, at reading body language, and at reading faces.

A remark on stereotypes. . . .

Are these stereotypes? Yes, many of them are (although, I must add, not all of them—for example, women's superiority in spatial memory and mathematical calculation). There seems to be a widespread assumption that if a sex difference conforms to a stereotype, the difference must have been *caused* by the stereotype, via differential expectations for boys and for girls. But of course the causal arrow could go in either direction: stereotypes might *reflect* differences rather than cause them. In fact there's an enormous literature in cognitive psychology which says that people can be good intuitive statisticians when forming categories and that their prototypes for conceptual categories track the statistics of the natural world pretty well. . . .

To sum up: I think there is more than "a shred of evidence" for sex differences that are relevant to statistical gender disparities in elite hard science departments. There are reliable average differences in life priorities, in an interest in people versus things, in risk-seeking, in spatial transformations, in mathematical reasoning, and in variability in these traits. And there are ten kinds of evidence that these differences are not *completely* explained by socialization and bias, although they surely are in part.

A concluding remark. None of this provides grounds for ignoring the biases and barriers that do keep women out of science, as long as we keep in mind the distinction between *fairness* on the one hand and *sameness* on the other. And I will give the final word to Gloria Steinem: "there are very few jobs that actually require a penis or a vagina, and all the other jobs should be open to both sexes."

Elizabeth Spelke

NO

The Science of Gender and Science: Pinker vs. Spelke Debate

(ELIZABETH SPELKE:) . . . I want to start by talking about the points of agreement between Steve [Pinker] and me, and as he suggested, there are many. If we got away from the topic of sex and science, we'd be hard pressed to find issues that we disagree on. Here are a few of the points of agreement that are particularly relevant to the discussions of the last few months.

First, we agree that both our society in general and our university in particular will be healthiest if all opinions can be put on the table and debated on their merits. We also agree that claims concerning sex differences are empirical, they should be evaluated by evidence, and we'll all be happier and live longer if we can undertake that evaluation as dispassionately and rationally as possible. We agree that the mind is not a blank slate; in fact one of the deepest things that Steve and I agree on is that there is such a thing as human nature, and it is a fascinating and exhilarating experience to study it. And finally, I think we agree that the role of scientists in society is rather modest. Scientists find things out. The much more difficult questions of how to use that information, live our lives, and structure our societies are not questions that science can answer. Those are questions that everybody must consider.

So where do we disagree?

We disagree on the answer to the question, why in the world are women scarce as hens' teeth on Harvard's mathematics faculty and other similar institutions? In the current debate, two classes of factors have been said to account for this difference. In one class are social forces, including overt and covert discrimination and social influences that lead men and women to develop different skills and different priorities. In the other class are genetic differences that predispose men and women to have different capacities and to want different things.

In his book, *The Blank Slate,* and again today, Steve [Pinker] argued that social forces are over-rated as causes of gender differences. Intrinsic differences in aptitude are a larger factor, and intrinsic differences in motives are the biggest factor of all. Most of the examples that Steve gave concerned what he takes to be biologically based differences in motives.

My own view is different. I think the big forces causing this gap are social factors. There are no differences in overall intrinsic aptitude for science and mathematics between women and men. Notice that I am not saying the genders are indistinguishable, that men and women are alike in every way, or even that men and women have identical cognitive profiles. I'm saying that when you add up all the things that men are good at, and all the things that women are good at, there is no overall advantage for men that would put them at the top of the fields of math and science.

On the issue of motives, I think we're not in a position to know whether the different things that men and women often say they want stem only from social forces, or in part from intrinsic sex differences. I don't think we can know that now.

I want to start with the issue that's clearly the biggest source of debate between Steve and me: the issue of differences in intrinsic aptitude. This is the only issue that my own work and professional knowledge bear on. Then I will turn to the social forces, as a lay person as it were, because I think they are exerting the biggest effects. . . .

Over the last months, we've heard three arguments that men have greater cognitive aptitude for science. The first argument is that from birth, boys are interested in objects and mechanics, and girls are interested in people and emotions. The predisposition to figure out the mechanics of the world sets boys on a path that makes them more likely to become scientists or mathematicians. The second argument assumes, as Galileo told us, that science is conducted in the language of mathematics. On the second claim, males are intrinsically better at mathematical reasoning, including spatial reasoning. The third argument is that men show greater variability than women, and as a result there are more men at the extreme upper end of the ability distribution from which scientists and mathematicians are drawn. Let me take these claims one by one.

The first claim . . ., is gaining new currency from the work of Simon Baron-Cohen. It's an old idea, presented with some new language. Baron-Cohen says that males are innately predisposed to learn about objects and mechanical relationships, and this sets them on a path to becoming what he calls "systematizers." Females, on the other hand, are innately predisposed to learn about people and their emotions, and this puts them on a path to becoming "empathizers." Since systematizing is at the heart of math and science, boys are more apt to develop the knowledge and skills that lead to math and science.

To anyone as old as I am who has been following the literature on sex differences, this may seem like a surprising claim. The classic reference on the nature and development of sex differences is a book by Eleanor Maccoby and Carol Jacklin that came out in the 1970s. . . . At the top of their list of myths was the idea that males are primarily interested in objects and females are primarily interested in people. They reviewed an enormous literature, in which babies were presented with objects and people to see if they were more interested in one than the other. They concluded that there were no sex differences in these interests. . . .

Let me take you on a whirlwind tour of 30 years of research. . . . From birth, babies perceive objects. They know where one object ends and the next one begins. They can't see objects as well as we can, but as they grow their object perception becomes richer and more differentiated.

Babies also start with rudimentary abilities to represent that an object continues to exist when it's out of view, and they hold onto those representations longer, and over more complicated kinds of changes, as they grow. Babies make basic inferences about object motion: inferences like, the force with which an object is hit determines the speed with which it moves. These inferences undergo regular developmental changes over the infancy period.

In each of these cases, there is systematic developmental change, and there's variability. Because of this variability, we can compare the abilities of male infants to females. Do we see sex differences? The research gives a clear answer to this question: We don't.

Male and female infants are equally interested in objects. Male and female infants make the same inferences about object motion, at the same time in development. They learn the same things about object mechanics at the same time.

Across large numbers of studies, occasionally a study will favor one sex over the other. For example, girls learn that the force with which something is hit influences the distance it moves a month earlier than boys do. But these differences are small and scattered. For the most part, we see high convergence across the sexes. Common paths of learning continue through the preschool years, as kids start manipulating objects to see if they can get a rectangular block into a circular hole. If you look at the rates at which boys and girls figure these things out, you don't find any differences. We see equal developmental paths.

I think this research supports an important conclusion. In discussions of sex differences, we need to ask what's common across the two sexes. One thing that's common is infants don't divide up the labor of understanding the world, with males focusing on mechanics and females focusing on emotions. Male and female infants are both interested in objects and in people, and they learn about both. The conclusions that Maccoby and Jacklin drew in the early 1970s are well supported by research since that time.

Let me turn to the second claim. People may have equal abilities to develop intuitive understanding of the physical world, but formal math and science don't build on these intuitions. Scientists use mathematics to come up with new characterizations of the world and new principles to explain its functioning. Maybe males have an edge in scientific reasoning because of their greater talent for mathematics.

[F]ormal mathematics is not something we have evolved to do; it's a recent accomplishment. Animals don't do formal math or science, and neither did humans back in the Pleistocene. If there is a biological basis for our mathematical reasoning abilities, it must depend on systems that evolved for other purposes, but that we've been able to harness for the new purpose of representing and manipulating numbers and geometry.

Research from the intersecting fields of cognitive neuroscience, neuropsychology, cognitive psychology, and cognitive development provide evidence for five "core systems" at the foundations of mathematical reasoning. The first is a system for representing small exact numbers of objects—the difference between *one, two,* and *three.* This system emerges in human infants at about five months of age, and it continues to be present in adults. The second is a system for discriminating large, approximate numerical magnitudes—the difference between a set of about ten things and a set of about 20 things. That system also emerges early in infancy, at four or five months, and continues to be present and functional in adults.

The third system is probably the first uniquely human foundation for numerical abilities: the system of natural number concepts that we construct as children when we learn verbal counting. That construction takes place between about the ages of two and a half and four years. The last two systems are first seen in children when they navigate. One system represents the geometry of the surrounding layout. The other system represents landmark objects.

All five systems have been studied quite extensively in large numbers of male and female infants. We can ask, are there sex differences in the development of any of these systems at the foundations of mathematical thinking? Again, the answer is no. . . .

[Studies] support two important points. First, indeed there is a biological foundation to mathematical and scientific reasoning. We are endowed with core knowledge systems that emerge prior to any formal instruction and that serve as a basis for mathematical thinking. Second, these systems develop equally in males and females. Ten years ago, the evolutionary psychologist and sex difference researcher, David Geary, reviewed the literature that was available at that time. He concluded that there were no sex differences in "primary abilities" underlying mathematics. What we've learned in the last ten years continues to support that conclusion.

Sex differences do emerge at older ages. Because they emerge later in childhood, it's hard to tease apart their biological and social sources. But before we attempt that task, let's ask what the differences are.

I think the following is a fair statement, both of the cognitive differences that Steve described and of others. When people are presented with a complex task that can be solved through multiple different strategies, males and females sometimes differ in the strategy that they prefer.

For example, if a task can only be solved by representing the geometry of the layout, we do not see a difference between men and women. But if the task can be accomplished either by representing geometry or by representing individual landmarks, girls tend to rely on the landmarks, and boys on the geometry. . . .

Because of these differences, males and females sometimes show differing cognitive profiles on timed tests. When you have to solve problems fast, some strategies will be faster than others. Thus, females perform better at some verbal, mathematical and spatial tasks, and males perform better at other verbal, mathematical, and spatial tasks. This pattern of differing profiles is not well captured by the generalization, often bandied about in the popular press, that women are "verbal" and men are "spatial." There doesn't seem to be any more evidence for that than there was for the idea that women are people-oriented and men are object-oriented. Rather the differences are more subtle.

Does one of these two profiles foster better learning of math than the other? In particular, is the male profile better suited to high-level mathematical reasoning?

At this point, we face a question that's been much discussed in the literature on mathematics education and mathematical testing. The question is, by what yardstick can we decide whether men or women are better at math?

Some people suggest that we look at performance on the SAT-M, the quantitative portion of the Scholastic Assessment Test. But this suggestion raises a problem of circularity. The SAT test is composed of many different types of items. Some of those items are solved better by females. Some are solved better by males. The people who make the test have to decide, how many items of each type to include? Depending on how they answer that question, they can create a test that makes women look like better mathematicians, or a test that makes men look like better mathematicians. What's the right solution? . . .

A second strategy is to look at job outcomes. Maybe the people who are better at mathematics are those who pursue more mathematically intensive careers. But this strategy raises two problems. First, which mathematically intensive jobs should we choose? If we choose engineering, we will conclude that men are better at math because more men become engineers. If we choose accounting, we will think that women are better at math because more women become accountants: 57% of current accountants are women. So which job are we going to pick, to decide who has more mathematical talent?

These two examples suggest a deeper problem with job outcomes as a measure of mathematical talent. Surely you've got to be good at math to land a mathematically intensive job, but talent in mathematics is only one of the factors influencing career choice. It can't be our gold standard for mathematical ability.

So what can be? I suggest the following experiment. We should take a large number of male students and a large number of female students who have equal educational backgrounds, and present them with the kinds of tasks that real mathematicians face. We should give them new mathematical material that they have not yet mastered, and allow them to learn it over an extended period of time: the kind of time scale that real mathematicians work on. We should ask, how well do the students master this material? The good news is, this experiment is done all the time. It's called high school and college.

Here's the outcome. In high school, girls and boys now take equally many math classes, including the most advanced ones, and girls get better grades. In college, women earn almost half of the bachelor's degrees in mathematics, and men and women get equal grades. Here I respectfully disagree with one thing that Steve said: men and women get equal grades, even when you only compare people within a single institution and a single math class. Equating for classes, men and women get equal grades.

The outcome of this large-scale experiment gives us every reason to conclude that men and women have equal talent for mathematics. Here, I too would like to quote Diane Halpern. Halpern reviews much evidence for sex differences, but she concludes, "differences are not deficiencies." Men and women have equal aptitude for mathematics. Yes, there are sex differences, but they don't add up to an overall advantage for one sex over the other.

Let me turn to the third claim, that men show greater variability, either in general or in quantitative abilities in particular, and so there are more men at the upper end of the ability distribution. . . .

[However] males and females [have been found to take] equally demanding math classes and major in math in equal numbers. More girls major in biology and more boys in physics and engineering, but equal numbers of girls and boys major in math. And they get equal grades. The SAT-M not only under-predicts the performance of college women in general, it also under-predicts the college performance of women in the talented sample. These women and men have been shown to be equally talented by the most meaningful measure we have: their ability to assimilate new, challenging material in demanding mathematics classes at top-flight institutions. By that measure, the study does not find any difference between highly talented girls and boys.

So, what's causing the gender imbalance on faculties of math and science? Not differences in intrinsic aptitude. Let's turn to the social factors that I think are much more important. . . . I will talk about just one effect: how gender stereotypes influence the ways in which males and females are perceived.

Let me start with studies of parents' perceptions of their own children. Steve said that parents report that they treat their children equally. They treat their boys and girls alike, and they encourage them to equal extents, for they want both their sons and their daughters to succeed. This is no doubt true. But how are parents perceiving their kids?

Some studies have interviewed parents just after the birth of their child, at the point where the first question that 80% of parents ask—is it a boy or a girl?—has been answered. Parents of boys describe their babies as stronger, heartier, and bigger than parents of girls. The investigators also looked at the babies' medical records and asked whether there really were differences between the boys and girls in weight, strength, or coordination. The boys and girls were indistinguishable in these respects, but the parents' descriptions were different.

At 12 months of age, girls and boys show equal abilities to walk, crawl, or clamber. But before one study, Karen Adolph, an investigator of infants' loco-motor development, asked parents to predict how well their child would do on a set of crawling tasks: Would the child be able to crawl down a sloping ramp? Parents of sons were more confident that their child would make it down the ramp than parents of daughters. When Adolph tested the infants on the ramp, there was no difference whatever between the sons and daughters, but there was a difference in the parents' predictions.

My third example, moving up in age, comes from the studies of Jackie Eccles. She asked parents of boys and girls in sixth grade, how talented do you think your child is in mathematics? Parents of sons were more likely to judge that their sons had talent than parents of daughters. . . .

There's clearly a mismatch between what parents perceive in their kids and what objective measures reveal. But is it possible that the parents are seeing something that the objective measures are missing? Maybe the boy getting B's in his math class really is a mathematical genius, and his mom or dad has sensed that. To eliminate that possibility, we need to present observers with the very same baby, or child, or Ph.D. candidate, and manipulate their belief about the person's gender. Then we can ask whether their belief influences their perception.

It's hard to do these studies, but there are examples, and I will describe a few of them. A bunch of studies take the following form: you show a group of parents, or college undergraduates, video-clips of babies that they don't know personally. For half of them you give the baby a male name, and for the other half you give the baby a female name. (Male and female babies don't look very different.) The observers watch the baby and then are asked a series of questions: What is the baby doing? What is the baby feeling? How would you rate the baby on a dimension like strong-to-weak, or more intelligent to less intelligent? There are two important findings.

First, when babies do something unambiguous, reports are not affected by the baby's gender. If the baby clearly smiles, everybody says the baby is smiling or happy. Perception of children is not pure hallucination. Second, children often do things that are ambiguous, and parents face questions whose answers aren't easily readable off their child's overt behavior. In those cases, you see some interesting gender labeling effects. For example, in one study a child on a video-clip was playing with a jack-in-the-box. It suddenly popped up, and the child was startled and jumped backward. When people were asked, what's the child feeling, those who were given a female label said, "she's afraid." But the ones given a male label said, "he's angry." Same child, same reaction, different interpretation. . . .

I think these perceptions matter. You, as a parent, may be completely committed to treating your male and female children equally. But no sane parent would treat a fearful child the same way they treat an angry child. If knowledge of a child's gender affects adults' perception of that child, then male and female children are going to elicit different reactions from the world, different patterns of encouragement. These perceptions matter, even in parents who are committed to treating sons and daughters alike.

I will give you one last version of a gender-labeling study. This one hits particularly close to home. The subjects in the study were people like Steve and me: professors of psychology, who were sent some vitas to evaluate as applicants for a tenure track position. Two different vitas were used in the study. One was a vita of a walk-on-water candidate, best candidate you've ever seen, you would die to have this person on your faculty. The other vita was a middling, average vita among successful candidates. For half the professors, the name on the vita was male, for the other half the name was female. People were asked a series of questions: What do you think about this candidate's research productivity? What do you think about his or her teaching experience? And finally, Would you hire this candidate at your university?

For the walk-on-water candidate, there was no effect of gender labeling on these judgments. I think this finding supports Steve's view that we're dealing with little overt discrimination at universities. It's not as if professors see a female name on a vita and think, I don't want her. When the vita's great, everybody says great, let's hire.

What about the average successful vita, though: that is to say, the kind of vita that professors most often must evaluate? In that case, there were differences. The male was rated as having higher research productivity. These psychologists, Steve's and my colleagues, looked at the same number of publications and thought, "good productivity" when the name was male, and "less good productivity" when the name was female. Same thing for teaching experience. The very same list of courses was seen as good teaching experience when the name was male, and less good teaching experience when the name was female. In answer to the question would they hire the candidate, 70% said yes for the male, 45% for the female. If the decision were made by majority rule, the male would get hired and the female would not.

A couple other interesting things came out of this study. The effects were every bit as strong among the female respondents as among the male respondents. Men are not the culprits here. There were effects at the tenure level as well. At the tenure level, professors evaluated a very strong candidate, and almost everyone said this looked like a good case for tenure. But people were invited to express their reservations, and they came up with some very reasonable doubts. For example, "This person looks very strong, but before I agree to give her tenure I would need to know, was this her own work or the work of her adviser?" Now that's a perfectly reasonable question to ask. But what ought to give us pause is that those kinds of reservations were expressed *four times more often* when the name was female than when the name was male.

So there's a pervasive difference in perceptions, and I think the difference matters. Scientists' perception of the quality of a candidate will influence the likelihood that the candidate will get a fellowship, a job, resources, or a promotion. A pattern of biased evaluation therefore will occur even in people who are absolutely committed to gender equity. . . .

From the moment of birth to the moment of tenure, throughout this great developmental progression, there are unintentional but pervasive and important differences in the ways that males and females are perceived and evaluated.

I have to emphasize that perceptions are not everything. When cases are unambiguous, you don't see these effects. What's more, cognitive development is robust: boys and girls show equal capacities and achievements in educational settings, including in science and mathematics, despite the very different ways in which boys and girls are perceived and evaluated. I think it's really great news that males and females develop along common paths and gain common sets of abilities. The equal performance of males and females, despite their unequal treatment, strongly suggests that mathematical and scientific reasoning has a biological foundation, and this foundation is shared by males and females.

Finally, you do not create someone who feels like a girl or boy simply by perceiving them as male or female. That's the lesson that comes from the studies of people of one sex who are raised as the opposite sex. Biological sex differences are real and important. Sex is not a cultural construction that's imposed on people.

But the question on the table is not, Are there biological sex differences? The question is, Why are there fewer women mathematicians and scientists? The patterns of bias that I described provide four interconnected answers to that question. First, and most obviously, biased perceptions produce discrimination: When a group of equally qualified men and women are evaluated for jobs, more of the men will get those jobs if they are perceived to be more qualified. Second, if people are rational, more men than women will put themselves forward into the academic competition, because men will see that they've got a better chance for success. Academic jobs will be more attractive to men because they face better odds, will get more resources, and so forth.

Third, biased perceptions earlier in life may well deter some female students from even attempting a career in science or mathematics. If your parents feel that you don't have as much natural talent as someone else whose objective abilities are no better than yours, that may discourage you, as Eccles's work shows. Finally, there's likely to be a snowball effect. All of us have an easier time imagining ourselves in careers where there are other people like us. If the first three effects perpetuate a situation where there are few female scientists and mathematicians, young girls will be less likely to see math and science as a possible life.

. . . Let me end, though, by asking, could biological differences in motives—motivational patterns that evolved in the Pleistocene but that apply to us today—propel more men than women towards careers in mathematics and science?

My feeling is that where we stand now, we cannot evaluate this claim. It may be true, but as long as the forces of discrimination and biased perceptions affect people so pervasively, we'll never know. I think the only way we can find out is to do one more experiment. We should allow all of the evidence that men and women have equal cognitive capacity, to permeate through society. We should allow people to evaluate children in relation to their actual capacities, rather than one's sense of what their capacities ought to be, given their gender. Then we can see, as those boys and girls grow up, whether different inner voices pull them in different directions. I don't know what the findings of that experiment will be. But I do hope that some future generation of children gets to find out.

POSTSCRIPT

Do Sex Differences in Careers in Mathematics and Sciences Have a Biological Basis?

From the 1940s to the 1960s boys tended to surpass girls in math and science, but those discrepancies have lessened more recently. Today girls and boys tend to be equal, especially in basic math skills. Although in advanced math, high school girls tend to outperform boys in the classroom. Even at the college level, although males receive higher scores on standardized tests such as the SAT, females tend to earn higher grades in college math courses. It has been suggested that numerous factors affect females' math performance, such as differential treatment of girls and boys in the classroom and girls' lower expectation and lower confidence because of cultural messages that math is a male domain and that girls are not supposed to do well. There was briefly a Barbie doll on the market that said "math is tough." Additionally, even highly competent girls may suffer from the stereotype threat in standardized testing situations. That is, although they may know they are good at math, the testing context arouses anxiety because of the stereotype; ironically, this can impair their performance. Research has suggested that girls who resist the pressure to conform to gender role expectations are more likely to take more math and science courses, compete in sports, and be more creative and achievement-oriented. Interestingly, it helps to not have a brother, especially an older brother. Birth order as well as the sex composition of the siblings makes a difference. Girls without brothers tend to have higher self-esteem and find it easier to resist the pressure to conform to gendered expectations. Jacque Eccles has proposed an Expectancy by Values Theory that helps explain girls' and boys' differential interest in math. She explains that one's expectations for success interact with the subjective value of various options. Women, as well as men, must believe they can do it and must enjoy doing it. Her research demonstrates that parental attributions are very important. Parents very strongly influence their children's beliefs about their skills, which in turn shapes their academic and ultimately, career choices. Very frequently men are socialized to value career over family and vice versa for women. This emphasis on the development of attitudes towards math and science and their impact on career choices is important because it gives us insight into why there is a gender wage gap and why so many single mothers find themselves on welfare. Recently organizations have launched campaigns to narrow the computer technology gap, which may contribute to the math and science gap for girls and boys. For example, in 2002 the American Association of University Women began the Nebraska Girls and Technology Project in cooperation with the Girl Scouts. The project includes *Girls Click,* which is a computer-based hands-on learning experience.

What does it mean if we find that cognitive sex differences are more heavily accounted for by biology or by environmental reason? If individuals are differently predisposed for cognitive skill, should we and can we do something about it? If so, what? For example, evidence suggests that testosterone is implicated in spatial abilities? Should we give females more testosterone to boost their spatial abilities? Does this sound preposterous considering that thousands of athletes (predominantly males) inject themselves with steroids daily to boost their muscle mass?

Feminist scholars are fearful of biological causal evidence because it renders the environment irrelevant and implies that cognitive sex differences are unchangeable. Rather, they believe that sociocultural evidence provides more hope for social change. How much truth can be found in either claim? Psychosocially caused behavior has often been very difficult to reduce or eliminate (e.g., sex and racial bias). Furthermore, biological mechanisms (e.g., hormones and brain structure) change in response to environmental input. Recent evidence shows, for example, that just as brain structures and functions have been found to impact the way people select and respond to the environment, environmental input and experience alter brain structure and function throughout the life course. If so, then a radical move like injecting females with testosterone is not necessary. Simply engaging individuals in certain activities (even the performance of cognitive tasks) can boost testosterone levels naturally. Thus, many scholars have argued for an interactionist approach to studying cognition, examining the interaction of biology and environment.

Rather than think of sociocultural and biological arguments as necessarily in opposition and mutually exclusive, we must consider how they interact to explain cognitive sex differences. For example, individuals differ in their genetic potential or predisposition for good spatial skills. But genetically predisposed children might select environments that provide more spatial opportunity, augmenting brain structure and further fostering the development of spatial ability. The environment also intercedes in either developing or thwarting this potential. The biological makeup of individuals in the home may also influence the family environment (e.g., parents' and siblings' biological predisposition as impacted by past experiences and environmental inputs). Likewise, individuals might recognize and directly respond to the child's predisposition for spatial ability and provide spatial experiences. Macro-level cultural influences may also act on biological predisposition (e.g., cultural prohibition of certain experiences.)

Scholars also urge that we need to go beyond descriptive and explanatory research to a consideration of what the differences *mean* for individuals and society, especially given differential societal valuation of the cognitive differences. Indeed, cognitive sex differences research has revealed the powerful effects of identification and reinforcement of sex role–appropriate behaviors, expectations, motivational variables, and explicit and implicit messages in cognitive sex differences. If individuals have poor mathematical or spatial skill, what does it mean to be excluded from opportunities because of these cognitive deficits (whether actual or presumed based on stereotypes)? Having cognitive deficits impacts identity and self-esteem: how we feel about our abilities, our role in society, and our potential for success. It also creates dependencies. (Think about how much more expensive life is for individuals who are not mechanically inclined.) Spending so much time in a devaluing environment provides constant reminders of the jeopardy incurred by cognitive sex differences to future income, status, and happiness. The restrictions to societal and occupational opportunities based on cognitive functioning have repercussions for individuals and also for society at large. How is society influence by the fact that the majority of engineers, mathematicians, chemists, mechanics, and airplane pilots are male? Of course, critics point out that the sex differences in occupational representation are grossly disproportionate to the magnitude of cognitive sex differences. Thus, even if there is biological evidence for cognitive sex differences, there seem to be other social factors at work in creating this gulf.

Suggested Readings

Deborah Blum, *Sex on the Brain: The Biological Differences Between Men and Women* (New York: Penguin Books, 1998).

Simon Baron-Cohen, *The Essential Difference: The Truth about the Male and Female Brain* (New York: Basic Books, 2003).

Girl Scouts, *The Girls Difference: Short-Circuiting the Myth of the Technophobic Girl.* (New York: Girl Scouts Research Institute, 2001).

Barbara A. Gutek, "Women and Paid Work," *Psychology of Women Quarterly, 25* (2001): 379–393.

Diane F. Halpren, *Sex Differences in Cognitive Abilities,* 4th ed. Mahwah, NJ: Lawrence Erlbaum.

Caryl Rivers and C. Barnett, *Same Difference: How Gender Myths Are Hurting Our Relationships, Our Children, and Our Jobs* (New York: Basic Books, 2005).

Janet Shibley Hyde and Kristen C. Kling, "Women, Motivation, and Achievement," *Psychology of Women Quarterly, 25* (2001): 364–378.

E. S. Spelke, "Sex Differences in Intrinsic Aptitude for Mathematics and Science? A Critical Analysis," *American Psychologist, 60* (2005): 950–958.

ISSUE 12

Is the Gender Wage Gap Justified?

YES: June O'Neill, from "The Gender Gap in Wages, circa 2000" (American Economy Association, 2003)

NO: Hilary H. M. Lips, from "The Gender Pay Gap: Concrete Indicator of Women's Progress Toward Equality" (Analyses of Social Issues and Public Policy, 2003)

ISSUE SUMMARY

YES: June O'Neill suggests that the gender gap is largely due to nondiscriminatory factors, most notably those associated with women's choices due to the division of labor in the home.

NO: Hilary M. Lips documents the continuing gender gap in wages and argues that a continuing undervaluing of women's work due to stereotypes and prejudice maintains the wage gap.

"Equal pay for equal work," "Equal pay for comparable work": These two phrases have been hallmarks of the women's movement's list of rights to which women are entitled. And there are several federal laws, enforced by the U.S. Equal Employment Opportunity Commission (EEOC), that are supposed to protect women from discrimination in their compensation. The Equal Pay Act states, "Employers may not pay unequal wages to men and women who perform jobs that require substantially equal skill, effort and responsibility, and that are performed under similar working conditions within the same establishment" but the act does allow for differences in pay under certain conditions: "Pay differentials are permitted when they are based on seniority, merit, quantity or quality of production, or a factor other than sex." These are known as "affirmative defenses" and it is the employer's burden to prove that they apply. Questions arise from these declarations. What constitutes "substantially equal"? By what criteria are judgments of "merit, quantity and quality of production or a factor other than sex" made? Classic studies in social psychology have shown repeatedly that the same work, whether it is an essay, a painting, or a resume, when attributed to a man receives a more favorable evaluation than when attributed to a woman. Decisions are made on a daily basis regarding who gets hired, who gets a pay raise, and who gets a promotion. To what extent do women's personality, interests, and choices affect these decisions and what extent do sexism and discrimination affect these decisions? Is the world of work so constructed that its practices and policies result in discrimination against women? These practices might include policies that require out-of-town travel to get a promotion and for the single mother in particular to have inadequate childcare. Or these practices might include tolerance for sexual harassment that forces a woman to quit her job or suffer in silence because she cannot afford to lose her job. Or perhaps there are policies that are intolerant of a single mother missing work because she has a sick child. So, under such institutional barriers to success women may be forced to forego certain careers and occupations "choosing" those more compatible with the gender roles society expects her to fulfill. Or, alternatively, perhaps it is the way women are constituted that makes the difference. Are women by nature less ambitious, less competitive, less assertive, and as a consequence less effective leaders? If so, they may freely choose careers and occupations that are more suited to their nature, careers and occupations that just happen to pay less.

In the following selections June O'Neill argues that women make employment choices that ultimately determine their wages. She suggests that the division of labor in the home plays a large role in the choices women make. She suggests that discriminatory factors are negligible. Hilary Lips could not disagree more. Lips argues that the continued undervaluing of women's work and prejudice against women in the workplace result in a continuing unjustifiable gender wage gap.

June O'Neill

The Gender Gap in Wages

The transition of women into the U.S. labor market was surely one of the most profound economic and social changes of the 20th century. In 1900 about 20 percent of women were in the labor force. This percentage rose to about 34 in 1950 and reached 61 percent in 2000; not far below the 75-percent participation rate of men. A key element in this change was the dramatic rise in market work among married women with children under the age of 18, whose labor-force participation increased from a rate of 18 percent in 1950 to 71 percent in 2000.

However, for much of the last 50 years the rise in women's labor-force activity and its growing convergence with that of men, did not appear to be matched by a narrowing of the gender gap in pay. Between 1955 and 1980, the most commonly cited measure of that gap, the female-to-male ratio of median annual earnings of full-time year-round workers, hovered around 60 percent. But using the same measure, the ratio began to rise after 1980, reaching 69 percent in 1989 and 74 percent in the mid 1990's, after which it leveled off. Based on a more appropriate measure, average hourly wage rates (available since 1979), the gender gap is smaller, but the pattern of change is similar, and the ratio rises from 66 percent in 1979 to 80 percent in 1993 and then stabilizes.

Through the years the gender gap in wages frequently has been a source of public concern and a puzzle to researchers. In this paper I examine evidence from the Current Population Survey (CPS) and the National Longitudinal Survey of Youth (NLSY79) on recent trends and current sources of the gender gap.

I. Unique Factors Underlying Gender Differences in Skills

In comparing the earnings of different demographic groups it is usually important to examine the effect of productivity differences between the groups that might account for any earnings differential. In the case of differences in earnings between racial and ethnic groups of the same sex,

From *American Economic Review*, vol. 93, no. 2, May 2003, excerpts from 309–314. Copyright © 2003 by American Economic Association. Reprinted by permission.

productivity differences most often stem from differences in the quantity and quality of education and other human capital acquired at home as well as in school. Differences in productivity between men and women, however, are not likely to be due to differences in educational background. Sisters and brothers are exposed to the same parental background and attend schools of the same quality. Their current educational attainment and their cognitive skills, as measured by achievement test scores, are similar.

Instead, the main source of productivity differences between women and men stems from the lesser amount of time and energy that many women can commit to labor-market careers as a result of the division of labor within the family. Even though women's home responsibilities have fallen dramatically over the past 50 years, they are nonetheless, still significant. Consequently, women are less likely than men to work continuously after leaving school and therefore are less likely to gain experience that can only be acquired on the job. In addition, anticipation of child-related work interruptions and the need to coordinate home responsibilities with market work are likely to influence choice of occupation and type of firm.

One can argue whether the source of these gender role differences is a form of discrimination rather than an outcome of biological and other deeply rooted psychological and cultural factors. However, by the time they are old enough to make choices, many women make different choices than men regarding the extent of career attachment.

Current data continue to show the strong effect of the presence of children, particularly young children, on work participation and on hours of work among those who do work. In March 2001, at ages 25–44, the prime period for career development, 34 percent of women with children under the age of six were out of the labor force, compared to 16 percent of women without children. Thirty percent of employed mothers worked part-time, compared to 11 percent of women with no children. Among men, however, the presence of children is associated with an increase in work involvement. Only 4 percent of men with children under the age of six are out of the labor force, and among employed fathers only 2 percent work part-time.

The expectation of withdrawals from the labor force and the need to work fewer hours during the week are likely to influence the type of occupations that women train for and ultimately pursue. More subtle factors such as the level of stress at work and the ability to take unplanned time off for family emergencies are also likely to influence the choice of occupation and work place. Thus, certain characteristics of jobs may affect women's occupational choices because they are particularly compatible or incompatible with women's dual home/market roles. These adaptive occupational choices will tend to lower the market earnings of women relative to men.

For example, some occupations require lengthy investment in skills with applicability only to highly specific market activities (e.g., aerospace engineer, surgeon, top management in large complex organizations). The payoff to such investments is obviously reduced when years in the labor force are reduced. Moreover, skills depreciate during periods of withdrawal from work and the rate of depreciation is likely to vary depending on the rate of technological change and obsolescence of the skills acquired. Fields such as physics, where knowledge depreciates rapidly have disproportionately fewer women. Other types of schooling and training are more general in their applicability to different situations and impart skills that are less prone to depreciate. For example, nursing and teaching skills are valuable to mothers and can be practiced widely in different settings with relatively little additional firm-specific training.

Certain characteristics of the workplace are more compatible with women's home responsibilities than others. The depreciation in skills and earnings related to complete withdrawal from the labor force may be ameliorated by work situations that accommodate the need for less demanding work while raising a family. Part-time work is the most obvious manifestation of this adjustment. Even if a woman does not always work part-time she may be more likely to choose an occupation or job setting that provides a shorter or more flexible work week in the event it may be needed, or a more informal work setting where time off for unpredictable events is acceptable.

Both work attachment and the choice of occupation are expected to be important determinants of women's earnings and important factors underlying the gender wage gap. . . .

II. Findings from the Current Population Survey: 1979–2001

The CPS analysis is based on data from the CPS outgoing-rotation-group files (CPS ORG) merged with data on occupational characteristics from the Department of Labor's Fourth Dictionary of Occupational Titles (DOT), 1991 revision. The analysis includes part-time and full-time wage and salary workers, ages 20–60.

The major changes that have occurred during the 1979–2001 period in the gender differential in earnings-related characteristics are as follows. Women continue to be much more likely than men to work part-time (19 percent versus 5 percent in 2001), although that difference narrowed. With respect to education, women gained relative to men at the college level. By 2001 they were somewhat more likely than men to be college graduates and were almost as likely to receive a higher degree. Women also have been entering occupations requiring more job-specific skills, as measured by SVP (specific vocational preparation), the time required to attain the average level of proficiency in an occupation—a DOT variable. The gender gap in SVP declined by almost half between 1984 and 1994 and has since declined further, but at a slower rate.

However, despite these changes, women and men remain in occupations that are disproportionately female or male. In 2001 women, on average, worked in occupations in which the percentage of female employees was close to 68 percent; men worked in occupations that were only 30-percent female. The percentage female in an occupation is one simple way of measuring the characteristics of an occupation that are conducive to women's particular needs. However, in the CPS analysis I have taken the more direct path of including specific characteristics of occupations as individual variables.

Returns to "potential experience."   —As a number of studies have shown, there is evidence that the years of work experience of employed women increased during the 1980's. In fact, the narrowing of the work-experience gap was a key factor causing the gender wage gap to narrow during the 1980's. Nonetheless, longitudinal data show that a significant experience gap remains. . . . Actual experience is reasonably close to potential experience for men. For women that is not the case. The return to potential experience is typically lower for women than for men, and the fact that the difference between actual and potential experience is larger for women than for men likely accounts for at least part of the difference in returns. Therefore, if women's actual experience has been catching up to their potential experience, one would expect that the effect of potential experience on the female wage rate would increase over time for women, and more so than for men, if the return to experience generally was rising for other reasons. [T]hat is in fact what has happened. . . .

Occupational characteristics explain a substantial portion of the wage gap. . . . The female/male wage ratio, increased from 84 percent in 1983 to 90 percent in 2001; the unadjusted ratio rose from 70 percent to 80 percent over the same period.

III. Findings from the NLSY

Analysis of data from the NLSY permits a more complete assessment of the extent to which important differences in human capital and job and occupational characteristics can explain the gender gap in wages. The analysis uses the 2000 NLSY when the cohort has reached ages 35–43.

. . . Here are the highlights:

(i) . . . Years of schooling and scores on the AFQT (Armed Forces Qualification Test) explain hardly any of the differential because women and men differ little in these characteristics.

(ii) Actual work experience accounts for much of the gap. . . .

(iii) The addition of occupational and workplace characteristics reduces the unexplained portion of the gap.

I have conducted additional analysis of the NLSY cohort separately by schooling level. Gender differences in work experience are much greater at the high-school level than they are for college graduates. Consequently, work experience accounts for a particularly large share of the gap. . . .

The unadjusted wage gap is larger for college graduates than it is at the high-school level. The field of college major, a harbinger of occupational choice, accounts for a significant amount of the gap.

IV. Concluding Comments

Understanding the gender gap in pay is important because even in the absence of any labor-market discrimination it is unlikely that the wage rates of women and men would be equal. As I have shown in this paper, the unadjusted gender gap can be explained to a large extent by nondiscriminatory factors. Those factors are unlikely to change radically in the near future unless the roles of women and men in the home become more nearly identical. Thus an unadjusted gender gap may be with us for quite a while.

NO ↩

Hilary M. Lips

The Gender Pay Gap: Concrete Indicator of Women's Progress Toward Equality

Media reports sometimes suggest that the gender pay gap is disappearing. Contrary to this optimistic conclusion, data released by such sources as the U.S. Census Bureau, the U.S. General Accounting Office, and the Internal Revenue Service (IRS) suggest that a significant gap between women's and men's earnings persists. According to the latest figures from the U.S. Census Bureau, women earned 73.25% of men's earnings in 2000. The IRS reported that the ratio of men to women in particular salary brackets is highest at highest income levels: For salaries of $1 million or more, the ratio of men to women is about 13:1, and it is necessary to drop down to the $25,000 to $30,000 range before the numbers of women and men in an income category are roughly equal. The U.S. General Accounting Office (2001) study, which focused on managers within a set of 10 industries between 1995 and 2000, found that, controlling for education, age, marital status, and race, women earned less than men in both 1995 and 2000 and that, in 7 of the 10 industries studied, the earnings gap between women and men had actually widened between 1995 and 2000. . . .

Research tells us that the pay assigned to work reflects, in certain important respects, the value that is attached to that work and to the person doing it. Thus, the gender pay gap may be thought of as an indicator of the regard in which women and their work is held by society, or even as an outcome variable in a grand social quasi experiment. The size of the gender pay gap is one of the most concrete ways of assessing women's progress toward equality. It is an indicator that should be of interest to psychologists.

Issues in Estimating and Reporting the Gender Pay Gap

One of the most basic issues in measuring and reporting the gender pay gap is the choice of measure used to indicate "average" income. Median income, less skewed by a few people making very high or very low earnings,

From *Analyses of Social Issues and Public Policy*, vol. 3, no. 1, 2003, excerpts from 87–96, 100–106.

is the indicator usually reported by U.S. government agencies such as the Census Bureau. . . .

The types of wages or salaries used in comparisons are also controversial. Agencies may present comparisons using ordinary hourly or weekly wages. Ordinary wages exclude overtime pay, bonuses, and other perks and awards. This measure makes the wage gap look smaller because men are more likely than women to have access to these "extras." The use of weekly of hourly, rather than annual, earnings makes the gap look smaller because men may work more weeks or more hours than women. . . .

A second problem with the reliance on an hourly measure of income is that it assumes equivalency between women and men in their choice to limit or expand the number of hours they work. However, men may be given more opportunities than women to work extra hours for extra pay; women, if they have family responsibilities, may be less free to accept such opportunities if they are presented. . . .

A third problem with the reliance on hourly income is one of practicality and social significance. When a woman applies for a mortgage or a car loan, she is not asked about her hourly income. The income statistic that affects whether or not she gets the loan, and indeed what kind of life she is able to afford, is her annual income.

It is obvious that it is difficult to find a comparison that is both inclusive and fair to women. The best solution to the problems noted above seems to be using median annual earnings of full-time, year-round workers. However, this strategy ignores part-time workers—and most of those workers are women. . . .

Much of the data used by governments around the world to measure the earnings gap between women and men is based on a model that makes men's pattern of working the standard—the norm against which women's outcomes are judged. If women cannot fit that model, they are omitted from the comparisons or their lower pay is said to be justified. However, the model of full-time, year-round, continuous participation in the workforce is not neutral, but gendered. Use of this model as the norm ignores the issues of family and domestic responsibilities that make it impractical for many women to fit this full-time, year-round, continuous model. It also ignores factors such as stereotyping, streaming, and discrimination that tend to channel women into low-paying work that is often part-time or seasonal.

There is, however, a strong tendency to brush such issues aside when talking about pay equity. . . .

[G]ender [is treated] as a factor that can be separated from such issues as hours worked, type of job, and family responsibilities. Yet, gender is strongly and seemingly inextricably associated with these very issues. The assertion that such issues can be somehow factored out of the pay-equity equation trivializes the importance of the earnings gap and promotes the assumption that women's route to pay equity lies in simply adopting a more male-like lifestyle. . . .

Documenting the Earnings Gap

A careful examination of the earnings of women and men in the United States reveals a significant and persistent gap that is evident in a variety of different comparisons. [W]hen the U.S. Census Bureau's reported median annual income of all workers, full- and part-time combined, is considered, the pattern revealed is more than half a century of earnings gaps favoring men. When the data are limited to full-time, year-round workers only a strong and persistent gap is still evident. . . .

Because the U.S. Census Bureau (2000c) has broken data down by race and ethnicity, at least for recent decades, it is possible to examine the gender pay gap within major racial and ethnic groups. . . . Only Asian American men approached the earnings levels of European American men, and within each racial group, women's earnings were less than men's.

The gender gap in earnings can also be examined within education levels—a comparison that is very important, in view of the widely held belief that education is one key to a higher income. Higher levels of education are indeed associated with higher levels of income for women however, the earnings gap does not become smaller with higher levels of education. . . .

The Earnings Gap and Occupational Segregation

Some have argued that the gender wage gap is simply an artifact of occupational choice. They assert that the difference in women's and men's median earnings does not reflect any devaluing of women's work or discrimination against women. Rather, it is an accidental result of the fact that women and men choose different occupational paths with different reward structures.

To evaluate this argument, it is instructive to examine U.S. Bureau of Labor Statistics data on earnings of women and men in various occupational subcategories. [I]n the 10 occupations in which women formed the largest majorities of full-time workers in 2001 and for which comparative data were available, in all but 2 of the occupations in which women formed the majority of workers, men's earnings were always higher than women's.

Women fare no better in occupations in which they form a minority of workers. Men's earnings were higher within all but one [male-dominated] occupation, electrical and electronic engineering, in which women's earnings were slightly higher than men's. . . . Clearly the gender wage gap does not exist simply because women and men choose different occupations. Within occupations, even within occupations in which women form the great majority of workers, there is an overwhelming tendency for women to earn less than men.

It may be tempting to think that at the high levels of education and awareness that characterize professional occupations and their institutional contexts, the gender pay gap is negligible. . . . An interesting case is the pattern of compensation for women in the teaching profession. Teaching at the elementary and secondary school level is dominated numerically by women. Women teachers earned 95% or less of what men teachers earned—a smaller earnings gap than exists in other professions, but one that translates into a significant economic advantage for men over years of continuing employment. The gap cannot be attributed to lower qualifications among women. . . .

The issue of occupational segregation is one that has been raised with enthusiasm by many people interested in closing the gender earnings gap. A variety of initiatives have been mounted to convince girls to choose such male-dominated career paths as engineering, business, and computing. Yet, these data suggest that the tendency for women to be paid less persists regardless of occupation. The explanation may well lie partly in the tendency to undervalue work that is done by women—a tendency that has been documented in the laboratory by psychologists. . . . [E]ven if the earnings gap can be partly attributed to gendered patterns of occupational choices (leaving aside the issue of how free or constrained such choices may be), it may not be easy to eliminate it by simply trying to change those choices. It is likely that as women enter occupations in large numbers, the prestige and earnings associated with those occupations tend to drop, leaving the earnings gap intact. . . .

The Earnings Gap Reflects a Long-Standing Pattern of Undervaluing Women

Why, in the face of years of focus on pay equity, does the gender earnings gap persist? As noted above, the gap appears within groupings of race/ethnicity and nationality; it is not diminished at higher levels of education; it cannot be explained easily or completely by women's and men's choices with respect to occupations; and, *if* it is closing, it is doing so at a glacial pace. It seems an inescapable conclusion that the gap reflects, in large part, a continuing tendency to undervalue women and the work they do: Even when women predominate in an occupational domain and perform at least as well as men, their work is valued and rewarded less than men's. In further support of this conclusion, I offer an examination of the gendered patterns in one final type of compensation and recognition for work produced: literary awards.

Literary awards have some monetary value, but that is only the tip of the iceberg in terms of the very tangible benefits they bring. Because literary prizes sell books, the recipient of such an award receives notice and status that may allow her or him to command a more prestigious position, with higher pay, and to be more sure that his or her next book will be published and that it will be likely to command a larger advance. The person may also be in a position to attract and mentor high-quality students and to place them by recommending them to others. Thus, the pattern of such awards is not a trivial matter. These and other awards are part of the pattern of the gender earnings gap.

When women appear scarce in the highest-paid echelons of various positions, such as engineers, computer scientists, and CEOs of Fortune 500 companies, the following explanation is often offered: Perhaps not as many women as men have the ability, qualifications, and/or interest to pursue such positions or to perform at top levels. In the field of literary endeavor, however, no such argument can be supported by the evidence. The literature on cognitive performance indicates that in the realm of verbal skills, there is no suggestion that males generally outperform females. . . . Clearly, the realm of writing and literature is one in which women should be primed to sweep the awards. However, that is definitely not what has happened.

Gender Differences in the Receipt of Pulitzer Literary Awards

The high-prestige Pulitzer awards are an interesting case. The overall ratio of men to women receiving these literary prizes is 4.25:1 over the life of the prize. Over the 86-year life of these awards, there have been 30 years in which men have won all of them—and only 1 year in which no men have won. . . .

Men defy the odds in winning these prizes. Here is a domain where women *should* have the advantage, but still the deck seems to be stacked against them. How are we to explain men's continuing dominance of these prestigious awards? It appears to reflect two forces that are intertwined and that underlie female–male differences in all types of compensation: greater male access to structural and decision-making power, and greater valuing of male than female contributions. The unacknowledged bias in the system is apparently so wide, so deep, and so long-standing that it remains virtually invisible and unassailable, even after decades of consciousness-raising efforts by activist women.

If women cannot obtain their share of the rewards in a domain in which, by objective measures, they appear to perform at least as well as, if not better than, men, what are we to anticipate for the more general, and perhaps even more intractable, problem of the gender earnings gap? What *cannot* be anticipated is that the gap will simply disappear without intervention. . . .

What Can Be Done?

Whereas there are many interventions that might reduce the gender pay gap in particular contexts, four broad recommendations appear plainly appropriate:

[1] Supporting Comparable Worth

Legislation that mandates comparable worth–the notion that people performing work of equal value should be paid the same–is resisted because businesses fear it will mire them in bureaucratic red tape. Yet there are strong reasons to support it. Because women and men tend to be segregated into different jobs, many gender disparities in pay are no covered by the requirement of equal pay for equal work. And research shows that it is difficult to evaluate the worth of an occupation independent of the gender labeling of that occupation. . . .

Comparable worth, once mandated, can be implemented through formal job analysis and evaluation—something in which industrial-organizational psychologists have strong expertise. Job analysis, already used in many settings (including the federal government) to determine appropriate salary levels, is not without problems. However, it provides a concrete strategy for comparing gender-segregated jobs and compensating them more fairly.

[2] Encouraging Family-Friendly Workplace Policies

If women's work tends to be undervalued, there may be nowhere it is more undervalued than in the context of home and family. Since women still do most unpaid domestic, child-rearing, or dependent-care work, and the average U.S. woman is also employed, most women are juggling two or three jobs. They suffer real economic costs when they must decrease their commitment to employment in order to meet other obligations. . . .

To the extent that family work prevents women from advancing in their occupations, the refusal of employers to accommodate these dual responsibilities contributes to the earnings gap. And whereas some may question whether employers are morally bound to support women (or men) in meeting their non-employment-related obligations, such support and acknowledgment is, at least, not without precedent. Employers sometimes give credit for military service—why not for child rearing? Employers sometimes grant paid or unpaid leave for employees to work for charity or to run for and hold political office—why not for dependent care?. . .

[3] Improving the Position of Part-Time Workers

As noted above, a large percentage of women work part-time, and the gender pay gap is much larger when part-time workers are included. One way to begin lifting the status, pay, and benefits associated with part-time work is to place information about those issues in the foreground of discussions about pay equity. This suggestion does not mean, however, that pay-equity analyses should rely on average hourly earnings. As noted above, such an approach may conceal more subtle forms of pay inequity. Reports on women's earnings should not focus only on full-time workers, as this marginalizes and excludes from consideration a large group of women workers. . . .

[4] Education About Gender Bias

Social psychological research abounds with examples demonstrating that both women and men are biased against women in terms of selecting them for positions, promoting them to higher positions, and evaluating their contributions. Over the years, social psychologists have demonstrated, for example, that under certain conditions, people tend to evaluate men's work more favorably than women's; prefer to hire and promote males than females; are more critical of females than males in positions of authority; dislike women, but not men, who promote their own competence; respond negatively to assertive or agentic women; and sabotage women who try to assert leadership in groups. In many of these cases, respondents were not aware of their biases in the evaluation of women. . . . Because biases are often subtle and organizations complex, changes produced by such education may be slow. However, there is a wealth of evidence that education can lead to attitude change.

POSTSCRIPT

Is the Gender Wage Gap Justified?

Historically, poor women have always worked, perhaps as a housekeeper or a nanny or a seamstress in a sweatshop. In recent U.S. history, women were most likely to enter the workforce in masses during times of war. Their presence was needed to compensate for the lack of male laborers. Rosie the Riveter became the patriotic role model. However, after each of the two major world wars women were encouraged to return to their rightful place in the home with as much enthusiasm as they had been encouraged to leave the home; Suzi homemaker became the new cultural icon for women. Issues of women's equal treatment in the workplace did not really come to the fore-front for debate until large numbers of women entered higher education, par-ticipated in the civil rights movement and the antiwar movement of the 1960s. The second wave of the women's movement was the result. Many believed that as more women obtained more education and began to climb the career ladder gender inequities would begin to dissipate. However, although in forty years there has been progress at the entry level for women, women at the top find themselves in a minority. The glass ceiling has not been broken. Some have suggested that women no longer "want it all"— career and family; rather, women are willingly choosing to opt out of the fast-paced, competitive rat race to be stay-at-home moms. There is evidence that some women with advanced degrees from some of the most prestigious insti-tutions in the United States have done this. However, these women are mar-ried to highly successful men who generate enough income to maintain an upper-middle-class lifestyle. Other women have opted out of the corporate race to the top because they realized they were not going to break through the glass ceiling. Women are a fast-growing group to start their own busi-nesses. However, such examples ignore the fact that the vast majority of people (women and men) do not have the resources to begin their own busi-nesses nor can they maintain a comfortable lifestyle without two incomes, and for single mothers it is not a question of lifestyle but a matter of survival. Economists Lommerud and Vagstad evaluated the notions of the mommy track and the fast track. The mommy track had originally been proposed as a career path that recognized women role as child-bearers; the idea was that a woman's career trajectory would be adjusted to allow for this reality without jeopardizing her chances of advancement. It did not work. Such a choice by women has resulted in subtle discrimination. Lommerud and Vagstad argued that a self-fulfilling prophecy occurred. An employer is more likely to put a male employee on the fast track, believing that he will not be distracted by childcare responsibilities like a female employee. As a result, they conclude that effort rather than talent is being rewarded. The man is expected to be on the fast track and to put forth more effort than his partner who is on the mommy track. They suggest that only permanent changes in public policy will remove the discrimination.

Suggested Readings

Francis Achampong, *Workplace Sexual Harassment Law: Principles, Landmark Developments, and Framework for Effective Risk Management* (Westport, CO: Quorum Books, 1999).

Jeanette N. Cleveland, Kevin R. Murphy, and Margaret Stockdale, eds., *Women and Men in Organizations: Sex and Gender Issues at Work* (Mahwah, NJ: Lawrence Erlbaum Associates, 2001).

Barbara A. Gutek and M. S. Stockdale, "Sex Discrimination in Employment," in F. Landy (ed.), *Employment Discrimination Litigation: Behavioral, Quantitative, and Legal Perspectives* (in press).

Catherine Hein, *Reconciling Work and Family Responsibilities: Practical Ideas from Global Experience* (Washington, DC: Brookings Institution Press, 2005).

International Labor Office, *Gender Equality and Decent Work. Good Practices at the Workplace* (Washington, DC: Brookings Institution Press, 2005).

Kjell Erik Lommerud and Steinar Vagstad (2000). *Mommy Tracks and Public Policy: on Self-Fulfilling Prophecies and Gender Gaps in Promotion* (London: The Centre for Economic Policy Research, 2000).

Linda Wirth, *Breaking through the Glass Ceiling: Women in Management* (International Labor Organization, 2001).

ISSUE 13

Are Gender Inequalities Primarily Responsible for the Increased Number of Low-Wage Single-Mother Families?

YES: Sarah Drescher, from "Why Welfare Fails: Addressing the Pre-Existing Gender Inequalities Contributing to the Feminization of Poverty," *The Oregon Advocate* (Summer 2000)

NO: Hilda Kahne, from "Low-Wage Single-Mother Families in this Jobless Recover: Can Improved Social Policies Help?" *Journal of Social Issues and Public Policy* (2004)

ISSUE SUMMARY

YES: Author Sarah Drescher contends that welfare reforms have inadequately addressed gender inequalities and have reinforced sex-segregated work and family roles thereby worsening the "feminization of poverty."

NO: Hilda Kahne makes the argument that incomplete education and few training programs, rather than gender discrimination, makes it more difficult for low-wage single mothers to raise their earnings.

According to the U.S. Census Bureau there are an estimated 98 million single mothers in the United States, a number that had tripled in the past 25 years and, as of 1998, there were an estimated 948,000 teen mothers age 15 to 19. About five-sixths of all single parents are women. Approximately 42 percent of single mothers have never married. From 1960 to 1980 the rate of divorce doubled, and although the rate has leveled off since, an increasing number of women find themselves in the role of single mother. Children, because they usually live with their mothers, are affected. Approximately two-thirds of divorces involve children and over one-half of children in the United States will experience parents' divorce. For these children their standard of living declines 30 to 40 percent and 25 percent of divorced mothers will fall into poverty within five years. Contributing to this poverty is the likelihood of not receiving child support even when entitled to it. Factors contributing to divorce, as well as single parenthood, for women include younger age of marriage, social attitudes more accepting of divorce, cohabitation and single-parenthood, as well as women's greater independence because of more opportunities in the workforce. At the same time, and perhaps ironically, the employment rates for single mothers has decreased from 73 percent in 2000 to 69.8 percent in 2003, and the steepest loss has been for black mothers.

Numerous debates surround these numbers. Issues being discussed include teen sexuality and unintended pregnancy as well as marriage initiatives. There is a strong belief among religious conservatives as well as economists that there is a relationship between marital stability, job stability, and earnings. One dimension of these debates relates to gender and whether welfare and work policies should be gender sensitive. There are stereotypes of welfare recipients, typically women, as lazy and irresponsible. However, stories of individual welfare recipients call welfare recipient stereotypes into question. In fact, it is common for poor women to combine welfare with work or to get welfare benefits between jobs. Many women use welfare to help them get more education—a critical factor in moving out of poverty. Many factors conspire against poor women: they can't find employment; they can't secure high enough pay, particularly if they have children in their care; they are financially penalized if married; and they have to endure public condemnation and discrimination.

Nevertheless, stereotypes of welfare mothers remain rigid and condemning. These stereotypes reflect three dominant perspectives or beliefs about the causes of poverty and wealth: (1) individualism contends that individuals are responsible for their own lot in life. Those who are motivated and work hard will make it. Those who do not make it (i.e., welfare recipients) have only themselves to blame; (2) social-structuralism asserts that due to economic or social imbalances (e.g., in education, marriage and family life, and even welfare programs themselves), opportunities are restricted for some people, overriding individual agency and affecting the likelihood of success; and (3) "culture of poverty," most often associated with African Americans who are thought to have developed a culture—some would say counterculture—of poverty with values, traits, and expectations that have developed from the structural constraints of living in poverty and that may be intergenerationally transmitted. Such logic demonstrates what social psychologists call the "fundamental attribution error;" that is, the tendency to blame individuals for their outcomes while ignoring the situational context. One situational context is gender. This is apparent in the selections that follow.

Sarah Drescher argues that welfare reforms have inadequately addressed gender inequalities and have reinforced sex-segregated work and family roles, thereby worsening the "feminization of poverty."

In contrast, Kahne does not discuss the role of gender. Rather, she suggests that wage-related social policies should be developed to improve educational and training opportunities for low-wage single mothers.

Sarah Drescher

 **YES**

Why Welfare Fails

Why are one in two female-headed families with children and over one quarter of elderly women in the United States living at or below the poverty line? To answer this question, one must explore the causes of poverty that place a disproportionate economic burden on women and contribute to a historic and contemporary phenomenon which has become known as the "feminization of poverty." An examination of empirical studies and present academic commentary demonstrates the presence of preexisting direct and indirect sources of women's economic insecurity. From unpaid domestic labor to the cost of children and gender inequality in economic and social spheres, gender-based economic burdens contribute to the disproportionate number of impoverished females in the U.S. Ultimately, the policy's inadequacy to address inherent gender inequalities and its reinforcement of sex-segregated roles, contributes to the excessive amount of women in poverty.

It should be noted that data used to support the aforementioned arguments made in this examination are drawn from national poverty rates, family income, per capita income, and the ratio of income-to-needs. Many statistics which trace economic disparities—such as one revealing that one third of black women and one fifth of white women with below-median incomes during marriage are living below the poverty line in the year following marital disruption—are insensitive to income change that remains above or below the poverty threshold and disregards the overall economic fluctuations in living wages.

While recent media accounts have begun to acknowledge this trend, the feminization of poverty has actually been occurring for many decades. State constructed poverty lines have been imposed that are analogous to the methodology proffered by Linda Barrington, Assistant Professor of Economics at Columbia University. She estimates that 12.8 percent of the poor resided in female-headed households in 1939, and that the number rose to 26.3 percent by 1959, and to 51.8 percent by 1979.[1] To understand how these statistics are achieved, and then to determine the direct and indirect causes, one must first understand the process by which the data is obtained. Linda Barrington and Cecilia Conrad explain: "The proportion of poor persons living in female-headed households is a function of the proportion of poor households that are female-headed, which in turn is a function of the number of and poverty rate among female-headed households, relative to that of male-headed households."[2]

Thus, the increase in female-headed households living in poverty cited above can be attributed to the increase in proportion of female-headed households that are poor or the propensity of females to form households relative to males. Sampling the 1940 and 1960 Public Use Microdata Samples (PUMS) of the US population census, one finds an increase in both of the aforementioned.[3] Contributing causes include (1) changes in the demographic composition of female-headed households, (2) a reduction in the minimum level of earnings deemed necessary for a woman to form an independent household, and (3) a shift in the earnings distribution.

Between 1939 and 1959 the home environment changed dramatically. Small houses replaced large farm houses, joint consumption and production in the home became less significant, electrification brought new appliances, and the reduction in time for homemaking produced larger savings in a larger household. However, the shift from extended families to more nuclear families during this time span contributed to a higher incidence of poverty. Barrington and Conrad calculate that the change in the demographic composition of households headed by white women generated an increase in the poverty rate of 7.8 percentage points, while the change by non-white women generated an increase in the poverty rate of 7.9 percentage points. "Clearly, for both whites and nonwhites, the change in the demographic composition of female-headed households contributed to the increasing poverty rate among these house-holds."[4] The choice of living arrangements made by divorced, widowed, and never-married women affects the proportion of female-headed house-holds among the poor. Female-headed households in 1960 had fewer adults and more young children than such households in 1940. This shift in the structure of family has a direct correlation to poverty levels of female-headed households:

> A female-headed family with earnings below the poverty line that is living in a larger male-headed household will not be counted as impoverished if the larger household's income exceeds the poverty line. If the same female-headed family forms an independent household, it will be counted as poor. If a female-headed family with low earnings was more likely to live in a larger male-headed household in 1939 than in 1959, then the poverty rate for female-headed families would have increased between 1939 and 1959.[5]

Conrad and Barrington are quick to point out that social norms could have also played a part in the reduction of threshold earnings. Living with adult children was a greater violation of norms in 1960 than in 1940, thus a shift that could encourage older women to form independent households at a lower earnings level in lieu of living with grown daughters. Additionally, ado-lescent pregnancy, higher rates of marital disruption, greater male mortality, and severely restricted economic opportunities have affected the household structure.

Whatever the attributing causes, the evidence suggests that among fami-lies with the lowest levels of earnings, a greater proportion formed indepen-dent households in 1959 than in 1939. This brings one to a closer examination of the female-headed households after the dissolution of marriage and probes one to question what role marriage plays in reducing or increasing economic vulnerability.

Karen Holden and Pamela Smock explain the disproportionate economic cost women pay following marital dissolution in the *Annual Review of Sociology:* "Longitudinal studies of the effects of divorce and widowhood indicate that both types of dissolution have negative and prolonged consequences for women's economic well-being."[6] Adding that this is not the case for men, Holden and Smock explain that marital dissolution often leads to an improved economic situation solely for men. Empirical evidence reveals that men are not only more financially secure compared to women following the dissolution of marriage, but they are situated in a position of greater economic stability compared to the previous economic status of the family as a whole. Unless women remarry, the economic deterioration they experience is likely to be significantly prolonged.

> Women's post-dissolution economic hardship is due to multiple interrelated factors, often only superficially coupled with the marital dissolution event. In particular, the division of labor during marriage, lower wages paid to women both during and after marriage, and the lack of adequate post-dissolution transfers to women imply that unless changes in women's work roles are mirrored by social policy initiatives and men's assumption of equal responsibility for children (both within and out of marriage), economic prospects for previously married women will remain poor.[7]

It is difficult to escape the conclusion that much of the association between marital dissolution and women's economic insecurity lies in the fact that "parenthood's costs are disproportionately borne by women even long after the children leave home."[8] Much of this disproportion can be attributed to the incompatibility of primary parenting and full-time work, the lack of affordable child care and women's disproportionate financial and time responsibility for children after the divorce.

Central to the conditions that cause greater economic insecurity for women are the lower wages paid to women both during marriage and after. In the "Cross-National Comparison of the Gender Gap in Income," Rachel Rosenfeld and Arne Kalleberg provide data which indicate that the greatest income inequality by sex is in the United States and the least in Sweden.[9] US women included in the analysis earn 57% of US men's earnings; Norwegian women, 58%; Swedish women, 64%. These figures, however, include the earnings of those working less than full-time, a more common situation among Scandinavian women. Among those employed at least 35 hours a week, the differences between these countries become sharper: the income for full-time employed women relative to that for full-time employed men is 58% in the United States, 74% in Norway, and 76% in Sweden.

Researchers argue that the primary reason for the gender gap in wages is sex segregation of jobs. Women are in jobs that pay less, and this sex segregation is predominantly lower in corporatist countries than in the dualist countries. The dualist countries, such as the United States and Canada, represent decentralized and non-inclusive employment and family policies, while

Norway and Sweden, representing corporatist countries, reveal greater income equality: "Women in Sweden tended to get greater returns to their job characteristics than men. For them, 'good' jobs are important for getting relatively better pay, while in other countries even good jobs tend to pay women less than men. The indirect effect of family policies on income through their effect on job location is thus an important area for further study."[10]

Women's union membership is more prevalent in these Scandinavian countries than in the US, and the returns from this membership in the Scandinavian countries provides greater income returns to women than men. Canadian women also get larger returns than men from union membership. Additionally, part-time workers in Scandinavia can get various health and other benefits because these are determined by the state rather than the employer. However, in the US, part-time employment usually means few—if any—benefits. This fact alone has serious economic implications on the ability of women in need of work, but also needed in the home. If part-time work isn't recognized in the United States as a means for single mothers to attain economic stability by compensating unpaid labor through benefits and government aid (such as is provided in Scandinavia), then the burden is not being alleviated, but exacerbated.

When examining the evidence, it is hard to ignore the discrepancy between ethnic and social class subgroups. For lower-class blacks and increasingly for poor Mexican-Americans and Puerto Ricans, reproduction occurs outside marriage and a large proportion of marriages end in divorce.[11] For these groups, female-headed households have become more common at both early and later stages of the family life course. Female hardship is becoming a lifelong phenomenon for many minority-group women, necessitating a demographic adaptation. Applying their analysis to the Survey on Aging (SOA), Jaqueline Lowe of the Population Issues Research Center at Pennsylvania State University and Ronald Angel at the University of Texas in Austin suggest:

> In the absence of economically active males, women often adapt by forming multigenerational female-headed households. Although men occasionally contribute economically in these households, for the most part women make up the permanent nuclear unit and must rely on one another or support.[12]

This proposition suggests that the growth in female-headed households among blacks and Hispanics is not a transitory characteristic, and we would expect a high proportion of unmarried older minority women not only to live with family, but to be the head of the household. Additionally, if extended living arrangements substitute institutionalization in the event of poor health and insufficient economic resources, the proportion of black and Hispanic women living with health problems and with family is going to be higher than non-Hispanic white women. Worobey and Angel conclude that the causes of specific living arrangements and of females being heads of household in later life are "unlikely to be due entirely to either health or poverty; instead they are more likely to be a complex response to poverty, with unknown consequences on the health of older women."[13]

The feminization of poverty has been the result of societal changes in the twentieth century. The government must address the inequality of gender, since there is little possibility that society can revert to the family model that existed earlier in the last century. Following the example of Western European countries, particularly Scandinavia, there are measures the government must take to end the impoverishment of women and children, and benefit society as a whole.

The current system of Welfare in the United States fails to address gender inequalities which contribute to the feminization of poverty, ignores the role of the primary caregiver as a labor worthy of compensation, and ultimately denies women of full citizenship benefits because of its ignorance.[14] More recent reforms, including the Personal Responsibilities Act passed under Clinton in 1996, subordinate poor single mothers in a separate system of law, forcing mothers to find economic security outside the home.

Gwendolyn Mink, Professor of Political Science at the University of California, Santa Cruz, argues that poor single mothers have always been judged by welfare policy, and developments in welfare policy have always either enhanced or undermined their rights, security, and ability to care for their children.[15] Single mothers are forced either by law or predicament to choose between children and wages. Mink explains:

> The broad support for disciplinary welfare reform is rooted in the view that mothers' poverty flows from moral failing. Both Democrats and Republicans emphasize the wrongs of mothers—their "unwillingness to work," their failure to marry (or stay married), their irresponsible sexuality and childbearing. Accordingly, the legislative debate about welfare was a contest among moral prescriptions, rather than a conflict between perspectives either on the role and responsibilities of government or on the rights and responsibilities of women.[16]

The Personal Responsibility Act [PRA] is a demonstration of a policy which substitutes a moral prescription for the economic mitigation of poverty. The Act not only ignores poor mothers' vocational freedom provided by the Thirteenth Amendment, which prevents coerced labor, but also endangers poor women's rights to make their own moral decisions about marriage, procreation, and family life. Under the PRA, poor mothers and their children do not have any legally enforceable claim to benefits. The PRA explicitly disclaims an entitlement for individuals in its statement of purposes, and requires states to allocate benefits not on need alone but also on moral conformity.

As Mink explains in her book, *Welfare's End,* there is some truth to the claim that welfare reform affects us all. Single mothers may be the most immediately harmed by the PRA, but the law's invasions of rights and protections affect all women. Congress impairs poor women's reproductive rights by paying states to reduce non-marital births, destroying the constitutional status of reproductive rights fundamental to all women's equality.

> Although the PRA requires disclosure of procreative relations from welfare mothers only, policymakers have proposed requiring mothers to identify

biological fathers outside the welfare context[17]. . . . Further, although poor single mothers are most directly endangered by the elimination of welfare's income entitlement, all mothers surrender equality in gender relations when government withdraws their safety net—their last gap means for economic independence from men.[18]

The initial welfare policies which emerged from the mothers' pension programs of the Progressive Era were based on the concept that welfare was to relieve poor single mothers of the necessity of wage-earning so that they might engage in the full-time care of their children. Today, the welfare policies have shifted in the opposite direction to remove women from the caregiving role inside the home and place them in a wage labor position.[19] Instead of forcing single mothers to choose children or wages, welfare policies must address the problems contributing to the feminization of poverty.

Karen Holden of the Department of Consumer Science and the Robert LaFollette Institute of Public Affairs and Pamela Smock of the Department of Sociology at the University of Wisconsin-Madison provide alternative financial assistance following the dissolution of marriage: "Households with children need continued sharing after marriage in the form of explicit transfers from husband to wife, either through the division of assets, child support payments, or insurance against death."[20] Another viable option is that children should continue to share the standard of living of the higher-income parent—who is usually the nonresidential father.

For households without children, when the husband dies or leaves their spouse alone, the woman should continue to share in the economic prosperity of the missing spouse through insurance against potential earnings lost. Particular emphasis in policy dialogues is thus placed on ensuring adequate child support, whether from the non-custodial parent or through governmentally guaranteed minimum benefit levels.

Part-time workers in the US should be given benefits in a manner similar to that found in other European countries. Part-time working mothers should have health care and government provided child-care so that women are not disadvantaged by being out of the labor force during their child-rearing years, nor do they have to choose full-time employment over their children to afford basic necessities.

The phenomenon of the feminization of poverty is not new. It has its roots in changes in living arrangements prior to 1960. The smaller, nuclear, female-headed families which have evolved from the previous status quo, consisting of larger, male-headed families have significantly impacted the economic status of many women in the United States. Research suggests that policy designed to combat the feminization of poverty cannot ignore the physical constitution of such families and the implications the constitution has upon the economic stability. Moreover, unless changes in female work roles are mirrored by social policy initiatives on several fronts as well as men's assumption of equal responsibility for children (both within and out of marriage), economic prospects for many women and children will continue to be grim.

Notes

1. Barrington, Linda, "At What Cost a Room of Her Own? Factors Contributing to the Feminization of Poverty Among Prime-Age Women." *Journal of Economic History,* Vol. 54, Issue 2, Papers Presented at the Fifth-Third Annual Meeting of the Economic History Association (Jun., 1994), 342–357.

2. Id. at 342

3. Id. at 343

4. Id. at 347

5. Id. at 348

6. Holden, Karen C., and Pamela Smock. "The Economic Costs of Marital Dissolution: Why do Women Bear a Disproportionate Cost?" *Annual Review of Sociology,* Vol. 17, 51–78

7. Id. at 52

8. Id. at 74

9. Rosenfeld, Rachel, and Arne Kalleberg. "A Cross-National Comparison of the Gender Gap in Income." *American Journal of Sociology,* Vol. 96, Issue 1 (July, 1990), 69–106.

10. Id. at 101

11. Worobey, Jacqueline Lowe, and Ronald Angel. "Poverty and Health: Older Minority Women and the Rise of the Female-Oriented Household," *Journal of Health and Social Behavior,* Vol. 31 (Dec. 1990), 370–383.

12. Id. at 372

13. Id. at 373

14. Mink, Gwendolyn. "Disdained Mothers, Unequal Citizens." Welfare's End. Ithaca: Cornell University Press, 1998.

15. Id. at 9

16. Id. at 5

17. For example, President Clinton's 1994 welfare bill sought the establishment of paternity for all non-marital hospital births.

18. Mink, p. 8

19. Regulating the Poor: The Function of Public Welfare. New York: Random House, 1971. Frances Fox Piven and Richard Cloward explain how this is a technique used to regulate the poor rather than aid them in their book.

20. Holden, Karen and Pamela Smock. "The Economic Costs of Marital Dissolution: Why Do Women Bear a Disproportionate Cost?" *Annual Review of Sociology,* Vol. 17 (1991), 51–78.

NO ↵

Hilda Kahne

Low-Wage Single-Mother Families in this Jobless Recovery: Can Improved Social Policies Help?

This article focuses on the experience of low-wage single-mother families and how they are affected by the current soft economy and jobless recovery that continues to display many of the earmarks of a recession. It suggests that these effects, bringing uncertainty and stress and often temporary loss of income and asset value for many people, are worse for low-wage earners, including single-mother families. They face a difficult labor market and must compete with more-skilled unemployed workers for available jobs, while carrying considerable family responsibilities, often with limited education and no income reserves for coping with emergencies. In the short run they need financial support through an updating of existing social policies that take account of changing economic realities and life style requirements. But their more permanent need is to increase earning ability that can only be assured if training and education programs make possible an increase in their skills and job versatility. . . .

Changing Economic Context

Long Run

The long-run changing economic context provides a valuable backdrop for understanding the linkage between production and well-being of societal groups. In a recent study of productive and related institutions over time, Michael Piore describes the changing nature of four key institutions between the 1950s and today—the family, corporate enterprises, trade unions, and the government. During the earlier period the family was structurally stable and defined as including a male earner and female homemaker. Corporate enterprises were organized for mass production with a labor force having defined skills and tasks. A strong trade union movement negotiated terms of employment. And a federal government provided regulatory legislation and oversight as well as a safety net for persons needing social support. . . .

From *Analyses of Social Issues and Public Policy,* vol. 4, issue 1, 2004, pp. 47–48, 52–56, 58–65. Copyright © 2004 by Blackwell Publishing, Ltd. Reprinted by permission.

More Recent Trends

Given Piore's insightful observations about long-run changing societal trends, what can be said about the shorter-run influences on the well-being of poor single-mother families and the possibility of their achieving an adequate standard of living as a participant in the creation of society's goods and services? How will they be affected by current changing trends? At present, 50% of persons in poverty live in female-headed families and of all female-headed families, over 25% have incomes below the poverty level. Can their existence be made more economically secure through policies that move them further toward economic independence? . . .

Female family heads experienced unemployment rates higher than the overall average. By February 2003, their unemployment rate was 9% compared with a rate of 5.8% for all workers. The higher rate was partly due to the lesser stability of frequently held low-skill jobs that were often temporary or contingent or part time. It was also probably higher than for other groups because some skilled laid-off workers, at least until they found other work, took low-skill jobs, replacing traditional low-skill workers who were then shuffled to the back of the queue and lacked needed abilities to compete for other openings. It was especially high for single mothers who lacked a high school degree—18% in 2002. In addition to high rates, unemployment has shown a continuing increase in its length. Women's long-term unemployment rates now match those of men. . . .

The causes of the growth in income disparity are multiple and economists do not agree on the relative importance among them. Growing earnings inequality undoubtedly explains much of it with rewards given for high skills and educational levels. Bonuses and stock option benefits have also increased income, especially at the high managerial levels, as have relatively greater tax reductions for high-income groups. Some of the disparity has also been due to the effects of technological changes and of globalization. At the other end of the income stream, changes in family structures, erosion of the value of the minimum wage, and a decline in union bargaining strength have undoubtedly had negative effects on income distribution. Continued gender wage discrimination can intensify these effects. But, whatever the causes of growing inequality, the fact remains that in recent years the inequality in income distribution has increased despite the economic growth that has taken place in society as a whole. Although in the past all groups benefited from rising productivity in reduced unemployment and rising wages, this has not happened in recent years. The distribution of income has become more, rather than less, unequal.

Changing Family Structures and Economic Status

. . . The family, as we know, has been a true anchor of social life. But its form and the roles of its members have varied across cultures and nations and through historical time. . . . [I]n the United States, at least, it is "structure" that statistically defines a family unit. Government data on families reflect particular structural forms and have yet to take account of the features that highlight the cohesion that family units represent.

Family data for the United States is reported by the U.S. Census as part of household data. The Census defines a family as two or more people related by birth, marriage, or adoption who reside together. Female householders were 12% of all households and almost one-fifth of all families in 2001. About 60% of all single householders are single parents. The U.S. Bureau of Labor Statistics also reports on several categories of female singlehood such as single women (with or without children), single mothers with one or more children (own and/or step and/or adopted), and female householders (who may or may not have children). If a single mother with children is living in her mother's residence, she may be excluded from a single-family head accounting. Thus, discussions about categories of female family heads must be carefully defined and interpreted.

. . . No regular account is taken of blended families as a category, not infrequently composed of two or more clusters of stepchildren. Nonfamily households that have grown at twice the rate of family households, although not considered to be "families," often fulfill the role of a family unit. Sometimes single mothers and children live in a grandparent household; increasingly, the grandparents alone are the parent figures. But they are not included as a distinct family form in statistics. Widows are often subsumed under other categories such as "single mothers" or "elders." In fact, there are characteristics and issues that are unique to them.

Whereas in the 1950s, about 90% of all families were married couples, with a large majority of wives being homemakers, by 2001, only 76.3% of all families were married couples and over one-half of wives were in the paid labor force. By way of contrast, 10% of all families were female householders with no husband present in 1959; in 2001, they numbered 13.1 million or 17.7% of all families. . . .

For middle-class traditionally married parents, it is often difficult to understand the complexities required of a single parent who must meet not only work demands of inflexible work hours and required production schedules, but also the many immediate family demands that involve time and money and issues of child safety. . . .

But more than this, a high proportion of single-mother families experience low income and high rates of poverty because of limited education and/or job skills. Their treatment as low-paid workers is often further marked not only by wage disadvantage relative to men in comparable jobs, but also by more frequent lay-offs, involuntary part-time work, job severance, and lack of health and pension benefits and severance pay. Their situation can be further compromised by the absence of child support and accompanying stress and always the complexities involved in having to combine paid work with home responsibilities. Income reserves with which to meet emergencies are often absent. Single-mother parenting and poverty reflect a connection that is only somewhat mitigated in recent years by the rising labor force participation of single mothers. . . .

The rapid growth of single-mother families, and their association with high rates of poverty, has led to a number of research studies seeking to identify the causes for the strong growth trend in this family structure. . . .

One factor influencing the rapid growth of the group has been the weakening of the time linkage between marriage and having a child. This extension of time between the two events, found to be true for both white and black women who marry, is perhaps encouraged by the wish to participate in the labor market. But among less-educated black women who do not marry and who have fewer skills, marriage may be postponed but child bearing prior to marriage is not and is more likely than for white women, though both groups more commonly than in the past have children before or without marriage. Other factors may also play a role in the growth of single-mother families, though with varying intensity and direction at any one time. For example, a poor labor market experience of low-skill men (in wages or employment) as well as a low production of marriageable men relative to women can lead to marriage avoidance and an increase in the pool of single mothers. Divorce, greater sexual freedom, the availability of cohabitation as a prelude or alternative to marriage, and a lack of effective birth control availability and usage can also influence the result. Not all factors have the same intensity and direction at any one time—but the fact of their multiplicity and differing strength for specific population groups has made for complexity in explaining growth trends of low-wage single-mother families. What is clear is that single parenting, for low-skill women especially, has grown in size and results for them, as for other single-mother heads, in a complexity of life's functioning and often financial difficulty and poverty in achieving and retaining economic self-sufficiency for the family reliant on the earnings of one low-wage earner who must fulfill and reconcile both work and home demands.

Poverty: Consequences for Single-Mother Families

Changes in family structures, reinforced by the fact that economic growth in itself does not ensure a dispersal of its benefits to all members of society, have resulted in increasingly wide differences in family incomes. Poverty is often the consequence for single-mother families. . . .

[W]e can expect that with increasing income inequality, reduced job creation and prolonged unemployment for those who lose jobs, that family poverty will be a concern for some time to come, even if economic improvement begins for more skilled groups. The interaction of the growth of economically challenged family structures, combined with an uncertain economy with high unemployment, and the lack of adequate social supports including skill training, will continue to frustrate the efforts of poor families to regain an economic foothold in society.

Social Policy Directions

Existing Social Policies to Improve Incomes

A broad range of wage-related social policy measures need consideration and improvement in order to address effectively the downward sliding position and earnings inadequacy of many single-mother families. Each in some way compensates for inadequate wages and has merit. But none provides a means for permanently increasing the skill and productivity, and hence earnings, of the single-mother providers. This concluding section evaluates existing wage-related income-supportive measures and points the way to policies that can help to establish what is most important—an earned income economic independence for the family unit.

1. *Unemployment Insurance.* Unemployment insurance fulfills a distinctive need of helping to stabilize an economy in troubled times and to providing partial earnings replacement to maintain consumer spending for regular workers who experience involuntary temporary job loss. . . .

   Problems in coverage and eligibility for unemployment benefits arise not only because of changes in the law, but because of the changing nature of work and of labor force work patterns since the law's original enactment. Originally, unemployment was viewed as a temporary employment rupture due to cyclical and seasonal variation in employment patterns. But with changing technological and globalization effects causing major and long-term need for structural adjustments, unemployment can require permanent change in job location and work skills. At the same time, regular full-time uninterrupted work affiliation with an employer, by choice or necessity, is no loner the norm for many workers, especially women, who are more likely to work in service and retail industries where nonstandard work is more common.

   Indeed, women and increasing numbers of men, may need to choose such jobs (part-time, part-year, temporary, or other contingent work offering limited benefits, as best) in an effort to balance work and family responsibility. . . . [Thus, t]he unemployment insurance program is in need of review and revision to adapt to the realities of today's work structures and work patterns and to the needs of all groups in the labor force.

2. *Minimum Wage.* Low wage earners need more than the national economic growth and full employment to assure a satisfactory standard of living. Their well-being also requires that they receive adequate earnings to enable them to support their families. Historically, minimum wage legislation has provided an earnings floor. . . .

   Two criticisms, in addition to the low level of the national minimum wage, are directed at the effectiveness of minimum wage policy in fulfilling its purpose. One criticism points to the low-wage teen-age individuals in the group, not all of whom live in poor families. But teenagers constitute only about one-fourth of the minimum wage workers. Their earnings, like those of other family members, help to meet a variety of expenditures, including family needs and education. They are entitled to equal pay for the equal work they perform.

The second criticism concerns the claim that, consistent with traditional economic theory, an increase in labor costs resulting from an increase in the minimum wage will negatively impact employment levels. Some studies have supported this result. But other recent scholarly research does not show this and, in fact, indicates that employment levels sometimes even increase as a consequence of worker increased motivation and satisfaction when the minimum wage is raised. . . .

3. *Earned Income Tax Credit (EITC).* Complementing the income support provided by the minimum wage is the Earned Income Tax Credit, a form of negative income tax credit applied to wages paid to low-income earners. Non-wage earners are not eligible for these benefits. . . . Single-mother families have especially benefited from the law's provisions. These benefits are viewed as being responsible for the large increase in their labor force participation in recent years.

Under the provisions of the federal law, a small credit is available to low-income single persons with no children and to childless couples. Substantially more, computed on a graduated scale, is payable to one-child families, and higher amounts to families with two or more children. . . .

The tax credit receives high praise from all political sectors. It is seen as providing a major stimulus for low-income single-mother heads of families and others to engage in paid work in order to qualify for an earned income benefit. And it provides a major boost to incomes of the 18.6 million low-wage family recipients. . . .

4. *Training and Education: A Missing Policy Link.* Each of these existing social supports have worthy goals and provide a measure of income support for the low earnings received by a worker or the absence of wages of a regular labor force participant temporarily and involuntarily unemployed. At present, the EITC is the strongest nation-wide measure in this category, giving tax credit and income rebate support specifically for low-earning family units. It provides a stimulus to potential earners in poor families to engage in paid work, with the result that poverty and the degree of family income inequality nationally can be somewhat lessened. It has been a major cause of the reduction of poverty for children and families.

Still, none of the national social policies, though supportive, has as a goal an increase in wages to a level adequate for family self-sufficiency. It is this that should be the long-run goal of social policy. This is what is needed to complement the income policies that buttress and supplement existing low wages.

Low wages and the increasing disparity in wages between low and high earners are thought by many economists to be linked in a major way to the relatively greater demand for more highly skilled and technically proficient workers. This demand is expected to continue to grow in the future as globalization and the use of technology intensify. Although wage supportive policies can buttress income for low earners, it is education and training that raise worker productivity and enable a move to more skilled jobs at higher wages. An added benefit of such a policy would be reducing the inequality in the distribution of income that now exists. . . .

Training and education programs are neither inexpensive nor easy to implement. Well-conceived programs must not only respond to employer and community skill needs but must take place for a period of time long enough to develop well-honed workplace talents. But all of society would benefit from the increased productivity that results from such programs. And the ameliorative social support that now buttresses low earnings would have as its complement a social policy that would both reduce national disparities in family incomes and, at the same time, make possible a permanent rise in the family standard of living for previously low-income families. That would be a welcome achievement for low-wage single mothers who have shown in earlier training programs an ability to respond well relative to other groups to training opportunities that have been offered them . It is time to develop constructive legislation to provide this meaningful steppingstone for single mother earners and other low-income groups to higher skills and more adequate family income.

POSTSCRIPT

Are Gender Inequalities Primarily Responsible for the Increased Number of Low-Wage Single-Mother Families?

A related controversy surrounds the incidence of conception and childbirth while the mother is a welfare recipient (i.e., "subsequent births"). Traditionally, welfare policies grant monetary benefits to families based on the number of children. Thus, the birth of another child would earn the family increased financial support. Critics charge these women with intentionally having additional children so as to increase their financial benefit and view them as irresponsible and promiscuous (though, on average, welfare recipients have fewer children than individuals not on welfare). Critics fear that subsequent births will promote long-term dependency on federal aid. The 1996 federal welfare reform law allows states discretion to adopt strategies for inhibiting subsequent births.

States have adopted a variety of programs that operationalize supposed solutions to the subsequent birth problem. Efforts include family caps on welfare benefits, enhanced family-planning services, directive counseling (telling mothers they should not have another baby and instructing them in how to prevent pregnancy), and financial incentives for young mothers who do not become pregnant. Additional incentives and programs aimed at keeping women from having additional children and keeping young women from having sex include the "Illegitimacy Bonus," which rewards states that reduce their out-of-wedlock birthrate while also reducing abortion rates for all women, not just those on welfare; the Abstinence-Only Standard" (see Issue 13), which offers financial incentives to states that teach abstinence as the expected or only standard; requiring unmarried mothers under the age of 18 to live with their parents; and enforcing child support by performing paternity tests to identify biological fathers and forcing women to turn in fathers of their children or lose benefits, regardless of the risk of physical or emotional harm to the woman or her children.

Most controversial are family cap provisions, which preclude a welfare recipient from receiving additional case benefits for a child conceived while the recipient parent was on welfare (albeit the child would be eligible for Medicaid coverage and other benefits). The desired outcome of family cap provisions would be fewer out-of-wedlock births.

Supporters of family caps believe that the traditional rule that welfare benefits are determined on the basis of the number of children in a family actually provides a financial incentive to have children while on welfare. Therefore, family caps are implemented to send a message to these women that they should not have more children until they can support them.

Opponents of family caps consider them to be in violation of a mother's right to determine whether or when to have children. Others fear that family caps wil increase welfare families' hardship and increase abortion rates. Interestingly, some evaluation studies of such programs also look for higher abortion rates as an outcome signifying program success. In fact, program evaluation research to date has been underwhelming, resulting frequently in inconclusive or disappointing results.

Another criticism is that efforts at the "rational econometric control" of reproduction are ignorant of the complexities involved in becoming pregnant. Typically, two individuals are involved in a social interaction that is not always volitional and often includes an array of pressures. To what degree can reproduction be controlled by incentive pressures? It is also noteworthy that males' role in fertility are largely ignored in programs aimed at reducing subsequent births.

Welfare legislation and statistics raise serious questions about gender dynamics and differentials. Why are most welfare recipients women? How is the societal construction of "mother" and "father" related to welfare statistics and policies? How is socioeconomic class associated with women's reproductive rights and freedoms? How do existing gender inequalities contribute to single mothers low-income status? How does racism amplify the problems for women of color?

Selected Readings

Children's Defense Fund, "Families Struggling to Make It in the Workforce: A Post Welfare Report" (December 2000).

Diane F. Halpern and S. E. Murphy, eds., (2005). *From Work-Family Balance to Work-Family Interaction: Changing the Metaphor* (Mahwah, NJ: Lawrence Erlbaum Associates, Inc. Publishers, 2005).

Diane F. Halpern, "How Time-Flexible Work Policies Can Reduce Stress, Improve Health, and Save Money," *Stress and Health*, 21, (2005).

K. Edin, L. Lein, T. Nelson, and S. Clampet-Lundquist, "Talking With Low-Income Fathers," *Poverty Research News*, 4, (2000).

M. C. Lennon, J. Blome, and K. English, "Depression and Low-Income Women: Challenges for TANF and Welfare-to-Work Policies and Programs," *Research Forum on Children, Families and the New Federalism, National Center for Children in Poverty* (Columbia University, 2001).

Martha Fetherolf Loutfi, ed., *Women, Gender and Work: What Is Equality and How Do We Get There?* (New Delhi: Rawat Publications, 2002).

Gary N. Powell, ed., *Handbook of Gender and Work* (Thousand Oaks, CA: Sage, 1999).

World Health Organization

The World Health Organization Web site provides access to many documents related to female genital mutilation.

http://www.who.int/mipfiles/2270/
241-FemaleGenitalMutilationforMIP.pdf

Information for Health

The INFO Project (Information and Knowledge for Optimal Health Project), based at the Johns Hopkins University Bloomberg School of Public Health's Center for Communication Programs, is focused on understanding how knowledge and information can improve the quality of reproductive health programs, practice, and policies.

http://www.infoforhealth.org/

Go Ask Alice!

Go Ask Alice! is a health question-and-answer site and is sponsored by Columbia University's health education program. The mission of this site is to provide in-depth, factual, and nonjudgmental information to assist individuals' decision making about their physical, sexual, emotional, and spiritual health. Questions about sexuality, sexual health, and relationships are frequent. This site includes hundreds of relevant links.

http://www.goaskalice.columbia.edu/

University of New Hampshire

The Crimes against Children Research Center (CCRC) at the University of New Hampshire provides high-quality research and statistics to the public, policy-makers, law enforcement personnel, and other child welfare practitioners. The center focuses on research about the nature of crimes including child abduction, homicide, rape, assault, and physical and sexual abuse as well as their impact. The center's definition of child sexual abuse includes adultlike romantic relationships between adults and minors.

http://www.unh.edu/ccrc/

National Organization to Halt Abuse and Routine Mutilation of Males

The Web site for the National Organization to Halt the Abuse and Routine Mutilation of Males: A Health & Human Rights Organization (NOHARMM) is dedicated to what it calls a campaign for genital integrity and provides information and links related to male and female circumcision.

http://www.noharmm.org/

PART 5

Gender and Sexuality: Double Standards?

*H*ow *do adolescents first experience sexual attractions—developing a "crush," falling in love, making the decision to "go all the way." How does a child grow into a sexual being? What does it mean to be sexual? How does a child learn to think about his or her own genitals? These are profoundly personal and important questions, the answers to which are shaped by our cultural understanding of sexuality.*

Many contemporary scholars view sexuality as a cultural construction. Cultures provide individuals with knowledge and "lenses" that structure institutions, social interactions, beliefs, and behaviors. Through cultural lenses or meaning systems, individuals perceive the "facts" of sex and gender. Conceptualizations of sex and gender and the importance of sex and gender as social categories vary from culture to culture. However, within a particular culture, because individuals are usually limited to their own cultural lens, definitions of sex and gender seem fixed or even natural. In fact, cultural scholars argue, culture so completely defines us that we are usually oblivious to its presence in our own society. We think of culture as something that other societies have.

In this section, we examine cultural constructions of sex and gender, especially messages sent to children and adolescents. Specifically, how are cultural institutions and mores structured by cultural definitions of the importance of sex and gender and by cultural gender proscriptions? What does culture dictate about the significance and characteristics of the social categories "male" and "female"? Does one's standpoint or location within the culture prescribe one's sexual experiences?

- Is Female Circumcision Universally Wrong?

- Should "Abstinence-Until-Marriage" Be the Only Message for Teens?

- Can Women's Sexuality Be Free From Traditional Gender Constraints?

- Are Adult–Child Sexual Relations Always Harmful?

Is Female Circumcision Universally Wrong?

YES: Gerald Mackie, from "Female Genital Cutting: A Harmless Practice?" *Medical Anthropology Quarterly* (2003)

NO: Carla Obermeyer, from "The Health Consequences of Female Circumcision: Science, Advocacy, and Standards of Evidence," *Medical Anthropology Quarterly* (2003)

ISSUE SUMMARY

YES: Gerald Mackie takes a scientific approach to challenge the argument that female genital cutting is not always harmful, citing multiple examples of physical and psychological harm.

NO: Carla M. Obermeyer argues that a lack of research precludes us from fully understanding female circumcision and claiming that it is responsible for a variety of harmful health outcomes. She includes examples of no harm.

According to the World Health Organization, female circumcision (also called female genital mutilation—FGM) involves the partial or total removal of the external female genitalia or other injuries to the female genital organs. These practices may occur for cultural, religious, or other nontherapeutic reasons. Is female circumcision a practice of some cultures that other cultures should respect? To what extent is it a fundamental violation of females' human rights? For those who conclude that it is, the basis of their claim is based on health concerns or on concerns surrounding the imposition of gender role constraints on women, the most fundamental being reduction in capacity for female sexual pleasure.

FGM is practiced primarily in Middle Eastern, African, Indonesian, and other Muslim countries. In Africa it is estimated that every year two million girls are subjected to FGM. The practice reduces their chances of having a normal sexual and reproductive life and jeopardizes their own survival, as well as that of their unborn children. Other complications include severe pain, shock, hemorrhage, urinary retention, ulceration of the genital region, and injury to adjacent tissue. Hemorrhage and infection can cause death.

The type of FGM and the age at which the practice is done varies across countries and regions, ranging from birth to early adulthood. The targeted age varies by the cultural meaning of the ritual. For example, if FGM is thought of as a rite of passage into adult womanhood, FGM is done at the age of 14 or 15. If FGM is done to control female sexuality, the procedure is performed at age 7 or 8. FGM has a disproportionate impact on girls of color. Mothers, grandmothers, and other female kin typically control FGM. Women who are not medically trained usually perform the procedures.

There has been heated debate about FGM as being in violation of universal human rights. Are there certain fundamental, inviolable human rights that transcend all cultural boundaries? Cultural universalists argue *yes*. But cultural relativists respond *no*, arguing that Western liberal individualism has biased the delineation of human rights, and thus current delineations of human rights cannot be seen as universal but as Western impositions on non-Westerners. Cultural relativists also maintain that scholars' prioritization of human rights differs in Western and non-Western societies, whereby Westerners value civil and political rights over social and cultural rights; non-Westerners tend to do the opposite. Universalists retort that relativists' toleration of FGM and other harmful cultural practices perpetuates the violation of human rights and reinforces the subjugation of women to the interests of their larger sociocultural group.

Some immigrants to the United States and Canada from Aboriginal, Christian, and Muslim families from some Muslim countries desire to continue the practice as a social tradition. It is also done at birth to some "intersex" infants for what are seen by some as medical reasons. One issue in the United States is the pressure to allow immigrants to continue this practice, where it is outlawed with prison sentences up to five years.

On the question of justified reaction to FGM, the universalist position has largely prevailed. Many legal and nonlegal strides have been made in the international campaign against FGM, including the passage of the Female Genital Multilation Act into U.S. law in 1996. On February 5, 2004, the World Health Organization reconfirmed its call to member states in the African region to eliminate female circumcision. In recognition of the first International Day on Zero Tolerance to FGM (observed on 6 February 2004), the WHO Regional Director for Africa (AFRO), Dr. Ebrahim M. Samba said, "I appeal to all (African) countries and their (development) partners to ensure that this practice is eliminated in our continent." But now the question has shifted from whether or not FGM is a human rights violation to how FGM can be eradicated, effecting lasting social change. Some argue that relativists' sensitivity to the cultural context may be more effective in bringing about change *from within*, since culture itself is the most formidable obstacle. Universalist critics argue that assertive condemnation is necessary to convey the moral imperative of the eradication of FGM, anything short of this stance may be counterproductive. In the following selections, Gerald Mackie represents the universalist stance, and Carla Obermeyer advocates a cultural relativist position on bringing about the eradication of FGM. As you read these selections, consider with which position you are most comfortable and why.

Gerry Mackie

➡ **YES**

Female Genital Cutting:
A Harmless Practice?

The stated purpose of a recent article in this journal (Obermeyer 1999) is to obtain a relative reduction of funding for research intended to assist affected peoples to abandon the practice of female genital cutting (FGC), labeled advocacy, and thereby obtain a relative increase of funding for the mass survey research preferred by the author, labeled science (p. 85). The article has entered public debate as warrant for the claim that FGC is of minimal harm, and, thus, that it should be legalized for minors in the United States (it is presently legal for consenting adults) and other immigrant-receiving countries; that claims for asylum based on FGC are spurious; and that international agencies such as WHO and UNICEF should cease supporting programs for abandonment of FGC in practicing areas of Africa.

The article speaks in the voice of science as the authoritative survey of the epidemiological, demographic, and anthropological evidence on the question. It was awarded the Polgar Prize by the Society for Medical Anthropology, for the best article published in volume 13 (1999) of the society's journal, *Medical Anthropology Quarterly*. The article is correct that some people have undifferentiated and exaggerated views about the forms, meanings, and risks of FGC, and that it would be better to have more research on the topic. Otherwise, many of its remarkable claims are mistaken, or so I shall argue. Because of the article's vigorous claim to authority, and because of its actual and possible effects on public policy and private health decisions, I call attention to ambiguities, inconsistencies, and errors that one ordinarily might leave unmentioned. . . .

Scientific Conclusions

The article presents itself as the scientific approach toward FGC, in opposition to the "moral advocacy" (p. 78) approach of policy makers, activists, and professionals in various fields concerned to end the practice. The article claims to be within the purely empirical scientific framework (p. 97), based on the sciences of epidemiology and demography, "two disciplines where the evaluation of empirical evidence is a central preoccupation" (p. 81). The moral advocacy position is said to lack nuance (p. 79) and moderation (p. 98).

According to the article, the moral advocacy position has aroused an international consensus and mobilization to end FGC based on two

From *Medical Anthropology Quarterly,* vol. 17, no. 2, 2003, excerpts from 135–154. Copyright © 2003 as conveyed via the Copyright Clearance Center. Reprinted by permission.

premises: (1) that the practices are widespread, and (2) that the practices have "extremely harmful consequences for those who undergo them" (p. 80). An unstated implication of such an argument is that if one of the premises were wrong, then the international consensus on advocacy would be wrong; the author states that the second premise is wrong. I say, however, that the international consensus and mobilization on FGC is based on two alternative premises: (1) that in general there is an absence of meaningful consent to the irreversible act of FGC, and (2) that complications are nontrivial. Liberals are reluctant to intervene against activities freely consented to by adults, or of trivial consequence. Prevalence is not morally relevant: If only one person suffers nontrivial complications in the absence of consent, then that is a matter for concern. Complications are relevant only if nontrivial, but such complications need not be precisely measured, especially frequent, or especially severe. . . .

The genius of epidemiology is to detect a causal relationship between an exposure, often subtle, and outcomes that are obscure, rare, or latent. There is no causal question, however, about the connection of the traumatic injury of FGC to immediate complications such as bleeding and infection, nor to many of the delayed complications cited in the literature. Nor is prevention obscure: Refrain from doing the FGC and the complications do not ensue. Effective strategies of prevention are a sociological question, not a medical one. Secondarily, epidemiology might establish frequencies and dose–response relationships. Such information might be very useful in crafting strategies of prevention, but it need not be, and in any case we would also want insights from many fields of inquiry, most of all from people involved in the practice and attempts to end it.

The [Obermeyer] article demands evidence that is *incontrovertible*; further, it states that those who claim nontrivial complications must present *irrefutable* (p. 91) and *indisputable* (p. 97) evidence for their case. An epidemiology textbook explains that since Hume it has been understood that induction fails to provide a foundation for conclusive causal inference (Rothman and Greenland 1998:22). Perhaps the author means that the claim must be beyond any reasonable doubt. But there is no reasonable doubt that FGC is a traumatic injury, nor, from an anatomical standpoint, that there are associated complications of nontrivial quality. Frequencies of complications are more vaguely apprehended, but, for purposes of public policy, these assessments should be made by the public-policy standard rather than by the laboratory standard of evidence. By either standard, the author has no warrant to claim as "fact that the most severe complications are actually rare events" (p. 93).

Similarly, the article's anticlimactic claim that FGC is "probably" not a matter of "relative safety," but that further studies are needed to attain greater certainty (p. 97), wrongly assumes that harm is harder to establish than safety and it commits an error of misplaced precision. There is insufficient evidence that FGC is safe. There is no reasonable doubt that FGC is harmful.

Theory: Idiographic or Comparative?

According to the [Obermeyer] article, "female genital surgeries" are practices that are ambiguous, variable, changing (p. 84); sociodemographic factors equivocally relate to them (p. 88); indeed, "it may not be possible to fully understand the complex forces that account for the persistence or decline of these practices" (p. 97). . . . The author believes that the only commonality among the practices is that they involve the cutting of women's genital areas (p. 89). But just as it is possible for the ethnographer to generalize despite the range of circumstances, motivations, and meanings across individual respondents, so is it possible for the comparativist to generalize across groups.

A commonality of major importance overlooked in the article is that FGC is found more or less contiguously within a zone of distribution, but is not found outside that zone (with a few exceptions that can be traced to diffusions in the historical era). Such a distribution demands theoretical attention. Also, adherents give different but overlapping reasons for the practice. When we look for patterns across lists, we notice that marriageability and tradition are offered as reasons in almost all groups. This commonality suggests that these two reasons usually play the causal role and that the remainder of reasons are either explained by marriageability and tradition or express noncausal associationist responses to the practice. . . .

The only way to abandon such a convention is if a critical mass of the families in an intramarrying group agrees to stop together at the same time, which preserves the marriageability of their daughters. This method worked to end the convention of footbinding in China. In Senegal, people in rural villages with almost no formal education were exposed in a basic education program to nondirective health, human rights, and other information that, among many other items, included information about FGC. They were further given information about how one village (later many) stopped FGC by means of collective deliberation culminating in public declaration that all would stop FGC at the same time. As predicted by the convention hypothesis, people in exposed villages decide to abandon FGC by the same process, and these are by far the largest abandonments in the FGC zone. Further abandonments now proceed through hundreds of villages by way of organized contagion. . . .

Trends and Variations

The [Obermeyer] article reports that in some places there is a (modest) decline in prevalence and shift to less severe forms. Elsewhere, persistence is robust (p. 87). There is an association of FGC with region and with ethnic group, but an equivocal association with urbanization, it says, and an equivocal association with education (p. 88). The equivocal association with education, it argues, "undermines a key presumption" in the literature, "that the spread of formal education, mass media, and 'modern' health care entails a convergence in worldviews towards biomedicine and the particular ways in which 'universal' values are defined . . . in international human rights documents" (p. 89). This discrepancy poses a puzzle to the intellect and imagination, it says (p. 89); FGC is perhaps even "unknowable" (pp. 97, 98).

The absence of an education effect on attitudes toward FGC is the second most important claim in the article (the first is the minimization of

Table 1

**Beh = Behavior = Prevalence, Percent Respondents Cut;
Att = Attitude = Percent Respondents Support Continuation of FGC.**

Country:	CAR		CDI		Egypt		Eritrea		Mali		Sudan	
Education:	Beh	Att	Beh	Att	Beh	Att	Beh	Att	Beh	Att	Beh	Att
Sec'ary+	23	11	23	na	91	61	92	18	90	48	98	55
Primary	45	29	25	na	100	87	93	34	94	76	98	84
None	48	36	55	na	100	93	95	71	94	78	83	82

Sec'ary+ = Secondary education or better
CAR = Central African Republic, CDI = Ivory Coast

Source: Carr 1997:69–74

complications); the finding is now repeated in policy debates. The claim contributes to further inferences: that the understanding of advocates and generalizers is shallow and ethnocentric (p. 90), that FGC continues because it is of minimal harm (pp. 91, 92, 94), and that the association of genital organs with sexual enjoyment is a social construction peculiar to the Western worldview (p. 96).

[However, it] helps to display further DHS [Demographic Health Surveys] results in tabular and more complete form, as in Table 1. Looking at the columns labeled *Beh* (Behavior), indicating percentage cut, it is plain that in five of the six countries there *is* an education effect (Sudan is the exception, and I surmise that ethnicity confounds education in this case).

. . . Looking at the columns labeled *Att* (Attitude) in Table 1, it is plain that large proportions of the more educated do *not* support continuation of FGC, and in larger proportions than the less educated. . . .

There are many who oppose the practice of FGC but nevertheless intend it for their daughters. If behavior matched attitude, then, among women who oppose continuation of cutting, 100 percent in each country would intend not to have their daughters cut. . . . The DHS findings suggest that the mothers are caught in a convention trap. . . .

Empirical Science versus Moral Advocacy

The [Obermeyer] article discourages generalizations about FGC (except to the extent permitted by the scientific demographic and health surveys) and encourages attention to the heterogeneity disclosed by ethnographic reports. It recommends that we investigate and understand the motivations of people who do FGC, "without dismissing others as ignorant, irrational and cruel" (p. 93). Yet, in its discourse about *advocates,* the article makes broad and extremely negative generalizations. Their discourse is not "supported by the evidence" (p. 79), which suggests that the advocates are ignorant. The advocates fail "to gain an insider's view of those societies that practice such surgeries" (p. 89), which suggests that they are irrational, as does their "false sense of knowledge" and "sensationalizing accounts" (p. 90). Their "reactions of rejection and contempt," their "neocolonial thinking," and their domineering role in "ongoing political struggles about legitimacy and authority, at both the local and the global levels" (p. 90), suggest that they are cruel.

The article demands the highest standards of evidence for the uncontroversial proposition that FGC entails nontrivial complications but offers no such evidence for its controversial propositions about the advocates. The negative characterization of them violates two further canons of science.

First, other than an assertion that "many" (pp. 89–90) sources, publications, and discussions of FGC deserve such characterization, the article presents no data of any kind concerning the distribution of views among those who prefer FGC to end. Shouldn't we appreciate the heterogeneity of views among advocates? The term includes everyone in the world who would like for FGC to end and contains everyone from African individuals who have worked a lifetime for reform to high school students writing term papers in Peoria.

Second, there is no controlled comparison of advocates' attitudes with respect to matched issues. To make the point that advocates are unusually in the grip of illegitimate motivations, the article would have to measure, say, American advocates' attitudes with respect to FGC in Africa, and American advocates' attitudes with respect to an American issue, perhaps abortion. Do all pro-choice advocates have a thorough and detailed grasp of the relevant evidence? Do they all sympathetically understand the motives of pro-lifers, and discuss them in tones of reserve and respect?

To conclude, is the article's claim merely that public opinion has a shallow understanding of a topic distant from respondents' experiences? Or does it intend to lodge the serious charge that the most informed and most practically involved advocates are factually and morally mistaken?

Frequency of Health Complications

The article excludes from evidence of health complications all anatomical inference, all history, all journalism, all ethnography, all policy forums, all public health reports, all clinical observations, and all personal experiences. . . .

The article concludes, then, that health complications "are the exception rather than the rule" (p. 92). Death from malaria is the exception rather than the rule, but no physician would put it that way to a patient about to travel to a malarial zone. A more responsible statement for the public would be that "complications are common, and can be serious." Summarizing the DHS research, Carr states that "women commonly report cutting-related health problems" (1997:6). The DHS surveys that the article considers authoritative measured self-reported complications in the Central African Republic, Egypt, and Eritrea. The DHS analysis extrapolated from the sample to estimate that one million women in those countries would self-report complications (Carr 1997:41), and in its summary reported that "medical problems related to genital cutting are a public health issue of some magnitude" (Carr 1997:6). For those one million women, complications would be the rule not the exception. . . .

Perils of Survey Research

The [Obermeyer] article warns that respondent women may not be able to accurately distinguish among complications and may be subject to recall bias with respect to both the operation and potential complications. I want to add that there are other major problems of causal attribution that would bias toward serious underreporting of FGC complications, and these must be considered in research design.

If FGC is nearly universal within an intramarrying group, then respondents themselves have no comparison group. In the worst case, they would mistakenly consider even immediate complications as normal background, and this would bias against both recognition and recall of complications. Respondents without close knowledge of untreated women may not suspect a causal relationship between FGC and complications. Writing about complications of infibulation in Islamic Northeast Africa, Hicks observes:

> Women do not even correlate subsequent physical discomfort, pain, and related gynecological and obstetric problems with having been circumcised. Such physical problems are perceived as being the common lot of women. That is because the problems are, to one degree or other, prevalent among the majority of infibulated women, they are not viewed as unusual. Logically then, neither the act of infibulation nor related sequelae (unless requiring emergency treatment) are high priority issues for women in these societies. [1996:73]

. . . A survey among such women would show very different results before and after the discovery of a causal relationship (the article, however, considers schooling or contact with women's organizations a biasing factor; p. 100). An excisors' future work depends on the repute of her skills in carrying out the cutting. I learned in Senegal that excisors, those who perform FGC, often for compensation, will, sincerely or opportunistically, minimize or misattribute immediate complications, which further contributes to causal misattribution in the population. . . .

There seems to be a universal human reticence about discussing matters relating to human sexuality. This is exacerbated in some localities by norms of female modesty and further in some localities by powerful norms of secrecy concerning FGC and its meanings. . . .

Prior to sensitization, a causal relationship was not suspected by those involved in the practice and would never have been discovered, because women did not disclose to one another, let alone to local men or to outsiders, information about the FGC and associated (though unrecognized) complications; complete silence was the powerful norm. After sensitization, and the suggestion of a causal relationship, women began to share experiences about complications, and discovered, to their horror, that what they thought were unassociated or idiosyncratic harms were associated and unacceptably prevalent. . . .

Survey results would drastically undermeasure complications in locations where there is a strong norm of secrecy—the norm of secrecy is itself a secret—and would mislead, compared to other approaches. It would not do to have flawed surveys paraded as science alongside the dismissal of anatomical inferences, clinical reports, personal experiences, and other data as worthless information. Poorly designed survey research would also suffer from extreme selection bias on the question of severe complications. The survey would undercount all complications sufficiently severe to remove the woman by death from the measured population. Such selection bias also probably obscures causal attribution within practicing populations. If the survey measures only ever-married women, then those who survive but are unmaniageable due to complications also go unmeasured. Interviewing sisters or mothers about family fatalities would fail if respondents were unaware of a causal relationship between FGC and complications, which is no imaginary problem. And even if respondents were aware of causal connection, perceived culpabilities for the loss may inhibit reporting.

Survey research is not equivalent to facts.

Harms and Benefits

Next, the [Obermeyer] article maintains that assessments of benefits and harms are culturally variable and socially constructed. It cites the benefits of beauty, marriageability, sexual alteration, and group conformity. What is the evidence for such benefits? Notice again an inconsistent standard: citations to five ethnographers. If, on the question of *benefits*, we demanded the same standard of evidence that the article demands on the question of *complications*—that ideally designed and executed demographic and health surveys carried out widely across space and time confirm that FGC *inevitably* provides *incontrovertible* benefits—then we would have to conclude that its critical discourse about benefits is insufficiently supported. Ethnographers' reports contain descriptions of perceived benefits, harms, and complications; thus, if ethnographers' reports are our standard of evidence, then nontrivial complications are well established.

The article deplores generalizing theories of FGC but, inconsistently; proposes one of its own: "the ill health and the death that these practices are thought to cause are difficult to reconcile with the reality of their persistence in so many societies" (p. 91, reiterated on pp. 92, 94). That a practice would persist because it is only minimally harmful seems to be a plausible hypothesis, but on reflection it is not. Do smoking and drinking persist because they are harmless? Does war? Did footbinding persist for a millennium because it was harmless? The convention hypothesis explains how certain harmful practices like FGC and footbinding stubbornly persist, and how they suddenly end. No other evidence is offered in the article to support the minimal-harm hypothesis.

A few simple observations will indicate the implausibility of the minimal-harm explanation for the persistence of FGC. . . . The minimal-harm hypothesis, would predict less persistence in groups with more severe FGC and more persistence in groups with less severe FGC. With the recent exception of organized abandonments in Senegal, where FGC has ended in groups regardless of severity of cutting, FGC is unusually persistent, for example, the severe practice of infibulation for 2,200 years among some Beja.

Inspection of DHS data does not suggest any relationship between severity of practice and proportion opposed to continuation of the practice. [Furthermore,] if complications were trivial, then education would not change attitudes. We have seen already, though, that more education means more opposition in attitudes toward continuation. . . .

The article suggests that education makes no difference in approval for the continuation of FGC, and from this it infers that the educated do not share the biomedical view of harm and the universalist view of human rights. The inference is confused: If one cannot escape from the tragic circumstance of having to suffer a harm in order to obtain a greater benefit, that does not mean that one believes there is no harm. Mothers worry and sorrow when daughters go under the knife. . . . For a girl to avoid the harm of FGC brings about for her the worse harm of unmarriageability.

The article . . . claims that ethnographic studies link FGC to "rites of passage and to the marking of membership in a social group such as a tribe or secret society" (p. 88). . . . [However,] contrary to expectation, FGC is *not* a rite of passage; . . . but rather a practice that is entirely oriented to marriageability.

A physician at a public health clinic in Senegal emphasized to me that the negative psychological consequences of FGC (for some individuals, not all) were not sufficiently appreciated. . . . Toubia and Izett (1998:31–33) say that the "cumulative evidence suggests that the [cutting] event is remembered as extremely traumatic and leaves a life-long emotional scar." . . .

Sexual Limitations

. . . Toubia, a physician originally from the Sudan, explains that, "by altering the normal anatomy of the sexual organs, FGM reduces the case with which sexual fulfillment is achieved, or makes it extremely difficult."

The [Obermeyer] article (pp. 96, 101) proposes, however, that Western anatomy's finding that the genital organs are related to sexual enjoyment is merely a social construction, as is female orgasm. The case reports on sexuality, it says, are from "unusual" women who have had contact with schooling or women's organizations. Further, case reports tend to be from groups with more severe cutting, and negative effects are improperly generalized to all forms of cutting. . . .

[In contrast,] numerous sources indicate that FGC is widely *intended* to limit female sexual capacity, often to encourage chastity or fidelity. The [Obermeyer] article, however, suggests that FGC is "not designed to obliterate sexual enjoyment," that humans in FGC cultures have a "very different conception of the link between an intact clitoris and orgasm," and that such a linkage is not a "physiological reality" but rather is "socially constructed" (p. 96). . . .

Conclusion

In sum, the article shifts standards of evidence without justification, and its hypotheses are falsified by evidence from sources it otherwise accepts. Its central conclusions are stated boldly, but dissolve with simple linguistic analysis. The conclusive proof it seeks of complications is not possible in any empirical investigation, and is not appropriate for evaluation of a health and human-rights issue such as FGC.

The claim that the advocates exaggerated estimates of prevalence is contradicted by evidence from a source otherwise relied on and considered ideal, as is the claim that more educated respondents do not adopt new attitudes on harm, bodily integrity, health, and informed consent. The article's extremely negative generalizations about the advocates are unjustified. Its claim of low frequency of health complications is unsupported by the laboratory standard of evidence demanded in the article, and is contradicted by the DHS data that it otherwise accepts. Its belief that evidence on health complications of FGC is peculiarly wanting is not tested against controlled comparisons, and it fails to consider more plausible alternative hypotheses to its proposal that the allegedly poor state of the evidence should be blamed on the advocates and on unnamed forces.

It is wrong to equate survey research to the facts: Survey research on FGC may underestimate harms because of norms of secrecy and of modesty, because of causal misattributions among respondents due to the local universality of the practice, and because of selection bias. It wants to explain FGC as a benefit, not grasping that to avoid the harm of FGC brings about the worse harm of unmarriageability. It minimizes the "discomfort" (p. 94) of "female genital surgeries" without reference to any source, a claim directly contradicted by a demographic study and by an ethnographic study cited elsewhere in its text. It suggests that FGC does not limit sexual capacity, but the very sources it cites in support, on examination, demand the opposite conclusion. It may take a relativist view toward biomedicine and morality, which would not cohere with its scientism and evaluative stance.

The article argues that the "international consensus" (p. 80) to support the abandonment of female genital cuttings is based on "the conviction that they have extremely harmful consequences" (p. 80). The article concludes that the evidence that they have extremely harmful consequences is insufficient (p. 97). Thus, the author is "motivated" (p. 80) to shift "resources" (p. 85) away from "groups working against the continuation of these practices" (p. 80).

I propose an alternative account: That the international consensus and mobilization to which the article objects is based primarily on something like the understanding that FGC is an irreversible limitation of a human capacity carried out in the absence of meaningful consent, that opposition is motivated by human-rights concerns. I argue that by appropriate standards of evaluation, FGC entails nontrivial complications. The foregoing debate over complications must not distract us, however, from the more important human-rights issues pertaining to FGC and the need to orient research toward the goal of abandonment.

NO ⤶

Carla Makhlouf Obermeyer

The Health Consequences of Female Circumcision: Science, Advocacy, and Standards of Evidence

T he opportunity to revisit a controversial article more than five years after it was written is an offer one cannot refuse. I appreciate the chance to clarify my position, dispel misrepresentations, and continue to insist on nuanced statements. Returning to the issue at this time is also the occasion to review the state of our knowledge in light of recent research, and I have chosen to devote part of this rejoinder to an update on the evidence. . . .

My Article Was Not an Attack against "Advocates"

. . . Although I expressed concern at the imbalance between research and advocacy, I did not portray them as being in competition. I see the two as complementary, and I referred to the "potential disparity between the mobilization of resources toward activism and the research base that *ought to support such efforts*" (p. 80; emphasis added). Although I disagreed with some specific claims in the advocacy literature, nowhere did I condemn advocacy efforts in general. I welcomed initiatives to bring together activists and researchers (p. 85). . . .

Mackie's argument is based on deliberately misreading my work and imputing to me misguided opinions and motivations. . . .

Nowhere did I say the things that are attributed to me. The supposed paraphrase has in fact been assembled from text found on three different pages. . . .

Mackie also engages in a detailed polemic about whether particular advocates more often under- or overestimated the prevalence of circumcisions globally. This is irrelevant, because the point is not whose guesses were accurate, or whether some guesses were better than none, but, rather, that many estimates were made by individuals who did not have the requisite competence, and that advocacy efforts were not based on reliable evidence. . . .

It may be true that research on circumcision is not unique and that many other widely held beliefs are not sufficiently supported by evidence. But when I reviewed the evidence in 1996, it was certainly shocking to find out how little attention had been directed to documenting harmful effects, given the global mobilization of attention and efforts toward eradicating female genital mutilation, precisely on the grounds that the operations caused death and ill health. It may well be more appropriate that advocacy efforts have since shifted to a discourse highlighting human rights, informed consent, and bodily integrity, and that research will be directed toward ascertaining how the practice violates these principles. This still does not dispose of the need for solid information on prevalence and health consequences. That was the goal of my article: to take stock of what was known about health effects and to assess how good the evidence was.

Claims about the Integrity of the Review Are Unfounded

Mackie repeatedly questions my use of sources, claiming that some reports, available at the time of writing, were excluded or presented inaccurately. But despite his sustained efforts over a three-year period to find fault with the quality of the review, he offers no credible evidence that I excluded reports about health effects, or that I misrepresented the findings of any study. I presented all the sources that were available to me and provided explicit criteria for inclusion and exclusion. My article included an extensive bibliography, so readers can easily verify that sources have been appropriately cited. While Mackie may disagree with my explicit exclusion of nonscholarly sources such as journalism or individual accounts, he cannot and does not point to any omissions or misrepresentations. . . .

Mackie contends that some of the sources that I cited in my discussion of the association between schooling and circumcision were insufficiently covered, and he tries to suggest that this was a deliberate attempt to conceal findings that did not support my argument. The point I had made was that whereas some studies showed lower prevalence of circumcision among educated women in some countries, in others, differences by education were very small or nonexistent (pp. 88–89). The lengthy discussion that Mackie engages in to try and disprove my point shows exactly the same results for each of the countries I had cited and provides similar figures from more recent surveys in two other countries. It unequivocally substantiates what I had said: that the direction of the association between schooling and prevalence is not uniform, that it is relatively weak, and that in several countries, the near totality of women with secondary schooling are circumcised.

The additional data that Mackie presents have no direct bearing either on the question of prevalence or on the question of health effects. The finding that in several countries, schooling is associated with lower expressed support for circumcision only allows us to speculate that practices may change in the future. And responses in surveys about the frequency of unspecified complications do not represent reliable evidence on health effects. It is for this simple reason, rather than other questionable motives, that I had not discussed such sources in detail. This example demonstrates how, despite his efforts, Mackie is unable to question the integrity of the review.

Multidisciplinarity Still Requires Specific Standards of Evidence

Mackie repeatedly claims that my analysis shifts standards of evidence. This allegation stems from a misunderstanding of what is involved when combining different disciplines to analyze a complicated topic. Each of the three disciplines that were brought to bear on the issue—demography, epidemiology, and anthropology—uses specific methods to gather and analyze data. Although it is important to consider the results of all research together, one cannot indiscriminately mix evidence across fields. Multidisciplinarity requires a degree of competence in each discipline and is a risky undertaking because it can, as I had stated, "make one vulnerable to critiques of specialists from each of them" (p. 80). It is thus somewhat ironic that my article is criticized by someone who is not familiar with any of the three disciplines I drew on.

Mackie misunderstands my approach. He appears at times to think that I advocate surveys unconditionally, while at other times he refers to "the laboratory standard of evidence demanded in the article," and yet elsewhere he states that as a relativist I do not endorse the biomedical view. Perhaps my review confused him because it did not privilege a single discipline. I had said as much in the introduction of my article: that my analysis was "motivated by the conviction that a single approach is not sufficient in itself to understand the issue" (p. 80). Each discipline brings a different contribution to the study of this complex problem. All involve trade-offs in attaining "gold standards" of evidence, but good research is about balancing these trade-offs in light of the reality of the field situation.

Concerning the prevalence of female circumcision, the best evidence would come from large-scale observations, but because clinical research of this kind is neither feasible nor desirable, the next best thing is to assume that women know whether they have been circumcised and to ask them to report on their own condition. This assumption is known to be fairly reasonable, and demography has wellestablished methods for making inferences from samples to large populations. That is why my presentation of the data on prevalence relied on demographic surveys.

Surveys, however, are not a good way to measure health effects, and this is obvious to those who obtain the most elementary training in any of the health sciences. The reasons for this include recall bias and differences in perceptions of general health and symptoms across individuals and across cultures. Another important reason is that health conditions may be caused by various agents—for example, reproductive health problems may result from any number of factors, such as malnutrition, sexually transmitted infections, poor obstetric care, exposure to radiation or chemicals, etc.—and individuals suffering from health problems are usually not qualified to draw conclusions about the connections. To ascertain the increased risks associated with a given factor, the frequency of the health outcome has to be measured by means other than respondents' reports and comparisons have to be made between groups where the factor is found and groups where it is not. . . .

How to Measure, and Not to Measure, Health Effects

The best way to determine whether a given factor represents a risk for a given health effect is to examine the statistical association between the two. Because experimental or prospective designs are rarely feasible, the most commonly used method in epidemiology is the case-control study. It ascertains the extent of exposure in a sample of "exposed" and "unexposed" individuals, compares the frequencies of the hypothesized health effect in the two groups, and applies statistics to measure the strength of the association. [W]e would have to measure the frequency of the reproductive health problem among women who have been subjected to cutting or hitting, compared to those who have not. To determine the health effects of female circumcision, there is no substitute for studies that include a comparison group and provide sufficient numbers for statistical analyses.

Mackie does not understand why certain sources were excluded from my analysis, and he denounces my exclusion of "all history, all journalism, all ethnography, all policy forums, all public health reports, all clinical observations, and all personal experiences." Although each of these sources is valuable for particular purposes, they are not equally relevant to the analysis of health effects. Mackie lumps them together indiscriminately, showing little awareness of differences in the quality of the information they provide on health effects. The individual stories and case reports that he would rely on are certainly useful as a preliminary step, to draw attention to possible connections with health conditions. But although anecdotal evidence and individual reports can be important bases for formulating hypotheses, they have limited value when trying to establish associations. They may over- or under-estimate health effects, depending on the population from which they are drawn. For example, reports from a clinic specializing in reproductive problems or surgical repair of lesions often overestimate complications because they come from facilities where the more complicated cases are referred; conversely, where awareness of health consequences is low, individuals may not report symptoms that they view as normal, and such reports underestimate complications. Thus, one cannot simply rely on an ad hoc collection of reports to convincingly establish increased risks, especially when measuring effects beyond those immediately observed.

Mackie consistently fails to distinguish the health effects of circumcision, measured by the methods of public health, from public policy judgments about preventing the practice and sociological analyses about abandonment. He argues that "proof of complications is not possible and not appropriate for human rights," and that because female circumcision is a social practice and not a pathogen or toxin, assessing the "frequencies of complications [. . .] should be made by the public-policy standard." Such assertions mix science and advocacy and confuse the domains of analysis of different disciplines. My article dealt with prevalence and health effects. It did not cover harmful effects other than health complications, nor address questions related to consent, ethics, or rights. That these dimensions of the practice are important does not mean that public policy or human rights standards can be substituted for epidemiological methods when measuring health consequences.

Ethnographic Reports Are Not Normative Statements or Scientific Endorsements

Throughout his critique, Mackie appears unable to refrain from entering public policy debates, even when reading descriptions of the practices found in other cultures. My article had included ethnographic reports on circumcision and relied on anthropology to help contextualize the practices and gain some insight into what they mean in the societies where they are found. Information about local views would help answer the question "How can they do this?" and lessen the reactions of horror or outrage that Shweder calls the "mutual yuck" response. Ethnographic descriptions are meant to give us a glimpse of the different valuations that surround circumcision and the way in which it is rationalized in the local culture. They are not arguments in a public policy debate. No one familiar with the anthropological approach could take my statement (p. 94) regarding the perceived benefits of circumcision as an endorsement of local beliefs, and then proceed to demand that I provide evidence for such benefits. Mackie also disagrees when I report (pp. 95–96) on local notions of gender and sexuality, or when I try (p. 94) to explain how individuals can disregard the risks of circumcision, mistaking my attempt to suspend belief and understand others' views for wholehearted approval.

The effort to set aside our own assumptions and consider foreign practices from the perspective of others is particularly challenging when dealing with the effects of circumcision on sexuality, and here Mackie does not seem to see the point of the exercise. My review of the very limited information documenting sexual effects led me to raise some questions about the experience of sex in cultures where women are circumcised. These questions arose from reports indicating that circumcised women said that they enjoyed sex and that some experienced orgasm. None of these reports were from studies specifically designed to address the many difficulties encountered in research on sexuality, and I was careful to say so (p. 95). But the unexpected finding in several of the studies—that sexual response persists despite the operations—casts some doubt on the blanket assertion that circumcision obliterates sexuality, and I called for careful research that would focus on the link between the physical reality of the operations and the experience of sex under those conditions.

I said that contemplating the possibility of such different notions of sexuality is unsettling, because it implies "that what is presented as an undisputable physiological reality may itself be socially constructed" (p. 96). Mackie interprets this as a complete denial of anatomy, an extreme constructivist view that rejects the connection between genital organs and sexual enjoyment. There is no room here for subtlety, and we are back to gross comparisons with cutting and amputating, along the lines of the domestic violence analogy.

My discussion of the consequences of circumcision on sexuality was not designed to provide answers, mainly because the evidence is so scant. I said that the practice of circumcision, and its consequences, strains our ability to understand, and, far from making definitive pronouncements about how others experience it, I had suggested that perhaps there were limits to how much we can understand it. That is why I had referred to the "unknowable" in the title of my article.

Anthropology's nonconventional ways of thinking about the contingency of social arrangements and ideas appear to be disturbing to Mackie. He finds it "worrisome" when I say that not everyone shares the biomedical point of view on circumcision. If I mention variations in the extent to which people in different societies think about risks to health, expect discomfort, or endure pain, he thinks I am denying that the operations cause pain. If I warn that conflating lesser and more extensive operations is an oversimplification, he concludes that I am opposed to comparisons and generalizations. Relativism makes him apprehensive, and he detects what he refers to as "undercurrents" of it when I put quotation marks around words like *facts, normal bodies,* or *healthy sexuality,* or use the word *powerful* to refer to the biomedical point of view. From all this, he deduces that I must be skeptical of science, of medicine, of universals, maybe even an adept of 'Foucault, for whom there is no truth or falsehood, right or wrong.

Oversimplification versus Nuanced Statements

Mackie is so impatient with the subtle distinctions I tried to make that he takes it on himself to restate my findings. He asks: "How might they read if we removed the ten qualifiers and readjusted phrasing?" And, of course, after such vigorous editing, they read exactly the way he would like them to read.

Instead of relying on Mackie to do so, let *me* sum up the "bottom-line" of the argument: Did I try to argue that circumcision was harmless from a health point of view as Mackie's title suggests? No, it depends on the type of operation: more extensive operations are more likely to cause damage. It also depends on the type of harm: some effects are well documented, others not. I offered comments to elaborate on these points.

First, I commented on the state of the available evidence that did not support some of the claims of harmful effects; I attributed this to the paucity and poor quality of the research rather than to the fact that the operations are completely safe (p. 97)—remember that it depends on the type of operation.

Second, I commented on the frequency of complications and said that serious complications were relatively infrequent. This is a statistical assessment, and it is made in contrast with claims that circumcision causes death and serious ill health. It was not meant to diminish the importance of individual pain and illness or to question the veracity of the many poignant stories and personal experiences. I had also qualified my statement about serious complications by saying that from a public health point of view, even low frequencies are too high if they are preventable (p. 92).

Finally, I commented on the context in which the debates about circumcision were taking place, pointing out the historical and political forces that shaped them.

Perhaps the reason my article has been controversial has to do with the passions that circumcision continues to elicit, with the surprise caused by the weakness of the evidence on what was thought to be patently obvious, and with the difficulty of accepting that the answer to the question of harmful effects is in shades of gray. I believe that as more evidence becomes available, it will confirm both the assertions that I did make and the caution I exercised in presenting my findings.

Update on the Evidence

A few months ago, I conducted a review of sources published between 1997 and 2002. Comparing the 440 recent sources to those reviewed in 1996 shows a small increase in the proportion of studies that present some evidence compared to those that do not. There remain fundamental problems in studies measuring health and other effects, such as lack of comparison groups, inconsistent numbers, or incomplete analyses, but there are a few well-designed studies and, one hopes, the start of a trend toward better research on health effects.

To facilitate comparisons with my 1999 article, I have prepared a summary table, grouping effects under headings similar to those I used in my earlier review: general health, bleeding, infections, reproductive problems, labor and delivery problems, lesions-scars-cysts, urinary problems, pain, and sexual problems. Findings have been separated depending on the type and strength of the evidence on which they are based. Studies that include a comparison group and provide information about statistical significance represent the strongest evidence. . . . Studies that do not include comparison group of women not subjected to circumcision are less conclusive. Many of these studies use loose definitions of effects and give no details about measurements in the field. This results in much less precise estimates of the frequencies of complications. . . .

In general, the quality of the information is better for measures that lend themselves to laboratory or clinical confirmation. Many of these come from a thorough study in the Gambia. The results indicate that some infections (bacterial vaginosis and herpes) are significantly more frequent among circumcised women, while others (syphilis) are significantly less frequent, and yet others (candida, chlamydia, or trichomoniasis) show no significant difference. Studies not including a comparison group show much wider, and less informative, estimates, for example 2–50 percent for edema, or 8–37 percent for unspecified infections.

Analyses of studies on infertility that have appeared in the last few years do not document significant differences, while studies of labor and delivery problems show mixed results: those with a comparison group do not find significantly higher risks of complications of labor and delivery, except where these are very loosely defined to include hospital practices such as c-sections and episiotomies; less rigorous studies suggest that difficulties in delivery, prolonged labor, c-sections, excessive bleeding, and various tears may be relatively frequent but do not make it possible to ascertain that the risks are statistically higher, or to estimate the magnitude of the increased risks.

Studies of gynecological problems find that some are significantly more frequent (unspecified complications), others (prolapse) significantly less so. Regarding urinary problems, [one] study did not find significant differences, whereas studies without comparison groups show a wider range in reported frequencies, reflecting the lack of standardized definitions, and inaccuracies in measurement.

Bleeding and scarring are, to a certain extent, self-evident consequences of any surgical operation, and it is important to document how serious they are and the magnitude of the health risks they represent. There is a disparate set of studies on bleeding, but given the lack of clear definitions and measurements (e.g., what is bleeding compared to excessive bleeding, or hemorrhage), it is difficult to interpret their results. On lesions, scars, and cysts, there are several series of case reports, and a number of frequency-only studies reporting a range of figures, but [a] controlled study did not find significant differences.

Studies of pain have concentrated principally on dysmenorrhea, and, whereas [one] study found significantly higher frequencies among circumcised women, [and another] found higher frequencies among uncircumcised women but the difference was not significant. Other studies without a comparison group report widely divergent estimates (9–87 percent), again showing the difficulty of ascertaining effects with suboptimal research designs.

Problems with quality are especially apparent in studies that have investigated sexual effects. Unlike other complications that can, in principle, be measured in purely medical fashion, assessing the effect of female genital cutting on sexuality requires inputs from the individual herself. To ensure accuracy and allow systematic comparisons, data collection methods have to be especially careful with terminology, the phrasing of questions, the circumstances of the interview, and the quality of the conversation with the researcher.

In addition, attention has to be directed to contextual factors that reflect the values of a given culture and influence the meanings attached by the respondent to her experience: admitting to sexual pleasure may, in some settings, be regarded as inappropriate with strangers, or there may be gendered values related to interest in sex, or modesty considerations that influence responses. Unfortunately, none of the available studies has taken the necessary care to ensure that concepts related to sexuality can be appropriately defined and translated, none has documented the conditions of interviews and women's understandings and reactions. This considerably weakens their findings. . . . [One] controlled study found no differences in dyspareunia. Other studies have reported on problems with intercourse and orgasm, but it is not clear how different these frequencies would be in an uncircumcised group of women.

In general, the studies summarized in this review show that circumcision is associated with significantly higher risks of selected complications, but that for many possible complications, the available evidence does not show significant differences. The summary also highlights two simple points: (1) where complications are not precisely defined, widely divergent frequencies of complications are found, and (2) studies without comparison groups do not provide conclusive results.

It is not clear to what extent the paucity of significant results can be attributed to the difficulty of designing appropriate studies. Certainly, the fact that most of the research summarized here has been conducted in countries where the lesser operations are prevalent—Burkina, Central African Republic, Côte d'lvoire, Egypt, the Gambia, Kenya, Mali, and Tanzania—needs to be noted. Some of the studies I had reviewed in my 1999 article had been conducted on populations where infibulation is practiced (Sudan and Somalia), and they suggested that the more extensive operations may be associated with a greater likelihood of complications. I cannot, on the basis of this recent review, comment on this possibility, because none of the studies on infibulated women included a control group, and all have been limited to immigrant populations (Somali immigrants to Canada, Horn of Africa immigrants to Australia, and Sudanese/Somali women in Saudi Arabia). It is all the more important that future research make special efforts to separate lesser operations from the more extensive ones (i.e., infibulation compared to others) in order to establish to what extent more extensive surgeries cause greater harm.

Conclusion

Despite the accumulation of information on health effects, large gaps remain in our understanding of the extent of harm that is caused by the various operations subsumed under the heading of circumcision. This is mainly because most of the available studies are not designed to document these effects. Some careful studies have shown higher risks for a few well-defined complications but no difference for most others, whereas less rigorous studies yield much wider ranges of estimates for a greater number of, often loosely defined, conditions. There is no doubt that better-designed studies can go a long way toward improving our estimates of the health risks of the operations, but the current state of the evidence does not allow hasty pronouncements about all the harmful effects attributed to circumcision.

My 1999 article drew attention to the complexity of measuring harms to health, pointed to the weakness of our understanding, and showed the inadequacy of simplistic judgments. While we may feel strongly that these practices are wrong, and for a variety of reasons apart from their health effects, the debates about female circumcision remind us of one of anthropology's central tenets—that "we see the lives of others through lenses of our own grinding and that they look back on ours through ones of their own." The multiculturalism of today's world makes it all the more pressing that we engage in discussions that are informed by evidence and that we develop better ways to bring together different perspectives to focus on this complicated issue.

POSTSCRIPT

Is Female Circumcision Universally Wrong?

Why has FGM been practiced for so long? What sociohistorical changes have made possible the recent campaigns against FGM? What are the major obstacles to the worldwide eradication of FGM?

When should a cultural practice that is a departure from established American culture be accepted or disallowed in the United States? Imagine you are a pediatrician and one of your new patients is a small female child whose family just immigrated to the United States from Northern Sudan, where FGM is very prevalent. Her mother asks you to perform FGM on the child. What would be your response? How far do U.S. principles of familial privacy and personal autonomy extend in such a situation? Should the parent's decision about her/his child be respected or rejected? How does this situation differ from the performance of surgical "correction" to intersexual infants and children? To what degree should the child's health and well-being and legal inability to consent be weighed in the decision?

Now imagine you are a gynecologist and an adult Sudanese woman of legal consenting age comes to you and asks to be reinfibulated. If the procedure to which she is consenting is prohibited under law, are we unconstitutionally limiting her personal autonomy? After all, Americans place high value on bodily autonomy and privacy.

Consider a new twist on nonmedically based genital surgery. "Sexual-enhancement" surgery is the hottest new trend in plastic surgery, including labiaplasty and vaginal tightening. A Canadian surgeon Dr. Stubbs, who performs these procedures, suggests that this is a natural extension of women's quest for beauty (see Issue 16): "After all the benchmarks of beauty have been obtained—Barbie Doll breasts, youthful face, sporty thighs—it appears that for a certain segment of female society, tidy genitals are worth the $1,500 to $2,500 price tag. If the labia are oversized, asymmetrical, too loose or triangular, they don't measure up to the ideal and are a candidate for cutting." According to Dr. Stubbs, women seeking the surgery are either the 25- to 35-year-old trophy wives of sports figures for whom the sexual and physiological ideal is the price of entry into that world, or women of all ages who have abnormally large labia that may be interfering with their sexual confidence and performance (see http://www.noharmm.org/mommy.htm).

What is the relationship between FGM and elective genital surgery for sexual enhancement? Is it truly elective or just a newer form of cultural pressures to look and feel the "right way"? What position do you think the universalists' and the cultural relativists would take on this new trend? Finally, what is the relationship between FGM and male circumcision? Is there really a difference?

Suggested Readings

C. L. Annas, "Irreversible Error: The Power and Prejudice of Female Genital Mutilation," *Contemporary Health Law and Policy* (1996).

Fauziya Kassindja, *Do They Hear You When You Cry?* (New York: Delta Books, 1998).

Ellen Gruenbaum, *The Female Circumcision Controversy: An Anthropological Perspective* (Philadelphia: University of Pennsylvania Press, 2001).

Mireya Navarro, "The Most Private of Makeovers," *New York Times* (November 28, 2004).

Rosemarie Skaine, *Female Genital Mutilation: Legal, Cultural and Medical Issues* (Jefferson, NC: McFarland, 2005).

C. J. Walley, "Searching for 'Voices': Feminism, Anthropology, and the Global Debate Over Female Genital Operations," *Cultural Anthropology* (1977).

ISSUE 15

Should "Abstinence-Until-Marriage" Be the Only Message for Teens?

YES: Bridget E. Maher, from "Abstinence Until Marriage: The Best Message for Teens," Family Research Council (2004)

NO: Debra Hauser, from *Five Years of Abstinence-Only-Until-Marriage Education: Assessing the Impact* (2004)

ISSUE SUMMARY

YES: Bridget E. Maher argues that far too much funding has gone into programs that teach young people about sexuality and contraception—programs that she concludes are ineffective.

NO: Debra Hauser, in an evaluation of numerous abstinence-only-until-marriage programs that received funding under the Title V Social Security Act, concludes that they show few short-term benefits and no lasting, positive effects; rather such programs may actually worsen sexual health outcomes.

$\mathbf{I}$n 1996, President Clinton signed the welfare reform law. Attached to this law was a federal entitlement program allocating $50 million per year over a five-year period to abstinence-only-until-marriage educational programs. This Act specifies that a program is defined as "abstinence-only" education if it:

- has as its exclusive purpose teaching the social, psychological, and health gains to be realized by abstaining from sexual activity;
- teaches that abstinence from sexual activity outside of marriage is the expected standard for all school-age children;
- teaches that abstinence from sexual activity is the only certain way to avoid out-of-wedlock pregnancy, sexually transmitted diseases, and other
- teaches that a mutually faithful monogamous relationship in the context of marriage is the expected standard of sexual activity;
- teaches that sexual activity outside the context of marriage is likely to have harmful psychological and physical side effects;
- teaches that bearing children out-of-wedlock is likely to have harmful consequences for the child, the child's parents, and society;

- teaches young people how to reject sexual advances and how alcohol and drug use increase vulnerability to sexual advances; and,
- teaches the importance of attaining self-sufficiency before engaging in sexual activity. (*Section 510(b) of Title V of the Social Security Act, P.L. 104-193*).

In order to access these funds, an entity must agree to teach all of these points, not just a few. Failure to do so would result in loss of the funding.

Those who support the teaching of comprehensive sexuality education disagree with the tenets that abstinence-only-until-marriage (AOUM) supports. They present research that demonstrates how comprehensive sexuality education programs help young people to delay the onset of risky sexual behaviors, and to use contraceptives more effectively once they do start engaging in these behaviors. Some argue that AOUM is exclusionary, excluding non-heterosexual youth; is fear- and shame-based, and is wildly out of touch with the reality in which young people are living. They are quick to point out that AOUM supports have yet to provide empirical evidence that their programs "work."

AOUM supporters believe that comprehensive sexuality education programs teach "too much, too soon." They believe strongly that providing information about abstinence, along with safer sex information, confuses teens, and gives them permission to become sexually active when the potential consequences for sexual activity are much more serious.

Take a look at the language of the legislation. The language refers to "sexual activity." We know that for many people "having sex" means only sexual intercourse. It does not include oral sex, for example. We know that many teens are having sexual intercourse outside of marriage, and although this number is going down, the number of youth engaging in oral sex is increasing. What does "sexual activity" mean to you? Would you be able to support the legislation if it included some behaviors, but not others? Are there some messages you agree with and not others? If you were an educator, would you be able to teach all eight points, especially given what you know about adolescent sexual behavior.

As you read these selections, think about any sexuality education classes you may have had—do you think they should have taught you more? Less? Consider, too, young people who are already sexually active. Would abstinence messages work for them? Did a more comprehensive program "fail" them?

In the following selections, Bridget E. Maher outlines some of the negative consequences of teen sex, and why abstinence is the only 100 percent effective option for avoiding those negative consequences. She argues that more comprehensive sexuality education programs, while purporting to teach about abstinence, actually rarely, if ever, do. Debra Hauser describes what she perceives to be flaws in the assertions made by AOUM proponents, such as the idea that if educators teach only abstinence, teens won't have sex. In reviewing abstinence-only programs, she concludes that although most show changes in attitudes towards abstinence, many actually discourage safe practices in youth who are sexually active and thereby increase the risks of the very problems the programs were designed to prevent.

Bridget E. Maher

 **YES**

Abstinence Until Marriage:
The Best Message for Teens

The federal government has provided some abstinence-until-marriage funding in recent years, but comprehensive sex education and contraception programs are vastly over-funded in comparison. In 2002, abstinence-until-marriage programs received $102 million, while teen-sex education and contraception programs received at least $427.7 million. In his last budget, President Bush proposed an increase of $33 million for abstinence-until-marriage programs, following upon his campaign promise to try to equalize funding between comprehensive sex education and abstinence programs. This is a good first step, but it still doesn't bring true parity between these programs. It's time for our government to get serious about fulfilling the president's promise to at least level the playing field with regard to funding of the positive and healthy message of abstinence-until-marriage versus that of promoting premarital sex and contraception.

Teens are greatly influenced by the messages they receive about sex in school. Unfortunately, the majority of schools teach "safe sex"—"comprehensive" or so-called "abstinence plus" programs—believing that it's best for kids to have all the information they need about sexuality and to make their own decisions about sex. Abstinence is downplayed while sexual activity and condom use are encouraged in these curriculums, because it's assumed that children are eventually going to have sex. A 2002 report by the Physicians Consortium, which investigated comprehensive sex programs promoted by the Centers for Disease Control, reveals that abstinence is barely mentioned and condom use is clearly advocated in these curriculums.

Abstinence-until-marriage programs, on the other hand, teach young people to save sex for marriage, and their message has been very effective in changing teens' behavior. Today, there are over one-thousand abstinence-until-marriage programs around the United States and one-third of public middle and high schools say that abstinence is "the main message in their sex education." Abstinence organizations do more than just tell teens to say no to unwed sex: they teach young people the skills they need to practice abstinence. Classes cover many topics including self-esteem building, self-control, decision-making, goal-setting, character education, and communication skills. Choosing the Best, Teen-Aid, Inc., and Operation Keepsake are just a few of the many effective abstinence programs in the U.S. . . . .

Teens want to be taught abstinence. Nearly all (93 percent) of teenagers believe that teens should be given a strong message from society to abstain from sex until at least after high school. A 2000 poll found that 64 percent of teen girls surveyed said sexual activity is not acceptable for high-school age adolescents, even if precautions are taken to prevent pregnancy and sexually transmitted diseases.

Those who do not abstain from sex are likely to experience many negative consequences, both physical and emotional. Aside from the risk of pregnancy, teens have a high risk of contracting a sexually transmitted disease (STD). Each year 3 million teens—25 percent of sexually active teens— are infected with an STD. About 25 percent of all new cases of STDs occur in teenagers; two-thirds of new cases occur in young people age 15–24. Teens who engage in premarital sex are likely to experience fear about pregnancy and STDs, regret, guilt, lowered self-respect, fear of commitment, and depression. . . .

Public opinion polls show that teens value abstinence highly. Nearly all (93 percent) of teenagers believe that teens should be given a strong message from society to abstain from sex until at least after high school.[1] A 2000 poll found that 64 percent of teen girls surveyed said sexual activity is not acceptable for high-school age adolescents, even if precautions are taken to prevent pregnancy and sexually transmitted diseases.[2] Moreover, teens who have not abstained often regret being sexually active. In 2000, 63 percent of sexually active teens said they wish they had waited longer to become sexually active.[3]

Negative Consequences of Unwed Teen Sex

Teens need to be taught to save sex for marriage, because premarital sex has many negative consequences, both physical and emotional. One of the most obvious outcomes of engaging in premarital sex is having a child outside marriage; today, one-third of all births are out-of-wedlock.[4] Teen birthrates have declined since the early 1990s, but the highest unwed birthrates are among those age 20–24, followed by those 25–29.[5] This shows that many young girls abstain from sex while they are in high school, but not afterward.

Teen unwed childbearing has negative consequences for mothers, children, and society. Unwed teen mothers are likely to live in poverty and be dependent on welfare, and only about 50 percent of them are likely to finish high school while they are adolescents or young adults.[6] Children born to teen mothers are more likely than other children to have lower grades, to leave high school without graduating, to be abused or neglected, to have a child as an unmarried teenager, and to be delinquent.[7] Teen childbearing costs U.S. taxpayers an estimated $7 billion per year in social services and lost tax revenue due to government dependency.[8] The gross annual cost to society of unwed childbearing and its consequences is $29 billion, which includes the administration of welfare and foster care programs, building and maintaining additional prisons, as well as lower education and resultant lost productivity among unwed parents.[9]

Aside from the risk of pregnancy, teens have a high risk of contracting a sexually transmitted disease (SID). Each year 3 million teens—25 percent of sexually active teens—are infected with an STD.[10] About 25 percent of all new cases of STDs occur in teenagers; two-thirds of new cases occur in young people age 15–24.[11]

Chlamydia and gonorrhea are two of the most common curable STDs among sexually active teens. According the Centers for Disease Control, gonorrhea rates are highest among 15- to 19-year-old females and 20- to 24-year old males, and more than five to 10 percent of teen females are currently infected with chlamydia.[12] If these diseases are untreated, they can lead to pelvic inflammatory disease, infertility, and ectopic pregnancy.[13] Studies have found that up to 15 percent of sexually active teenage women are infected with the human papillomavirus (HPV), an incurable virus that is present in nearly all cervical cancers.[14]

In addition to being at risk for STDs, unwed sexually active teens are likely to experience negative emotional consequences and to become both more promiscuous and less interested in marriage. Teens who engage in premarital sex are likely to experience fear about pregnancy and STDs, regret, guilt, lowered self-respect, fear of commitment, and depression.[15] Also, adolescents who engage in unwed sex at a younger age are much more likely to have multiple sex partners. Among young people between the ages of 15-24 who have had sex before age 18, 75 percent had two or more partners and 45 percent had four or more partners. Among those who first had sex after age 19, just 20 percent had more than one partner and one percent had four or more partners.[16] Premarital sex can also cause teens to view marriage less favorably. A 1994 study of college freshmen found that non-virgins with multiple sex partners were more likely to view marriage as difficult and involving a loss of personal freedom and happiness. Virgins were more likely to view marriage as "enjoyable.". . .[17]

"Safe Sex" or "Comprehensive Sex Education" Programs

In addition to the influence of their parents, teens are also affected by the messages on sex and abstinence that they receive in school. Unfortunately, the majority of schools teach "safe sex," "comprehensive," or so-called "abstinence plus" programs, believing that it is best for children to have all the information they need about sexuality and to make their own decisions about sex.[18] Abstinence is downplayed and sexual activity and condom use are encouraged in these curriculums, because it is assumed that kids are eventually going to have sex. A 2002 report by the Physicians Consortium, which investigated comprehensive sex programs promoted by the Centers for Disease Control, reveals that abstinence is barely mentioned and condom use is clearly advocated in these curriculums. Not only do students learn how to obtain condoms, but they also practice putting them on cucumbers or penile models. Masturbation, body massages, bathing together, and fantasizing are listed as "ways to be close" in one curriculum. . . .[19]

The Effectiveness of Abstinence-Until-Marriage Programs

Abstinence-until-marriage programs, on the other hand, teach young people to save sex for marriage, and their message has been very effective in changing teen's behavior. According to the Physicians Resource Council, the drop in teen birth rates during the 1990s was due not to increased contraceptive use among teens, but to sexual abstinence.[20] This correlates with the decrease in sexual activity among unwed teens. In 1988, 51 percent of unwed girls between the ages of 15 and 19 had engaged in sexual intercourse compared to 49 percent 1995. This decrease also occurred among unwed boys, declining from 60 percent to 55 percent between 1988 and 1995.[21]

Today, there are over one thousand abstinence-until-marriage programs around the United States, and one-third of public middle and high schools say both that abstinence is "the main message in their sex education" and that abstinence is taught as "the only option for young people."[22] Started by non-profit or faith-based groups, these programs teach young people to save sex for marriage. However, abstinence organizations do more than just tell teens to say no to unwed sex: They teach young people the skills they need to practice abstinence. Classes cover many topics including self-esteem building, self-control, decision making, goal setting, character education, and communication skills. Sexually transmitted disease, the realities of parenthood and anatomy are also discussed.[23] The effectiveness of birth control may be discussed, but it is neither provided nor promoted in these programs.

Choosing the Best, an abstinence program based in Marietta, Georgia, and started in 1993, has developed curriculum and materials that are used in over two thousand school districts in 48 states. Students in public or private schools are taught abstinence by their teachers, who have been trained by Choosing the Best's staff. Appropriate for 6th through 12th graders, the curriculum teaches students the consequences of premarital sex, the benefits of abstaining until marriage, how to make a virginity pledge, refusal skills, and character education. Choosing the Best involves parents in their children's lessons and teaches them how to teach abstinence to their children. . . .

This abstinence program has contributed to lower teen-pregnancy rates in Georgia. In Columbus, Georgia, Choosing the Best's materials were used in all 8th grades for a period of four years. A study requested by the Georgia State Board of Education to examine the effectiveness of this curriculum found a 38-percent reduction in pregnancies among middle-school students in Muscogee County between 1997 and 1999. Other large school districts that did not implement Choosing the Best's program experienced only a 6-percent reduction in teen pregnancies during those same years.

Teen-Aid, Inc., based in Spokane, Washington, has been promoting abstinence until marriage and character education for over twenty years. This program seeks to teach young people the knowledge and skills they need to make good decisions and to achieve goals. Parent-child communication is a key component of the Teen-Aid curriculum, as parents are involved in every lesson. In 1999–2000, over 41,000 families in public schools, churches, and community organizations used these materials.

A 1999 study conducted by Whitworth College in Spokane, Washington found may positive results among teens in Edinburg, Texas who were taught the Teen-Aid curriculum. On the pretest administered to students after the course, 62 percent said "having sex as a teenager would make it harder for them to get a good job or be successful in a career," compared to 71 percent on the post test. When asked if they were less likely to have sexual intercourse before they got married, 47 percent responded yes on the pretest, compared to 54 percent after taking the course. . . .[24]

Operation Keepsake, a Cleveland, Ohio-based abstinence program started in 1988, has its "For Keeps" curriculum in 90 public and private schools in the greater Cleveland area. It is presently taught to over 25,000 students, including those in middle and high school, as well as college freshman. Along with a classroom component, this program also includes peer mentoring, guest speakers, opportunities to make an abstinence pledge, and parental involvement.

Case Western Reserve University evaluated Operation Keepsake's program in 2001, finding that it is having a positive impact on adolescents' beliefs and behavior regarding abstinence. Over nine hundred 7th and 8th graders completed the pretests and post tests. According to the study, the program had "a clear and sustainable impact on abstinence beliefs" because students in the program had "higher abstinence-until-marriage values" at the follow-up survey than did those in the control group, who did not attend the abstinence program. . . .[25]

Virginity pledges are also successful in encouraging sexual abstinence among unwed teens. A 2001 study based on the National Longitudinal Study of Adolescent Health . . . found that teens who take a virginity pledge are 34 percent less likely to have sex before marriage compared to those who do not pledge, even after controlling for factors such as family structure, race, self-esteem, and religiosity. . . .[26]

Conclusion

These are only some of the many abstinence-until-marriage programs in the United States. Their success in changing young people's views and behavior regarding abstinence is due to their telling the truth about sex to young people: that it is meant to be saved for marriage and that it is possible to live a chaste life. Along with this message, they give kids the encouragement and skills they need to save themselves for marriage. . . .

Notes

1. "The Cautious Generation? Teens Tell Us About Sex, Virginity, and 'The Talk,'" National Campaign to Prevent Teen Pregnancy, April 27, 2000.
2. Ibid.

3. "Not Just Another Thing to Do: Teens Talk About Sex, Regret and the Influence of Their Parents," National Campaign to Prevent Teen Pregnancy, June 30, 2000.

4. Joyce A. Martin et al., *Births: Final Data for 2001,* National Vital Statistics Reports 51, December 18, 2002, National Center for Health Statistics, Table C.

5. Bridget Maher, *The Family Portrait: A Compilation of Data, Research and Public Opinion on the Family,* Family Research Council, 2002, p. 73, 162.

6. Rebecca Maynard, *Kids Having Kids: Economic and Social Consequences of Teen Pregnancy,* The Urban Institute, 1997, p. 2–5.

7. Ibid, p. 205–229, 257–281, Judith Levine, Harold Pollack and Maureen E. Comfort, "Academic and Behavioral Outcomes Among the Children of Young Mothers," *Journal of Marriage and Family* 63 (May 2001): 355–369 and Amy Conseur et al., "Maternal and Perinatal Risk Factors for Later Delinquency," *Pediatrics* 99 (June 1997): 785–790.

8. Rebecca A. Maynard, ed., *Kids Having Kids: A Robin Hood Foundation Special Report on the Costs of Adolescent Childbearing,* The Robin Hood Foundation, 1996, p. 19.

9. Ibid, pp. 20, 88–91.

10. The Alan Guttmacher Institute, "Teen Sex and Pregnancy," *Facts in Brief,* 1999.

11. Linda L. Alexander, ed., et al., "Sexually Transmitted Diseases in America: How Many Cases and at What Cost?" The Kaiser Family Foundation, December 1998, 8.

12. Centers for Disease Control, *Tracking the Hidden Epidemics: Trends in the United States 2000,* 4.

13. The Alan Guttmacher Institute, "Teen Sex and Pregnancy."

14. Ibid. See also the Kaiser Family Foundation, "HPV (Human Papillomavirus) and Cervical Cancer," *Fact Sheet,* July 2001.

15. Tom and Judy Lickona, *Sex, Love and You,* (Notre Dame: Ave Maria Press, 1994), 62–77.

16. Centers for Disease Control, "Current Trends: Premarital Sexual Experience Among Adolescent Women—United States, 1970–1988," *Morbidity and Mortality Weekly Report* 39 (January 4, 1991): 929–932. Available at www.cdc.gov/mmwr/preview/mmwrhtml/00001869.htm.

17. Connie J. Salts et al., "Attitudes Toward Marriage and Premarital Sexual Activity of College Freshmen," *Adolescence* 29 (Winter 1994): 775–779.

18. Tina Hoff and Liberty Greene et al., "Sex Education in America: A Series of National Surveys of Students, Parents, Teachers, and Principals," Kaiser Family Foundation, September 2000, 16.

19. The Physicians Consortium, "Sexual Messages in Government-Promoted Programs and Today's Youth Culture," April 2002.

20. Cheryl Wetzstein, "Drop in Teen Birthrates Attributed to Abstinence," *The Washington Times,* February 11, 1999, A6.

21. Joyce C. Abma and Freya L. Sonenstein, *Sexual Activity and Contraceptive Practices Among Teenagers in the United States, 1988 and 1995,* Series 23: Data from the National Survey of Family Growth, National Center for Health Statistics, Washington, D. C., April 2001, Table 1.

22. Tina Hoff and Liberty Greene et al., "Sex Education in America: A Series of National Surveys of Students, Parents, Teachers, and Principals," 14.

23. Barbara Devaney et al., "The Evaluation of Abstinence Education Programs Funded Under Title V Section 510: Interim Report," Mathematica Policy Research, Inc., April 2002, 14.

24. Raja S. Tanas, "Report on the Teen-Aid Abstinence-Education Program Fifth-Year Evaluation 1998–1999, Whitworth College, Spokane, WA, July 1999.

25. Elaine Borawski et al., "Evaluation of the Teen Pregnancy Prevention Programs Funded Through the Wellness Block Grant (1999–2000), Case Western Reserve University, March 23, 2001.

26. Peter S. Bearman and Hannah Bruckner, "Promising the Future: Virginity Pledges and First Intercourse," *American Journal of Sociology* 106 (January 2001): 859–912.

NO ↩

Debra Hauser

Five Years of Abstinence-Only-Until-Marriage Education: Assessing the Impact

Introduction

Since 1991, rates of teenage pregnancy and birth have declined significantly in the United States. These are welcome trends. Yet, teens in the United States continue to suffer from the highest birth rate and one of the highest rates of sexually transmitted infections (STIs) in the industrialized world. Debate over the best way to help teens avoid, or reduce, their sexual risk-taking behavior has polarized many youth-serving professionals. On one side are those that support comprehensive sex education—education that promotes abstinence but includes information about contraception and condoms to build young peoples knowledge, attitudes and skills for when they do become sexually active. On the other side are those that favor abstinence-only-until-marriage—programs that promote "abstinence from sexual activity outside marriage as the expected standard" of behavior. Proponents of abstinence-only programs believe that providing information about the health benefits of condoms or contraception contradicts their message of abstinence-only and undermines its impact. As such, abstinence-only programs provide no information about contraception beyond failure rates.

In 1996, Congress signed into law the Personal Responsibility & Work Opportunities Reconciliation Act, or "welfare reform." Attached was the provision, later set out in Section 510(b) of Title V of the Social Security Act, appropriating $250 million dollars over five years for state initiatives promoting sexual abstinence outside of marriage as the only acceptable standard of behavior for young people.

For the first five years of the initiative, every state but California participated in the program. (California had experimented with its own abstinence-only initiative in the early 1990's. The program was terminated in February 1996, when evaluation results found the program to be ineffective.) From 1998 to 2003, almost a half a billion dollars in state and federal funds were appropriated to support the Title V initiative. A report, detailing the results from the federally funded evaluation of select Title V programs, was due to be released more than a year ago. Last year, Congress extended "welfare reform" and, with it, the Title V abstinence-only-until-marriage funding without benefit of this, as yet unreleased, report.

As the first five-year funding cycle of Title V came to a close, a few state-funded evaluations became public. Others were completed with little or no fanfare. This document reviews the findings from the 10 evaluations that Advocates for Youth was able to identify. Advocates for Youth also includes evaluation results from California's earlier attempt at a statewide abstinence-only initiative.

Available Evaluations

Ten states made some form of evaluation results available for review. For Arizona, Florida, Iowa, Maryland, Minnesota, Oregon, Pennsylvania, and Washington, Advocates was able to locate evaluation results from state Title V programs. For Missouri and Nebraska, Advocates located evaluation findings from at least one program among those funded through the state's Title V initiative. Finally, the evaluation of California's abstinence-only program was published in a peer-reviewed journal and readily available.

Funding*

During the first five years of abstinence-only-until-marriage Title V programming, the 10 states received about $45.5 million in federal funds. To further support the initiatives and to cover their required funding match, these states appropriated about $34 million in additional funds over the five years. In addition, California spent $15 million in state funds between 1991 and 1994 to support its abstinence-only initiative. In sum, the program efforts discussed in this paper cost an estimated $94.5 million in federal and state dollars.

Program Components

For the most part, Title V funds were administered through states' departments of health and then sub-granted to abstinence-only contractors within each state. Program components varied from state to state and from contractor to contractor within each state. However, all programs discussed in this document included an abstinence-only curriculum, delivered to young people in schools or through community-based agencies. Popular curricula included: *Education Now Babies Later (ENABL)*, *Why Am I Tempted? (WAIT)*, *Family Accountability Communicating Teen Sexuality (FACTS)*, *Choosing the Best Life*, *Managing Pressures before Marriage*, and AC Green's *Game Plan*, among others. Some programs included peer education, health fairs, parent outreach, and/or *Baby Think it Over* simulators. Some states supplemented their educational programs with media campaigns, also funded through Title V.

Evaluation Designs

The 11 evaluations summarized in this document represent those Advocates for Youth could uncover through extensive research. The quality of the evaluation designs varied greatly. Most evaluations employed a simple pretest/post-test survey design. Slightly fewer than half (five) assessed the significance of changes from pre- to posttest, using a comparison group. Additionally, seven evaluations included some form of follow-up to assess the program's impact over time, although results are not yet available for two. Three of these seven also included a comparison group. For those programs that included follow-up, surveys were administered at three to 17 months after students completed their abstinence-only-until-marriage program. . . .

Summary of Results

Evaluation of these 11 programs showed few short-term benefits and no lasting, positive impact. A few programs showed mild success at improving attitudes and intentions to abstain. No program was able to demonstrate a postive impact on sexual behavior over time. A description follows of short- and long-term impacts, by indicator.

Short-Term Impacts of State Abstinence-Only Programs

In 10 programs, evaluation measured the short-term impact of the program on at least one indicator, including attitudes favoring abstinence, intentions to abstain, and/or sexual behavior. Overall, programs were most successful at improving participants' attitudes towards abstinence and were least likely to positively affect participants' sexual behaviors.

Attitudes endorsing abstinence   10 evaluations tested for short-term changes in attitudes.

- Three of 10 programs had no significant impact on attitudes (Maryland, Missouri, and Nebraska);
- Four of 10 showed increases in attitudes favorable to abstinence (Arizona, Florida, Oregon, and Washington);
- Three of 10 showed mixed results (California, Iowa, and Pennsylvania).**

Intentions to abstain   Nine evaluations measured short-term changes in intentions.

- Four of nine programs showed no significant impact on participants' intentions to abstain (California, Maryland, Nebraska, and Oregon);
- Three of nine programs showed a favorable impact on intentions to abstain (Arizona, Florida, and Washington);
- Two of nine programs showed mixed results (Iowa and Pennsylvania).**

Sexual behaviors   Six evaluations measured short-term changes in sexual behavior.

- Three of six programs had no impact on sexual behavior (California, Maryland, and Missouri).
- Two of six programs reported increases in sexual behavior from pre- to posttest (Florida and Iowa). It was unclear whether the increases were due to youth's maturation or to a program's effect, as none of these evaluations included a comparison group.
- One of the six programs showed mixed results (Pennsylvania).**

Long-Term Impacts of State Abstinence-Only Programs

Seven evaluations included some form of follow-up survey to assess the impact of the abstinence-only programs over time. Results from two of these are not yet available (Nebraska and Oregon). Of the remaining five, three were of statewide initiatives (Arizona, California, and Minnesota). Two were evaluations of programs within statewide initiatives (Missouri's *Life Walk* Program and Pennsylvania's LaSalle Program). All five evaluations included questions to assess changes in participants' attitudes and behaviors between pretest/posttest and follow-up. Four also measured changes in intentions to abstain. Three evaluations included a comparison group.

Attitudes endorsing abstinence   Five evaluations included assessment of changes in attitudes.

Four of five evaluations showed no long-term positive impact on participants' attitudes. That is, participants' attitudes towards abstinence either declined at follow-up or there was no evidence that participating in the abstinence-only program improved teens' attitudes about abstinence relative to the comparison groups, at three to 17 months after taking the abstinence-only program (Arizona, California, Missouri, and Pennsylvania's LaSalle Program).

Follow-up surveys in Minnesota showed mixed results.

Intentions to abstain   Four evaluations measured long-term intentions to abstain.

Three of four evaluations showed no long-term positive impact on participants' intentions to abstain from sexual intercourse. That is, participants' intentions either declined significantly at follow-up or there was no statistically significant difference in participants' attitudes relative to controls at follow-up (Arizona, California, and Minnesota).

In one of the four (Pennsylvania's LaSalle Program), evaluation showed a positive impact at follow-up on program participants' intentions to abstain relative to comparison youth.

Sexual behavior   Five programs measured long-term impacts on sexual behavior.

No evaluation demonstrated any impact on reducing teens' sexual behavior at follow-up, three to 17 months after the program ended (Arizona, California, Minnesota, Missouri, or Pennsylvania's LaSalle Program).

Comparisons of Abstinence-Only-Until-Marriage versus Comprehensive Sex Education

Two evaluations—Iowa's and the Pennsylvania Fulton County program—compared the impact of comprehensive sex education with that of abstinence-only-until-marriage programs.

- In Iowa, abstinence-only students were slightly more likely than comprehensive sex education participants to feel strongly about wanting to postpone sex, but less likely to feel that their goals should not include teen pregnancy. There was little to no difference between the abstinence-only students and those in the comprehensive sex education program in understanding of why they should wait to have sex. Evaluation did not include comparison of data on the sexual behavior of participants in the two types of programs.
- In Fulton County, Pennsylvania, results found few to no differences between the abstinence-only and comprehensive approaches in attitudes towards sexual behavior. Evaluators found that, regardless of which program was implemented in the seventh and eighth grades, sexual attitudes, intentions, and behaviors were similar by the end of the 10th grade.

Discussion

These evaluation results—from the first five-year cycle of funding for abstinence-only-until-marriage under Section 510(b) of Title V of the Social Security Act—reflect the results of other studies. In a 1994 review of sex education programs, Kirby *et al* assessed all the studies available at the time of school-based, abstinence-only programs that had received peer review and that measured attitudes, intentions, *and* behavior. Kirby *et al* found that none of the three abstinence-only programs was effective in producing a statistically significant impact on sexual behaviors in program participants relative to comparisons. In a 1997 report for the National Campaign to Prevent Teen Pregnancy, Doug Kirby reviewed evaluations from six abstinence-only programs, again finding no program that produced a statistically significant change in sexual behavior. This was again confirmed in 2000 when another review by Kirby found no abstinence-only program that produced statistically significant changes in sexual behaviors among program youth relative to comparisons. This failure of abstinence-only programs to produce behavior change was among the central concerns expressed by some authors of the evaluations included in this document. [For examples of authors' remarks on behavior change, see quotations under Arizona, Florida, Missouri, and Pennsylvania in the state-by-state analyses that follow.] It is important to note that a great deal of research contradicts the belief that changes in knowledge and attitudes alone will necessarily result in behavior change.

A few evaluators also noted the failure of abstinence-only programs to address the needs of sexually active youth. Survey data from many of the programs indicated that sexually experienced teens were enrolled in most of the abstinence-only programs studied. For example:

- In Erie County, Pennsylvania, researchers found that 42 percent of the female participants were sexually active by the second year of the program.
- In Clinton County, Pennsylvania, data collected from program participants in the seventh, eighth, and ninth grades showed a dramatic increase in the proportion of program females who experienced first sexual intercourse over time (six, nine, and 30 percent, respectively, by grade).
- In Minnesota, 12 percent of the eighth grade program participants were sexually active at posttest.
- In Arizona, 19 percent of program participants were sexually active at follow-up. Concurrently, Arizona's evaluators found that youth's intent to pursue abstinence declined significantly at follow-up, regardless of whether the student took another abstinence-only class. Eighty percent of teens reported that they were likely to become sexually active by the time they were 20 years old.

Abstinence-only programs provide these youth with no information, other than abstinence, regarding how to protect themselves from pregnancy, HIV, and other STIs.

A third, related concern of evaluators was abstinence-only programs' failure to provide positive information about contraception and condoms. Evaluators noted more than once that programs' emphasis on the failure rates of contraception, including condoms, left youth ambivalent, at best, about using them.

- In Clinton County, Pennsylvania, researchers noted that, of those participants that reported experiencing first sexual intercourse during ninth grade, only about half used any form of contraception.
- Arizona's evaluation team found that program participants' attitudes about birth control became less favorable from pre- to posttest. They noted that this was probably a result of the "program's focus on the failure rates of contraceptives as opposed to their availability, use and access."

Conclusion

Abstinence-only programs show little evidence of sustained (long-term) impact on attitudes and intentions. Worse, they show some negative impacts on youth's willingness to use contraception, including condoms, to prevent negative sexual health outcomes related to sexual intercourse. Importantly, only in one state did any program demonstrate short-term success in delaying the initiation of sex; none of these programs demonstrates evidence of long-term success in delaying sexual initiation among youth exposed to the programs or any evidence of success in reducing other sexual risk-taking behaviors among participants.

Notes

* In federal fiscal year 2003, the 10 states discussed here with evaluations of Title V programs received $8,810,281 in federal funds. Under the law, states are required to provide matching funds of three state-raised dollars for every four federal dollars received. Thus in 2003, the 10 states supplied $7,268,060 in state dollars, bringing the total of public monies to Title V funded abstinence-only-until-marriage programs to $16,078,341.

** Mixed results indicated that attitudes changed in both desired and undesired directions, either by survey questions within one initiative, or by individual programs within an initiative.

POSTSCRIPT

Should "Abstinence-Until-Marriage" Be the Only Message for Teens?

The Healthy People 2010: Understanding and Improving Health report (U.S. Department of Health and Human Services, 2000) suggests that as many as 50 percent of all adolescents are sexually active. The *National Youth Risk Behavior Survey* (1998) reported similar findings, with rates higher for boys than girls, and with 7.2 percent of youth having sexual intercourse before age 13. The *National Survey of American Attitudes on Substance Abuse IX: Teen Dating Practices and Sexual Activity* found that 28 percent of 12-year-olds have sexually active friends, and this rises to 79 percent for 17-year-olds. The high rates of sexual activity among young people are especially troubling, given that a large and disproportionate percentage of sexually transmitted diseases and unintended pregnancies occur among adolescents. Approximately 25 percent of teenagers who are active sexually will acquire a STD in a given year, nearly as many sexually active adolescent females (20 percent) become pregnant, and the overwhelming majority (85 percent) of these pregnancies are unplanned.

In reality we know that during the teen years, young people go through many powerful hormonal, emotional, and social changes. They discover sexual feelings without fully understanding their meaning or what to do with them. They often end up engaging in sexual activity that is not pleasant (especially females) and often do not practice safe sex (using condoms or dental dams, for example). There are powerful gender-related dating and sexual scripts that make it more difficult for adolescents to negotiate their sexual experiences. These scripts guide expectations: notions of "real" sex, who is supposed to initiate, and what the experience is supposed to be like (e.g., an ideal), as well as the consequences for engaging (or not) in sexual activity. Males may feel like they have to be sexually active to be seen as a "real" man and run the risk of being called "gay" if they refrain. Females have to deal with the stereotypes of "prude" or "slut." Many adolescent girls report they engage in oral sex to be popular.

Each side of the sexuality debate is working with what it considers to be a logical presumption. For AOUM proponents, the surest way to avoid an unintended pregnancy. or STI is to not do anything sexually until in a committed, monogamous relationship—which, to them, is only acceptable within the context of marriage. If people do not engage in the behaviors, they cannot be exposed to the negatives. Since AOUM supporters also believe that marriage is a commitment that is accompanied by a promise of monogamy, or sexual exclusivity, it is, for them, the only appropriate choice for teens.

For comprehensive sexuality education proponents, the logic is that sexual exploration is a normal part of adolescents' development. They believe that the "just say no" approach to sexual behaviors is as unrealistic as it is unhealthy. Rooted in education, social learning, and health belief theories, comprehensive sexuality education programs believe that youth can make wise decisions about their sexual health if given the proper information. Comprehensive programs can address the psychosocial issues, and the role of gender-role expectations in ways that AOUM cannot.

Suggested Readings

Charles Abraham, Mary Rogers Gillmore, Gerjo Kok, and Herman P. Schaalma, "Sex Education as Health Promotion: What Does It Take? "*Archives of Sexual Behavior, 33* (2004): 259–269.

Paul Florsheim, (2003). *Adolescent Romantic Relations and Sexual Behavior: Theory, Research, and Practical Implications* (Mahwah, NJ: Lawrence Erlbaum Associates, 2003).

Douglas Kirby, "The Impact of Schools and School Programs upon Adolescent Sexual Behavior," *The Journal of Sex Research, 9* (2002): 27–33.

J. Mark Halstead, and Michael J. Reiss, *Values in Sex Education: From Principles to Practice* (London: RoutledgeFalmer, 2003).

Karen J. Maschke, ed., *Reproduction, Sexuality, and the Family: Gender and American Law: The Impact of the Law on the Lives of Women* (New York: Garland Publishing, 1997).

ISSUE 16

Can Women's Sexuality Be Free From Traditional Gender Constraints?

YES: Elizabeth Sheff, from "Polyamorous Women, Sexual Subjectivity and Power," *Journal of Contemporary Ethnography* (June 2005)

NO: Cheryl B. Travis, Kayce L. McGinnis, and Kristin M. Bardari, from "Beauty, Sexuality, and Identity: The Social Control of Women," *Sexuality, Society, and Feminism: Psychological Perspectives on Women* (2000)

ISSUE SUMMARY

YES: Elizabeth Sheff conducted an ethnographic study that suggests that engaging in nontraditional romantic and sexual relationships can help women reject sexual objectification and enlarge their sexual subjectivity.

NO: Cheryl B. Travis and her colleagues argue that society's social construction of beauty has so deeply affected the socialization of girls that it plays a key role in controlling women's sexuality. Their analysis of the impact of the beauty myth calls into question whether any woman can truly have a sexual self that has not been shaped by societal ideals.

Sexuality has been identified by feminists as a culturally important domain for gender relations and politics. In Victorian times, self-control, discipline, delayed gratification, self-sacrifice, and repression characterized sexuality. Religious authorities defined the moral boundaries of right and wrong sexual activities. Contemporary conservative religious perspectives continue to restrict sexuality to procreation in the family context. Women's individual pleasure, exploration, and sexual identity are seen as antithetical or even threatening to procreative sexuality within the family. The patriarchal influence of Victorian times castigated women into a role of sexual subordination and ignorance, shame, and passivity. The pleasures of the body were considered "dirty."

The locus of definition and control then shifted to a medical model, proscribing sexual activity outside of a procreative model as abnormal and evidence of illness. In the medical model, sexuality is seen as located within the person as a set of natural physiological drives. The dominant medical model of sexuality, the Human Sexual Response Cycle (HSRC) was advanced in 1966 by William Masters and Virginia Johnson. The HSRC describes the sequence of physiological changes that occur during sexual activity and presumes that the sexes have the same sexual response cycles. Critics argue that this model of sexuality is biased toward men's sexual interests. They argue that although men's and women's sexuality may be more similar than different physiologically, gender inequality is a social reality that impacts that HSRC. Furthermore, sexuality is not just an internal or genital sensation of desire, arousal, and orgasm. There are also important *social* sexual realities.

Some contemporary sexologists (scholars who engage in the scientific study of sexuality) challenge a biological or "natural" approach to sex by arguing that the sociocultural context is central in defining everything about sexual experience. The sociocultural context creates and shapes sexuality by defining "sexual scripts," which are enacted in physical performance. Sexual scripts, of which expectations are a key element, guide sexual behavior by helping participants define the situation and plot out appropriate behavior.

Males are socialized to be more sexually aware, active, assertive, and entitled. They learn to value varied sexual experience and sexual gratification, for which they are often rewarded with the esteem of peers. Females generally are socialized to limit sexual activity and to tie sex to romance and beauty in which there is greater concern for affection than for sex. They learn to value intimacy and emotional communion. Females are often treated as and consequently see themselves as sexual *objects,* not subjects with sexual agency of their own. Many scholars argue that sex role socialization creates fundamental gender differences and inequalities, leading to heterosexually based scripts and experience.

Indeed, it seems that females are in a no-win situation regarding their sexuality. While heterosexual females are rewarded early on for abstinence, later they receive pressure from male partners to have sex. Such females are considered "prudes" if they do not have sex, "sluts" or "loose" if they to have sex. Females learn that sex is "dirty" but they feel like their worth as a female is determined by their ability to attract and please males. HIV prevention educator Carolyn Laub explains how such sexual gender ideology is related to the practice of safer sex strategies and sexual risk. According to Laub, a female who is prepared for sex (e.g., carrying condoms) signals that she is sexually aware and therefore "easy" or dirty. Likewise, a female who talks with a potential sex partner about safer-sex issues may imply that she has been sexually active and therefore "loose."

The following selections illustrate a stark contrast between patriarchally delimitted women's sexuality and the possibility of sexual freedom and power for women. Elizabeth Sheff describes her study of polyamorous women—women who she says, by engaging in long-term romantic, sexual, and/or affective relationships with multiple people (female or male) simultaneously, are able to reject sexual objectification and find a subjective sexuality that is free of societal constraints. Her analyses suggest that polyamorous women report feelingless constrained by gender roles, an increased sex drive, deeper connections with other women, and more powerful. In contrast, Cheryl Travis and her colleagues begin their analysis of women's sexuality and identity by asserting that beauty, as it has been socially constructed, is a key factor in defining and controlling women's sexuality.

Elizabeth Sheff

YES

Polyamorous Women, Sexual Subjectivity and Power

In the shifting gendered and sexual social landscape of the early twenty-first century, multiple-partner relationships remain eroticized and undertheorized. Pornographic films and magazines frequently present images of multiple-partner sex, most often of multiple women or a man with several women. Rather than challenging gendered and sexual roles or enlarging women's sexual sphere, these scenes actually reinforce heteronormativity. These highly sexualized images fail to capture the lived experiences of the people, especially the women, who actually engage in multiple partner relationships. Feminist theorists have criticized such androcentric images of women's sexuality and have argued instead for an agentic female sexual subjectivity.

Polyamory is a form of relationship in which people have multiple romantic, sexual, and/or affective partners. It differs from swinging in its emphasis on long-term, emotionally intimate relationships and from adultery with its focus on honesty and (ideally) full disclosure of the network of sexual relationships to all who participate in or are affected by them. Both men and women have access to additional partners in polyamorous relationships, distinguishing them from polygamy. . . .

The study of polyamory is essential to forming a more complete understanding of women's sexual subjectivity and power. My analysis provides empirical evidence that suggests new complexities associated with multiple-partner relationships and expands sociological understanding of women's sexuality by investigating a previously unexamined area of sexual subjectivity. To explore polyamorous women's potential to enlarge the concept of sexual subjectivity through engagement in nontraditional relationships and their attempts to reject sexual objectification, I analyzed data based on seven years of participant observation and in-depth interviews. . . .

While social theorists have examined multiple-partner relationships in the context of bisexuality, open marriage, adultery, and swinging, these discussions have focused on variations within a conventional sexual framework. Analysis indicates that swingers maintain conservative attitudes regarding gender roles, heterosexuality, and politics. . . . Addition of polyamory to the catalog of women's sexual identities augments contemporary sociological

From *Journal of Contemporary Ethnography*, vol. 34, no. 3, June 2005, excerpts from 251–267, 269, 271–273, 275–280. Copyright © 2005 by Sage Publications. Reprinted by permission.

research by acknowledging an alternate form of sexuality that offers women expanded horizons of choice.

[S]exual subjectivity [is] "a person's experience of herself as a sexual being, who feels entitled to sexual pleasure and sexual safety, who makes active sexual choices, and who has an identity as a sexual being. Sexual desire is at the heart of sexual subjectivity." . . . Sexual subjectivity for girls and women contrasts heterocentric, patriarchal objectification in which female sexuality is commodified or colonized in the service and convenience of men. Sexual subjectivity is integrally linked with power—the power to appropriate sexuality, relational power, and social power connected to defining versions of sexuality outside rigidly controlled norms as deviant. Women with no access to their own sexual subjectivity have bodies that Tolman terms "silent," disempowered by being spoken for and defined by masculine ideas and desires. . . . Some women refuse the mandates of androcentric versions of sexuality and redefine themselves as sexual agents. . . .

By simultaneously challenging and participating in aspects of sexual subjectivity and sexual objectification, polyamorous women inhabit the borderland between *emphasized femininity,* or a version of womanhood that is "defined around compliance with this subordination and is oriented to accommodating the interests and desires of men" and an alternative, noncompliant form of femininity. . . .

If, conventional sexual arrangements are designed to silence women's authentic spirits, then an alternative erotic system could offer women a more authentic expression of sexual subjectivity from which to "rise up empowered." Through their involvement in polyamory, the women in my sample explored new roles and avenues of sexuality while shifting the balance of power in their relationships. . . . In this article, I explore the impact the alternate sexual system of polyamory exerts on some women's lives. In so doing, I detail some of the ways in which polyamorous women expand "normal" social roles, discuss their sexual lives and identities, and explore the novel and traditional forms of power polyamorous practice engenders for these women's relationships.

Method

This article is part of a larger project based on participant observation and in-depth interviews I conducted during a seven-year period (1996 to 2003). . . .

My data for this article come from extensive participant observation, including attendance at support group meetings, workshops, and national polyamorists conferences, as well as informal conversations and forty in-depth interviews (twenty women and twenty men). Reflecting mainstream polyamorous communities in the Western United States, my respondents were in their mid-30s to late 50s and tended toward middle- and upper-middle-class socioeconomic status, usually college educated, overwhelmingly white, and frequently employed as professionals in computer or counseling/therapy fields. I used semistructured interviews that lasted from one and one half to two hours, a format that yields data suitable for answering questions about members' interpretations, actions, and interactions. . . .

I analyzed the interview data and my field notes by adjusting analytical categories to fit the emerging theoretical concepts. Once the theoretical concepts emerged, I constructed clusters of participant's experiences to further develop my theories. I used subsequent interviews and field observation to verify the validity of these theories, as well as checking for the boundaries and variations of common themes.

[Concepts and Themes]

[1] Expanded Roles

Some polyamorous women who felt constrained and disempowered by monogamy reported a sense of release upon embarking on polyamorous relationships. Departure from accepted forms of relationships required polyamorous women to form new roles or expand roles previously available to them as monogamists. The women in my sample expanded their familial, cultural, gendered, and sexual roles.

[a] Family and monogamous culture.   Peck, a thirty-six-year-old white magazine editor and mother of three, rejected the traditional wifely role she observed in her family of origin and had originally replicated in her monogamous marriage: "Women got married, had children, raised the children and stayed in the home, that's what I was taught and brought up with. And that was the role I was following. . . . That period in my life, I was thinking and wanting things different and was starting to get my own empowerment as a woman, changing roles, and wanting more." "Wanting more" involved not only pursuing higher levels of education but also rejecting a form of sexuality and family that was not working for her and forging a polyamorous alternative. Polyamory provided the impetus for Peck to shift long-standing roles she found ill fit. . . .

[b] Gender roles.   The majority of the polyamorous women in my sample reported shifting gender roles resulting from, or precipitating, participation in polyamory. Yansa, a twenty-nine-year-old African American health care provider and stepmother of one, related her reasons for agreeing to monogamous relationships even though she knew she desired multiple partners.

> I didn't want to hurt my partner's feelings. I felt that I wanted to be the righteous one and do the right thing for them and for the relationship. . . . When we became committed and like kind of in a monogamous relationship I think the relationship immediately went down hill from there. And it was more of a situation where he had sown his wild oats. He was tired of playing around. I was the one, but I had just begun and it was like, quelled this desire and I was just like, this is not enough for me. And he was like, this is enough for me, and I said, we have a problem.

Yansa initially conformed to a traditionally feminine role of ignoring her own desire for multiple partners in favor of being "righteous" and engaging in the monogamy her partner desired. Eventually, she came to define their disparate needs as "a problem" and transitioned to a polyamorous relationship style and identity. . . .

[c] Sexual roles.   Sexuality was one of the primary areas in which polyamorous women reported expanding their roles. Julia, a forty-one-year-old Lebanese American software consultant, found polyamory to be instrumental in redefining the cultural ideal of sex and sexuality that failed her personally:

> My motive of expressing my sexuality has really changed a lot since finding polyamory. . . . On the face of it, you could just say that it's been limited a lot and the things that other people usually call sex, things that involve genital contact and bringing one another to orgasm, mostly I don't do that anymore because it's too emotionally wrought for me. It's too, I just can't do it with integrity anymore. . . . So for me, when I talk about any sexual relationships or interactions I have had they've been relationships dominated overwhelmingly by what other people might just call smooching or a lot of breathing and gazing into each other's eyes and caressing and things where for me arousal is what's enjoyable and orgasm is not.

. . . [P]olyamorous women rejected a sexual and gender system that separated people with a false emphasis on small differences between men and women. Many of these polyamorous women embraced forms of sexual subjectivity that allowed them to redefine mores and social institutions such as sexuality and monogamy to better fit their own needs. Some consciously refused the subject/object dichotomy that cast women as passive objects of men's sexual satisfaction. Others simply forged novel roles without theorizing a social context. . . .

[2] Sexuality

Polyamorous women frequently discussed sexuality in support groups, social gatherings, and with their partners. These discussions emphasized sexuality in relation to polyamorous women's high sex drives, connections with other women, and bisexual identities.

[a] High sex drive.   In direct opposition to cultural mandates of female sexual submission and a double standard that requires women restrain their sexual desires, a number of polyamorous women reported viewing themselves as highly sexual people. Louise asserted that

> I have such a high sex drive and literally feel I need sex on a regular basis to feel grounded, to feel clear, to feel good, and it's just, it's very, it's like exercise for me. It feels good. I enjoy it. . . . If I haven't had sex in a while, after about three to four weeks I start climbing the walls and I get very bitchy

and I'm just not in a good mood and I don't feel good and I feel on edge. Whereas if I get sex on a regular basis, I'm calm, I'm fine, I'm happy.

This description of sexual appetite would be unremarkable coming from a man, but from a woman, it contrasts dominant cultural scripts mandating women's disinterest in sex except to meet masculine needs. . . . Risking defamation by eschewing the constraints of coupledom, polyamorous women reject the power dynamic embedded in the persistent sexual double standard that continues to limit women's sexual choices and stigmatize those who refrain from living by its mandates. . . .

[b] Connections with other women.   The majority of the women in my sample viewed sexuality as a source of unity with other women, even some who had previously experienced sexuality as divisive. Louise discussed the new sense of connection she had developed with women since finding the polyamorous community:

> One of the things that has probably been the best thing about finding the poly community is meeting women that I can relate to because I haven't had women friends before now. This is the first time in my life, with a few exceptions, that I have really had close women friends. It's been wonderful to meet women who are highly sexual who don't feel threatened that I'm highly sexual. . . . And it's brought me a closeness with women that I thought I'd never have.

. . . Facile connection with other women was not universal, however, and feelings of jealousy or strife often plagued relationships among polyamorous women. . . .

[c] Bisexuality.   Bisexual women were quite numerous in polyamorous communities. In fact, bisexuality was so common among women in the polyamorous community that they had a standing joke that it allowed them to "have their Jake and Edith too!" Bisexual women were also among the highest status members of the subculture because they were most often sought as additions to existing female/male dyads to create the coveted and elusive F/M/F (female, male, female) triad. While the high status of the role might have encouraged some women to experiment with bisexuality, others had identified as bisexual long before their association with the polyamorous community. Some polyamorous women sought independent sexual relationships with other women, while others preferred group sexual encounters involving both women and men. Women in polyamorous communities interacted with varying degrees of sexuality that created social space for multiple definitions of bisexuality to coexist. . . .

Even those women who questioned the legitimacy of their bisexual identity because of their greater attraction for men made it clear that they had felt attractions to and engaged in sexual relationships with women as well as men. . . .

Clearly, the relationship between gender and bisexuality within the polyamorous community is complex. On one hand, women were sometimes sexualized as "hot bi babes" and sought to endow a new level of eroticism upon established male/female sexual relationships. On the other hand, men were sometimes objectified as sex toys but excluded from emotional relationships. In the relationally intricate world of polyamory, both scenarios operated simultaneously. Still, in patriarchal societies, men generally retain greater social and financial power on average, endowing their definitions of a given situation with greater weight. Power remains a complex issue within polyamorous relationships.

[3] Power

While both men and women involved in polyamorous subcultures tended to view women as retaining more power in polyamorous relationships, women who had initiated the entree into polyamory themselves seemed more secure in their perceived enhanced power than did women who engaged in polyamory at the behest of their male partners. Yet both types of women endured stigma and the attendant loss of power that accompanies deviation from cherished social norms such as monogamy.

[a] Women in power. Some polyamorists perceived women to have greater power in polyamorous subcultures. Emmanuella felt women's greater control of sexuality within polyamorous communities endowed them with increased social power in a potentially highly sexualized setting.

> The women seem to have more of a sexual parlance because the women decide whether sex is available and there are still some incredibly conventional notions about who approaches whom. The men seem to swing between being very sort of kid in a candy store, elated, can't believe this whole practice is happening to them, but yeah, buddy, let's get it on of thing. And the other extreme is feeling very dour about the fact that their woman is participating in this and really uncertain whether they want to have that, but are going along with it because there might be sex involved. . . .

[b] Power shifts. Other polyamorous women viewed power as more equally shared. . . .

[Some] polyamorous women maintained the ostensibly equitable balance of power via rigorous communication, an esteemed ideal of polyamorous relationships. Some discussed a division of labor with their partner(s) that included some task division but ultimately established parity, while others explained how they shared all tasks with their partners and split everything equally.

Some women asserted that polyamorous men supported and indeed sought relationships based on equality in relationship. Louise said that she found that the polyamorous men "just think differently." She explained:

> They are much more nontraditional. They aren't looking, most men that I've seen that are polyamorous aren't looking for a relationship with a woman they can control or be in charge of. They like independent women

who are highly sexual, who are exciting. They like that. That's why they're attracted to this kind of lifestyle is because they like strong women. And because of that, they're looking for an equal relationship in most cases.

This perception of equality stood in sharp contrast to some other polyamorous women's experiences with both polyamorous and monogamous men who became increasingly uncomfortable with multiple-partner sexuality as the relationship became more serious. . . .

[c] Women disempowered.   Some polyamorous relationships retained elements of a traditional power structure in which men relied on their female partners to perform a greater share of the emotional maintenance. These relationships seemed to regularly self-destruct. Louise reported encouraging Max, her husband of thirteen years and the father of two of her children, to deepen emotional intimacy with her and facilitate her attempts at friendly contact with his other lovers. Max reported feeling that these demands were excessive and refused to meet them because they "invade my privacy." . . .

Some women reported an increased sense of insecurity in their relationships with the advent of polyamory. Shelly was eloquent regarding the numerous personal costs of polyamory. She had chosen to engage in polyamory at the behest of Sven, her forty-two-year-old white bisexual husband employed as a computer consultant. Sven hoped to find another bisexual man with whom he and Shelly could establish a long-term triad. This ideal relationship proved difficult to establish, and Shelly felt some emotional pain in connection with Sven's desire for outside relationships. . . .

Regardless of potential power shifts in intimate relationships, polyamorous women retained their positions relative to the power base of monogamous society. This created some problems for them, primary among which was the anomic pain borne of failing to fit in to a monogamous society. Many discussed the social intolerance and fear of censure that sometimes accompanied their polyamorous lifestyle. Dylan described this as "being profoundly unacceptable on many levels." Peck detailed the legal difficulties that plagued her when she was married to one man but had a child with another and wanted the "real" father's name listed on the birth certificate. Ultimately she chose to divorce, partially to disentangle herself from legal issues surrounding multiple-partner relationships. . . .

Conclusions

The polyamorous women who participated in this ethnographic study related their experiences of attempting to expand their social roles, explore sexuality (especially bisexuality), and create and maintain the assorted power arrangements associated with polyamorous relationships, with varied results. Many of the women in my sample discussed feelings of power, with feelings of empowerment and disempowerment coexisting in the same relationships. While very few of the respondents explicitly linked access to shifting power dynamics and social arrangements with race, the impact of race and class privilege cannot be ignored. The fact that the majority of these polyamorous women have considerable financial and cultural capital to fall back on should their nontraditional relationships fail made this complex and somewhat risky relationship style more accessible to them than it might have been to women with fewer social or personal resources. It is no coincidence, then, that women with class and race privilege reported feeling greater freedom in relationship style. The ample resources they commanded conferred increased ability to transgress social boundaries since their cultural cachet created the safety net that allowed them to challenge monogamous social norms while simultaneously weathering the storms of the complex relationship style. My findings thus support [the] conclusion that those with power are at greater liberty to alter the social fabric around them.

The women in my sample recognized and rejected the propensity to define female sexual desire in male terms. Many were aware of their transgressions and sought the company of others who supported their efforts to reshape dominant forms of female sexuality in a way that better met their needs. They experienced some success at a gynocentric redefinition of sexuality, gaining greater social power within polyamorous communities and relationships. By rejecting conventional social mores, polyamorous women were forced to create their own roles and examine their sexual relationships. . . .

Shifts in the base of relational power may have endowed polyamorous women with greater power because their ostensible greater ease in finding additional partners translated to greater capital within the relationship. . . . Increased access to other lovers amplifies the resources of the more sought-after lover. In this market-based relationship model, successful polyamorous women (and especially bisexual women)would indeed have greater power in their relationships because of their superior market worth. At least for some polyamorous women, the expanded horizons of choice conferred greater power than that which they experienced in monogamous relationships.

This dynamic could shift as the polyamorous population ages and elderly polyamorous women potentially outnumber their male counterparts. Such numerical imbalance might empower the relatively fewer men choosing from a comparatively larger pool of female partners. . . .

Though numerous women in my sample reported feelings of empowerment, they simultaneously discussed experiences that left them feeling disempowered in their own relationships or larger, monogamous society through the impacts of stigma. Sexuality remains a contested region, and women who challenge it often do so at a cost. The promise of sexual freedom, which theoretically accompanied the sexual revolution beginning in the 1960s, translated into increased sexual freedom for men, but not for women. Feminist theorists hypothesize that it "released" women's sexual appetites in the service of male sexual desire and retained an androcentric focal point. Many polyamorous women experienced the lingering affects of this stalled sexual liberation when they felt periodically objectified as sex toys. Others grated at the assumption that they would perform the majority of emotional management in an extremely high-maintenance relational style. While polyamorous women offered new visions of expanded sexual subjectivity and alternative roles for women, many continued to struggle under the yoke of an androcentric society that demands that women's sexuality function in the service of men. Even though they reported varying degrees of success in their attempts to create new roles and power dynamics within their own relationships, they continued to live with the impacts of stigma attributed by a monogamous society that views their actions as deviant. In both cases, they were unable to completely reform power dynamics in either their own relationships or society at large.

. . . Ultimately, polyamorous women's attempts at self-redefinition were active resistance to suppression. Even though their defiance was imperfect and left their emancipation unfinished, they still attempted to forge lives outside of the narrow confines allowed by heterocentric patriarchal culture. Any attempts at liberation serve to undermine the suppression of women and sexual minorities and are worthy of recognition in their myriad forms.

NO ↵ Cheryl Brown Travis, Kayce L. McGinnis, and Kristin M. Bardari

Beauty, Sexuality, and Identity: The Social Control of Women

This chapter is based on the premise that beauty has become a key factor in defining and controlling women's sexuality. Socially constructed, narrow definitions of beauty and, thereby, sexuality are used as mechanisms to maintain social, political, and economic control by those who benefit from traditional patriarchal structures. We propose that the conflation of physical appearance and sexuality is detrimental to women on individual, interpersonal, and systemic levels and that it ultimately sustains gender-based oppression. . . .

The Social Construction of Sexuality and the Social Control of Women

. . . Despite traditional notions that sexuality is based in anatomy and biology, we contend that sexuality is a socially constructed phenomenon; sexuality is negotiated between people and groups and emerges as a result of normative standards about what is both typical and desirable. The social framework of sexuality provides rules about who can be sexual and under what circumstances sexual behavior is appropriate. The social framework of sexuality even defines what counts as sex. Ultimately, individual experiences of being sexual and sexually aroused are determined, at least in part, by these socially constructed realities.

Although sexuality may be experienced as a personal and highly private aspect of the self, social and political frameworks fundamentally shape the ways in which we think about and experience sexuality. These frameworks encompass norms, expectations, labels, habits, customs, judgments, values, and social scripts of sexuality and sexual behavior. Socially constructed definitions assign meanings and determine whether behaviors are seen as flirtatious, titillating, provocative, salacious, or criminal. The experience of desire and the formulation of what even constitutes sexuality have developed within a social and political context.

Most important, the social framework determines who has the power to exercise choice and authority. Socially constructed definitions of sexuality do not occur randomly but derive from the interests of privileged groups.

From SEXUALITY, SOCIETY, AND FEMINISM, Cheryle Brown Travis and Jacquelyn W. White, editors, January 2000, excerpts from 237–272. Copyright © 2000 by American Psychological Association. Reprinted by permission.

Those who are in power (political, economic, and social) have the most influence in establishing the social framework and are in positions to exert more influence over its design, usually for their own comfort. The sociopolitical context in most societies has consistently advantaged men at the expense of women. . . .

The Beauty = Sex Equation

A primary mechanism used to monitor and control women's sexuality resides in the realm of beauty. For women, sexuality is inextricably linked to physical appearance. Sexuality is distorted as ornamental and observable rather than being viewed as a quality that emanates from the context of women's lives and relationships. Thus, the shape of a woman's body, the size of her breasts, and the color of her hair, are all features commonly used to assess her value as a sexual being.

Ideas about sexual appeal and beauty are not benign expressions of aesthetic preference, but are symbolically constructed systems of knowing and meaning. The social construction of women's sexuality as embedded in attractiveness constitutes a conflation between beauty and sexuality. This merger moves sexuality into the public realm, making it concrete and external, and thereby amenable to inspection, definition, social monitoring, and control. Equating physical appearance with sexuality facilitates a pervasive and ready monitoring of whether women are adhering to an appropriate sexual identity and, most important, an appropriate social role. . . .

By linking women's identity to observable markers and signs that are readily available for public monitoring, comment, and sanction, the social control of women is sustained. Under the framework, women whose identities are not centered on the display of sexuality through beauty and who instead may be focused on obtaining power through educational and economic pursuits are pejoratively labeled as unfeminine, asexual, or lesbian. Woman who live in poverty or who are unable to effectively pursue normative standards of beauty are viewed as lazy and even mentally ill. . . . The social construction of women's identity demands selflessness; healthy, good women attempt to meet the needs of others, specifically, the needs of men. A consequence of the internalization of the beauty-sexuality-identity equation is that normative standards and expectations that are destructive for women often are unseen and unchallenged.

By emulating beauty ideals and attracting and pleasing men, women are taught that sexuality is generated and made real by the responses of men. Sexuality is not promoted as a sensual benefit for women, but is defined as the capability to evoke sexual arousal in others. To be sexual, for women, means to be an object of desire. Thus, whether or not one is sexual is determined almost exclusively by the judgments and experiences of others. Others, then, largely define women's sense of identity and worth. . . .

It is important to note that the social construction of beauty, sexuality, and identity is most compulsory with respect to women; it doesn't operate in the same way for men. Despite the fact that there are normative appearance standards for men, they are not singularly used to perpetuate oppression and disempowerment. . . .

Internalize False Dreams

Ultimately, women come to internalize these beliefs and standards, rendering the elements of social control even more transparent. Women themselves promote the value of breast enlargement surgery, the perfectly matched cosmetic set. Women themselves become members of the social police who monitor and judge other women for failing to embody the ideal. Women themselves equate personal success with the ability to attract attention from men. Women are proud when they have been able to teach their daughters to pursue similar success. The internalization process is multilayered and generated by social, occupational, economic, and legal policies that inherently support patriarchy (i.e., policies that benefit men, for example, in the areas of reproduction, prostitution, childcare, marriage and divorce, etc.). Internalization also is fostered by billion dollar advertising campaigns that prey on insecurities regarding identity and acceptance. Most important, internalization is crystallized through the administration of moderate rewards to women who cultivate their physical attractiveness in accordance with normative expectations.

Despite the fact that these rewards are often fleeting, women who are willing and able to elicit sexual desire from men through the use of beauty are often able to achieve a certain level of self-worth and validation. . . . Sexuality and beauty are strategies for survival for women who face disadvantages of discrimination, harassment, and crime. . . . Unfortunately, to the extent that these constructions of beauty and sexuality are internalized, women will continue to experience ongoing anxiety regarding their identity and social standing, especially in times of financial crisis, divorce or death of spouse, and when the inherent promises of acceptance and safety are ultimately found to be flimsy and unfulfilling. . . .

Whether women embody the ideal or reject it, they face detrimental consequences. The equation of beauty and sexuality creates profound effects in many areas. Here we concentrate on three: body manipulations, health effects, and implications for selfhood and identity.

Body Manipulations

To the extent that beauty ideals are internalized, women themselves are likely to see beauty work as a personal preference and to feel badly about themselves when they do not quite meet the standard. Women regularly report an ideal body image that is thinner, lighter, taller, more muscular, with larger breasts and longer hair compared with their actual physical characteristics. In fact girls and women are encouraged to experiment with various looks and body manipulations very much as if they themselves were objects. Although cosmetic surgery is the primary culprit—and clearly the most potentially dangerous—dysfunctional eating, tattooing, and body piercing also are forms of body manipulation.

Approximately 2 million cosmetic procedures are performed annually in the United States. . . . For example, more than a third of face-lift patients are age 50 or younger. Cosmetic surgery fosters the notion that being unattractive is a form of pathology. It has been suggested that cosmetic surgery exists to cure women of their ugliness, despite the fact that ugliness is not a biological disease, but rather a socially created disease. . . .

Because Western ideas of sexuality are projected onto women's breasts, various means of shaping and enlarging breasts have become common. . . . [A]s a society [we continue] to view breast size as an important maker of sex appeal and beauty.

New technologies have expanded the range and degree of invasiveness possible in the pursuit of beauty. Liposuction (the surgical vacuuming of subcutaneous fat) is now one of the most common procedures. New techniques break up fat cells with ultrasound and suction with a smaller cannula than used in earlier methods that allow for removing pounds as well as reshaping the body. . . .

Health Effects for Adolescent Girls

The fundamental dilemma conveyed to adolescent girls is that if they develop their own autonomy and agency—and thus refuse to participate in the quest for beauty—they may risk their social acceptance and eventually jeopardize future social roles as wives and mothers. In general, these roles depend on the affirmation of a man who finds them attractive and who will choose them as a partner. Messages about the importance of attractiveness begin early, and even elementary school girls have definite ideas about how women should look (e.g., tall, thin, blonde, matching clothes) and, thus, be. Girls learn early that the most important part of who they are is their physical appearance. . . .

One ethnographic study revealed that ideals of beauty, as portrayed in the media, constitute a major theme that may block girls' success. As young women enter college, they are reminded, for example, of the importance placed, not on their education, but on their bodies.

Internalizing beauty ideals by merging one's sense of self-worth with physical attractiveness in order to obtain social rewards creates the potential for serious health problems for adolescent girls. Intensified focus on the body may increase the risk of eating problems an compulsive weight-management behavior. Eating disorders are alarmingly prevalent among adolescent girls, and a substantial portion of these girls will require hospitalization because they are dangerously starved. . . .

As are all complex behaviors, eating disorders are multiply determined, and depending on the constellation of relationships, the disorder may represent either acquiescence or resistance. In some instances an eating disorder may represent the efforts of a young girl to retain her connection to her parents, even if it means rejecting physical maturation. In other instances, the phenomenon may reflect the last means available to the girl by which she can express any form of resistance to control. . . .

Smoking is another health risk behavior that often coexists with dieting and efforts to control weight. Tobacco companies have associated smoking with freedom, adulthood, and sexual allure. Ad slogans such as "slim and sassy" are used to promote smoking among adolescent girls. The result is that 19% of 14–17-year-old girls are regular smokers. Since nicotine dependence is one of the most pernicious addictions, it is likely that girls who become regular smokers in adolescence will carry throughout their lives significant increased risks for low birth weight babies, heart disease, and lung cancer.

The ubiquitous message that external beauty is the sin qua non of sexual allure sends a parallel message to girls that the proof of their sexuality lies not in their own experience so much as the experience of others (i.e., boys and men). In some respects, girls are not considered sexual until they elicit sexual desire in others. This dynamic leads one to question who possesses girls' sexuality—girls themselves or those who are attracted to them? Contributing to this ambiguity is the fact that many girls are discouraged from masturbating. A healthy exploration of one's body for personal pleasure is often condemned in spite of the fact that initiations to erotic stimulation with boys is expected and culturally condoned. . . .

This blurring of boundaries creates implications for health with regard to sexual behavior. Sexual experimentation and intercourse is common among teens, and national data indicate that 30% of 14–15-year-old girls and 58% of 16–17-year-old girls have had intercourse. Less than half of adolescent girls report condom use, and nearly one third report using no contraception at all. The normative model that seems to be operative is that sex involves little or no planning and little or no talking. The popular image is that people are swept away by the lure of romance and interpersonal intimacy. . . .

Consequences of unprotected intercourse for adolescent girls involve high rates of sexually transmitted diseases. . . . The highest rates of gonorrhea and chlamydia are among teen females. . . . Unprotected intercourse results in approximately 1 million pregnancies to unmarried teen girls annually. . . . These disturbing statistics lead us to question the social construction of adolescent sexuality. What is negotiated in these arrangements? What are the implicit assumptions of sexuality and identity? Whose version of reality is constructed that fosters these destructive outcomes?

Fragmented Identity

Another profound effect of the social construction of sexuality and beauty is a fragmented sense of identity for both girls and women. Fragmentation occurs in part because society encourages women to be desirable according to certain beauty ideals while simultaneously encouraging them to deny their sexuality. Women are expected to be sexually attractive while at the same time being punished for being promiscuous and denied adequate access to contraception and reproductive care. In effect, women are left trying to incorporate their real experiences into a framework of fantasy. The missing images of women's realities makes women's experiences seem less valid and only vaguely visible.

An insidious effect of beauty ideals and their relation to sexuality is the transformation of women's (and men's) sexuality away from variable, emergent, and personal experiences to a sexuality that is external, impersonal, and rigidly fixed. Women learn that their sexuality is for others and that being sexual means being an object rather than an agent. . . . In a sense, the women themselves become invisible while the interests and desires of men become figural. To the extent that women internalize the idea that their sexuality, physical appearance, and identity are united, their sense of worth and well-being will depend in large part on their ability to meet whatever impossible standards are popular at the time. . . .

We propose that problems with body image, sexual dysfunction, and other psychological disorders are not the result simply of a failure to achieve the right look but are the product of striving for an impossible fantasy. Rather than feeling satisfied, affirmed, and included, women are more likely to feel vaguely anxious, inadequately, vulnerable, and needy. Rather than feeling empowered or enjoying an expanded social life, women are likely to feel insecure and defeated. Ultimately, as long as women continue to have a vested interest in their appearance for lack of another choice, they will continue to be controlled through objectification. . . .

POSTSCRIPT

Can Women's Sexuality Be Free From Traditional Gender Constraints?

Within feminism, women's sexual freedom was initially advanced as a central cause. Shortly thereafter, women's sexual victimization was added to the feminist agenda. Many say that although women's sexual victimization is a critical cause, attention to it supplanted the advancement of women's sexual freedom.

Over the last three decades, women's sexuality has changed—by some accounts dramatically—in ways more commensurate with men's sexuality. In general, women are gaining greater sexual experience. They engage in intercourse at a younger age, they have more sex partners, they engage in sexual intercourse more frequently, and they are increasingly likely to engage in casual sex. Yet, despite this trend toward sex equality in behaviors, traditional gender socialization and the sexual double standard continue to act as an interpretive filter for sexual experience. Women continue to experience guilt and shame in response to sexual experience and be seen by others as "dirty" or promiscuous.

Caution must be exercised in defining sexual equality for women. Many argue for commensurate sexual permissiveness for males and females. But does that necessarily mean women achieving a sexuality akin to men? Competitiveness, assertiveness, and coercion often characterize males' sexual experience. Males' self- and peer-esteem are linked to sexual experience and performance. Many future-oriented sexologists caution that in striving for sexual equality, we must not limit ourselves to a preset "male" definition of sexual freedom.

Psychologist and sex researcher Leonore Tiefer argues that we need to encourage women's sexual experimentation and explore sexual possibilities. Furthermore, new ideas need to be developed about desire and pleasure. To facilitate this, there needs to be freely available information, ideas, images, and open sexual talk. Tiefer asserts that if women develop sexual knowledge and self-knowledge, they can take more responsibility for their own pleasure.

Traditional sex education programming has overlooked the possibility of female desire and sexual pleasure (see Issue 15). Some argue that sex education programs can be used to help females not allow themselves to be treated as objects but think of themselves as sexual subjects. Women as sexual subjects would feel free to seek out sexual pleasure and know that they have a right to this pleasure. This argument supports the assertion that we also need to raise boys to avoid treating females as sexual objects. The challenge for sex education programming is to inform women about the possible risks of sexual relationships without supporting the double standard that limits, inhibits, and controls their sexuality.

Ideally, sex education programming would include education specifically about gender ideology, as it influences sexual perceptions, decisions, and experiences. Conformity to gender-based norms and ideals for sexual activity is the most important source of peer sexual pressure and risky sex among youth; youth "perform" gendered roles in sexual relations to secure gender affirmation.

Other scholars also argue that catalyzing women's sexual freedom necessitates more far-reaching changes in gender role socialization. Tiefer comments, "A person would have to feel comfortable, safe, and entitled in order to focus wholly on his or her tactile experience. Can we assume that most women can be thoroughly relaxed in sexual situations given the inequality of so many relationships, given women's concern with their appearance, given women's worries about safety and contraception?"

Advocates of sex education reform also call for incorporating definitions of "good sex"—sex that is not coercive, exploitative, or harmful. They caution not to impose rigid definitions of "sexual normality"; rather, identify some dimensions of healthy sexuality as examples upon which individuals can explore and develop their own unique sexual identity and style. It has been observed that a central practice in the social construction of gender inequality is *compulsory heterosexuality* or societal pressure to be heterosexual. Many sexual revolutionaries argue that an important condition of sexual freedom is freedom from pressures to be a particular "type" of sexual being.

What cultural pressures exist to be a certain kind of sexual being? How can these cultural pressures be transcended? What would women's sexuality be like if it were not so socially restricted? How do media images of the "ideal" woman contribute to these restrictions? Do you think, as Sheff's research suggests, that it is possible to be free of societal constraints?

Suggested Readings

Ruth Bell, *Changing Bodies, Changing Lives: Expanded Third Edition: A Book for Teens on Sex and Relationships* (New York: Three Rivers Press, 1998).

Boston Women's Health Book Collective, *Our Bodies, Ourselves: A New Edition for a New Era* (New York: Touchstone, 1998).

Patricia Hill Collins, *Black Sexual Politics: African Americans, Gender, and the New Racism* (New York: Routledge, 2004).

Jean Kilbourne and Mary Pipher, *Can't Buy My Love: How Advertising Changes the Way We Think and Feel* (New York: Simon & Schuster, 2000).

K. Thompson and L. Smolak, *Body Image, Eating Disorders, and Obesity in Youth: Assessment, Prevention, and Treatment* (Washington, DC: American Psychological Association, 2001).

Leonore Tiefer, "Arriving at a 'New View' of Women's Sexual Problems: Background, Theory, and Activism," *Women and Therapy, 24* (2001): 63–98.

Deborah Tolman, *Dilemmas of Desire: Teenage Girls Talk about Sexuality* (Cambridge, MA: Harvard University Press, 2005).

Naomi Wolf, *The Beauty Myth: How Images of Beauty Are Used Against Women* (New York: HarperCollins, 2002).

ISSUE 17

Are Adult-Child Sexual Relations Always Harmful?

YES: Sonja Grover, from "On Power Differentials and Children's Rights: A Dissonance Interpretation of the Rind and Associates Study on Child Sexual Abuse," *Ethical Human Sciences and Services* (Spring 2003)

NO: Bruce Rind, from "An Empirical Examination of Sexual Relations Between Adolescents and Adults," *Journal of Psychology and Human Sexuality* (2004)

ISSUE SUMMARY

YES: Sonja Grover argues that any sexual contact with a minor by an adult under any circumstances violates the human rights of a child.

NO: Bruce Rind suggests that it is important to distinguish adult-child from adult-adolescent sexual relationships, suggesting that the latter may not be harmful because adolescents are likely to interpret the relationship differently than children.

The media headlines call our attention to child predators, the child sex slave industry, and pedophile priests. Even Oprah Winfrey has taken up the cause of getting child predators off the streets and into jail. Three men whose pictures were posted on October 4, 2005 on her Predators' Watch List have been captured as of this writing (December 17, 2005). Little stirs the public's ire more. Few people in the United States consider sex between children and adults acceptable. However, there are those who find it permissible, even understandable, under conditions of mutual consent. First, there is the North American Man/Boy Love Association, which advocates for the personal sexual freedom of all men and boys. Also, consider the sensational cases of student–teacher sexual relationships that have made the national news, and consider too the public's as well as legal system's responses. There was the case of Mary Kay Letourneau who served six months in prison (although originally sentenced to serve seven years) for her sexual affair with a sixth grade student, by whom she became impregnated. They were married on May 20, 2005, by which time the young man was 21 years old, and have had a second child. At the time of the original affair the boy declared he was "in love." In another case, reported by CNN.com (http://archives.cnn.com/2002/fyi/teachrs.ednews/06/13/teacher.student.sex.ap/), a judge was quoted as having said, when sentencing a 43-year-old female teacher to probation rather than jail, for having sex with a 13-year-old, that the relationship may have satisfied the boy's sexual needs and "I don't see anything here that shows this young man has been psychologically damaged by her actions. And don't forget, this was mutual consent." It is impossible to imagine that a judge would ever say that a 43-year-old man was meeting the sexual needs of a 13-year-old girl. These are just two of the cases that made the news; there are many more. The underreporting is substantial according to experts. Although no one knows for sure how much sexual abuse goes on in schools by employees toward students, Charol Shakeshaft of Hafstra University, in a draft report she has prepared for the Department of Education estimated approximately 290,000 cases from 1991 to 2000. What we do not know is how many cases involved male employees and female students and vice versa. What does appear to be apparent is a double standard. Female teachers who have relationships do not usually receive the same public condemnation or legal sanctions that male teachers do. This double standard rests on the implied assumption that boys are more sexual than girls and will not be harmed, that in fact they likely consented. But is mutual consent ever possible? Kathleen Parker, in an editorial, said, "But lately our cultural understanding of what's acceptable is on shaky ground. After all, a consenting teenage boy is getting when he wants from a wiling adult woman, right? And certainly a compliant 16-year-old girl can seem womanly enough to her twenty-something-year-old geography teacher?" She goes on to discuss the issues of trust and power in relationships and the dependency that children and adolescents have on adults who are in positions of authority, such as priests and teachers. This sentiment is echoed in the selection by Sonja Grover. She offers a children's rights perspective. She critiques Rind's conclusion that mutual sex between adolescents and adults can be consensual and not necessarily harmful. Rind argues that it is important to distinguish between adult-child and adult-adolescent sexual relationships. He came to his conclusion based a review of the literature on child sexual abuse that suggests that psychological harm is not inevitable. Grover offers a dissonance theory interpretation of an apparent no-harm outcome. Dissonance theory proposes that people experience psychological distress when there is a discrepancy between their beliefs/attitudes/values and behaviors/experience. One way to reduce the negative emotions associated with the discrepancy, especially when the behavior or experience is irreversible is to change one's cognitions about the experience. She suggests that some victims of childhood sexual abuse minimize the perceived harm. She concludes, in accord with legal definitions, that all sexual contact between an adult and a minor (including adolescents) is sexual abuse because the minor cannot give informed consent.

Sonja Grover ➡ **YES**

On Power Differentials and Children's Rights: A Dissonance Interpretation of the Rind and Associates (1998) Study on Child Sexual Abuse

This article illustrates that social science research can affect our perception of power relationships in society even when this is not the express purpose of the researcher. The social scientist as a member of an elite (the academic community accorded a certain social class status, prestige and moral authority) is in a position to alter conceptions of social reality through his or her research. The case study examined here concerns the research of Rind, Tromovitch, and Bauserman (1998) on the long-term effects of childhood sexual abuse. This research group attempts to redefine our understanding of the nature of child sexual abuse. This has implications for how we perceive the power relationships which form the context for sexual contact between adults and adolescents or younger children.

The Rind and colleagues, study has the unique, if unwelcome, distinction of being the only psychological study to have triggered a congressional resolution condemning a scientific work. The American Psychological Association (APA), which had published the work, asked for an independent review of the paper by the American Association for the Advancement of Science. The latter found nothing clearly amiss in the methodology or otherwise: "... we saw no clear evidence of improper application of methodology or other questionable practices on the part of the article's authors" ... (cited in McCarty, 1999, pp. 2–3). Given the history of the debate concerning the Rind and colleagues (1998) study, this paper concerns itself solely with an evaluation of the Rind and associates data interpretations and with the implications drawn by these authors about the concept of child sexual abuse.

Rind and coworkers state their research objective as examining whether child sexual abuse (CSA) causes intense harm across both genders and whether it does so pervasively in the general population. They conducted a meta-analysis of 59 studies, all based on college students retrospectively self-reporting on the immediate and longer-term effects of their childhood sexual experience with an adult. The authors contend that the college population

From *Ethical Human Sciences and Services*, vol. 5 (1), 2003, pp. 21–33. Copyright © 2003 by Springer Publishing Company. Reprinted by permission.

"is useful in addressing questions regarding the general population because about 50% of US adults have some college exposure" (Rind et al., 1998, p. 26). Current psychological status was examined via self-reports on standardized psychological measures. Rind and associates found that the reports of harm were neither as pervasive nor intense as commonly held nor were they equivalent across genders. The authors then extrapolated from [these] data to suggest that the concept of child sexual abuse ought not be applied to all adult sexual contact with minors but only to a subset of such contact which meets certain criteria, as will be discussed.

In a later reply to some critics, Rind, Tromovitch, and Bauserman appear to see their findings as countering a view they term "sexual victimology." They lament the tendency to pathologize experiences and to infer psychological damage where they hold none exists. . . . They suggest that the erroneous notion of "sexual victimology" has been applied also to adult sex with minors, resulting in an overbroad concept of "child sexual abuse." Rind and colleagues suggest that not all non-adolescent or adolescent children exposed to CSA experience psychological harm or are non-consenting, and thus not all can properly be considered to be victims. . . . Rind and associates then further suggest that current notions of "abuse," which they hold to be value-laden and inappropriately applied to all adult sexual contact with minors, cloud empirical issues. . . .

Rind and colleagues specifically suggest that minors who experience sexual contact with adults, but who make causal self-attributions of consent (what Rind terms "willingness"), and who *perceive* no harm cannot be considered to have been victimized by the experience. Rind and associates suggest that the term "abuse" is a socio-moral and legal concept implying psychological harm, and that the use of the term "child sexual abuse" when used to refer to all adult sexual contact with minors is incorrect and "unscientific" since psychological harm is not pervasive in such situations. . . .

Rind and colleagues' attempt to redefine our understanding of what is meant by *child sexual abuse* is reflected by the fact that a section of their 1998 paper is entitled "Child Sexual Abuse as a Construct Reconsidered." Rind and associates suggest that, where the minor perceives he or she is willing and has no negative reaction to the sexual contact with an adult, the term *abuse* should be replaced with the "value-neutral" terms *adult-child sex* or *adult-adolescent sex*. Thus, they hold that the use of the term "child sexual abuse" should be restricted to situations where children perceive that they were coerced and report negative reactions or harm. . . .

Is any terminology value-neutral? All terminology reflects a particular perspective, chosen from among alternatives, and one that represents a particular philosophical framework. The notion of certain non-abusive categories of adult sexual contact with minors thus implies certain criteria for assessing the presence or absence of harm, which is not value-free. As will be discussed, Rind and colleagues' criteria for the presence of harm does not include the harm inflicted on the child's human dignity, given the violation of certain fundamental human rights independent of any self-reports of perceived psychological harm. . . .

Dissonance and Self-Attributions of Consent in the Child Sexual Abuse Situation

Dissonance refers to psychological discomfort that one can experience, for example, when confronted with having chosen a course of action that leads to negative consequences. It arises from the knowledge that one has *voluntarily* exposed oneself to harm or unpleasantness. According to dissonance theory there is an impulse to reduce this discomfort, which may involve minimizing the perception of harm arising from the perceived choice. The question arises, then, whether children and adolescents who experience sexual contact with adults are provided cues that lead them to falsely perceive that they have chosen to be in the situation. One such false cue leading to causal self attributions of consent may be the behavioral compliance itself. . . .

The CSA occurs generally in private with only the minor and adult present, and the victim is often reluctant to reveal the experience to others due to embarrassment, inappropriate guilt, threats, pressure, fear, or various other factors. Thus, independent others, with whom the minor can verify his or her evaluation regarding voluntariness, choice, and blame, are rarely available. Also, the youth is often coached by the abuser to assign self-blame for the sexual experience and may be exposed to repeated sexual assaults. In Rind and colleagues' college sample, a weighted mean percentage of 46% had been sexually assaulted as children or adolescents more than once. Further, a child or adolescent who is emotionally dependent on an adult, or who has been led to trust that adult, may have intense emotional responses, which impact cognitive interpretation of the situation. [There is] evidence that emotions impact cognitive assessments of risk and are an essential determinant of behavior in risky and uncertain situations apart from any "rational" cognitive cost/benefit analysis. [A]ccurate risk perception in unfamiliar situations, even by adults, requires sufficient contextual information.

Research on attribution and risk assessment has demonstrated that our interpretation of social reality and of risk is highly dependent on social and emotional cues. The world of human interaction is notoriously ambiguous, and we therefore tend to depend heavily upon feedback from others in mutually constructing the shape of our social reality. However, unless physical force is involved, the abuser is unlikely to make salient for the child or adolescent the myriad of other coercive elements in the situation. In sum, recognizing whether one is consenting or has consented requires complex cognitive processing of available social, emotional, and physiological cues, placing a child or adolescent at particular risk for errors in interpretation. Rind and colleagues, however, do not discuss the socio-emotional dimension of the CSA situation. Rather, these authors focus on cognitive appraisal separate and apart from the child's emotional and physiological state. . . .

Social Reconstruction of the Personal Past by Child Sexual Abuse Victims

Rind and associates' data on college students is comprised of *self-reports* concerning current psychological status and retrospective and current reports of level of *perceived* harm relating to CSA. It is essential not to make the mistake of equating self-report and perception of harm or lack of harm with actual level of harm. Discrepancies between perception and reality arise partly because individuals do not simply recall their past as if dredging up a carbon copy of events and feelings experienced originally. Rather, adults' recall of their past is an interpretive and social reconstruction process. [T]he context in which remembering takes place influences the reconstruction of the past and that the responses of others often influence our own reconstruction of our life story or events in that story.

College students being interviewed about CSA and given psychological tests may wish to present themselves as psychologically and socially competent (i.e., communicate the story that they have integrated the CSA experience and minimize any perceived harm). Consistent with such a hypothesis is the finding by Rind and colleagues (1998) that the CSA group scored as high on internal locus of control (perceiving they were in control of their life) as did the non-abused college student group. On a measure of locus of control, the CSA group was as well-adjusted as the non-CSA group, while for all other 17 measures of psychological symptoms studied, "CSA participants as a group were *slightly less* well-adjusted than control participants" (p. 32, emphasis added). It may be that in this resilient CSA group, not perceiving oneself as a victim, but rather as in control, was a coping mechanism. In addition, the subjects may have determined that little was to be gained from reporting one's psychological issues, given the lack of follow-up support in most, if not all, of these studies. Such individual reconstructions of the past, however, may differ in a different context, such as a counseling setting, as discussed by Pasupathi (2001). There, disclosing one's struggles and psychological frailties is expected and occurs where trust and familiarity have been cultivated with a particular counselor, and emotional support is anticipated.

In sum, there may have been pressures arising from the subject's psychological needs and the research study context itself which were conducive to those with a CSA history reconstructing their personal past to underreport actual harm. This, combined with the dissonance phenomena previously discussed, could create both significant minimization of perceived harm and decreased reporting of harm (although this is not to suggest that long-term psychological harm occurred in all cases).

A Dissonance Interpretation of the Rind and Colleagues (1998) Key Findings

Compelling evidence from the Rind and colleagues study supports a dissonance interpretation of the minimization of perceived harm, as follows:

1. Force: Force is a salient cue for coercion. Rind and associates found the largest effects in terms of reports of negative reactions when force was used by the adult in the CSA situation. . . . Thus where force was involved, the young person had the clearest cue regarding coercion. This cue frees individuals from dissonance and the need to negate their emotional reactions to the experience. In contrast, where the

adult's goal is accomplished in graduated steps over a long period such a cue may not be available. Those exposed to violations using force reported negative reactions significantly more often (medium size effect), though the increase in reported psychological symptoms on the standardized psychological measures in the CSA group was not a large effect. It may be, for example, that these college students (a non-clinical sample) were resilient and did not suffer long-term psychological harm, or that they were reluctant to report such symptoms, or that the measures chosen were not the optimal ones to reveal lasting distress.

In addition, it should be noted that the Rind and associates (1998) finding that the CSA group showed only small significant increases in self-reported psychological symptoms compared to the non-CSA group is not necessarily a finding that CSA subjects were not harmed. . . .

2. Incest: Incest was significantly related to both the reporting of current psychological symptoms and negative reactions to the sexual experience (Rind et al., 1998, p. 35), although the effect size was much smaller than for the force variable. In the case of a parent or close relative as abuser, the minor has no frame of reference for understanding that such individuals would under any circumstances risk significantly harming them. Further, the minor may be loyal to and emotionally dependent on the adult abuser. Therefore, the child often comes to erroneously infer that he or she must have at least partly freely consented to the situation, and minimization of *perceived* harm may follow. Further, sexual abuse, unlike other forms of physical abuse, often involves apparently loving touch and words from the abuser, providing further miscues to the abused in a more private, intimate context. All of these factors then contribute to an underestimation in the reporting of perceived harm in regard to sexual abuse generally, including incest.

   Rind and colleagues (1998) found that non-sexual abuse (i.e., physical abuse) and neglect by close family members are better predictors of self-reports of psychological *symptoms* (p. 38) than is CSA. This is consistent with the dissonance interpretation as both physical abuse and many forms of neglect (i.e., lack of food) provide salient cues to the child's non-voluntariness. Where incest is accompanied by force, one would expect less of a tendency in self-report to minimize negative reactions or the harm done. . . . [T]he *child's interpretation of the CSA experience as abusive or non-abusive* (consensual or non-consensual) varies as a function of "family environment." Thus, where there is denial in the family, and no physical force is used, for example, the child may come to *misperceive* the incestuous experience as non-abusive or non-harmful, leading to more resilience.

3. Gender effects: The gender effects reported by Rind and colleagues were importantly related to level of perceived consent to sexual contact with an adult. College women were twice as likely as men to have experienced some form of direct or implied use of force (presumably this occurred more often also in the case of incest involving female victims although this was not specifically addressed by Rind and his colleagues). The incidence of incest in this college sample was found

to be low and women experienced incest twice as often as men (p. 30). The weighted mean percentage of college women experiencing force or threat of force was 41% compared to 23% for the men (p. 31). As women had more access to the salient cue of coercion (force), this may account for the fact that 72% of them perceived themselves to have had a negative reaction to the CSA at the time compared to 33% of the men. (p. 36)

When the men reported the CSA experience as "unwanted," they too were freed, to an extent, from the effects of dissonance and from the tendency to underreport psychological symptoms. . . . [S]elf-reported psychological symptoms as adults were greater for men when they identified the childhood sexual abuse as an *unwanted* rather than a wanted sexual experience. Many women might more easily accept a self-perception as victim since society traditionally acknowledges that women may be powerless to effectively resist sexual assault. Thus, consistent with dissonance theory, Rind and associates (1998) found "a stronger association between CSA and adjustment problems for women than for men when all levels of consent were considered," but this gender effect disappeared "when unwanted sex only was contrasted" (p. 43). . . .

One need not conclude, however, contrary to the Rind and colleagues (1998) view, that the college students in the studies they examined were any less harmed due to CSA when they perceived the experience as "wanted" compared to when they perceived it as "unwanted." . . . [D]issonance accounts for how perceived level of consent impacts upon *perceived* harm and may thus ultimately affect level of resilience. . . .

The evidence thus suggests that self-reports of harm regarding CSA reflect cognitive judgments about the sexual experience that are subject to biasing effects just as are any other cognitive judgments. Such judgments or perceptions are, for example, in part a function of: (a) various factors occurring in the abuse situation (i.e., the identity of the abuser, the presence or absence of force, etc.) and their impact upon the victim's interpretation of the experience as well as: (b) the context in which the victim is being asked to self-report (i.e., a research study versus a counseling setting). It is when the individual with a CSA history becomes attuned to the coercive aspects in adult-minor sexual contact (i.e., the inherent power differential, the subtle manipulative pressures at play, the abuser's possible use of implied or actual threats) that he or she is more likely to become cognizant of the harm done.

Power Differentials in the Child Sexual Abuse Situation: Implications for Conceptions of "Abuse"

Adult-child sex (or *adult-adolescent sex*), to use the Rind and colleagues' terminology, also involves significant coercive elements due to the power differential in the situation. In this regard CSA situations are not heterogeneous. Abusers typically try to shift the responsibility for the sexual contact to the victim, for example, by reference to the alleged sexual precociousness of the young child or adolescent (this pattern is typical for those who perpetrate non-sexual forms of abuse as well). The distinction between "wanted" and "unwanted" sexual involvement with an adult in the Rind and colleagues meta-analytic study was based on phenomenological (often retrospective) reports from the abused. While quite informative as to psychological issues, such reports are not necessarily accurate as to the *inherent* coercive elements present in the situation. . . .

There is a power advantage for the adult in sexual scenarios such that compliance, assent, or approval by the child or adolescent to the sexual contact is not directly correlated to, nor an indicator of, either "informed consent" or "choice" in any meaningful sense. Thus, resilient individuals with a CSA history or those who for other reasons, such as community standards, do not perceive and/or report harm from the CSA experience cannot be considered to have freely consented and thus not to have been abused.

The child or adolescent who has sexual contact with an adult is, due to the power differential, very much a victim. . . . Children and adolescents who are exposed to sexual experiences of one sort or another with an adult have been cheated out of their opportunity to experience sexual contact in a situation of genuine choice in the context of an equal power relationship. They may also have been fooled into making faulty self-attributions of consent. In addition, there is always injury in terms of the affront to human dignity arising from having bodily and psychological integrity infringed without giving informed consent independent of any resultant psychological symptoms, level of resilience, or reports of psychological harm.

The notion of an "affront to human dignity" connotes both a psychological and a moral-legal conception. In this regard, it should be noted that Rind and associates' concept of the "willing" child or adolescent participant in adult sexual contact with a minor (p. 46) is no less entangled in moral-legal assumptions. . . . Rind and colleagues (1998) refer to socio-historical trends in moral codes and changes in the social acceptability of certain sexual behaviors (as reflected in the *DSM-IV*) to attempt to support their arguments that not all adult sexual involvement with children and adolescents should be considered pathological (p. 45). Rind's concept of *adult-child sex* or *adult-adolescent sex* is thus no more value-neutral or removed from legal and socio-political considerations than is the concept of CSA.

The facts of adult sexual contact with a minor will not change regardless of the socially sanctioned "sexual scripts" in a particular society and whether or not that society views adult sexual contact with a child or adolescent as pathological. Rind and associates make reference to the universal occurrence of sexual abuse often involving adolescents, and they suggest that such behaviors may be normal because they are commonplace: "Furthermore, unlike adult-child sex, adult-adolescent sex has been commonplace cross-culturally and historically, often in socially sanctioned forms, and may fall within the 'normal' range of human sexual behaviors" (p. 46). There is no question that sexual abuse, particularly of adolescents, is and has long been a fact of life, just as the abuse of women and other vulnerable groups. Adult sexual contact with a child or adolescent remains nonetheless exploitative and thus abusive independent of cultural context.

Rind and colleagues advance the notion that "consent" issues can be dis-entangled from "power" issues in sexual matters, but that is not the case. *It is in large part the trivialization of the power differential in CSA situations that allows Rind and colleagues to propose that such contact can in some cases be non-abusive.* This is a central point distinguishing the Rind and associates position from the one espoused here. . . .

[T]he age discrepancy between adult and minor is one of the essential aspects defining the CSA situation as an exploitative one involving a significant power differential. Therefore, incest has much to do with other types of sexual contact between adults and minors in that *they all share this essentially exploitative and hence abusive nature.* CSA involves the adult in usurping the protective role and utilizing a position of greater power to further their adult sexual agenda. While the parent or guardian has a preeminent role in protecting and nurturing the child or adolescent, so too the other adults in the society have an obligation to the young people in their community not to abuse their power or position of trust. The right to security of one's bodily and psychological integrity is an *inherent universal right* which every person possesses—including every child and adolescent—*independent of any state codification in law.* One essential harm resulting from sexual contact between an adult and a child or adolescent is then this violation of a fundamental human right to integrity of the person.

Acceptance of such behavior under any set of circumstances weakens our respect for the child or adolescent as a person with the inherent basic human right to make *informed choices* about matters that significantly impact upon his or her own bodily and psychological integrity. *Such respect for the child or adolescent as a person requires protecting that person from sexual exploitation in situations characterized by a significant power differential related, for example, to adult-child or adult-adolescent age discrepancies.* Consider now the contrast with sexual contact between two minors where no coercion is involved (nor adult involvement of any kind), and the minors are roughly equivalent in terms of degree of vulnerability (i.e., psychologically or cognitively). Such a scenario raises quite different issues than does sexual contact between an adult and a minor. Consensual sex between roughly matched peers who are minors may be inadvisable for a host of reasons; however, such sexual contact is not inherently exploitive as there is no power differential.

It is true that adults violate young people's bodily and psychological integrity in many non-sexual contexts (i.e., vaccination programs, psychiatric treatment). Each of these situations also raises human rights issues that society must resolve by examining, for example: (a) whether or not the child's or adolescent's best interests were of paramount concern and not the self-interest of some other party; (b) whether or not the violation results in a demonstrable benefit to the child or adolescent, which is foreseeable and sufficiently probable; (c) whether the probability of benefit to the health and development of the child or adolescent is great enough, and the risk and nature of any potential harm small enough, to warrant the violation; and (d) whether there is no other more appropriate alternative to ensure the well-being of the child or adolescent than to take this action (risk) at this time. The latter calculus does not favor adult sexual contact with a child or an adolescent because the adult is acting from a position of self-interest. Further, there is no compelling imperative that the child or adolescent engages in the behavior with an adult at that time or any other. . . .

Conclusion

It is misguided to believe that social scientists can examine human interactions within various power contexts in a way that does not simultaneously conceptualize the nature of the human rights issues implicit in the situation. Yet, this is Rind and colleagues' assumption. It is reflected in their erroneous view that moral and ideological stances can be sectioned out of social science theorizing and research if only one has the correct mindset and terminology. It further leads to their contention that distinctions between so-called abusive versus non-abusive adult sexual contact with minors make matters more objective and "scientific." The risk is that the underlying assumptions regarding human rights will not be scrutinized but rather accepted as part of the "package deal" along with the data interpretations they inform.

. . . A fundamental principle underlying all human rights movements and reflected in international human rights documents is that human rights abuses are not context-dependent. Basic human rights (i.e., the right to integrity of body and mind) are universal and independent of socio-legal situation and of victim perceptions of harm.

References

McCarty, R. (1999, November/December). A brief comment by APA executive director for science. *Psychological Science Agenda, 12*, 2–3.

Rind, B., Tromovitch, A., & Bauserman, R. (1998). Meta-analytic examination of assumed properties of child sexual abuse using college samples. *Psychological Bulletin, 124*, 22–53.

NO ↩

Bruce Rind

An Empirical Examination of Sexual Relations Between Adolescents and Adults

How do adolescents react to sexual encounters with adults? In America today, these encounters are referred to as "child sexual abuse," and the widespread view is that such encounters are traumatic and psychologically scarring. This American view has spread to other countries and has re-shaped public policy regarding this issue in both the U.S. and abroad. The purpose of my talk is to examine the scientific validity of this view.

The current heightened concern about child sexual abuse in America can be traced back to the early 1970s. The women's movement campaigned against inadequate social response to the problem of rape, which they characterized as a crime of violence motivated by the need to exert power and control over one's victims. Feminists made dramatic progress in changing public attitudes and social policy. With this success in hand, they next campaigned against incest, using the rape model to characterize it. Mental health professionals incorporated feminist theory in their attempt to deal with these problems. But soon, the 5-year-old girl's suffering at the hands of her step-father through repeated episodes of unwanted sexual abuse became the basis for understanding all sexual interactions between minors and adults. The documented trauma of repeated incestuous rape became the assumed reaction of the adolescent, even if years into puberty and voluntarily, if not enthusiastically, sexually involved with an unrelated adult.

Combining children and adolescents into a single category when it comes to sex with adults is problematic. Adolescents are not children in a biological sense, their cognitive functioning is much more similar to that of adults than children, and they are sexual beings with desires and fantasies. In almost all societies except for the modern West, they have been treated as and have functioned as young adults rather than older children in terms of their activities and responsibilities, which have often included sex and even marriage. Thus, conceptually it seems wrong to call an adolescent's sexual interaction with an adult "child" sexual abuse. Empirically speaking, how an adolescent reacts to sex with an adult

From *Journal of Psychology and Human Sexuality*, vol. 16, 2004, pp. 55–62. Copyright © 2004 by Haworth Press. Reprinted by permission.

should not be assumed to be inferable from how a young child reacts. Yet it is this type of inference that has dominated social, political, and professional discourse over the past few decades.

In order to examine the validity the sweeping view that adolescent-adult sex is traumatizing, in this paper I will focus on two types of adolescent-adult relations–those between heterosexual adolescent boys and women and those between homosexual adolescent boys and men. Studies based on clinical and forensic samples certainly show that such relations can be traumatic for the teenager, but these samples are selective, biased to the more negative episodes. To investigate the nature of these experiences, it is important to examine data from the general population. I now present such data.

Heterosexual Adolescent Male Sexual Relations with Women

The non-clinical empirical data show that heterosexual adolescent boys react predominantly positively to sexual relations with women. For example, in studies in America, half the males reacted positively to sex with women when they were boys, with only a quarter reacting negatively. In [another] study, 70% of the teens reacted positively and just 10% reacted negatively. In [other] studies, more than 80% reacted positively, and virtually none reacted negatively. These high proportions of positive reactions have to do with the high degree of interest and willingness on the part of the boys involved. For example, boys saw themselves as consenting to sex with women more than 85% of the time. Negative reactions were associated with incestuous contacts and with feeling coerced, which was relatively rare, as just discussed. In these studies, many youths felt that they benefited from the sexual experiences. In [one of the studies] 60% of teens felt the effect was positive, while only 3% felt the effect was negative. In [another], 37% of the boys thought their sexual functioning was improved by the encounters, while only 13% thought it was harmed.

There has been a genre of coming-of-age films about adolescent boys' sexual awakenings with their interest in and positive experience with women. The best known example in America is *The Summer of 42* in which a 15-year-old boy is initiated into sex by a woman in her mid-20s, whose husband is away at war. The boy's positive and nonproblematic reaction is consistent with the empirical data, and is something that many men recognize as resonating with their own adolescence. This film presents a far superior model for the heterosexual teenage boy's experience than the rape or incest model.

Homosexual Adolescent Boys' Sexual Experiences with Men

The analogue to the heterosexual adolescent boy's experience with a woman is the homosexual adolescent boy's experience with a man. Non-clinical research in this area yields findings quite similar to the research just discussed on heterosexual adolescent boys with women. [In one study it was] found that most encounters between homosexual adolescent boys and men in [an]

English college sample were positive. [In] data on over 1,000 male homosexuals aged 16–77 across the United States [obtained] through mail questionnaires, [it was] reported that, in the case of the respondent's first youthful experience with an adult, it was usually stressed by the respondent that it was he who made the first advance, he who desired and initiated the encounter, and that coercion was rare. [D]ata from over 4,000 gay male respondents aged 14–82 [revealed] that boyhood crushes and fantasies regarding older males were common. When asked whether sexual contacts with adults were helpful or not, most answered positively (69%) or neutrally (12%). The scientific studies are buttressed by a huge literature in autobiographical narrative among gay males in terms of their coming-of-age experiences with older males, which have much more in common with the "Summer of 42" model than the rape or incest models.

To elaborate on psychological research in this area, I next review a study I published a year ago in the *Archives of Sexual Behavior* (Rind, 2001) examining data already collected by Cornell University psychologist Ritch Savin-Williams, who was investigating gay development but in the process gathered data about sexual relations between gay or bisexual male teens and older men. The study included 129 gay and bisexual college-aged men in the state of New York, most of whom were attending college. Each subject was intensively interviewed. Twenty-six of the men (20%), when they were between the ages of 12 and 17, had sexual relations with men involving genital contact.

Savin-Willians measured two factors relevant to psychological adjustment: the subjects' self-esteem and the age at which they achieved a positive sexual identity, if they ever did. Previous research done by researchers at Penn State University showed that these two factors are the best predictors of current mental health for gay and bisexual college-aged men. In the current study, the self-esteem of those who had sex with men as teenage boys was just as high as that of those who did not. Moreover, those who had sex with the men achieved a positive sexual identity earlier than those who did not— the proportion in both groups reaching this milestone was the same. These results indicate that, in this sample, teenage boys' having sex with men was not associated with psychological maladjustment. In fact, in the case of the self-acceptance measure, there was evidence for somewhat better adjustment.

Many Anglophone researchers would refer to these relations as "child sexual abuse." Contrary to the term "child," however, implying naïveté and an unreadiness for sexual experience, in nearly 100% of the cases, before they had sex with the men, the boys had already reached puberty and had already become aware of their own sexual attractions to other males. Often, the subjects in this sample were actually more erotically drawn to men than to same-aged peers. Contrary to the term "sexual abuse," the vast majority of sexual encounters with men were experienced as positive (77%). Only a small minority was experienced as negative (15%). The relations were characterized by consent, not coercion. In almost a quarter of the cases, it was the boy rather than the man who initiated the contact, and in another two-thirds of the cases involvement was by mutual agreement and interest.

Positive reactions were associated with having relations with friends rather than strangers, greater duration of the relationships, and greater frequency of sexual episodes. But reactions were not affected by the boys' ages or the men's ages: younger teenage boys reacted just as positively as older teenage boys, and reactions to sex with older men were the same as reactions to sex with younger men.

In four of the 26 cases the subjects reacted negatively. The interviews reveal that it was the circumstances rather than the sex per se that was behind the negative reaction. For example, an older adolescent felt dirty about engaging in sex in a cemetery with a stranger to whom he was not attracted. A middle adolescent felt accomplishment at first by having anonymous sex with a man in a gay movie theater that he sneaked into, but later felt negative about it because he felt cheap about having sex that way.

But it was positive reactions that predominated. For example, a young adolescent said he "practically had to force sex" on a 22-year-old man with whom he had become friendly, and said it was "great" when it finally occurred. Another young adolescent had a 10 year relationship with a 35-year-old family friend; he described the sex with him as "physically great" and said he fell in love with the man. Still another young adolescent initiated sex with a 38-year-old family friend on a camping trip, which he found "incredibly erotic," "a tremendous release," and "very pleasurable;" the relationship went on for four more years.

Calling these encounters "child sexual abuse," as is so often done in anglophone countries, is scientifically problematic. The subjects were adolescents already with homosexual desires when they had the encounters, rather than naïve children shocked by strange, confusing, and unwelcome events. Savin-Williams (1997), the researcher who did the interviews, noted in his book ". . . And Then I Became Gay" that the subjects usually did not construe their early sexual encounters with men as abusive, but often saw the sex as serving an important function. For example, he noted that one "benefit of many age-discrepant relationships was that they helped a youth feel better about being gay. This was seldom anything but an extremely positive outcome." He added that the youths were often grateful for the experience and its positive influence on their development.

Conclusion

An important goal of this paper was to examine the assumption, widespread in anglophone countries, which sex between adolescents and adults is by nature traumatic. To this end, I focused on non-clinical, non-forensic data to avoid biases inherent in the clinical and forensic populations. I focused on male adolescents involved with adults of the gender they preferred. This focus served as a test of the assumption of inevitable and invariant trauma, although it is important to point out that conclusions cannot be extended to other adolescent-adult combinations (e.g., adolescent girl-man) without specific examination of them.

For heterosexual adolescent boys involved with women and for gay/bisexual adolescent boys involved with men, the non-clinical empirical data are strongly at odds with the assumption of trauma. Simply put, the rape and incest models, developed 30 years ago in America to describe the horrors of rape of women by men and incestuous assault of young girls by their male guardians, are inappropriate when applied to adolescent boys sexually involved with adults of the gender they prefer. In these relations, the data point more directly to psychological benefit than harm.

Recently enacted EU-legislation requires all EU member states to criminalize a good deal of contacts of a sexual nature engaged in by persons under 18 years of age (with partners over, and also even under, the age of 18). This proposal has as its aim to prevent the exploitation of children. If this is indeed the true aim, then the proposal is flawed from a scientific, empirical viewpoint, because adolescents are not children, though they are considered children by the proposal, and because adolescents, especially male adolescents, are not at serious risk for the exploitation that the proposal imagines. Either the proposal is misinformed in the ways just discussed, or it is disingenuous in alleging to protect sexually mature persons when in fact it is intending to control them.

POSTSCRIPT

Are Adult-Child Sexual Relations Always Harmful?

Sexuality has multiple meanings that may imply sexual identity, sexual preference, and/or sexual behavior. It may be defined in physiological, intrapersonal, or interpersonal terms. Throughout our lives we continue to learn more about ourselves as sexual beings. A newborn has no idea what it means to be sexual, in spite of the fact that infants experience genital arousal. Over time society shapes the meaning of such physiological feelings. Thus, it is not too difficult to imagine the kinds of messages that children receive about sexuality when they are subjected to various circumcision rituals. This is true for girls and boys. Across all societies boys learn that manliness is in some way associated with the penis and power, whereas girls are more likely to learn that there is pain, shame, embarrassment, and passivity associated with their genitals. In the United States the research of Masters and Johnson, while revealing in great detail the physiological side of the human sexual response, actually moved us away from thinking more deeply about the sociocultural-emotional side of sexual feelings and activities. Abstinence-only sex education programs, or what Leonore Tiefer has called "organ recitals," do little to improve on the situation. Mary Boyle has suggested there are four major themes that characterize contemporary discourse on sexuality: It is a property of the individual, is an energy system, can be understood through science, and is associated with gender relations. Cultural rituals and societal scripts reinforce traditional gender roles; males are assertive sexual agents and females are passive, nonsexual recipients. "Good" girls are not interested in sex; if they are, they must be "sluts" or "ho's." How often have women, especially from earlier generations, reported that the main message of their sex education was just "lie there and wait for it to be over"? Femininity was tied to surrendering the body (and the self) to men. Women were a sexual problem; they needed men to teach them mature sexual responsiveness. Women who reject these roles are psychologically flawed. What does this say about polyamorous women? Are they deviant because they actively choose to have sexual relationships that defy the gender-based scripts? Have they successfully defied the myth that beauty defines sexuality? It is probably not a coincidence that the third aspect of feminism is associated with the girl-power movement. Young women are actively taking control of their lives, developing Web sites, on-line zines; their goal is empowerment. For example, angelgirl.com defines *Riot Grrrl* as "activist music, 'zines, meetings, and other activity that builds a supportive environment for women and girls and is concerned with feminist issues such as rape, abortion rights, bulemia/anorexia, beauty standards, exclusion from popular culture, the sexism of everyday life, double standards, sexuality, self-defense, fat oppression, racism and classism" (http://www.angelfire. com/rant/RGC/explanaion.html, accessed 12/18/05). As women work

318

to establish more sexual agency in their personal lives, we might assume that with agency comes greater power to truly consent to sexual activity. Does this means that girls/women, as well as boys/men should have the personal freedom to engage in sexual activity with whomever they choose?

Much of the discussion about the appropriateness of sexual relationships between adults and minors revolves around three issues, mutual consent, power, and harm. Consent implies that each person fully understands the "what" and "why" of the relationship. Developmental psychologists tell us that most minors, even older adolescents, are neither cognitively nor emotionally mature enough to make a fully informed decision about having sexual intercourse. Even if adolescents have received good sex education regarding the risks of sexually transmitted diseases and unintended pregnancies, they probably cannot grasp the long-term psychological implications of sexual intimacy. Thus, relationships with powerful others, such as priests, teachers, or other trusted adults, hold the potential, even the inevitability, of abuse. Pamela Schultz, in an analysis of the rhetoric of survivors and perpetrators of child sex abuse, concludes that the stories of abuse perpetuate the power hierarchy of the social structure, between children and adults, and between women and men. When we add to the mix dimensions of race and class, the potential for the abuse of power is amplified. The American Psychological Association and the American Psychiatric Association both recognize the danger of sexual relationships in inequitable power relationships and as a result ban all sexual activity between therapists and clients. If these organizations acknowledge that power can be abused in relationships between adults, it follows that the abuse of power is inherent in adult-minor relationships, with resultant harm. Or does it? Bruce Rind and others point out that many studies suggest that not every victim of child abuse suffers harms, especially in adult-adolescent relationships. This brings us to the question of the definition of harm: psychological or physical, short-term or long-term? Should harm be the only criterion for deciding whether adult-minor sexual relationships are acceptable?

Suggested Readings

Claudia Bernard, *Constructing Lived Experiences: Representations of Black Mothers in Child Sexual Abuse Discourses* (Hampshire, England, Aldershot and Burlington, VT: Ashgate, 2001).

Jon R. Conte, ed., *Critical Issues in Child Sexual Abuse: Historical, Legal, and Psychological Perspectives* (Thousand Oaks, CA: Sage, 2002).

Julia O'Connell Davidson, *Children in the Global Sex Trade* (Cambridge: Polity, 2005).

Paula Reavey and Sam Warner, *New Feminist Stories of Child Sexual Abuse: Sexual Scripts and Dangerous Dialogues* (London: Routledge, 2003).

Pamela D. Schultz, *A Critical Analysis of the Rhetoric of Child Sexual Abuse* (Lewiston, NY: Mellen Press, 2001).

Danial Jay Sonkin and Lenore E. A. Walker, *Wounded Boys Heroic Men: A Man's Guide to Recovering from Child Abuse* (Adams Media Corporations, 1998).

On the Internet . . .

Intersex Society of North America

The Intersex Society of North America (ISNA) is a peer support, education, and advocacy group for intersexuals. This Web site includes annotated bibliographies on intersexuality, scholarly and popular press resources on intersexuality, and numerous links to related sites.

http://www.isna.org

The Zuni Man-Woman

The Zuni Man-Woman page includes discussion of and excerpts from Will Roscoe's book entitled *The Zuni Man-Woman—In Life Where There Are Only Differences, "Good"/"Bad" Are Merely Ideas* (University of New Mexico Press, 1991). This book describes the Zuni berdache.

http://www.ratical.org/many_worlds/
onlyDifferent.html

The Gender Identity Center of Colorado, Inc.

This educational Web site by The Gender Identity Center of Colorado, Inc., is about gender identity nontraditionality. It includes an interesting discussion of gender dysphoria and additional writings by Katherine K. Wilson.

http://www.transgender.org/gic/

The World Health Organization

The World Health Organization's Web site on women's mental health provides facts on the gender disparities in mental health, discusses gender bias, and gender-specific risk factors.

http://www.who.int/mental_health/prevention/
genderwomen/en/

LGBT Health Channel

This Web site for the LGBT Health Channel provides information on a number of transgender health topics, including health care, mental health, hormone therapy, transgender surgery, and gender identity disorder.

http://www.gayhealthchannel.com/transgender/

America Online

This Web site provides data regarding what is known about the "gay gene." It is described as "a forum for the discussion of the scientific, social, political and religious implications of research into the origins of sexual identity."

http://members.aol.com/gaygene/

PART 6

Girl Interrupted: Gender and Mental Health

*T*herapists will tell you that they treat people, not disorders. However, the health and mental health literature is filled with guidelines and research findings that suggest one's sex is central to the etiology, symptoms, diagnosis, treatment, and prognosis of psychological disorders. The same set of symptoms often leads to one diagnosis for women and a different one for men. What contributes to these differences: hormones or cultural constructions of sex and gender? Is it possible to ignore gender? In this section underlying assumptions about gender and mental health are explored by examining one example of an assumed hormonally based disorder—premenstrual syndrome, which is generalizable to other assumed hormonally based problems. This section also explores the implications for what we know about sexual orientation and transgenderism and mental health. These selections reveal new ways to think beyond gender as two categories and to consider that psychopathology may lay within culture not within the person.

- Is Premenstrual Syndrome a Hormonally Based Disorder?

- Is Reparative Therapy Effective in Changing One's Sexual Orientation?

- Can Gender Identity Be a Psychological Disorder?

ISSUE 18

Is Premenstrual Syndrome a Hormonally Based Disorder?

YES: Torbjörn Bäckström and colleagues, from "The Role of Hormones and Hormonal Treatments in Premenstrual Syndrome," *CNS Drugs* (2003)

NO: Joan Chrisler, from "PMS as a Culture-Bound Syndrome," *Lectures on the Psychology of Women* (2004)

ISSUE SUMMARY

YES: Torbjörn Bäckström and colleagues describe the relationship between hormones and premenstrual syndrome, also discussing the effects of hormones on the brain and various treatment options.

NO: Joan C. Chrisler argues that PMS is a culturally constructed disorder whose symptoms are tied to cultural meanings and social norms. PMS, as understood in U.S. women, does not manifest itself the same in all cultures.

$\mathbf{A}$ number of disorders are attributed to women's hormones: premenstrual syndrome (PMS), menopause, and post-partum depression. The assumption is that patterns of symptoms that women show in various social contexts are the result of fluctuating hormones. Although the evidence is clear that there are correlations between mood and hormone levels, there remains the pesky concern about correlation and causation. A focus on PMS exploded by the 1980s. Women's magazines began to popularize the idea of PMS and hormonal problems, in spite of little empirical evidence. All sorts of female "emotional" problems were attributed to it and it was used as a reason why women should be denied access to certain areas of power (in the workplace, politics, and the military). A host of physical, psychological, neurological, gastrointestinal, and dermatological symptoms has been associated with the few days before the onset of menstruation. In a 2005 report by Tara Strine and colleagues found that, based on the 2002 National Health Interview Survey of over 11,000 women aged 18 to 55 percent, only 19 percent reported menstrual-related problems. These problems included anxiety, depression, insomnia, fatigue, and pain, as well as several negative moods such as sadness, worthlessness, and hopelessness. Women who were white (non-Hispanic), previously married, less-educated, or working outside the home were more likely to report symptoms than their counterparts. These women also tended to smoke, drink heavily, and be overweight. Other research has suggested that premenstrual symptoms are higher in women who have experienced more sexist events. Consider as well a study by Sarah Earl-Novell and Donna Jessop (2005) in which they monitored undergraduate women's class performance, PMS symptoms, and beliefs. They found that the students reported that PMS disrupted their academic work, but in fact found no significant relationship between the number of symptoms reported and any indicator of classroom performance. Other studies cite that although most women report some premenstrual mental and physical changes, only a very small number (2 to 6 percent) meet the criteria for a formal diagnosis of PMS. Given the relatively low percentage of women reporting problems and the specific social factors associated with the problems, one may reasonable ask, if PMS is a hormonally based disorder why don't more women report problems? Is there something about the social and work contexts of subgroups of women that increase the likelihood of menstrual-related problems? The selections here present two contrasting views. In the Backstrom work there is an unquestioned acceptance that fluctuating hormones are related to PMS symptoms and can and should be treated with hormones. Chrisler, in contrast, takes a close look at historical and cultural attitudes toward menstruation and concludes that PMS is a culture-bound syndrome. As you read these articles, think about gender-specific hormonally based disorders and consider whether the same arguments can be made.

Torbjörn Bäckström, et al. ➡ **YES**

The Role of Hormones and Hormonal Treatments in Premenstrual Syndrome

The effect of ovarian hormones on mood and CNS-related disorders is of great interest, especially since the discovery that some ovarian hormones are potent modulators of neurotransmitter systems in the brain. Ovarian hormones have been discussed as aetiological factors in premenstrual syndrome (PMS)—a menstrual cycle-linked, CNS-related condition—since the syndrome was first described. PMS has long been debated, but today increased knowledge and agreement on diagnostic criteria have helped to make PMS research more comparable.

Both patients and clinicians have been confused, and often in disagreement, over whether PMS should be considered a disease or merely a normal phenomenon not requiring treatment. This is largely because of a failure to appreciate that PMS severity varies tremendously. Although most women experience mild mood and somatic symptoms premenstrually, a small but significant number are severely disabled by the disorder. Furthermore, scientists in the field of PMS have not agreed on which terminology to use. It was not until the publication of diagnostic criteria for PMS in the American Psychiatric Association's DSM-IV that a distinct diagnosis of a severe form of PMS with mood symptoms—premenstrual dysphoric disorder (PMDD)—could be made.

In this review, we discuss the hormonal back-ground of and possible treatments for PMS.

1. Diagnostic Procedure and Criteria

The correct diagnosis of disease is essential for successful treatment. The diagnostic criteria for PMS have until now been a long-standing problem. . . .

To fulfil the criteria for PMDD (or severe PMS), patients need to present with at least five of the following specific symptoms during the premenstrual week: depression, irritability, anxiety/tension, affect lability, decreased interest, difficulty in concentrating, fatigue, feeling out of control, insomnia, change in appetite, breast tenderness and breast swelling. At least one of these symptoms must be a mood symptom. The symptoms must be severe

From *CNS Drugs*, vol. 17, issue 5, 2003, excerpts from 326–342. Copyright © 2003 by Adis Online. Reprinted by permission.

enough to interfere with usual activities. Patients must be devoid of symptoms in the follicular phase to ensure that the premenstrual complaint is not merely an exacerbation of an underlying mood disorder. The PMDD diagnosis must be confirmed by prospective ratings for at least 2 months. As none of the symptoms of PMDD/PMS are unique to the syndrome, patients need to keep a daily diary of symptoms for at least 2 months to establish the temporal relationship between the onset of symptoms and the premenstrual period. Furthermore, ovulation should be diagnosed, for example by measuring leuteal progesterone.

Among 82 consecutive patients seeking help for cyclical mood changes at a PMS clinic, only 30% were free of symptoms during the preovulatory period and 14% did not show a significant mood change between preovulatory and premenstrual periods. The remaining 56% showed a significant number of days with preovulatory symptoms (premenstrual aggravation group). This shows the need for more objective criteria for diagnosis than a case history alone. We have found daily prospective self ratings to be a great help in this respect.

2. Epidemiology

A higher prevalence of premenstrual changes is reported in retrospective questionnaires compared with prospective ratings. Up to 75% of fertile women retrospectively report changes in mental and physical symptoms in the premenstrual week. Over 50% of the participants in community sample studies report the presence of PMS, but only 2–6% of them met the criteria for PMDD. Most women consider PMS to be a normal phenomenon and not a disease state. This implies that when women say they have PMS, they are usually not referring to a medical condition. Rather, they refer to various changes during the premenstrual phase in some menstrual cycles, changes most women can manage by themselves. . . .

In community samples, severe and uncomfortable premenstrual symptoms are found in 2–17% of fertile women. These figures are somewhat higher than the estimated prevalence of PMDD of 1–7%, reported in studies using prospective daily ratings, with recurrent occupational impairment and conforming to the DSM-IV criteria. From studies in community samples, 6–14% of fertile women state that they wish to consult a physician regarding their premenstrual symptoms. In US-based reports, approximately 10–30% of the respondents took prescription or over-the-counter medications to relieve premenstrual symptoms.

3. Aetiology

The temporal symptom variations experienced during the menstrual cycle and the close link to the luteal phase indicate that a factor produced by the corpus luteum of the ovary is involved in provoking premenstrual symptoms. . . .

Despite numerous efforts to identify endocrine disturbances in patients with PMS, there are very few consistent endocrine findings. The relationship between symptom development and the progester-one peak in the luteal phase is obvious, but apart from that there is a general agreement on the absence of peripheral markers of hypothalamus-pituitary-gonadal axis dysfunction in PMS. The most important finding by far is the necessity of ovulation and corpus luteum formation for PMS development. During anovulatory cycles, spontaneous or induced, when a corpus luteum is not formed, the cyclicity in symptoms disappears. . . .

3.1 Ovarian Steroids and Symptoms

Although no differences in progesterone and estradiol plasma levels have been shown between patients with PMS and control individuals, these sex steroids appear to have an impact on symptom development and severity within patients. Particular attention has been paid to estradiol, progesterone and progesterone metabolites active on the GABA$_A$ receptor in the brain. . . .

Both estradiol and progesterone seem to be of importance, as symptoms were induced with both estrogen and progesterone in women with PMS in whom the ovarian function had been interrupted with GnRH agonists. Increased estradiol and progesterone plasma levels during the luteal phase were found to be related to more severe symptoms when compared with cycles in the same individuals with lower luteal phase estradiol and progesterone levels. The symptom severity was in particular related to the luteal estradiol levels. In addition, a subgroup of patients with higher luteal phase estradiol levels showed more severe symptoms compared with patients with lower luteal phase estradiol. . . . The conclusion is that an increase in the estrogen dose accentuates negative mood and physical symptoms during the progestogen phase of sequential HRT but not in the absence of a progestogen.

This finding is consistent with the follicular phase of the menstrual cycle, when estrogen dominates and reaches its highest levels. At the preovulatory phase, women with PMS feel at their best and estradiol does not seem to provoke symptoms. Obviously, estradiol and progesterone acting together seem to induce a different response in the CNS than when they act separately.

3.2 Indications of Different Sex Steroid Sensitivity

If there is no difference in sex steroid levels between patients with PMS and control individuals, some other difference must exist, as not all women react to the substances produced by the corpus luteum. At least two other possibilities exist, namely that an as yet unknown provoking factor is produced from the corpus luteum in women with PMS, or that the sensitivity in the brain to the steroids differs between patients and control individuals. There exists some evidence for the latter hypothesis.

3.3 Neurosteroids

. . . Although plasma levels of neuroactive steroids may or may not differ between PMS patients and control individuals, neuroactive steroids might still play a role in the symptom provocation of PMS if the differences between women with and without PMS are based on neuroactivity within the brain.

3.4 Pathogenesis Within the Brain

As discussed [above], there are strong indications that the steroids from the corpus luteum are the provoking factor. However, there must exist a response system within the brain where the action takes place. The classical hormonal receptors for estradiol and progesterone exist in the brain and are specifically distributed to certain areas. . . .

The serotonin and GABA systems are considered the two transmitter systems most involved in PMS aetiology. The serotonin system is considered mainly because SSRIs are effective treatments for PMS and PMDD. The direct mechanism by which they work is unknown, but many studies indicate a connection between the serotonin system and PMS. . . .

4. Treatment

There are two main principles for the treatment of PMS. One treatment strategy focuses on hormonal treatments of different types, mainly by inducing an anovulatory state. The other treatment strategy focuses on effects within the CNS that ameliorate or block the effects of the provoking factor; this latter strategy is related to the similarities and interactions between PMS and major depression and aims at modulating serotonergic neurotransmission. The treatments that have shown benefit over placebo treatments are SSRIs; treatments that induce anovulation, such as GnRH agonists, high dosages of estrogen, low dosages of danazol (an antigonadotrophin) and surgical oophorectomy; and spironolactone (an aldosterone, androgen and progesterone antagonist).

5. Conclusion

Despite the significant understanding now held regarding hormones and CNS function, more research into the pathogenesis behind menstrual cycle-linked mood changes is needed. A consensus on how to define the condition, diagnostic criteria and diagnostic procedure has been reached. Good clinical trials show some treatments to be effective. With a deeper knowledge of the pathogenesis, new treatments, especially those that block symptom-provoking factors, will appear.

Sound diagnostic procedures are compulsory prior to the administration of treatment. A significant number of women at a fertile age are severely burdened by menstrual cycle-linked symptoms. Ovulation is needed for the symptoms to develop. Progestogens given alone or in combination with estrogen can induce symptoms similar to those seen in PMS and are therefore suspected as symptom-provoking factors. The response systems within the brain that are known to be involved include serotonin and GABA. Certain progesterone metabolites, such as allopregnanolone, are allosteric agonists to the $GABA_A$ receptor with a similar action as benzodiazepines, barbiturates and alcohol. Patients with PMS have a decreased sensitivity to $GABA_A$ receptor active substances compared with control individuals. These substances, including allopregnanolone, at low dosages are known to induce adverse mood effects in some humans and animals. Well designed clinical trials show that SSRI preparations have positive effects on PMS symptoms. Substances inhibiting ovulation, such as GnRH agonists, have proven to be effective treatments. To avoid adverse effects when high dosages of GnRH agonists are used, add-back HRT is recommended. Oral contraceptives have no treatment effect over placebo. Spironolactone has a mild effect and may be an alternative if the patient cannot take any of the previously mentioned treatments.

NO 👆

PMS as a Culture-Bound Syndrome

When I first began to study changes related to the menstrual cycle in the 1970s, so few studies existed in the literature that I could honestly say that I'd read every word ever written about premenstrual syndrome (PMS). The literature has expanded so dramatically that no one could say that today. . . .

What happened? How did PMS go from a little-known experience of tension in the few days preceding menstruation to a syndrome consisting of dozens of possible symptoms that occur during the weeks preceding menstruation—an experience so common that most women complain about it and an experience so well known that jokes about it appear everywhere? In this lecture, we'll consider the sociocultural and political meanings of PMS and how they contributed to its rise from relative obscurity to cultural icon in a mere 30 years.

What Is PMS?

A variety of physiological and psychological changes have been associated with phases of the menstrual cycle. Those changes that occur premenstrually (usually days 23 to 28 of the cycle) have been called premenstrual tension or premenstrual syndrome. The most frequently reported premenstrual change is fluid retention, particularly in the breasts and abdomen. Other symptoms have been classified as follows:

- *Psychological.* Irritability, depression, anxiety, lethargy, sleep changes, low morale, crying spells, hostility
- *Neurological.* Headaches, vertigo, backaches
- *Gastrointestinal.* Nausea, vomiting, constipation, increased craving for sweet or salty foods
- *Dermatological.* Acne

It has also been suggested, although there is no scientific evidence for this, that premenstrual women have difficulty concentrating, poorer judgment, lack of coordination, decreased efficiency, and lowered school or work performance.

From LECTURES ON THE PSYCHOLOGY OF WOMEN, THIRD EDITION, 2004, excerpts from 111–127. Copyright © 2004 by McGraw-Hill Companies. Reprinted by permission.

Although the data do indicate that women experience cyclic changes, it is difficult to know how common such changes are. Estimates of the prevalence of premenstrual symptoms, which depend on how the data were collected, have ranged from 2 percent (using the strictest criteria of a 30 percent change in intensity of selected emotional and physical experiences charted daily over three menstrual cycles) to 100 percent (using the loosest criteria, "Have you ever experienced a cyclic change in physiological or psychological state?"). Despite efforts by the Society for Menstrual Cycle Research, the National Institute of Mental Health, and the American Psychiatric Association to produce a standard definition, there is little agreement on how many symptoms must be experienced or how severe the symptoms must be in order to be classified as premenstrual syndrome. So many different definitions exist in the literature that results cannot easily be compared with each other. Even the timing of the premenstrual phase of the cycle is not clear. Some researchers have described it as five to seven days before the start of menstruation; others have described it as the time between ovulation and menstruation (about two weeks). The problem of estimates is made more complicated by the fact that premenstrual experience is highly variable and personal. All women do not experience the same changes, and the experience of any given woman may vary from cycle to cycle. In addition, PMS has been so frequently discussed in recent years that the results of surveys and questionnaire studies have undoubtedly been affected by a response bias in the direction of the cultural stereotype of the premenstrual woman.

What is the cultural stereotype of the premenstrual woman? You probably don't need me to tell you! A recent walk through a shopping mall turned up a bumper sticker ("A woman with PMS and ESP is a bitch who knows everything"), buttons ("It's not PMS, I'm psychotic," "It's not PMS, I'm always bitchy"), greeting cards ("Some special advice for the birthday girl—never cut your cake during PMS"), a calendar of cartoons about a woman with a particularly bad case of PMS ("Plagued by a raging hormonal imbalance, Melinda devours Hershey, Pennsylvania"), and several "humorous" books (*Raging Hormones: The Official PMS Survival Guide, PMS Attacks and Other Inconveniences of Life,* and *Hormones from Hell*). . . .

Karen Levy and I performed a content analysis of 78 articles about PMS that were published in American magazines from 1980 to 1987. The articles described a confusing array of symptoms and contradictory treatment recommendations. No single symptom was mentioned in every article; 131 different symptoms were described, including sallow skin, feeling fat, and changes in the way one's perfume smells. Treatment recommendations included drinking wine and limiting alcohol intake, limiting fluid intake and drinking plenty of water, and limiting protein intake and eating a high-protein diet. Although no biochemical differences have yet been found between women who suffer from PMS and women who don't, the journalists implicated hormone levels as the cause of PMS. The menstrual cycle was referred to as the "cycle of misery," a "hormonal roller coaster," the "inner beast," and the "menstrual monster." The premenstrual and menstrual phases of the cycle were described as "weeks of hell," during which women are "hostages to their hormones," and premenstrual women were described as "cripples" and "raging beasts." Among the titles of the articles we read were "Premenstrual Frenzy," "Dr. Jekyll and Ms. Hyde," "Coping with Eve's Curse," "Once a Month I'm a Woman Possessed," and "The Taming of the Shrew Inside of You."

Cartoons about violent women and journalistic representations of frenzied, "raging beasts" could easily make one lose sight of the fact that women commit fewer than 5 percent of all violent crimes. How did this violent image of premenstrual women arise? In 1981, two court cases in Great Britain gained worldwide attention as Sandie Smith and Christine English, on trial for murder, were found guilty of manslaughter. They were given probation because the judges accepted pleas of diminished responsibility after Dr. Katharina Dalton testified that they had PMS. When she first began working on PMS in the 1950s, Dr. Dalton did not believe that it was a problem that affected large numbers of women. By the early 1980s, she would suggest that most women have PMS, although they might not know it. The British trials resulted in an explosion of media interest in PMS. Images of violent premenstrual murderesses merged with ancient images of women as dangerous beings who lured men to their doom, but now there was a "scientific" basis to women's hostility and duplicity—hormones—and everyone was talking about them. Sociologist Sophie Laws has noted that few people bothered to ask how it is possible that the hormones of millions of women could be out of balance.

PMS a Disease? An Illness? A Syndrome?

A disease is defined as a pathological condition of the body that has clinical signs, symptoms, and laboratory findings that are specific to it and that allow us to discriminate it from normal or other pathological states of the body. PMS is not a disease. There are no laboratory findings that can discriminate PMS sufferers from nonsufferers. The symptoms of PMS are not specific to it; some are common in men and in premenarcheal girls and postmenopausal women. The only clinical sign specific to PMS is that it is generally followed by menstruation. However, there are many menstruating women who don't experience PMS, and some women who don't menstruate (for example, women who have had hysterectomies) do complain of PMS.

In medicine, it is common to distinguish between disease and illness. Diseases are tangible and have elements that can be measured. Illnesses are highly individual and personal. When we speak of illness, we are generally referring to psychological experiences such as pain, suffering, and distress. . . . PMS can be categorized as an illness. Those women who have severe symptoms are distressed and may be described as suffering. However, you should consider carefully the definition of an illness before you apply it to yourself. If you experience only a few premenstrual changes that can be described as mild or moderate, are you ill?

"Illness behavior" refers to "the way in which symptoms are conceived, evaluated, and acted upon by a person who recognizes some pain, discomfort, or other sign of malfunction." Illness behavior is significantly affected by society's definition of symptoms and malfunctions and by the roles and expectations society holds for individuals who experience them. . . .

Cultural images and social roles and stereotypes shape women to notice menstrual cycle–related changes and to label them as pathological rather than as normal. Thirty years ago, a woman who was experiencing tension or depression before her menstrual period would have thought to herself, "I'm tense (or blue) today." Now she thinks, "I have PMS." The modern woman engages in illness behavior; she feels ill, tells others that she's ill, and treats her illness (with Pamprin, a day off, etc.). In the past, she would have coped in other ways and considered her mood to be part of the normal ups and downs of life. The reason we found 131 different symptoms in our analysis of magazine articles is that the menstrual cycle has become so salient as problematic that American women attribute almost any change to it. If a man has a headache, he may think of several possible reasons for it—work pressure, hunger, or too much beer last night. If a woman has a headache, she can make any of those same attributions, but she's unlikely to do so. Three weeks out of four, she'll probably attribute here headache to her menstrual cycle—same symptom, very different illness behavior.

A syndrome is a group of symptoms that are related to each other by some anatomical, physiological, or biochemical peculiarity. This definition does not insist that a common cause be known, simply that the symptoms be related in some way. The menstrual cycle is the physiological or biochemical peculiarity that links the "symptoms" of PMS, which appear or are intensified during the premenstrual (luteal) phase. Thus, PMS can be said to meet the definition of a syndrome, although the "symptoms" may never be found to have a common cause.

What Is a Culture-Bound Syndrome

To understand PMS, we have to take an interdisciplinary approach. So far, we've considered evidence from psychology, sociology, and medicine. Now it's anthropology's turn. Anthropologists invented the term "culture-bound syndrome" to help them understand illnesses that occur in some societies but not in others. Examples of culture-bound syndromes include illnesses that result from voodoo, gypsy curses, and other "magical" spells. Until recently, the literature on culture-bound syndromes focused on illnesses in other societies that the Western anthropologists found mystifying because there was no measurable disease process involved. Members of highly technological societies such as ours expect that a biomedical cause and cure will ultimately be found for every illness. Now, however, anthropologists are suggesting that the illness behavior that surrounds conditions with which we are very familiar (for example, obesity and menopause) may constitute culture-bound syndromes.

A culture-bound syndrome is a constellation of symptoms that have been categorized as a dysfunction or disease in some societies but not in others.

PMS a Culture-Bound Syndrome?

I believe that PMS is a culture-bound syndrome, and I'll try to convince you to agree with me [by considering the following six features of a culture-bound syndrome]. . . .

[1] PMS cannot be understood apart from its specific cultural or subcultural context. In order to understand PMS, one must have, at the most basic level, a concept of menstruation as cyclic, which is necessary in order to anticipate it. Menstruation is a rare event in societies in which women are pregnant or lactating much of their adult lives. Therefore, members of those societies would not develop the same expectations of the menstrual cycle as members of more technologically advanced societies, and they would not have the familiarity with it to notice that certain changes are related to its events. There would thus be no PMS, merely a coping with individual symptoms as they emerged.

[I]n order to understand PMS, one must live in an industrialized society. Before industrialization, people worked in tune with natural rhythms—seasonal for farmers, circadian for skilled laborers. Now that most of us work at jobs in offices and factories that require sustained labor throughout the year and reward discipline of the mind and body, lapses in such discipline are noted. . . .

Industrialization may contribute to the belief in many societies that one can and should exercise self-control in order to feel and behave the same way all the time. Our culture encourages people to believe that we can have more control over our lives and bodies than is actually possible. This belief in control contributes not only to PMS but to eating disorders and compulsive exercise. But that's another lecture.

Finally, there would be no PMS without strong negative attitudes toward menstruation. . . . Americans are uncomfortable talking about menstruation and believe that the menstrual cycle has negative effects on women's personality, behavior and physiology. . . .

[2] PMS summarizes and symbolizes core meanings and behavioral norms of the culture. Among the core meanings and behavioral norms reflected in PMS are mind-body dualism, which contributes to our belief that people are not responsible for emotional or behavioral symptoms of disease; individuals' need for control and fear of noncontrol; the raging-hormones hypothesis, which promotes the belief that women are emotionally unstable; and the industrialized society's preference for stability of affect and behavior. Because stability is so highly valued, changeableness, rhythmicity, and emotionality have come to be viewed as inherently "unhealthy."

PMS also reflects the behavioral norms of the feminine gender role. Women are expected to be soft-spoken, nurturing, patient, and kind. Any woman who is turned inward or otherwise unapproachable is thought to have something wrong with her. Blaming the "unfeminine" parts of one's personality or behavior on PMS can be a survival strategy for women in that it can allow women to hold onto a self-definition of "good/proper" women. The premenstrual week is the only time of the month some women "allow" themselves to be angry because they can attribute their anger to their hormones rather than to any of the many things in the world that could "legitimately" anger them. However, this strategy also works against women. There's nothing more frustrating than expressing anger about something only to hear others say, "She must be on the rag" or "That's PMS talking."

. . . PMS can be seen as a collection of negative beliefs about women's "nature," a nature that "requires" medical management and the protection of men, who are stronger and "healthier" than menstruating women. Don't miss the point: If women are emotionally unstable and inherently unhealthy, it's for their own good and the good of society that women's roles in public life are limited.

[3] *Diagnosis of PMS relies on culture-specific technology as well as ideology.* To diagnose PMS, one must have a knowledge of hormones and their actions and accept the idea that hormones influence affect and behavior. There are no reliable laboratory tests for PMS, but calendars, thermometers, hormone assay techniques, nutrient deficiency measures, and self-report questionnaires have been used in attempts to document its existence. Technology may be involved in the cause as well as the detection of premenstrual symptoms. Landers has suggested that PMS may be an iatrogenic disease (i.e., an illness caused by medical intervention) because it frequently begins or worsens when a woman is using an IUD or stops using oral contraceptives or after she has had a hysterectomy, a tubal ligation, or an abortion.

The ideologies on which the diagnosis of PMS relies include the raging-hormone hypothesis, an assumption that cyclic change is inherently pathological, an acceptance of stereotypical gender roles as accurate and appropriate descriptions of healthy behavior for women and men, and a social contract between the patient and physician that allows patients to trust their physicians as experts who are able to make a diagnosis in a case in which the symptoms are so vague and numerous. . . .

. . . When others hear women complaining about PMS, it reinforces these ideologies and persuades others that women cannot be trusted to do important work or to make decisions that have serious implications.

[4] *Successful treatment is accomplished only by participants in that culture.* The act of being diagnosed has a therapeutic effect for many women who suffer from premenstrual changes, whether or not the symptoms are alleviated. Women are accustomed to having their complaints dismissed by powerful others, and the diagnosis may represent one of the few times someone has listened to the women in a way that made them feel worthy of attention. The use of the label PMS indicates that the physician and the patient accept society's standards and the cultural assumptions discussed earlier, which may, in a way, be comforting.

One of the characteristics that women who complain of PMS share is a strong placebo response.

Women may be more likely than men to have external health locus of control—that is, to be less likely than men to think that they can affect their health by their own actions. Seeking treatment for PMS, then, can be empowering for women because they will have to be put in charge of their health and self-care. . . .

[5] *Treatment judged as successful in one cultural context may not be understood as successful from another perspective.* The purpose of treating PMS is to help women to function more smoothly in their traditional, subordinate, "feminine" role "in an uncomplaining, cheerful way." Dalton has suggested that it is a woman's duty and obligation to be treated for PMS. Adherence to rigid gender roles may not be seen as a successful treatment even within subcultural contexts of our own society! . . .

[6] *The symptoms of PMS may be recognized and similarly organized elsewhere but are not categorized as the same dysfunction or "disease."* The symptoms associated with PMS are numerous and vague and have considerable overlap with those of other conditions. They could easily be recognized but organized differently. Many of the symptoms—headaches, backaches, irritability, tension, crying spells—are also associated with stress. It is agreed that stress worsens PMS, but perhaps stress actually causes these PMS "symptoms" just as it does in men.

None of the symptoms associated with PMS are unique to menstruation. What seems to be important to Western medicine is cyclicity, which is seen as instability. If cyclic or rhythmic changes were seen as normative or natural, then emotional, behavioral, and physiological changes would be accepted and expected. They would not be pathologized.

Thinking about our premenstrual experience in a different way would also change our illness behavior. Instead of considering yourself as "overreacting," consider yourself "sensitive." Changing your attributions about premenstrual changes would also make you feel better. If you know you are premenstrual, thinking "Water retention makes my tear ducts feel full" is probably more accurate than thinking "I am depressed and about to cry." Consider whether some of the changes associated with PMS should even be considered symptoms. If we lived in a society that preferred loose clothing such as robes or saris, then water retention might not even be noticed. In our weight-obsessed society, the small weight gain from premenstrual fluid retention is actively feared by many women. Probably only in the United States could an occasional urge to eat a candy bar or a salty snack be seen as a sign of a medical condition!

. . . The results of studies support the idea that culture shapes which variations in mood and physical sensations are noticed and which cause concern. Further support for cultural influence comes from study of women in the United States. She found that the most severe menstrual complaints came from strict Catholics and Orthodox Jews who strongly adhered to the feminine gender role.

Why Has PMS Become So Significa

Why has PMS become so well known in the last 30 years? With hindsight, we can see how the development of interest in PMS coincided with the conservative political shift in the United States and Great Britain in the 1970s and 1980s. It is part of the backlash against feminists so clearly delineated by Susan Faludi. In fact, now that the backlash has made it so unpopular to embrace feminism publicly, we may want to consider whether women's willingness to embrace PMS serves a similar function in facilitating resistance to sociocultural demands. Whereas 30 years ago a woman might have said, "I refuse to diet, to achieve a perfectly clean house, and to stifle my anger because I will not collude with patriarchal demands," she now says, "I cannot lose weight, get all of my work done perfectly, and stay calm and happy all the time because I have PMS."

To understand the significance of PMS, one must consider who benefits from it. Women? To some extent, yes—if they can excuse behavior others disapprove of by suggesting it was caused by PMS. If physicians or others pay attention to women and take them seriously, women may be said to benefit from seeking help for PMS, yet the benefits to women are few and the drawbacks many. The existence of PMS encourages women to think of themselves as unstable and potentially ill for at least half of each month. It encourages men to think of us that way, too, which limits our opportunities for self-expression and career advancement. Now that the American Psychiatric Association has placed in the fourth edition of its *Diagnostic and Statistical Manual* a mental illness called premenstrual dysphoric disorder, there will be additional ways to stigmatize women and use PMS to our disadvantage. . . .

Who benefits from PMS? The physicians who treat the many women who seek relief from it benefit greatly from the widespread belief that PMS is a disease. Gynecologists and psychiatrists have been battling each other over who has the "right" to treat PMS. Medical researchers and other scientists who work in the biomedical model have benefited greatly from the interest in PMS, as they have been given government and corporate grants to find a cause and cure for PMS. Pharmaceutical companies sponsor research conferences and medical education seminars on PMS in the hope that some drug they can manufacture will be the long-awaited cure. If the publicity about PMS has convinced most women that they have a monthly illness, think what the profits could be on a drug millions of women would buy every month! . . .

The greatest beneficiary of PMS is the status quo. PMS serves to keep women in their place; it is a form of social control. It's a culture-bound syndrome because it is only necessary in societies in which women have made major gains toward equality of rights and opportunities. If women are preoccupied with rhythmic changes in their bodies and emotions instead of preoccupied with winning political power, social institutions are safe. For example, women who are thought to have PMS are told to slow down the busy pace of their lives, sometimes in ways that can hurt their chances for successful careers. Self-help books advise women to tell their bosses about their PMS and tell them not to schedule important business meetings or travel during the second half of their menstrual cycles.

What do women learn from the label PMS? [I]t tells women that their problems are internal and individual; warns women not to express the entire range of their emotions because some of their feelings and behaviors are inappropriate; isolates women from the social, cultural, and environmental context of their lives by defining their experience as a medical problem; alienates women from each other and from their collective experience; and silences women from speaking out about the oppressive conditions of their lives.

PMS is bad news.

POSTSCRIPT

Is Premenstrual Syndrome a Hormonally Based Disorder?

A question that always arises when discussing hormonally based disorders in women is: Do men have cycles too? The answer is yes. The level of testosterone increases by about sixfold at puberty, and later begins to decline. Studies have shown that testosterone also fluctuates within a 24-hour period. Interestingly, levels are the lowest at night when crimes are most often committed and highest in the morning when people are more likely to be asleep. By the age of 55 most men will have lowered levels of testosterone, and by age 80 the levels will have returned to pre-pubertal levels. The syndrome associated with testosterone decline is known as *andropause* or *viropause*, and has two forms, one showing a rapid decline and the other a gradual decline. The form associated with a rapid drop in testosterone level is similar to menopause in women. The gradual decline is more confusing because its effects may be confused with depression, that is, male midlife psychological adjustment disorders. Men's symptoms are different from women. Women turn inward and are diagnosed as dependent or histrionic or depressed; men turn outward and are diagnosed with an antisocial personality or an adjustment disorder. They are more likely to turn to alcohol, drugs, and other behaviors that afford them the sense of being strong and in charge. They have difficulty admitting to having problems and in talking about them. The question is do the hormonal changes themselves cause these problems? Ron Levant, the president of the American Psychological Association (2005), discusses the problem of "normative male alexithymia"—a phrase used to describe men who cannot express their emotions. Society tells men and women how to be "sick" and how to (or not to) express their emotions. On the one hand, women's reproductive functions are seen as a source of problems and used to justify the claim that women are biologically inferior to men. On the other hand, hormonal changes in men are ignored and not considered a source of problems. Whereas women's problems are attributed to their own internal weaknesses, men's problems are attributed to situational factors beyond their control. How does the social construction of men as strong and active and women as weak and passive help shape the messages each receive about how to "appropriately" cope with life's problems?

Selected Readings

Malcolm Carruthers, *Maximising Manhood* (London: Harper Collins, 1997).

Jpan C. Chrisler and Paula Caplan, "The strange case of Dr. Jekyll and Ms. Hyde: How PMS became a cultural phenomenon and a psychiatric disorder," *Annual Review of Sex Research, 13* (2002): 274–306.

Sidney Crown and Alan Lee, eds., *Gender and Mental Health* (Basingstoke: Macmillan, 1999).

Anne Fausto-Sterling, *Sexing the Body: Gender Politics and the Construction of Sexuality* (New York: Basic Books, 2000).

Gail Sheehy, *Understanding Men's Passages: Discovering the New Map of Men's Lives* (New York: Random House, 1998).

ISSUE 19

Is Reparative Therapy Effective in Changing One's Sexual Orientation?

YES: Robert L. Spitzer, from "Can Some Gay Men and Lesbians Change Their Sexual Orientation? 200 Participants Reporting a Change from Homosexual to Heterosexual Orientation," *Archives of Sexual Behavior* (October 2003)

NO: Helena M. Carlson and Lisa M. Diamond, from "Commentary: Peer Commentaries on Spitzer," *Archives of Sexual Behavior* (October 2003)

ISSUE SUMMARY

YES: Robert L. Spitzer reports on a study that identified a subgroup of gay men and lesbians who reported at least some minimal change in some aspect of their sexual orientation.

NO: Helena M. Carlson and Lisa M. Diamond, in separate critiques, note numerous flaws in Spitzer's methods and conceptualization of sexual desire. Both argue that his conclusions are flawed.

T here are three fundamental questions regarding sexual orientation. First, is it a choice? Second, assuming it is "wrong," should efforts be made to change it? Finally, is change possible? Because of varying criteria for defining sexual orientation, it is difficult to establish an accurate estimate of the number of gays and lesbians. Most research depends on a person's self-identification. With these qualifications, it has been estimated that approximately 6 percent of men and 3 percent of women are gay and lesbian, respectively. These numbers do not appear to be related to race, class, ethnicity, geographical locale, or mental health status. With regard to choice, there is a great deal of controversy. Some research suggests that there is a "gay gene" or "gay brain." However, the evidence is correlational. The now classic 1991 study of brain structure by Simon LaVay, a gay neuroscientist, was initially touted as evidence for a gay brain. In comparing the brains of gay men who had died of AIDS with those of heterosexual men, he identified a structure within the hypothalamus (the INAH 3) that differed in size in the two groups. However, a careful reading of the study indicates that LaVay himself never made the claim that genetics

339

might be causal. He went on to write a book in 1996 discussing how research into homosexuality has been used and abused. However, to the present research continues to seek the biological roots of sexual orientation. For example, the National Institutes of Health is sponsoring a genetic study of sexual orientation and there are ongoing twin studies (of gay brothers) at Temple University. Some evidence suggestive of a genetic link hints that the genetic base may be stronger in men than women, with there being a genetic marker on the X chromosome in men. Also, if one twin is homosexual, 50 percent of the identical twins are as well, a rate 10 times higher than base rate. There is also some evidence that the recurrence of gays/lesbians in biological, but not adoptive, families is greater than chance. Some studies have also sought to find early childhood experiences and types of parenting that might be associated with sexual orientation, with evidence that the first behavioral manifestations may appear as early as age two. However, the research findings are correlational and mixed.

This leads to the second and third questions, regardless of whether sexual orientation is biologically based or the result of early childhood experiences, can it, and should it, be changed? Opinions range from yes it can be changed through prayer and counseling to no. Those adopting a conservative and religiously based view believe that homosexuality is a sin and should be changed. A more liberal perspective views homosexuality as one of many natural possibilities and as such, homosexuals should be granted the same individual rights and freedoms as heterosexuals. Some evidence suggests that the behavioral manifestations can be altered, although it is not clear that the orientation itself can be changed (see http://www.religioustolerance.org/hom_fixe.htm for a comparison of the most conservative to the most liberal views). These differing views are presented in the selections. Robert Spitzer describes a study in which there is evidence that a portion of self-selected gays and lesbians reported at least some minimal change in their sexual orientation at least five years after some form of reparative therapy. Reparative therapy is defined as any form of therapy aimed at changing sexual orientation, often supported by "ex-gay" ministries. The critiques of Spitzer's study focus on both methodological flaws, as described by Helena Carlson, and conceptual flaws, as described by Lisa Diamond. Carlson questions the self-selected, and therefore nonrepresentativeness of the sample, and Diamond raises the fundamental question of the definition of sexual orientation and evaluates the best indicators of "change."

YES

Robert L. Spitzer

Can Some Gay Men and Lesbians Change Their Sexual Orientation? 200 Participants Reporting a Change from Homosexual to Heterosexual Orientation

Introduction

In recent years, there has been a marked change about both the desirability and feasibility of attempts to alter a homosexual sexual orientation. In the past, such change was generally considered both desirable and possible. An increasing number of clinicians believe that such change rarely, if ever, occurs and that psychotherapy with this goal often is harmful by increasing self-loathing, lowered self-esteem, hopelessness, and depression. Several authors have argued that clinicians who attempt to help their clients change their homosexual orientation are violating professional ethical codes by providing a "treatment" that is ineffective, often harmful, and reinforces in their clients the false belief that homosexuality is a disorder and needs treatment.

At the present time, only a very small number of mental health professionals (primarily psychologists, social workers, mental health counselors, and pastoral ministers) provide therapy with the goal of helping their clients change their sexual orientation from homosexual to heterosexual. Therapy with this goal is often referred to as "reparative therapy." There are also religious "ex-gay" ministries that offer individual counseling and group support to gay men and lesbians who wish to change their sexual orientation. An example is Exodus International, an interdenominational Christian organization that promotes the message of "Freedom from homosexuality through the power of Jesus Christ." Finally, there are a small number of 12-step programs, such as Sexual Addicts Anonymous.

Many individuals receiving reparative therapy from a mental health professional also get support or counseling from an ex-gay ministry. In this article, any help from a mental health professional or an ex-gay ministry for the purpose of changing sexual orientation will be referred to as "reparative

From *Archives of Sexual Behavior*, vol. 32, no. 5, October 2003, excerpts from 403–417. Copyright © 2003 by Springer Journals (Kluwer Academic). Reprinted by permission.

therapy" or simply as "therapy." Reparative therapists believe that same-sex attractions reflect a developmental disorder and can be significantly diminished through development of stronger and more confident gender identification. Reparative therapists say that their gay male patients (who comprise the majority of their caseload) suffer from a lifelong feeling of "being on the outside" of male activities and "not feeling like one of the guys." When therapy succeeds in demystifying males and maleness, their romantic and erotic attractions to men diminish and opposite-sex attractions may gradually develop. A prominent reorientation therapist estimates that only about a third of the male clients that pursue a course of reparative therapy actually develop heterosexual attractions, another third diminish their unwanted male attractions and decrease their unwanted same-sex behaviors but do not develop heterosexual attractions; the remaining third remain essentially unchanged.

"The Surgeon General," the American Academy of Pediatrics, and all of the major mental health associations in the United States, representing psychiatry, psychology, social work, and counseling have each issued position statements warning of possible harm from such therapy and asserting that there is no evidence that such therapy can change one's sexual orientation. For example, the 1998 American Psychiatric Association Position Statement on Psychiatric Treatment and Sexual Orientation states:

> . . . there is no published scientific evidence supporting the efficacy of reparative therapy as a treatment to change one's sexual orientation. . . .
> The potential risks of reparative therapy are great, including depression, anxiety, and self-destructive behavior.

Is this seemingly authoritative position statement true, that there is "no published scientific evidence" supporting the efficacy of reparative therapy to change sexual orientation? The answer depends on what is meant by "scientific evidence." If scientific evidence requires a study with randomized assignment of individuals to a treatment condition, reliable and valid assessment of target symptoms before treatment, when treatment is concluded, and at follow-up, then it is certainly true that there are no such studies of reparative therapy. However, the same can be said about many widely used types of psychotherapy, including gay affirmative therapy, whose efficacy has never been subjected to a rigorous study. There is, however, a large literature relevant to the issue of the possibility of changing sexual orientation. Adams and Sturgis critically reviewed 37 studies of behavior therapy to change sexual orientation and concluded that, "Although sexual orientation techniques have achieved moderately positive results, research is needed to improve the efficacy of the procedures."

Of 19 studies, [only] one is perhaps the most informative regarding change from a homosexual or bisexual orientation to an exclusively heterosexual orientation. [In] a follow-up of 101 former clients, several years after having been treated in a form of psychoanalysis called "anticomplaining therapy," [e]leven (11%) of the patients had experienced a "radical change," defined as "no homosexual interests except for occasional and weak homosexual 'flashes' at most and the restoration of full heterosexuality."

Although providing some evidence for the efficacy of reparative therapy, all of the 19 studies have one or more serious methodological shortcomings, including no assessment of specific changes in sexual orientation (e.g., changes in masturbatory fantasies), no detailed sexual history, no follow-up assessment, no informants, no consecutive series, no objective measures, and possible bias in that the researcher conducted the therapy.

The 2000 American Psychiatric Association "Position Statement on Therapies Focused on Attempts to Change Sexual Orientation" noted that "there have been no scientifically rigorous outcome studies to determine either the actual efficacy or harm of 'reparative' treatments. . . . APA encourages and supports research . . . to further determine 'reparative' therapy's risks versus its benefits." This study attempts to contribute to that research by studying whether some individuals receiving reparative therapy do, in fact, change their sexual orientation from homosexual to heterosexual.

Critics of reparative therapy acknowledge that the therapy can change homosexual behavior by the individual resisting acting on homosexual feelings and can also succeed in getting the individual to relabel his or her homosexual orientation as heterosexual. They claim, however, that homosexual orientation itself remains unchanged. For the purposes of this study, homosexual orientation is operationalized by multiple measures of same sex attraction, arousal, fantasy, and yearning as well as overt behavior.

This study tests the following hypothesis: Some individuals whose sexual orientation is predominantly homosexual can become predominantly heterosexual following some form of reparative therapy (which can take the form of psychotherapy, counseling, or participation in an ex-gay ministry program).

This study involves systematically interviewing a large group of individuals who report that their sexual orientation had been predominantly homosexual, but who now report that because of some kind of therapy they have sustained for at least 5 years some change to a heterosexual orientation. If such individuals are found, the specific changes in components of sexual orientation and their magnitude are examined as well as changes in overt homosexual behavior, self-identity, and how bothered the individuals are by homosexual feelings. In addition, because sexuality in gay men and lesbians may be experienced and expressed differently, as is the case with heterosexual individuals, gender differences in the reported changes are also examined.

Method

Participant Recruitment and Entry Criteria

Announcements aimed at recruiting participants requested individuals who had sustained some change in homosexual orientation for at least 5 years. To be accepted into the study, however, it was necessary for an individuals to satisfy two criteria: (1) predominantly homosexual attraction for many years, and in the year before starting therapy, at least 60 on a scale of sexual attraction (where 0 = *exclusively heterosexual* and 100 = *exclusively homosexual*);

(2) after therapy, a change of at least 10 points, lasting at least 5 years, toward the heterosexual end of the scale of sexual attraction. These criteria were designed to identify individuals who reported at least some minimal change in sexual attraction, not merely a change in overt homosexual behavior or self-identity as "gay" or "straight." It should be noted that individuals who satisfied these criteria were not excluded from the study if they had had homosexual sex during or following therapy.

Over a 16-month period (January 2000 to April 2001), 274 individuals were recruited who wanted to participate in the study. Of these, 200 (143 males, 57 females) satisfied the entry criteria and constitute the study sample. . . .

Forty-three percent of the 200 participants learned about the study from ex-gay religious ministries and 23% from the National Association for Research and Therapy of Homosexuality, a group of mental health professionals and lay people who defend the right of gay men and lesbians to receive sexual reorientation therapy. In all but a few cases, these individuals were not chosen by these organizations; the individuals decided on their own to participate after reading repeated notices of the study that these two organizations had sent to their members. . . .

The New York State Psychiatric Institute Institutional Review Board approved the study protocol and waived the requirement of written informed consent.

Sample Description

The mean age of the 143 male participants was 42 years ($SD = 8.0$) and for the 57 females it was 44 years ($SD = 8.5$). Seventy-six percent of the men and 47% of the women were married at the time of the interview ($\chi^2(1) = 14.2$, $p < .001$). Twenty-one percent of the males and 18% of the females were married before beginning therapy. Almost all were Caucasian (95%). Most had completed college (76%). . . .

Most participants were Christian (Protestant 81%, Catholic 8%, Mormon 7%). Three percent were Jewish. The vast majority (93%) of the participants reported that religion was "extremely" or "very" important in their lives. Nineteen percent of the participants were mental health professionals or directors of ex-gay ministries.

Almost half of the participants (41%) reported that they had at some time prior to the therapy been "openly gay." Over a third of the participants (males 37%, females 35%) reported that they had had serious thoughts of suicide, related to their homosexuality. The majority of participants (78%) had publicly spoken in favor of efforts to change homosexual orientation, often at their church.

Description of Structured Interview and Interview Measures

A structured telephone interview was developed with 114 closed-ended questions. . . . Sixty of these questions addressed sexual feelings, fantasy, and behavior. There were also several open-ended questions (e.g., "What were the most important things you talked about in your therapy?"). . . .

There were 10 self-report measures used to assess different aspects of sexual orientation. . . .

There were three measures for participants having heterosexual sex: (1) frequency of sex . . . (2) emotional satisfaction with heterosexual relationship . . . (3) physical satisfaction with heterosexual sex (as earlier). . . .

Participants wanted to not only change their sexual orientation, but to function well heterosexually. For the purpose of this study, a variable called "Good Heterosexual Functioning" was created, defined as requiring all five of the following criteria: (1) during the past year, the participant was in a heterosexual relationship and regarded it as "loving"; (2) overall satisfaction in the emotional relationship with their partner (at least 7 on a 1–10 scale where 10 is *as good as it can be* and 1 is *as bad as it can be*); (3) heterosexual sex with partner at least a few times a month; (4) physical satisfaction from heterosexual sex at least 7 (the same 1–10 scale); (5) during no more than 15% of heterosexual sex occasions thinks of homosexual sex.

Participants were asked about 11 possible reasons they had for wanting to change their sexual orientation (list of possible reasons developed during a pilot study). For each reason, participants in the study were asked how important the reason was for them with response categories of "not at all" to "extremely important." . . .

Assessment of Marital Relationship

To assess the quality of marital relationships, after the interview the participants were mailed two copies of the Dyadic Adjustment Scale (Spanier, 1976), a validated instrument. Participants and their spouses were instructed to complete the forms independently and mail them to the author.

Results

Motivation to Change

Most participants noted more than one of the 11 reasons asked about. The most commonly reported reasons were that the individual did not find life as a gay man or lesbian emotionally satisfying, conflict between their same sex feelings and behavior and the tenets of their religion, and desire to get married or stay married.

Brief Description of Therapy

The great majority (90%) of the participants reported using more than one type of therapy. Almost half (47%) reported that seeing a mental health professional was the only or most helpful kind of therapy. . . .

To learn something about the focus of the therapy, individuals were asked, "What were the most important things you talked about in your (therapy)?" Topics often mentioned were dysfunctional family relationships and traumatic childhood experiences, and a variety of other psychological issues (e.g., under-lying motivations for same sex attraction). Only 5% of the participants mentioned a topic with a religious content (e.g., relationship with God, what God expects).

Participants were also asked, "How did you translate what you learned into actually changing your feelings?" Often mentioned were linking child-hood or family experiences to the development of their sexual feelings, hav-ing nonsexual relationships with individuals of the same sex (often in the context of an ex-gay support group), thought stopping (e.g., "When I got such thoughts, I didn't go down that route"), avoiding "tempting" situations, and gradually falling in love with a member of the opposite sex. . . .

Homosexual–Heterosexual Measures Prior to Therapy

Most of the participants reported that they "often" or "very often" had same sex attraction as teenagers. In contrast, many participants as teenagers "never" or "only rarely."

Although all of the participants had been sexually attracted to members of the same sex, a small proportion had never engaged in consensual homo-sexual sex. Significantly more males than females had engaged in consensual homosexual sex with more than 50 different sexual partners during their life-time. Significantly more males than females had not experienced consensual heterosexual sex before the therapy effort. . . .

To summarize the results on all 10 measures assessing homosexuality, they have been dichotomized at a point that the author regarded as indicating more than a slight level of homosexuality. . . . [T]here was a marked reduction on all change measures. This was not only on the three measures of overt behavior and sexual orientation self-identity, as critics of reparative therapy might expect, but also on the seven variables assessing sexual orientation itself. On 5 of the 10 measures at PRE and at POST, females showed significantly less homosexuality and more heterosexuality than males.

Good Heterosexual Functioning

At PRE, none of the females and only 2.1% of the males satisfied the crite-ria for Good Heterosexual Functioning. Sixty-six percent of the males and 44% of the females satisfied the criteria for Good Heterosexual Functioning at POST. . . .

Fifty-six participants (28%) had regular heterosexual sex both at PRE and at POST (in all but one case with the same person, their spouse). As would be expected, very few of these 56 participants reported Good Heterosexual Func-tioning at PRE. In contrast, 84% of these participants reported Good Hetero-sexual Functioning at POST.

[A]t POST a marked increase in the frequency of heterosexual sex, more satisfaction in the emotional relationship with their spouse, and more physical satisfaction with heterosexual sex [was found.]

Participants were presented with a list of several ways that the therapy might have been "very helpful" (apart from change in sexual orientation).

Notable were feeling more masculine (males) or more feminine (females) (87%) and developing intimate nonsexual relations with the same sex (93%).

Discussion

This study had a number of advantages over previous studies of attempts to measure change in sexual orientation. The assessment of the participants was far more detailed than the assessment in previous studies, which were usually limited to one or two global measures of sexual orientation. The sample size was larger than any previous study of sexual orientation change in which the participant himself or herself was directly assessed. The use of a structured interview makes it possible for others to know exactly how the participants were evaluated. The near perfect interrater reliability of the coding of the participants' responses indicates no bias in interviewer coding of the participant responses. An important feature of the study is that the entire data set and the audiotapes are available for review.

There are several limitations to the study. Ideally, the research interviewer in a study is blind to the research hypothesis and has no vested interest in the results. Because the author conducted the interviews, this was not the case in this study. . . . The fact that the study results are based on a structured interview reduces, but does not eliminate, the possibility that interviewer bias influenced the participants responses.

The study relied exclusively on self-report, as is almost always the case in psychotherapy treatment efficacy studies. . . .

Given the fallibility of memory for past events, it is impossible to be sure how accurate individuals were in answering questions about how they felt during the year before starting the therapy, which on average was about 12 years before the interview. . . .

Are the participants' self-reports of change, by-and-large, credible or are they biased because of self-deception, exaggeration, or even lying? This critical issue deserves careful examination in light of the participants' and their spouses' high motivation to provide data supporting the value of efforts to change sexual orientation. . . .

If there was significant bias, one might expect that many participants would report complete or near complete change in all sexual orientation measures at POST. Only 11% of the males and 37% of the females did so. One might also expect that many participants would report a rapid onset of change in sexual feelings after starting therapy. In fact, participants reported that it took, on average, a full 2 years before they noticed a change in sexual feelings. . . .

If systematic bias was present, one would expect that the magnitude of the bias for females would be similar to that for males. However, marked gender differences were found. On the 10 change measures, females at PRE and at POST never had values closer to the homosexual end of the respective scale than did the males.

The married participants, as were all participants, were motivated to provide evidence for the benefits of reparative therapy. If their reports of marital adjustment were biased to show how helpful the therapy was for their marriage, one would expect that the married participants would report a level of marital adjustment higher than that of the normative reference group. . . . Most participants who were married before starting therapy did report significant improvement in marital adjustment. However, they did not report a current level of adjustment higher than that of the normative reference group for this instrument.

Finally, real change in sexual orientation seems plausible (again, at least to the author) as the participants used change strategies commonly effective in psychotherapy. . . .

It is unclear how many gays and lesbians in the general population would want to change their sexual orientation or how representative the study sample is of those who would be interested in therapy with that goal. Obviously, this study cannot address the question of how often sexual reorientation therapy actually results in the substantial changes reported by most of the participants in this study. . . .

The participants in the study all believed that the changes they experienced were due primarily to their therapy. However, the lack of a control group leaves the issue of causality open. It is logically possible that a small proportion of gay men and lesbians change their sexual orientation without therapy and that the changes experienced by the participants were causally unrelated to their therapy. The issue of causality can only be answered by a study with random assignment of gay men and lesbians wishing to change their sexual orientation to either a treatment group (some form of reparative therapy) or a control group. . . .

This study indicates that some gay men and lesbians, following reparative therapy, report that they have made major changes from a predominantly homosexual orientation to a predominantly heterosexual orientation. The changes following reparative therapy were not limited to sexual behavior and sexual orientation self-identify. The changes encompassed sexual attraction, arousal, fantasy, yearning, and being bothered by homosexual feelings. The changes encompassed the core aspects of sexual orientation. Even participants who only made a limited change nevertheless regarded the therapy as extremely beneficial. Participants reported benefit from nonsexual changes, such as decreased depression, a greater sense of masculinity in males, and femininity in females, and developing intimate nonsexual relations with members of the same sex.

There is no doubt about what the participants in the study reported. The key question is judging the credibility of their self-reports. One possibility is that some of the participants actually changed their predominantly homosexual orientation to a predominantly heterosexual orientation. Another possibility is that all of the individuals constructed elaborate self-deceptive narratives (or even lied) when they claimed to have changed, at least to some extent, their sexual orientation. . . .

. . . Consider the many cases in this study who made substantial changes in sexual attraction and fantasy, and were now for the first time enjoying heterosexual sex but the change in sexual attraction was not complete. For example, there may occasionally be lustful fantasies of low intensity seeing someone of the same sex who reminded the participant of a previous same sex partner. Because such a change is not complete, strictly speaking such a participant continues to have a "tendency to same sex attraction." It makes no clinical sense to ignore such a change and this would never be done in the case of evaluating the efficacy of any psychosocial or pharmacological therapy.

It probably is the case that reparative therapy rarely, if ever, results in heterosexual arousal that is as intense as a person who never had same sex attractions. However, advocates of reparative therapy do not make that claim. . . .

Critics of reparative therapy assert that the claims of success in changing sexual orientation are limited to anecdotal reports of individuals who have had the reparative therapy, or of therapists who provide such therapy. This study, with the database available to other researchers, clearly goes beyond anecdotal information and provides evidence that reparative therapy is sometimes successful. For the participants in our study, there was no evidence of harm. To the contrary, they reported that it was helpful in a variety of ways beyond changing sexual orientation itself. . . .

These findings of considerable benefits and no obvious harms in the study sample suggest that the current recommendation by the American Psychiatric Association (2000) that "ethical practitioners refrain from attempts to change individuals sexual orientation" is based on a double standard: It implies that it is unethical for a clinician to provide reparative therapy because there is inadequate scientific evidence of effectiveness, whereas it assumes that it is ethical to provide gay affirmative therapy for which there is also no rigorous scientific evidence of effectiveness and for which, like reparative therapy, there are reports and testimonials of harm.

Helena M. Carlson

 **NO**

A Methodological Critique of Spitzer's Research on Reparative Therapy

In Spitzer's study of the effectiveness of reparative therapy in changing sexual orientation, he reports that gay men and lesbians indicate that they have made major changes in their sexual orientation from homosexual to heterosexual. He also notes that even those who made only limited change in sexual orientation still found the therapy beneficial.

The criteria for acceptance into the study required subjects to have had a predominantly homosexual orientation before entering reparative therapy. They should be able to report that after reparative therapy they have sustained for at least 5 years some change toward a heterosexual orientation. The acceptance criteria also required participants to report in a telephone interview on their sexual behavior for the year before they entered reparative therapy and then also report on their behavior in the year before the current research interview. Spitzer reports that there was, on average, an interval of 12 years between the time of entry into reparative therapy and the telephone interview. This places a heavy burden on memory and Spitzer acknowledges there is greater fallibility in such long range memory.

Participants in the study come from a very narrow stratification of the population: 97% were Christian, 95% were Caucasian, the mean age for males was 42 years, the mean age for females was 44 years, 76% of the males were married, and 47% of the women were married, Some participants were directors of ex-gay ministries and some had publicly spoken favorably of efforts to change sexual orientation, often at their church. Thus, this is a population of highly religious, White, Protestant, middle aged, and middle class men and women. There is little evidence that they are representative of a diverse gay community.

Participants in this study were asked in a telephone interview to report on their sexual fantasies, masturbation fantasies, lustful looks, use of gay pornography, homosexual thoughts, and overt sexual behavior. A key question is the credibility of the participants' self-report. It should be recognized that 93% of participants reported that religion was extremely or very important to them.

From *Archives of Sexual Behavior*, vol. 32, 2003, excerpts from 425–431. Copyright © 2003 by Springer Journals (Kluwer Academic). Reprinted by permission.

No consent form was administered and participants' identity was known to the interviewer. Ethical guidelines for informed consent for research issued by the American Psychological Association (2002) require not only protection of confidentiality for participants but that a consent form should clearly state that participants may withdraw from research at any time. Without a consent form, it is possible that participants were wary that their confidentiality would not be protected. The total reliance on self-report in this study can be disturbing when one considers that fundamentalist religious beliefs tend to be strongly opposed toward any acceptance of homosexuality.

Martin (2000) has pointed out that when the research topic is an emotion-laden issue, then individuals might not wish their true feelings to be known, particularly when these feelings differ from socially accepted practices in their community. It seems that this highly religious Christian sample would be particularly vulnerable to feelings of shame and embarrassment if they had to report that they had engaged in condemned behavior. There is a significant risk for self-deception and even lying in highly religious participants when responding to questions about sexual behavior that is strongly condemned by their religion. These participants would also be highly motivated to providing supportive data for the possibility of change of sexual orientation.

Another methodological concern is that all the telephone interviews were done by the investigator alone. This raises the methodological issue of interviewer bias. An interviewer can subtly influence respondent's answers by inadvertently indicating approval or disapproval. Interviewers may also bring their own expectations to their interviews and that can bias their interpretation of responses. Although no research method is absolutely free of bias, the interview is more open to bias than most other research methods. It would have been better to have trained and used other interviewers, preferably those blind to the hypothesis of the study. A research assistant did independently rate audio recordings of 43 of the 200 interviews and Spitzer reports they achieved .98 interrater reliability based on this sampling. It would be helpful if one had some details on the background of the research assistant in order to evaluate more fully the interrater reliability.

Another issue of concern was the diversity and background of the therapies or counseling offered. Although all were described as reparative or conversion, with the goal to change sexual orientation from homosexual to heterosexual, the therapists came from different educational and training backgrounds. The majority (43%) were from ex-gay religious ministries, primarily Protestant, who focused on conversion to heterosexuality; 23% came from a group of primarily psychoanalytic mental health professionals and lay people with the same focus; 9% were recruited as participants by their former therapists; and 25% were a variety of sexual reorientation counselors, including social workers, ministers, and lay people.

Despite the diverse educational and training background, Spitzer lumps all types of counseling together as reparative therapy. Since religious approaches may well be in the form of prayer, it is difficult to see how this form of counseling can be combined in data from the treatments used by trained psychoanalysis. This presents confusion since it is unclear to which particular type of therapy any reported changes can be attributed.

Spitzer used a numerical scale of sexual attraction to determine whether participants had a predominantly homosexual or heterosexual orientation before entering therapy and to assess any changes in sexual orientation by comparing scores on this measure after they had received reparative therapy. He defined participants in the study as predominantly homosexual if they scored at least 60 on the scale of sexual attraction before seeking therapy. He also required before acceptance in the study that participants report a change of at least 10 points, lasting at least 5 years, toward the heterosexual end of the scale.

It is difficult to assess data from this Sexual Attraction Scale, which appears to have been designed for this study. This is a 100 point scale (where 0 = *exclusively heterosexual* and 100 = *exclusively homosexual*). Spitzer defined a score ≥ 20 as homosexual and used the same score on the Sexual Orientation Self-Identity Scale. It appears that, for example, participants who scored 25 on this scale will be recognized as homosexual and similar to participants who scored 100 on this scale.

Spitzer reported that married couples were mailed copies of the Dyadic Adjustment Scale. They were asked to complete this questionnaire independently of their partner and to mail it in. Spitzer reported a 72% response rate from married participants and that, on average, subjects reported the same degree of marital adjustment as the instrument's normative reference group. It is difficult to assess data from this measure because no description was given of it, no complete reference for it was given, and no validity cited. There was also no control over when and how the respondents actually completed the measure.

There was no control group in this research, although admittedly that would be hard to obtain. This means that causality cannot be demonstrated. Spitzer acknowledged that there are fundamental methodological problems with the research but also claims that it provides support for the possibility of reparative therapy to change sexual orientation from homosexual to heterosexual. Spitzer cited some nonsexual benefits from this therapy. He noted that participants reported that after therapy they had a greater sense of masculinity in males and femininity in females. This needs more clarification in light of the many studies of the complexities of gender roles.

In conclusion, even the limited hypothesis that some individuals whose orientation is predominantly homosexual can become predominantly heterosexual following reparative therapy is not supported by this study. It may be possible that some of the research participants might have a more fluid sexual orientation, such as bisexuality.

NO ⬅

Lisa M. Diamond

Reconsidering "Sexual Desire" in the Context of Reparative Therapy

Clarifying the Question

First things first: Is Spitzer's study really "about" changing sexual orientation? In order to answer this question, we need to agree on a definition of sexual orientation and its defining criteria. But, of course, these issues have long been topics of heated debate. Is sexual orientation an innate sexual pre-disposition or a learned behavioral pattern? Does it primarily influence sexual desire or does it also shape affiliative preferences, affectional feelings, and gender-typed behavior? Such debates might seem shopworn at this point, but they are neither resolved nor irrelevant. To the contrary, the more we learn about the diversity of same-sex sexuality across different populations and contexts, the more we must regularly reevaluate our implicit and explicit models of this phenomenon and the hypotheses they prompt us to test.

Spitzer's central question—whether homosexuals can change into heterosexuals—presumes a fairly reductionistic sexual taxonomy that has garnered increasing scientific skepticism over the years. Kinsey et al. (1948) were perhaps the first and most famous to caution that "The world is not to be divided into sheep and goats" (p. 639) and empirical data increasingly buttress this perspective. For example, representative studies of American adolescents and adults have found that most individuals with same-sex attractions *also* report experiencing other-sex attractions, and both changes in, and disjunctures among, sexual behaviors, attractions, and identity are widespread.

Spitzer's research question and methodology do not acknowledge these complexities. Rather, he uncritically treats sexual attractions, fantasies, and emotional longings as coordinated indices of one's underlying "sheep" or "goat" status, despite the fact that (1) it is increasingly unclear whether these discrete types even *exist* as natural categories and (2) it is similarly unclear whether "sheepness" or "goatness" could ever be reliably diagnosed by coordinated and stable patterns of fantasy, desire, and affection. Given these problems, some researchers have argued that "it makes more sense to ask about specific aspects of same-gender behavior, practice, and feelings during specific periods of an individual's life rather than a single yes-or-no question about whether a person is homosexual." What, then, might we learn from Spitzer's study if we jettison extrapolations to "sexual orientation" and focus instead on domain-specific changes?

Interpreting the Findings: The Meaning and Experience of Desire

Unfortunately, a number of factors hamper interpretation of Spitzer's data, such as the significant and obvious problems of self-selection and self-report biases. Yet, I will leave aside these concerns. Granting for the sake of argument that some of Spitzer's participants did, in fact, experience declines in their self-reported same-sex desires, how should we interpret such changes?

First of all, as noted above, the phenomenon of plasticity in sexual desire over time has already been documented in several prospective studies, and is not newsworthy in and of itself. Spitzer, however, is more concerned with *effortful* changes effected through cognitive–behavioral strategies, such as "thought stopping," avoidance of situations that trigger same-sex attractions, and social support mobilization. Can these techniques actually alter one's subjective desires? Of course they can—just as attending Weight Watchers meetings and keeping "forbidden" foods out of the house can attenuate a dieter's natural, evolved cravings for salty, fatty, calorie-dense foods. Furthermore, any reader of Shakespeare or Jane Austen will recognize that these cognitive and behavioral techniques have been used for hundreds of years by individuals who had the misfortune of becoming attracted to partners of the right sex, but the wrong family, wrong social class, wrong nation, etc.

Yet, we are already ahead of ourselves—this entire discussion skirts a far more important but unanswered question lying just beneath the surface of this and other studies of sexual orientation: *Just what do we mean by "desire?"* Given that sexual desire is generally considered the primary indicator of one's sexual orientation, one might expect that researchers would have spent considerable time validating and cross-checking our conceptualizations and measures of its phenomenology, but this has not been the case. Instead, we typically ask respondents to estimate their balance of same-sex and other-sex desires without clarifying what types of experiences "count" as desire, naively assuming that (1) these experiences are fairly uniform from person to person and (2) we all "know them when we feel them."

Yet, qualitative research increasingly demonstrates that individuals have strikingly different personal definitions and experiences of "desire" and "attraction," including, for example, "liking to look at a woman's face or body"; "the urge to have sex"; "a fluttery feeling in my belly"; "wanting to be physically near someone"; "not needing to care about her personality"; "feeling really really happy around someone"; "electric energy"; "wanting to talk all night long." Such ambiguity makes it impossible to reliably interpret self-report data on everything from "age of first attractions" to "ratio of same-sex to other-sex attractions" to—most notably— "stability of attractions."

Which types of feelings might Spitzer's respondents have been talking about? How might it influence our interpretation of his findings if, for example, an individual's "fluttery belly feelings" exhibited little change, but "liking to look at face/body" changed markedly? How exactly do these phenomena relate to the specific frequency with which one's sexual fantasies are populated with same-sex versus other-sex individuals? We currently have no empirical or theoretical basis on which to interpret such phenomenological nuances and their relevance for models of sexual orientation, just as we have long lacked clear-cut conceptualizations of the specific relevance of love and affection for such models. Without greater empirical and theoretical rigor, we will remain hamstrung in our attempts to interpret the causes and implications of *any* self-reported changes in same-sex sexuality.

Final Evaluations: What Gets Repaired?

Where does this leave us ? Does reparative therapy work? What does it work *on*? On this point, it bears noting that perhaps the most salient and striking changes recollected by Spitzer's research participants concerned their overall happiness and self-concept. Prior to the therapy, they were bothered by their same-sex feelings, they were at odds with their own personal or religious beliefs, many were unhappily unmarried, and one third were suicidal. After the therapy, over 75% of the men and over 50% of women were married, less than 10% reported that they were still bothered by their same-sex attractions, and measures of "heterosexual functioning" (participation in a "loving" heterosexual relationship, regular and satisfying sex with partner, etc.) had apparently improved markedly.

Are these successful outcomes? For individuals embedded in social-relational contexts that fundamentally forbid same-sex sexuality and prioritize traditional marriage, how can they not be? Of course, such outcomes could have been achieved through therapeutic interventions *other* than effortful control, redirection, and reconditioning of sexual and affectional feelings; at the very least, these individuals might have attempted to change—or escape—their stigmatizing and restrictive social contexts instead of their sexuality.

But for some this is not an option. Living in Salt Lake City (the worldwide headquarters of the Church of Latter Day Saints), I have come to know numerous men and women who have struggled with the gulf between their same-sex sexuality and their passionate devotion to the Mormon faith, *both* of which may be experienced as inextricably woven into one's deepest sense of self. As long as some individuals' chosen communities (whether based on faith, ethnicity, geography, etc.) invalidate the possibility of living openly with same-sex desires, clinicians must develop, analyze, test, and validate different approaches for helping members of those communities to make peace with, and decisions about, their irreconcilably conflicting life choices and chances.

At the very least, our evaluations of "reparative" interventions must be scrupulously attentive to clients' motives and the unique nature of their experiences in order to guard against inappropriate generalizations about "sexual orientation." Studies such as Spitzer's provide valuable information about how individuals with stigmatized experiences actively manage those experiences, in concert with their own narratives of adjustment, coping, and personal growth. In the final analysis, however, such studies have little to tell us about "change in sexual orientation" or even "change in sexual desire." If anything, Spitzer's findings should prompt sex researchers to revisit our own assumptions about the phenomenology and ontology of same-sex and other-sex desires, fantasies, and attractions in order to improve the validity and interpretability of future research on these phenomena over the life course.

POSTSCRIPT

Is Reparative Therapy Effective in Changing One's Sexual Orientation?

The definition of sexual orientation is complex. Should it be based on desire or behavior? How does the basis of the definition alter our understanding of change in sexual orientation? If one's behavior changes, that is, one no longer engages in sexual behavior with a person of the same sex, has her/his sexual orientation changed? Consider the implications of this logic for being heterosexual. If a person no longer engages in heterosexual activity, has her/his sexual orientation changed? Bisexuality becomes relevant to this discussion. Bisexuality is defined as emotional and sexual attachment to both women and men. Is bisexuality "real" or a reflection of people who are confused or indecisive? Are bisexuals people who flip-flop between being heterosexual or bisexual? Recently it has been suggested that perhaps it is a revolutionary concept, forcing us to consider the possibility that we are sexually attracted to people, not gender categories (see Issue 20 for further exploration of these issues). If this is the case, why is there a need to change anyone's pattern of affectional and erotic attractions?

The focus on reparative therapy gives rise to several issues regarding what constitutes therapy and its purpose. Psychotherapy rose out of the mental health movement. It was an effort to assist individuals who could not function in everyday life. This was premised on the assumption that abnormal and normal behavior could be distinguished. In the 1970's Thomas Szasz challenged the traditional approach to psychiatry, suggesting that mental illness is a cultural construction. He, and many critics since, suggested that the mental health movement has been an instrument of those in power to control the behavior of individuals to meet the traditional conventions and expectations of society. Consider for example the diagnosis of *drapetomania*, a psychosis described as "an irrestrainable propensity to run away." Many African slaves in the pre–Civil War history of the United States received this diagnosis when they attempted to escape their plantations owners. The recommended treatment was amputation of the toes. Clearly, this "disorder" no longer exists. It was a socially constructed "disorder" that met the sociopolitical needs of the powerful at a particular point in time. So, does the claim that sexual orientation is a "problem" to be fixed serve a similar soiciopolitical need at this point in history?

Alternative forms of therapy have arisen to challenge traditional approaches that have focused on individual change, including drugs and institutionalization to accomplish this goal. Consider feminist therapy. Feminist therapy, as discussed by Judith Worell and Pamela Remer, focuses on empowerment of individuals within their social context. This approach asserts that power is the basis for social arrangements and that gender is socially constructed. Thus, therapy must recognize multiple levels of change: the personal, the interpersonal, and the sociopolitical. Therapy must go beyond, and perhaps even defy, the demand that an individual conform to existing social norms. Rather growth, resilience, and empowerment are the goals. Empowerment is defined as "helping one become more independent and assertive about attaining her/his goals and achieving psychological growth." If "abnormal" behavior is socially constructed, then as debates about homosexuality continue, do you think we can expect to see changes in attitudes towards it and changes in opinions about the need to change one's sexual orientation?

Suggested Readings

Tiffany Yvette Christian, "'Good Cake': An Ethnographic Trilogy of Life Satisfaction among Gay Black Men," *Men and Masculinities, 8* (2005): 164–174.

Simon LeVay, *Queer Science: The Use and Abuse of Research into Homosexuality* (Cambridge, MA: MIT Press, 1996).

Aaron H. Oberman, "Relationship Therapy With Same-Sex Couples," *Family Journal: Counseling and Therapy for Couples and Families, 13* (2005): 511–512.

Nikki Sullivan, *A Critical Introduction to Queer Theory* (Edinburgh: Edinburgh University Press, 2003).

Thomas S. Szasz, *The Manufacture of Madness: A Comparative Study of the Inquisition and the Mental Health Movement* (New York: Harper Row, 1970).

Judith Worell and Pamela Remer, *Feminist Perspectives in Therapy: Empowering Diverse Women* (New York: John Wiley & Sons, 2002).

ISSUE 20

Is Transgenderism a Psychological Disorder?

YES: American Psychiatric Association, from "Gender Identity Disorder," *Diagnostic and Statistical Manual of Mental Disorders,* Fourth Edition (2000)

NO: Carla Golden, from "The Intersexed and the Transgendered: Rethinking Sex/Gender," *Lectures on the Psychology of Women* (2004)

ISSUE SUMMARY

YES: The DSM-IV, the official manual of the American Psychiatric Association, presents the diagnostic criteria that must be met in order for a person to be diagnosed with a gender identity disorder.

NO: Carla Golden argues that the diagnosis of gender identity disorder is problematic. It is the socially constructed nature of sex and gender that has problematized some forms of gender expression while privileging others.

Psychosexuality, or psychological behaviors and phenomena presumably associated with biological sex, has typically been defined as having three components: gender identity, gender role, and sexual orientation. A fundamental assumption is that these are congruent. Transgenderism present a case of incongruence that challenges the traditional understanding of psychosexuality.

Gender identity is one's sense of self as belonging to one sex: male or female. Cognitive developmentalists such as Lawrence Kohlberg add the criterion of gender constancy. Gender constancy starts with the ability of a child to accurately discriminate females from males and to accurately identify her or his own status correctly, and develops into the knowledge that gender is invariant. The acquisition of gender identity is often affectively loaded and sometimes marked by negative emotion, otherwise known as gender dysphoria.

The term *gender role* refers to attitudes, behaviors, and personality characteristics that are designated by society (in particular sociohistorical contexts) as appropriately masculine or feminine (i.e., typical of the male or female role, respectively). Thus, assessments of gender role behavior in children have included toy preferences, interest in physical activities, fantasy role and dress-up play, and affiliative preference for same-sex versus opposite-sex peers.

Sexual orientation refers to the match between one's own sex and the sex of the person to whom the person is erotically attracted. Typically, sexual orientation has been considered categorically as heterosexual, homosexual, or bisexual. However, current thinking reflects a more complicated view. Sexual orientation is seen as dimensional with diversity in the object of one's sexual attraction, affectional attraction, and erotic attraction. Furthermore, one's thoughts, feelings, and behaviors do not have to coincide. How would you label someone who feels strong sexual attraction to members of one's own sex but engages in sexual behaviors only with members of another sex?

Are gender roles solely cultural productions? There is considerable controversy about this issue. Many social scientists view gender roles as primarily social in origin. In contrast, some researchers have shown that in lower animals some gender role behaviors, such as rough-and-tumble play, are influenced by prenatal sex hormones. Perhaps, they suggest, phenotypically related behaviors in humans also have a biological component.

Gender Identity Disorder (GID) is defined as a strong psychological identification with the opposite sex and is signaled by the display of opposite sex-typed behaviors and avoidance or rejection of sex-typed behaviors characteristic of one's own sex. It is not related to sexual orientation. Distress or discomfort about one's status as a boy or a girl frequently accompanies these behaviors. The age of onset is 2 to 4 years. Some children self-label as the opposite sex, some self-label correctly but wish to become a member of the opposite sex. Other children do not express cross-sex desires but exhibit cross-sex-typed behavior. Some children cross-dress, sometimes insistently. Less characteristic are cross-sex-typed mannerisms (e.g., body movements, voice, pitch). Cross-sex peer affiliation preferences, poor peer relations, and alienation are typical. Although not extensively studied, genital dysphoria (distress about genitalia) is sometimes present. Children with GID are not typically biologically intersexed.

Child referrals for GID have increased in the last two decades. Speculations about the cause of this increase include the heightened sensitivity to gender identity issues among schools, doctors, parents, and others. Boys are about six times as likely as girls to be referred for GID. Three explanations have been offered: (1) perhaps boys have greater biological vulnerability to anomalous development, (2) social factors reflect less tolerance of cross-gender behavior in boys, thereby creating greater dysphoria, or (3) different base rates of cross-gender behavior (i.e., boys are less likely to display feminine behavior than are girls to display masculine behavior) make boys' cross-gender behavior more noticeable.

In the following selections, the *Diagnostic and Statistical Manual, 4th. ed., (DSM-IV)* diagnostic criteria for GID are presented. Then Carla Golden critically analyzes the classification of GID as a disorder, and offers a social constructionist view as an alternative to atypical gender identities.

YES ⬳ American Psychiatric Association

Gender Identity Disorder

Diagnostic Features

There are two components of Gender Identity Disorder, both of which must be present to make the diagnosis. There must be evidence of a strong and persistent cross-gender identification, which is the desire to be, or the insistence that one is, of the other sex (Criterion A). This cross-gender identification must not merely be a desire for any perceived cultural advantages of being the other sex. There must also be evidence of persistent discomfort about one's assigned sex or a sense of inappropriateness in the gender role of that sex (Criterion B). The diagnosis is not made if the individual has a concurrent physical intersex condition (e.g., partial androgen insensitivity syndrome or congenital adrenal hyperplasia) (Criterion C). To make the diagnosis, there must be evidence of clinically significant distress or impairment in social occupational, or other important areas of functioning (Criterion D).

In boys, the cross-gender identification is manifested by a marked preoccupation with traditionally feminine activities. They may have a preference for dressing in girls' or women's clothes or may improvise such items from available materials when genuine articles are unavailable. Towels, aprons, and scarves are often used to represent long hair or skirts. There is a strong attraction for the stereotypical games and pastimes of girls. They particularly enjoy playing house, drawing pictures of beautiful girls and princesses, and watching television or videos of their favorite female characters. Stereotypical female-type dolls, such as Barbie, are often their favorite toys, and girls are their preferred playmates. When playing "house," these boys role-play female figures, most commonly "mother roles," and often are quire preoccupied with female fantasy figures. They avoid rough-and-tumble play and competitive sports and have little interest in cars and trucks or other nonaggressive but stereotypical boys' toys. They may express a wish to be a girl and assert that they will grow up to be a woman. They may insist on sitting to urinate and pretend not to have a penis by pushing it in between their legs. More rarely, boys with Gender Identity Disorder may state that they find their penis or testes disgusting, that they want to remove them, or that they have, or wish to have, a vagina.

Girls with Gender Identity Disorder display intense negative reactions to parental expectations or attempts to have them wear dresses or other feminine attire. Some may refuse to attend school or social events where such clothes may be required. They prefer boys' clothing and short hair, are often misidentified by strangers as boys, and may ask to be called by a boy's name. Their fantasy heroes are most often powerful male figures, such as Batman or Superman. These girls prefer boys as playmates, with whom they share interests in contact sports, rough-and-tumble play, and traditional boyhood games. They show little interest in dolls or any form of feminine dress-up or role-play activity. A girl with this disorder may occasionally refuse to urinate in a sitting position. She may claim that she has or will grow a penis and may not want to grow breasts or to menstruate. She may assert that she will grow up to be a man. Such girls typically reveal marked cross-gender identification in role-playing, dreams, and fantasies.

Adults with Gender Identity Disorder are preoccupied with their wish to live as a member of the other sex. This preoccupation may be manifested as an intense desire to adopt the social role of the other sex or to acquire the physical appearance of the other sex through hormonal or surgical manipulation. Adults with this disorder are uncomfortable being regarded by others as, or functioning in society as, a member of their designated sex. To varying degrees, they adopt the behavior, dress, and mannerisms of the other sex. In private, these individuals may spend much time cross-dressed and working on the appearance of being the other sex. Many attempt to pass in public as the other sex. With cross-dressing and hormonal treatment (and for males, electrolysis), many individuals with this disorder may pass convincingly as the other sex. The sexual activity of these individuals with same-sex partners is generally constrained by the preference that their partners neither see nor touch their genitals. For some males who present later in life (often following marriage), the individual's sexual activity with a woman is accompanied by the fantasy of being lesbian lovers or that his partner is a man and he is a woman.

In adolescents, the clinical features may resemble either those of children or those of adults, depending on the individual's developmental level, and the criteria should be applied accordingly. In a younger adolescent, it may be more difficult to arrive at in accurate diagnosis because of the adolescent's guardedness. This may be increased in the adolescent feels ambivalent about cross-gender identification or feels that it is unacceptable to the family. The adolescent may be referred because the parents or teachers are concerned about social isolation or peer teasing and rejection. In such circumstances, the diagnosis should be reserved for those adolescents who appear quite cross-gender identified in their dress and who engage in behaviors that suggest significant cross-gender identification (e.g., shaving legs in males). Clarifying the diagnosis in children and adolescents may require monitoring over an extended period of time.

Distress or disability in individuals with Gender Identity Disorder is manifested differently across the life cycle. In young children, distress is manifested by the stated unhappiness about their assigned sex. Preoccupation with cross-gender wishes often interferes with ordinary activities. In older children, failure to develop age-appropriate same-sex peer relationships and skills often leads to isolation and distress, and some children may refuse to attend school because of teasing or pressure to dress in attire stereotypical of their assigned sex. In adolescents and adults, preoccupation with cross-gender wishes often interferes with ordinary activities. Relationship difficulties are common, and functioning at school or at work may be impaired.

Specifiers

For sexually mature individuals, the following specifiers may be noted based on the individual's sexual orientation: **Sexually Attracted to Males, Sexually Attracted to Females, Sexually Attracted to Both,** and **Sexually Attracted to Neither.** Males with Gender Identity Disorder include substantial proportions with all four specifiers. Those who are attracted to males usually first experience the disorder beginning in childhood or early adolescence, while those males attracted to females, both genders, or neither usually report their gender dysphoria beginning in early to mid-adulthood. Those men attracted to neither gender are often isolated individuals with schizoid traits. Virtually all females with Gender Identity Disorder will receive the same specifier—Sexually Attracted to Females—although there are exceptional cases involving females who are Sexually Attracted to Males.

Recording Procedures

The assigned diagnostic code depends on the individual's current age: if the disorder occurs in childhood, the code 302.6 is used; for an adolescent or adult, 302.85 is used.

Associated Features and Disorders

Associated descriptive features and mental disorders   Many individuals with Gender Identity Disorder become socially isolated. Isolation and ostracism contribute to low self-esteem and may lead to school aversion or dropping out of school. Peer ostracism and teasing are especially common sequelae for boys with the disorder. Boys with Gender Identity Disorder often show marked feminine mannerisms and speech patterns.

The disturbance can be so pervasive that the mental lives of some individuals revolve only around those activities that lessen gender distress. They are often preoccupied with appearance, especially early in the transition to living in the opposite sex role. Relationships with one or both parents also may be seriously impaired. Some males with Gender Identity Disorder resort to self-treatment with hormones and may very rarely perform their own castration or penectomy. Especially in urban centers, some males with the disorder may engage in prostitution, which places them at high risk for human immunodeficiency virus (HIV) infection. Suicide attempts and Substance-Related Disorders are commonly associated.

Children with Gender Identity Disorder may manifest coexisting Separation Anxiety Disorder, Generalized Anxiety Disorder, and symptoms of depression. Adolescents are particularly at risk for depression and suicidal ideation and suicide attempts. In adults, anxiety and depressive symptoms may be present. In clinical samples, associated Personality Disorders are more common among males than among females. Adult males who are sexually attracted to females, to both males and females, or to neither sex usually report a history of erotic arousal associated with the thought or image of oneself as a woman (termed *autogynephilia*). In most cases, the individual would qualify, at least in his past, for a diagnosis of Transvestic Fetishism. In others, however, the individual's favorite fantasy emphasizes feminine attributes other than clothing. Some men, for example, masturbate while picturing themselves as nude women, focusing on their imagined breasts and vulvas; others masturbate while picturing themselves engaged in some stereotypically feminine activity such as knitting.

Associated laboratory findings   There is no diagnostic test specific for Gender Identity Disorder. In the presence of a normal physical examination, karyotyping for sex chromosomes and sex hormone assays are usually not indicated. Psychological testing may reveal cross-gender identification or behavior patterns.

Associated physical examination findings and general medical conditions   Individuals with Gender Identity Disorder have normal genitalia (in contrast to the ambiguous genitalia or hypogonadism found in physical intersex conditions). Adolescent and adult males with Gender Identity Disorder may show breast enlargement resulting from hormone ingestion, hair denuding from temporary or permanent epilation, and other physical changes as a result of procedures such as rhinoplasty or thyroid cartilage shaving (surgical reduction of the Adam's apple). Distorted breasts or breast rashes may be seen in females who wear breast binders. Postsurgical complications in genetic females include prominent chest wall scars, and in genetic males, vaginal strictures, rectovaginal fistulas, urethral stenoses, and misdirected urinary streams. Adult females with Gender Identity Disorder may have a higher-than-expected likelihood of polycystic ovarian disease.

Specific Age and Gender Features

Females with Gender Identity Disorders generally experience less ostracism because of cross-gender interests and may suffer less from peer rejection, at least until adolescence. In child clinic samples, boys with this disorder are referred for evaluation much more frequently than are girls. In adult clinic samples, men outnumber women by about two or three times. In children, the referral bias toward males may partly reflect the greater stigma that cross-gender behavior carriers for boys than for girls.

Prevalence

There are no recent epidemiological studies to provide data on prevalence of Gender Identity Disorder. Data from smaller countries in Europe with access to total population statistics and referrals suggest that roughly 1 per 30,000 adult males and 1 per 100,000 adult females seek sex-reassignment surgery.

Course

For clinically referred children, onset of cross-gender interests and activities is usually between ages 2 and 4 years, and some parents report that their child has always had cross-gender interests. Only a very small number of children with Gender Identity Disorder will continue to have symptoms that meet criteria for Gender Identity Disorder in adolescence or adulthood. Typically, children are referred around the time of school entry because of parental concern that what they regarded as a "phase" does not appear to be passing. Most children with Gender Identity Disorder display less overt cross-gender behaviors with time, parental intervention, or response from peers. By late adolescence or adulthood, about three-quarters of boys who had a childhood history of Gender Identity Disorder report a homosexual or bisexual orientation, but without concurrent Gender Identity Disorder. Most of the remainder report a heterosexual orientation, also without concurrent Gender Identity Disorder. The corresponding percentages for sexual orientation in girls are not known. Some adolescents may develop a clearer cross-gender identification and request sex-reassignment surgery or may continue in a chronic course of gender confusion or dysphoria.

In adult males, there are two different courses for the development of Gender Identity Disorder. The first is a continuation of Gender Identity Disorder that had an onset in childhood. These individuals typically present in late adolescence or adulthood. In the other course, the more overt signs of cross-gender identification appear later and more gradually, with a clinical presentation in early to mid-adulthood usually following, but sometimes concurrent with, Transvestic Fetishism. The later-onset group may be more fluctuating in the degree of cross-gender identification, more ambivalent about sex-reassignment surgery, more likely to be sexually attracted to women, and less likely to be satisfied after sex-reassignment surgery. Males with Gender Identity Disorder who are sexually attracted to males tend to present in adolescence or early adulthood with a lifelong history of gender dysphoria. In contrast, those who are sexually attracted to females, to both males and females, or to neither sex tend to present later and typically have a history of Trasnsvestic Fetishism. Typically, after sex reassignment, those males who were attracted to females wish to live with another woman in either a lesbian relationship or as sisters. If Gender Identity Disorder is present in adulthood, it tends to have a chronic course, but spontaneous remission has been reported.

Differential Diagnosis

Gender Identity Disorder can be distinguished from simple **nonconformity to stereotypical sex-role behavior** by the extent and pervasiveness of the cross-gender wishes, interests, and activities. This disorder is not meant to describe a child's nonconformity to stereotypic sex-role behavior as, for example, in "tomboyishness" in girls or "sissyish" behavior in boys. Rather, it represents a profound disturbance of the individual's sense of identity with regard to maleness or femaleness. Behavior in children that merely does not

---

Diagnostic Criteria for Gender Identity Disorder

A. A strong and persistent cross-gender identification (not merely a desire for any perceived cultural advantages of being the other sex).

In children, the disturbance is manifested by four (or more) of the following:

(1) repeatedly stated desire to be, or insistence that he or she is, the other sex
(2) in boys, preference for cross-dressing or simulating female attire; in girls, insistence on wearing only stereotypical masculine clothing
(3) strong and persistent preferences for cross-sex roles in make-believe play or persistent fantasies of being the other sex
(4) intense desire to participate in the stereotypical games and pastimes of the other sex
(5) strong preference for playmates of the other sex

In adolescents and adults, the disturbance is manifested by symptoms such as a stated desire to be the other sex, frequent passing as the other sex, desire to live or be treated as the other sex, or the conviction that he or she has the typical feelings and reactions of the other sex.

B. Persistent discomfort with his or her sex or sense of inappropriateness in the gender role of that sex.

In children, the disturbance is manifested by any of the following: in boys, assertion that his penis or testes are disgusting or will disappear or assertion that it would be better not to have a penis, or aversion toward rough-and-tumble play and rejection of male stereotypical toys, games, and activities; in girls, rejection of urinating in a sitting position, assertion that she has or will grow a penis, or assertion that she does not want to grow breasts or menstruate, or marked aversion toward normative feminine clothing.

In adolescents and adults, the disturbance is manifested by symptoms such as preoccupation with getting rid of primary and secondary sex characteristics (e.g., request for hormones, surgery, or other procedures to physically alter sexual characteristics to simulate the other sex) or belief that he or she was born the wrong sex.

C. The disturbance is not concurrent with a physical intersex condition.

D. The disturbance causes clinically significant distress or impairment in social, occupational, or other important areas of functioning.

Code based on current age:

302.6 Gender Identity Disorder in Children
302.85 Gender Identity Disorder in Adolescents or Adults

Specify if (for sexually mature individuals):

Sexually Attracted to Males
Sexually Attracted to Females
Sexually Attracted to Both
Sexually Attracted to Neither

---

fit the cultural stereotype of masculinity or femininity should not be given the diagnosis unless the full syndrome is present, including marked distress or impairment.

Transvestic Fetishism occurs in heterosexual (or bisexual) men for whom the cross-dressing behavior is for the purpose of sexual excitement. Aside from cross-dressing, most individuals with Transvestic Fetishism do not have a history of childhood cross-gender behaviors. Males with a presentation that meets full criteria for Gender Identity Disorder as well as Trnasvestic Fetishism should be given both diagnoses. If gender dysphoria is present in an individual with Transvestic Fetishism but full criteria for Gender Identity Disorder are not met, the specifier With Gender Dysphoria can be used.

The category **Gender Identity Disorder Not Otherwise Specified** can be used for individuals who have a gender identity problem with a

concurrent congenital inter-sex condition (e.g., partial androgen insensitivity syndrome or congenital adrenal hyperplasia).

In **Schizophrenia**, there may rarely be delusions of belonging to the other sex. Insistence by a person with a Gender Identity Disorder that he or she is of the other sex is not considered a delusion, because what is invariably meant is that the person feels like a member of the other sex rather than truly believes that he or she is a member of the other sex. In very rare cases, however, Schizophrenia and severe Gender Identity Disorder may coexist.

Carla Golden

The Intersexed and the Transgendered: Rethinking Sex/Gender

Let me first define what transgender means, and then I'll give you some idea of the diversity that exists under the umbrella of the transgender community. "Trans" means *across* or *beyond,* and thus transgender means that which moves across or beyond gender (as it is defined by the culture). As applied to people, it refers to someone who moves across or beyond gender boundaries. Leslie Feinberg, who first used the term and continues to elaborate on it, identifies as a transgendered person, as well as a "he-she," and a masculine female. Even as s/he travels around the country speaking and raising consciousness on transgender issues, s/he lives and passes as a man in daily life because s/he fears for her safety as an openly transgendered person. Kate Bornstein, a genetic male and a self-described "gender outlaw," sees herself as beyond gender. In both her writing and speaking, she is emphatic that she is not a man, despite having lived as one for 37 years, and "probably not a woman either," though to look at her you would think she was. Riki Wilchins adopts the label "transgender" at the same time as she rejects it. She points out that transgender is not some natural fact or true identity but a political category that people like her are forced to take on when they construct their sex and gender according to their own definitions and desires.

You may be wondering at this point what's the difference between people who call themselves transsexuals and those who call themselves transgendered. The answer is that it's very much a question of chosen identity. The word "transsexual" has been around much longer and has been used by psychologists to describe people whose gender is at odds with their biological sex. Feinberg, Bornstein, and Wilchins are politically active feminists who have self-consciously constructed their own identities as transgender. They have also used the term "transpeople" (also written as "trans people," or "trans" for short). Still, they have not completely discarded the word "transsexual." In writings from within the transgender community, one will see abundant references to ftms (female to male transsexuals, also called transsexual males) and mtfs (male to female transsexuals, also called transsexual females).

Transsexuals and transgendered people are a diverse group, and the transgender activists previously cited do not speak for all tanssexuals. For example, Margaret O'Hartigan vigorously rejects a transgender identity in favor of a transsexual one because to her thinking she did not change her *gender;* she changed her *sex.* As a postoperative transsexual, she moved from one sex category (male) to the other (female), but she had always considered herself a girl or woman. In her experience of self, there are only two categories, and she is a *woman*—not a man, not in-between, not beyond gender. Many transsexuals tell the story of being "trapped in the wrong body," a powerful metaphor that rests on the essentialist belief that there exist only two sexes and two corresponding genders, each of which is fundamentally different from the other. If the gender doesn't match the body's sex, then the body is wrong (a trap) and must be altered. Although it is impossible to provide numerical estimates, it is probably the case that more transsexuals see themselves as trapped in the wrong body than think in terms of transgender identities.

This essentialist dichotomy shows up also in the diagnostic category of gender identity disorder (GID), which entered the third edition of the American Psychiatric Association's *Diagnostic and Statistical Manual of Mental Disorders (DSM)* in 1980. It is perhaps not surprising that the narrative told by so many transsexuals resonates with the psychiatric diagnosis they must have if they want to be considered acceptable candidates for surgical and hormonal treatments. The specific criteria that one must meet in order to be given a diagnosis of GID are completely dependent on binary models of sex and gender—specifically, the belief that a person is either male *or* female, a man *or* woman; there is no beyond or in-between. The criteria also rest on the assumption that one's sex and gender must match, and if they don't, something is profoundly wrong and warrants a psychiatric diagnosis.

It is worth considering the diagnosis of gender identity disorder in greater detail as it is presented in the *DSM-IV.* The first diagnostic criterion is "a strong and persistent cross-gender identification," which can manifest itself in a number of different ways. . . .

The second criterion is "persistent discomfort with his or her sex or sense of appropriateness in the gender role of that sex." . . .

There are two additional criteria for diagnosis; one specifies that "the disturbance" is not related to intersexuality and the other that it causes "clinically significant distress or impairment" in the life of the person so diagnosed. In the section on differential diagnosis, it is noted that gender identity disorder is not the same thing as "simple nonconformity to stereotypical sex role behavior" and that it is distinguishable from this "by the extent and pervasiveness of the cross-gender wishes, interests, and activities."

From a feminist psychological perspective, the diagnosis of gender identity disorder is both problematic and suspect. Cross-gender interests and activities? Feminist psychologists had already established that interests and activities are not, and should not, be constrained by one's sex/gender. Just because trucks are marketed to boys doesn't mean that a girl who wants to play with them (even exclusively) has "cross-gender interests." Consider another symptom: the conviction that one has the typical feelings and reactions of the other sex. Is a woman who feels angry, or sexual, or aggressive, or ambitious having the feelings of the other sex? You might agree with me that these so-called symptoms are questionable. But what about the desire to physically alter one's sexual characteristics through hormones and surgery? That's pretty extreme and a legitimate criterion of mental disturbance, isn't it? It all depends on how you think about it. What about the large numbers of nontranssexual women (i.e., biological females who consider themselves to be women) who are both dissatisfied and preoccupied with their secondary sex characteristics to the point of undergoing breast augmentation or reduction surgeries; electrolysis; frequent shaving of legs, underarms, and "bikini" lines; weight-reduction regimens; hormone replacement therapy—all of which are designed to alter the natural female body. Such practices on the part of women reflect the nonconscious ideology that females are born—if not the wrong sex—the second sex, or "the never-good-enough-as-you-are" sex, yet women who choose to change their bodies in these ways are considered quite normal in our culture!

Finally, consider the "clinically significant distress" that must be present for the person to receive a diagnosis of GID. As with any condition of difference in our culture, one can question whether the distress comes from the condition itself or from other people's reaction to the difference. If transsexuals are distressed (as required for a diagnosis of GID), is it because they have "cross-gender" identifications and interests, or because in a culture where sex and gender are dichotomized, we are intolerant of people who step outside the dichotomies? Suppose a person has a ". . . sense of inappropriateness in the gender role of that sex"? So what?! What is the appropriate gender role of each sex, anyway?! Each sex doesn't have one and only one appropriate gender role. Sex and gender aren't linked in any necessary or inevitable way. The diagnostic category of gender identity disorder, like so many other gender-and sexuality-related diagnoses, is highly problematic for feminists or anyone in the process of rethinking the meaning of sex and gender and their relation to each other.

The social constructionism of the transgender activists is more enlightening than the essentializing and pathologizing language of the *DSM,* so let me return to consideration of transgender issues as they emerge from *within* that community rather than from outside of it. One question that often arises has to do with the relative frequency of transsexualism in females and males. Early discussions of the topic pointed to a much lower frequency in biological females. The *DSM-IV* offers no data on prevalence of the disorder but does suggest that in terms of those who seek sex-reassignment surgery, the ratio is 3:1 in favor of biological males. It is difficult to know with any certainty, but recent estimates made from within the transsexual community are that there are probably as many ftms as there are mtfs. In just the past few years, numerous works have appeared that have broadened our exposure to females who cross and sometimes move beyond the gender divide. Holly Devor's (1997) book *FTM: Female-to-Male Transsexuals in Society* offers more than 600 pages of description and analysis of her interviews with 45 ftms. Loren Cameron has produced an eye-opening set of photographs of ftms under the title *Body Alchemy: Transsexual Portraits,* and a documentary film called *You Don't Know Dick*[1] features female to male transsexuals talking about their lives.

Trans people can be anywhere in the process of moving across or beyond gender, from being preoperative to postoperative to any of a number of places in-between, including nonoperative. In contrast to essentialist transsexuals, transgender activists talk about choosing their gender as well as making choices about what kinds of bodies they want. Their chosen gender may or may not correspond to their genitals. Apparently, more and more transsexuals are choosing not to have genital surgery not only because it's extremely expensive (and often results in subsequent complications) but also because it's increasingly seen as unnecessary. The belief in two sexes/genders is challenged, to say the least, by women with breasts and penises and men with beards and clitorises!

Trans people are as heterogeneous a group as any other group of people. In addition to the diversities of thought, personality, and interests that you would find in any group, there are differences among them as they relate to sex, gender, and identity. Some specifically identify as transgender, whereas others do not. They have been variously described as gender blenders (or gender benders), masculine females, feminine males, and gender variants. Among them are those who consider themselves to be women, or men, or intermediate, or neither, or in-progress, or just "different" from what their culture dictates a man or woman should be. Some say they have chosen their gender; others say it was not a choice. Some have decided to have genital surgery, and others have decided against it. Some elect to change other parts of their bodies, and some do not. Their sexualities cover a broad range of possibilities. Their performance of gender reveals its multiplicity and range of complexity. And they are only one segment of the larger whole that makes up the transgender community.

If we understand transgender to mean across or beyond gender lines, then there are many more people who might claim (or be claimed for) membership in the transgender community. The International Foundation for Gender Education (founded in 1987) estimates that 6 percent of the U.S. population are cross-dressers, also known as transvestites. In the *DSM-IV*, transvestites are identified as heterosexual males who cross-dress. I wouldn't argue that we need to expand the criteria for inclusion in the *DSM*, but clearly there are some gay men (known as drag queens) as well as women (less well known, but referred to as drag kings) who don the clothes not considered appropriate for their sex. According to the *DSM-IV*, transvestism is classified as a "fetish," which means that there is some sexual arousal that accompanies cross-dressing in men. Psychologists and others have doubted that there are parallels between men's and women's cross-dressing, believing that for women cross-dressing is more socially acceptable and has no related sexual component. Pat Califia disagrees, pointing to the discrimination, condemnation, and even violence directed toward biological females who cross-dress.[2] She also describes the sexual rush she feels when she is in male drag and notes that her conversations with other women suggest that this is not uncommon. Like transsexuals, cross-dressers constitute a diverse group of men and women with a range of identities and practices. Cross-dressers have existed across history (e.g., Joan of Arc, Mulan) and although some have attempted to claim them as trans people, it's not so easy to say how they thought of themselves. In contemporary times, cross-dressing carries many meanings, and people do it for different reasons. It may or may not be related to sexual orientation, or to transsexuality, and it may or may not include a sexual component. Whatever the case, the very notion of "cross" dressing warrants its inclusion under the umbrella of the transgender community.

In addition to transsexuals and cross-dressers, self-identified inter-sexuals belong within the transgender community. Intersexual activists are raising awareness about the harm done to infants and children who are subject to genital surgeries they do not need. A federal law passed in 1996 bans genital cutting in the United States, and although the law was aimed at halting the practice among recent immigrants from countries where female genital mutilation is widely practiced, intersexual activists are seeking ways to use the law to ban medically unnecessary intersex surgeries as well. Taking a stand against surgery is not a simple issue for the transgender community, which is hardly monolithic. Movement across and beyond gender lines can work in multiple and sometimes contradictory ways. While intersexual activists are organizing and calling for a halt to intersex surgery, transsexuals are fighting for the right to surgically alter their bodies. Although there is a difference in informed consent (infants can't give it), a feminist social constructionist like me resonates best to the idea of people keeping whatever bodies and genitals they have and performing gender in whatever way suits them. As I see it, the most progressive trend in the transgender community is the one that challenges the requirement that the sex of the body must match the gender of the performance.

Intimate partners of intersexuals and transgendered people deserve inclusion within the transgender community. One shouldn't assume that intersexuals and transgender people are lonely and have difficulty establishing meaningful sexual relationships with others. Nor should it be assumed that they will always or most often relate intimately with other people like them. Any person sexually involved with a man who has breasts or with a woman who has a penis is crossing gender boundaries regardless of their own particular body or identification.

There are still others to be included. Lesbians, gays, and bisexuals might consider themselves part of a broadly defined transgender community. Through their partnerships, self-presentations, and ideas, many lesbians, gays, and bisexuals cross and go beyond conventional gender lines. For that matter, so do some heterosexuals. There are a diversity of ways to cross and go beyond gender boundaries, from the mundane to the more unusual. Consider the report of a 31-year-old "normal" married heterosexual male who requested breast enlargement (which was accomplished via estrogen treatment), so that he could experience more sexual pleasure in his nipples during sexual activity with his wife.

Finally, there are contemporary boys and girls who are gender nonconformists, sometimes aided and encouraged by feminist parents and teachers, all of whom might be included within the transgender community for expanding the possibilities of what gender means. Girls especially seem to me to be stretching the boundaries, moving in-between and beyond gender. In conversations with young girls, I have found the concept of "tomboy" to be on the wane. One 7-year-old whom I asked to point out the tomboys in her class said she wasn't sure about that, but she could identify the "really girly girls" and the "sometimes girly girls" and "the kid kids," a category that included both boys and girls.

The Fluidity of Gender

I hope by now your head is spinning with the dazzling diversity of gendered expressions and with a sense of possibility. It all started out so neat and clear, with sex being defined as biological and gender as a social construction. Then I presented information on the intersexed and suggested that sex wasn't so neatly packaged into two and only two categories and that gender wasn't something we *have* or *are* but a performance. This was followed by a necessarily brief reference to members (or potential members) of the transgender community. The people I have described may or may not consider themselves to be part of a transgender community. But the fact that they might not consciously think of themselves as part of a larger coalition of gender benders or gender performers doesn't stop us from seeing them that way. Performances are seen and interpreted by others, and those of us who are in the process of learning to see differently can learn a lot from other people's performance of gender. Probably most important is that they can help us to imagine the gender possibilities for *ourselves* and to see that gender is fluid—a process, a work-in progress, something not yet finished—not just for *them*, but for *all* of us.

What we can learn from the experiences and performances of those within the transgender community is that neither bodies nor genders are fixed and unchanging. This has led some feminist psychologists to question the notion that a stable and fixed gender identity is desirable or even possible. Research over the past decade on the fluidity of women's sexuality has shown that fixed sexual orientation categories don't adequately describe many women's experience of sexual desire and identity. In the same vein, it is possible that fixed gender identities don't capture the multiplicities of our gendered selves, either. Some psychologists have begun to challenge the longstanding claim of mainstream developmental psychologists that the developing child *must* attain a fixed gender identity, and that doing so is a sign of maturity. Virginia Goldner suggested that learning to tolerate the ambiguity and instability of gender categories is a more appropriate developmental goal than achieving a gender-unified and coherent sense of self. Robert May has argued that, in men, a fixed gender identity may be the result of an inhibition of gender ambiguities and contradictions and as such reflects an impoverishment of character rather than a mature developmental outcome. Sandra Bem argued that, in a gender polarizing and androcentric culture that requires men to repress any "feminine" tendencies, the security of their gender identity will be under constant threat; thus, men will work ceaselessly to prove their masculinity. Sarah Pearl-man described gender identity *destabilization* as healthy and elaborated on the opportunities for creative self-expression that can arise from such destabilization of fixed gender identity in women. For the most part, however, these views are too radical to have reached the mainstream of developmental psychology texts.

Conclusion

There are at least five "sex/gender principles" that can be extracted from this lecture, and they are based on what we have learned from the intersexed and the transgendered, broadly defined. First, there exists a lot more diversity in biological sex than we have previously acknowledged; our belief in the existence of only two sexes is a social construct. Second, because both sex *and* gender are socially constructed and because they don't always match, it is no longer so useful to distinguish between them. It made more sense to do so when we thought that gender was a social construct and sex was a biological fact, but our thinking has shifted. Third, people can choose their gender, and this includes moving away from or beyond the gender that had been imposed upon them as children. What they choose may not correspond to their genitals, and what that means is that genitals need not be the central marker of our sex/gender. Fourth, identities are not necessarily fixed, stable, and coherent, and thus a fixed gender identity is neither necessary nor advantageous to mental health. Just as our age-related or ethnic identities can change over the life course, so, too, can our gender identities. Fifth, the possibilities for gender fluidity, as well as gender ambiguity and contradiction, are enormous, as demonstrated by the members of the broadly defined transgender community.

In my early days as a feminist, I used to think that, in order to achieve equality between the sexes, we would need to deemphasize gender by constantly refocusing attention away from the differences between women and men. But that strategy was frustrating because it wasn't effective. People still focused on the differences, despite a body of research demonstrating that there are more similarities than differences. That was before I realized that gender is a mode of performance and that *more* of it might be better than less. The more we do gender, the more we can stretch it and in the process diversify and multiply the possibilities. Rather than aiming for a gender-free utopia, my vision now is for a world that would be gender-full, where there would be so many different ways to be women, men, in-between, and beyond, that in the end the categories themselves would lose meaning and what we would be left with is a diversity of ways to be. And I don't just mean that the categories woman and man would lose meaning, but so, too, would all cultural constructs grounded in gender, and that includes femininity and masculinity as well as heterosexuality, homosexuality, and bisexuality. A world of multiple gender expressions, where bodies, selves, and desires can combine in all possible ways will be one where there is a lot to see, to be, to do, and to learn—and being female or male, woman or man will have little to do with it. If we take social construction theory seriously, we must remember that those possibilities aren't merely "out there" to be discovered; they are to be actively created by us. Gender is not just what the other presents; it is what we do and what we see. Feminism is, after all, about seeing differently.

Notes

1. This film is distributed by the University of California (at Berkeley) Extension Center for Media and Independent Learning.
2. The notion that women can wear men's clothing without negative social consequence is belied by the experience of Brandon Teena who in 1995 was killed for a having a female body at the same time that s/he presented as a man.

POSTSCRIPT

Is Transgenderism a Psychological Disorder?

The etiology (cause) of GID is still more unknown than known. The biological perspective explores the effects of prenatal androgens and maternal prenatal distress on gender atypicality. This research is primarily conducted on lower animals or on intersexual humans (even though GID is not typical in intersexuals). Social scientists examine sex-related socialization practices, including parental attitudes, social reinforcement processes (consistently and without ambiguity rearing a child as a boy or a girl, including encouragement of same-gender behavior and discouragement of cross-gender behavior), and self-socialization. An interactionist perspective suggests that sexual biology makes some individuals more vulnerable to certain psychosocial rearing conditions.

Different ideologies about whether or not GID is a disorder seem to rest on this question: do we view sex, gender, and sexual orientation as distinct domains or as inextricably linked? Phyllis Burke notes in *Gender Shock: Exploding the Myths of Male and Female* (Anchor Books, 1996) that "when you look at what society pathologizes, you can get the clearest glimpse of what society demands of those who wish to be considered normal." It appears, then, that our society expects congruence among sex, gender, and sexual orientation and believes that to be the norm. But some critics caution that the biodiversity of nature is greater than our norms allow us to observe. Moreover, we have little understanding, beyond stereotype and presumption, of the association between this biodiversity and gender identity and behavior. For example, how many of us have biological evidence (beyond visible external genitalia) that we are the sex that we believe ourselves to be? There have been cases where female athletes were surprised to find that they have a Y chromosome, yet by other biological measures they are clearly female. What, then, is this individual's "appropriate" gender identity?

Throughout history all societies have had differently gendered people, with varying statuses. These range from examples of women such as Joan of Arc who presented as men, without necessarily hiding their femaleness, so they could fight in wars. The *Hijras* in India were male-to-female transgender people who were believed to be possessed with a spirit of the opposite sex and participated in a religious cult. Other societies have also presumed that transgender people had special spiritual powers, such as the Xaniths in Oman and the Berdache among Native Americans. Clearly, beyond biology, societal norms define what traits and behaviors are "normal" and what status should be accorded individuals who manifest various traits and patterns of behavior. Deviation from conventional social norms may lead either to

376

elevation of status, such as to that of a spiritual leader in some cultures, to that of depraved in other cultures.

What is the future of gender? Are there only two genders (predetermined by the sex binary) or are genders unlimited in form and function, able to be individually and uniquely constructed? Many contemporary scholars remark that the boundaries of gender have been challenged in recent times and that the future holds promise for the "transcendence" of gender. They foretell movement beyond traditional gender roles to refashioned and more flexible gender motifs or perhaps even to the eradication of gender altogether. What would a gender-transformed or gender-irrelevant future look like and what will enable the attainment of such future visions? What do current societal trends indicate? Are our ideas about sexual deviance changing? Are we moving toward or away from gender redefinition and transcendence?

Suggested Readings

Jennifer Finney Boylan, *She's Not There: A Life in Two Genders* (Random House, 2004).

Mildred L. Brown and Chloe Ann Rounsley, *True Selves: Understanding Transsexualism—For Families, Friends, Coworkers, and Helping Professionals* (Jossey-Bass).

Judith Butler, *Undoing Gender* (New York: Routlege, 2004).

Pat Califia, *Sex Changes: The Politics of Transgenderism* (1997).

Paula J. Caplan, *They Say You're Crazy: How the World's Most Powerful Psychiatrists Decide Who's Normal* (Perseus Books, 1995).

G. Herdt, *Third Sex, Third Gender* (Zone Books, 1994).

N. K. Sandnabba and C. Ahlberg, "Parents' Attitudes and Expectations About Children's Cross-Gender Behavior," *Sex Roles* (February 1999).

D. Scholinski and J. M. Adams, *The Last Time I Wore a Dress* (Riverhead Books, 1997).

K. J. Zucker and S. J. Bradley, *Gender Identity Disorder and Psychosexual Problems in Children and Adolescents* (Guilford Press, 1995).

Contributors to This Volume

EDITOR

JACQUELYN W. WHITE is Professor of Psychology and former director of Women's and Gender Studies, at the University of North Carolina at Greensboro. She received her Ph.D. in social psychology from Kent State University.

Dr. White has conducted research in the area of aggression and violence for over 30 years, publishing numerous articles and chapters. She has conducted one of the only longitudinal studies of sexual assault and dating violence among adolescents and college students (funded by NIMH, NIJ, and CDC). Recent publications reflect an ecological developmental perspective to aggression and violence. She is a frequent speaker at national and international conferences. She is co-editor with Dr. Cheryl Travis of the University of Tennessee on *Sexuality, Society, and Feminism: Psychological Perspectives on Women,* published by the American Psychological Association. She recently completed the "Gendered Aggression" chapter for the *Encyclopedia of Gender* (Academic Press) and "A Developmental Examination of Violence Against Girls and Women" for the *Handbook of the Psychology of Women and Gender (Wiley).*

In addition to her research activities, Dr. White served as the editor of the *Psychology of Women Quarterly* (2000–2004) and is a consulting editor for *Aggressive Behavior.* She has been president of the Southeastern Psychological Association and is currently the treasurer of the International Society for Research in Aggression. She has been a consultant on a project with the US Navy examining the impact of pre-military experiences with physical and sexual abuse on military experiences. She has been the

STAFF

Larry Loeppke	Managing Editor
Jill Peter	Senior Developmental Editor
Nichole Altman	Developmental Editor
Beth Kundert	Production Manager
Jane Mohr	Project Manager
Tara McDermott	Design Coordinator
Bonnie Coakley	Editorial Assistant
Lori Church	Permissions
Julie J. Keck	Senior Marketing Manager
Mary S. Klein	Marketing Communications Specialist
Alice M. Link	Marketing Coordinator
Tracie A. Kammerude	Senior Marketing Assistant

recipient of a number of awards, including the Women's History Committee Service Award given by the Commission on the Status of Women and the Greensboro YWCA and Kent State University's Honors Alumna of 2000. She was UNCG's 1996 Senior Research Excellence Award recipient, the highest research honor the university can bestow on a faculty member. She is also a fellow of the American Psychological Association and a member of APA's Council of Representatives.

AUTHORS

AMERICAN PSYCHOLOGICAL ASSOCIATION'S COUNCIL OF REPRESENTATIVES is the elected governing body of the American Psychological Association. Among various activities it creates task forces charged with drafting resolutions based on research reviews that the Council can then consider for adopting as official APA policy.

AMERICAN PSYCHIATRIC ASSOCIATION publishes the Diagnostic and Statistical Manual (DSM-IV), which is the official manual providing diagnostic criteria for psychological disorders.

CARL F. AUERBACH is an associate professor of psychology at the Ferkauf Graduate School of Psychology at Yeshiva University, is the founder and co-dirctor of the Yeshiva Fatherhood Project. He has collaborated extensively with Louise B. Silverstein.

TORBJÖRN BÄCKSTRÖM, M.D. and colleagues are members of the department of clinical Science, Obstretics and Gyneocology at Umea University in Sweden and have published numerous articles on the effects of female hormones.

KRISTIN BARDARI, Ph.D., is in private practice in South Carolina.

GARY BERNTSON is a Professor at Ohio State University. His research focuses on the elucidation of the functional organization of brain mechanisms underlying behavioral and affective processes, with a special emphasis on social neuroscience.

BARRIE BONDURANT, a former professor of psychology at Lyon College, where she received the 2002–2003 Excellence in Teaching award, is a counselor at New River Valley Community Services in Blacksburg, VA. She has published several chapters and research articles related to violence against women.

JOHN T. CACIOPPO, social psychologist and Tiffany & Margaret Blake Distinguished Service Professor in the department of psychology at the University of Chicago, specializes in social neuroscience, affect and emotion, and social connectedness and health. He is director of the center for cognitive and social neuroscience. Among many awards he received the 2002 American Psychological Association Distinguished Scientific Contribution Award.

ANNE CAMPBELL, professor of psychology at Durham University, studies sex differences in aggression with special emphasis upon female aggression.

She is the author of *Mind of her own: The evolutionary psychology of women*. Oxford: Oxford University Press, 2002.

HELENA M. CARLSON, professor emerita at Lewis and Clark College in the department of psychology, has conducted research on a variety of topics ranging from community policing to women, racial and sexual minorities. She has also studied women and homelessness and the psychological effects of unemployment, sexual harassment, and acquaintance rape.

MARCIA J. CARLSON is an assistant professor of social work and sociology at Columbia University. Her current research focuses on linkages among family structure, mother-father relationships, father involvement, and child well-being for a cohort of children born outside of marriage. She calls these family structures "fragile families."

JOAN C. CHRISLER is a professor and chair of the psychology department at Connecticut College and is editor of *Sex Roles*. She is also the 2005–2007 president of the Society for the Psychology of Women. She has published five books, including *Lectures on the Psychology of Women* (2003, McGraw-Hill) along with Carla Golden and Patricia Rozee, which received a distinguished publication award from the Association of Women in Psychology.

DAVID B. COHEN, retired clinical psychologist from the University of Texas at Austin, has, in addition to authoring *Stranger in the Nest: Do Parents Really Determine a Child's Personality, Intelligence, or Character?* (John Wiley & Sons, 1999), has recently published a book for parents entitled *Where Did THAT Child Come From!* (Templegate Publishers, 2003).

TIMOTHY J. DAILEY, senior research fellow at the Center for Marriage and Family Studies, has a Ph.D. in religion and specializes in issues threatening the institutions of marriage and the family. He has authored three books, including *Dark Obsession: The Tragedy and Threat of the Homosexual Lifestyle* (Broadman and Holman, 2003).

DENA S. DAVIS is a professor at the Cleveland-Marshall College of Law at Cleveland State University. She was a Fellow in Bioethics at the Cleveland Clinic and has published in the areas of church and state and bioethics and teaches and conducts research in biomedical ethics, church and state, torts.

LISA M. DIAMOND associate professor of psychology and gender studies at the University of Utah, focuses her research on the nature and development of affectional bonds and the nature and development of same-sex sexuality, publishing numerous articles on both topics.

PATRICIA L. N. DONAT, Professor of Psychology and Associate Vice President of Academic Affairs at Mississippi University for Women, has published several chapters and articles related to her research interests in women's issues and violence against women.

SARAH DRESCHER is currently a lawyer in Oregon. In 2004, as a law student and ACLU volunteer, Drescher represented the prisoners of Jackson County OR in a jail overcrowding case. She successfully negotiated with state officials reaching a settlement that was approved by a U.S. district judge. Later that year, Drescher was awarded the Outstanding Service Impact Award from the University of Oregon Law School.

RICHARD B. FELSON, is a professor in the department of crime, law & justice and sociology at Pennsylvania State University, has received numerous grants, and published extensively in the field of aggression. He received the PSU 2004 Distinction in the Social Sciences Award from the College of Liberal Arts.

CARLA GOLDEN, professor of psychology at Ithaca College has published several articles on women's issues, including articles related to sexual orientation. She is co-editor, along with Joan Chrisler and Patricia Rozee of *Lectures on the Psychology of Women* (2003, McGraw-Hill), which received a distinguished publication award from the Association of Women in Psychology.

SONJA GROVER, associate professor in the faculty of education at Lakehead University, teaches in the area of Special Education and Children's Human Rights. Her work has focused on both global and domestic issues concerning the rights of marginalized children such as street children, poor or minority children, or refugee children. She is currently a Policy Research and Analysis Consultant for the Canadian International Development Agency (CIDA) project "Improving Services to Youth at Risk in the Russian Federation."

TARA GRUENEWALD is an Assistant Researcher with the Division of Geriatric Medicine at the David Geffen School of Medicine at UCLA.

REGAN R. A. GURUNG is the Associate Dean of Liberal Arts and Sciences and Associate Professor of Psychology at the University of Wisconsin-Green Bay. His research interests include healthy behaviors in schools and colleges, cultural differences in health, and clothing and body image.

DEBRA HAUSER, MPH, is the Vice President of Advocates for Youth. Advocates for Youth is an national, nonprofit organization that creates programs and supports policies that help young people make safe, responsible decisions about their sexual and reproductive health.

BERNICE L. HAUSMAN, Associate Professor of english and former Director of Women's Studies at Virginia Tech, is the author of *Mother's Milk: Breastfeeding Controversies in American Culture* (Routledge, 2003) and *Changing Sex: Transsexualism, Technology, and the Idea of Gender* (Duke University Press, 1995). She also received the Schachterle Award for "Sex before Gender: Charlotte Perkins Gilman and the Evolutionary Paradigm of Utopia," Society for Literature and Science, in 1997.

HILDA KAHNE, professor emerita at Wheaton College in Massachusetts and a member of the Women's Studies Research Center Scholars Program and a Resident Scholar at Brandeis University. Her research at the Women's Studies Research Center (WSRC) focuses on low-wage single-mother families and how their earnings can be increased to a level of long-run financial adequacy. In her earlier years, Dr. Kahne also held positions at Wellesley

College, Radcliffe College, Harvard University, Harvard School of Public Health, and the Social Security Administration in Washington, D.C.

LAURA COUSINO KLEIN, Ph.D. is Assistant Professor of biobehavioral health at Penn State University. Her research interests include the biobehavioral effects of stress on drug abuse in humans and animals, sex differences in neuroendocrine and behavioral stress responses, and nicotine regulation of stress reactivity.

MARY P. KOSS, a clinical psychologist and professor in the Mel and Enid Zuckerman College of Public Health at the University of Arizona, is an international authority on sexual violence and has authored two books and over 175 articles on sexual assault. She received the 2000 American Psychological Association Award for Distinguished Contributions to Research in Public Policy. She currently serves as a member of the management committee of the Sexual Violence Research Initiative, an initiative of the Global Forum of the World Health Organization.

LAWRENCE A. KURDEK, clinical psychology professor at Wright State University, is interested in developmental psychology and the effects of family structure and family process on children's and adolescents' development. He is also interested in the issue of relationship quality in gay, lesbian, and heterosexual couples. He has published over 150 referred journal articles and edited book chapters.

BRIAN P. LEWIS was formerly an assistant professor of psychology at Syracuse University.

HILARY M. LIPS, a professor of psychology and the director of the Center for Gender Studies at Radford University, has published numerous books and articles related to the psychology of gender, including *Sex and Gender: an Introduction* (2000, Mayfield).

GERALD MACKIE, assistant professor of political science at the University of California, San Diego. He has been Research Fellow, Social and Political Theory Program, Research School of Social Sciences, Australian National University, and Junior Research Fellow in Politics, St John's College, University of Oxford. He is the author of *Democracy Defended*.

BRIDGET E. MAHER, policy analyst at the Center for Marriage and Family Studies at Family Research Council. She has authored several Family Research Council publications including two editions of *The Family Portrait*, a comprehensive book of data, research, and polling on the family.

KACY L. McGINNIS-PAYNE, Ph.D, is a clinical psychologist who teaches courses in the areas of clinical and counseling psychology at Peace College in North Carolina. She was the Advisor of the Year, 2004–2005. She is interested in the connections between women's reproductive health and clinical psychology.

SARAH S. McLANAHAN is professor of sociology and public affairs and director of the Bendheim-Thoman Center for Research on Child Well-being at Princeton University. She is Editor-in-Chief of *The Future of Children*. She is the author of many articles and books including *Fathers Under Fire: The*

Revolution in Child Support Enforcement (1998). The James S. Coleman Fellow of the American Academy of Political and Social Sciences and the Distinguished Scholar Award from the American Sociological Association Family Section are two of the many honors she has received.

MARTHA McCLINTOCK is the Director of the Institute for Mind and Biology, co-director of the Center for Interdisciplinary Health Disparities Research (CIHDR), and holds joint appointments in the Department of Psychology, the Committee on Biopsychology, the College Committee on Evolutionary Biology, the Committee on Neurobiology, and the Committee on Human Development at the University of Chicago. She is a leading figure in the study of human pheromones and social modulation of aging, immune function and susceptibility to disease. She studies the reciprocal interactions between social behavior, neuroendocrinology and gene expression, particularly those that affect reproduction and health throughout the life span.

CARLA M. OBERMEYER, scientist for the World Health Organization's Department of HIV and adjunct associate professor in the Department of Population and International Health at Harvard University, has been chair of the Committee on Reproductive Health of the International Union for the Scientific Study of Population and a member of the US National Science Foundation Senior Review Panel for Anthropology. Her research has addressed the links between health and social factors and has included population policy and gender in Arab countries, the Safe Motherhood initiative in Morocco, the health effects of female circumcision, and a multisite study of therapeutic decision making at menopause. She is the author of three books: Changing Veils: Women and Modernization in Yemen (1979); Family Gender and Population in the Middle East (1995); Cross-Cultural Perspectives on Reproductive Health (2001).

CRAIG T. PALMER, an instructor in the department of a anthropology at the University of Colorado, conducts research primarily in the field of evolutionary psychology. He recently co-authored a paper with Randy Thornhill evaluating reactions to their book (Straw men and fairy tales: Evaluating reactions to *A Natural History of Rape,* in *Journal of Sex Research, 40,* 2003).

STEVEN PINKER is now the Johnstone Family Professor of Psychology at Harvard University. Until 2003 he was in the department of brain and cognitive sciences at MIT. His empirical studies focus on linguistic behavior. He also conducts theoretical analyses of the nature of language and its relation to mind and brain. He has authored several books including *The Blank Slate: The Modern Denial of Human Nature* (Penguin Books, 2003).

ROSAMOND RHODES is a professor of medical education and director of bioethic education at the Mount Sinai School of Medicine. She was guest editor, along with Daniel A. Moros, on the theme of "Issues in medical ethics understanding professionalism and its implications for medical education" in the *Mount Sinai Journal of Medicine* (2002).

BRUCE RIND, a professor of psychology at Temple University, is now best-known for a paper he published with Robert Bauserman and Philip

Tromovitch in *Psychological Bulletin* in 1998. The paper, questioning the presumed negative effects of childhood sexual abuse, caused an uproar both within the academic and therapeutic communities. Congress also weighed in on the issue, by voting unanimously on July 12, 1999 to denounce the Rind et al. study. Matt Salmon (R-Arizona), the resolution's sponsor called the study "the emancipation proclamation of pedophiles."

DONALD L. RUBIN, professor of speech communication and language and literacy education at the University of Georgia, focuses his research on social identity (e.g., gender, nationality, and ethnicity) and style in writing. He has published extensively on oral and written communication.

ELIZABETH SHEFF, assistant professor of sociology at Georgia State University, is currently studying issues of sexuality, gender, family, deviance, and communities. She has taught courses in sexuality, gender, families, introductory sociology, social theory, and research methods. Her current research interests involve examining the norms and ethics of practitioners of various types of sexual activities, including bondage, domination, and sadism.

JOHN F. SHERIDAN is the Associate Director of the Institute for Behavioral Medicine Research of Ohio State University. His research interests include viral immunology, regulation of T-cell responses during viral infection, cytokine and chemokine gene expression during infection (influenza, herpes simplex and coxsackie viruses), and stress-induced modulation of anti-viral immune responses and viral pathogenesis.

LOUISE B. SILVERSTEIN, professor at the Ferkauf Graduate School of Psychology at Yeshiva University is the founder and co-director of the Yeshiva Fatherhood Project, along with Carl F. Auerbach. She received the Association for Women in Psychology's Distinguished Publication Award for her paper on "Deconstructing the Essential Father" (*American Psychologist*, 1999). She has co-authored with T. J. Goodrich, among numerous articles and chapters, *Feminist Family Therapy: Empowerment in Social Location* (American Psychological Association Books, 2003). She is also a family therapist.

ELIZABETH SPELKE, the Marshall L. Berkman Professor of Psychology at Harvard University. Her most recent honors include the William James Award, American Psychological Society 2000; Distinguished Scientific Contribution Award, American Psychological Association, 2000; Ipsen Prize in Neuronal Plasticity, 2001; America's Best in Science and Medicine, Time Magazine, 2001; Fellow, American Association for the Advancement of Science, 2002. She is currently publishing research on numerical cognition in infants and young children.

ROBERT L. SPITZER, a psychiatrist, is Chief of Biometrics Research and professor of psychiatry at Columbia University of Psychiatry at Columbia University. He was instrumental in getting homosexuality removed as psychiatric disorder from the diagnostic manual of disorders.

PETER SPRIGG is vice president for policy at the Family Research Council. He oversees research, publications, and policy formulation, and coordinates the work of Center for Human Life and Bioethics and Center for Marriage and Family Studies. His areas of policy expertise are human sexuality and the homosexual agenda; religion in public life; and the arts and entertainment. He has authored *Outrage: How Gay Activists and Liberal Judges Are Trashing Democracy to Redefine Marriage* (Regnery, 2004).

SHELLEY E. TAYLOR, social psychologist and professor at the University of California, Los Angeles, is co-director of the Health Psychology program at UCLA and director of the social neuroscience lab. Her research interests are in the areas of social cognition and health. She has written several books and among several awards, including the American Psychological Association's Distinguished Scientific Contribution to Psychology Award and the Outstanding Scientific Contribution Award in Health Psychology.

RANDY THORNHILL, zoologist and distinguished professor of biology at the University of New Mexico, has published extensively on evolutionary and ecological aspects of animal social psychology and behavior. His current research foci include evolution of human social psychology and behavior and the evolution of female sexuality.

CHERYL B. TRAVIS, professor of psychology and chair of Women's Studies at the University of Tennessee, is author of numerous books, chapters and articles on various aspects of women's health. She has been president of the Society for the Psychology of Women, Editor Psychology of Women Book Series, and received the American Psychological Association's Committee on Women Career Achievement Award. She also recently edited *Evolution, Gender and Rape.* (2003, MIT Press).

JOHN UPDEGRAPH is an assistant professor of psychology at Kent State University. His research focuses on the cognitive and emotional processes that underlie well-being and adaptation to stress.

RICHARD WILSON, a former research fellow at the University of Sheffield, is currently a Medical Research Council-funded student in Medical Sociology at the Royal Holloway College at the University of London. He is also an assistant editor of the journal *Sexualities, Evolution and Gender.*

LAURA L. WINN, assistant professor of communications at Wayne State University, focuses her research on interpersonal communication, family communication and research methodology. She recently published "Weddings as text: Communicating cultural identities through ritual" in *Journal of Social and Personal Relationships* (2004).

JUNE O'NEILL, Wollman Professor of Economics and Finance at the Zicklin School of Business is also the Director of the Center for the Study of Business and Government, School of Public Affairs, at Baruch College, City University of New York. Dr. O'Neill is the chairwoman of the Board of Scientific Counselors of the National Center for Health Statistics. Between 1995 and 1999, she served a term as Director of the Congressional Budget Office (CBO) in Washington D.C. O'Neill is currently a member of a Panel of Economic Advisors for the CBO. She has authored books pertaining to welfare, income and earnings differentials, women in the economy, health insurance, social security, and education finance.

JULIA T. WOOD, professor of communications studies at the University of North Carolina at Chapel Hill, is an expert on gender, communication, and culture; personal relationships; and feminist theories. She has authored or edited 20 books and over 50 articles and chapters in books. She received the 1998 Board of Governors award for teaching at the University of North Carolina at Chapel Hill and the 1998 Case/Carnegie Award for North Carolina Professor of the Year.

Index